CALIFORNIA
MISSION LANDSCAPES

Architecture, Landscape, and American Culture Series

Katherine Solomonson and Abigail A. Van Slyck, Series Editors

Medicine by Design: The Architect and the Modern Hospital, 1893–1943
ANNMARIE ADAMS

Churches for Today: Modernism and Suburban Expansion in Postwar America
GRETCHEN BUGGELN

Building Zion: The Material World of Mormon Settlement
THOMAS CARTER

Little White Houses: How the Postwar Home Constructed Race in America
DIANNE HARRIS

California Mission Landscapes: Race, Memory, and the Politics of Heritage
ELIZABETH KRYDER-REID

Manhood Factories: YMCA Architecture and the Making of Modern Urban Culture
PAULA LUPKIN

Fallout Shelter: Designing for Civil Defense in the Cold War
DAVID MONTEYNE

Designing the Creative Child: Playthings and Places in Midcentury America
AMY F. OGATA

Women and the Everyday City: Public Space in San Francisco, 1890–1915
JESSICA ELLEN SEWELL

194X: Architecture, Planning, and Consumer Culture on the American Home Front
ANDREW M. SHANKEN

A Manufactured Wilderness: Summer Camps and the Shaping of American Youth, 1890–1960 ABIGAIL A. VAN SLYCK

The Architecture of Madness: Insane Asylums in the United States
CARLA YANNI

CALIFORNIA MISSION LANDSCAPES

Race, Memory, and the Politics of Heritage

ELIZABETH KRYDER-REID

Architecture, Landscape, and American Culture Series

UNIVERSITY OF MINNESOTA PRESS
MINNEAPOLIS • LONDON

The University of Minnesota Press gratefully acknowledges financial assistance provided for the publication of this book by the David R. Coffin Publication Grant of the Foundation for Landscape Studies.

Published by the University of Minnesota Press
111 Third Avenue South, Suite 290
Minneapolis, MN 55401-2520
http://www.upress.umn.edu

Printed in the United States of America on acid-free paper

22 21 20 19 18 17 16 10 9 8 7 6 5 4 3 2 1

Library of Congress Cataloging-in-Publication Data
Names: Kryder-Reid, Elizabeth, author.
Title: California mission landscapes : race, memory, and the politics of heritage / Elizabeth Kryder-Reid.
Description: Minneapolis : University of Minnesota Press, 2016. | Series: Architecture, landscape, and American culture series | Includes bibliographical references and index.
Identifiers: LCCN 2016039455 (print) | ISBN 978-0-8166-2839-1 (hc) | ISBN 978-0-8166-3797-3 (pb)
Subjects: LCSH: Spanish mission buildings—California. | Cultural landscapes—California. | Cultural property—Political aspects—California. | Cultural property—Social aspects—California. | BISAC: ARCHITECTURE / Landscape. | HISTORY / United States / State and Local / West. | ARCHITECTURE / History / General.
Classification: LCC F862 .K79 2016 (print) | DDC 979.4—dc23
LC record available at https://lccn.loc.gov/2016039455

This book is dedicated to my parents,
who supported my dreams from the beginning;
to my family, Tom, Emily, Caroline, and Grace,
who have stood by me in every way imaginable;
and to all those whose lives have been entwined in the missions,
especially the Native people, who have seen such profound loss
and inspiring renewal in the California landscape.

Contents

Preface

For a number of years psychologist Alan Dienstag led a creative writing group for people suffering from Alzheimer's disease. The experience, which he recounted on a broadcast of *On Being* in March 2015, gave him insights into the power of sharing memories to break through the isolation of people with dementia.[1] Sharing their experiences provided a sense of commonality, a way to be recognized. And through the group's writings others could know them, even when they were gone.

Dienstag's words struck home because my father had recently died after living with Alzheimer's for about six years. Over the course of the disease this brilliant scholar gradually lost not only his mastery of his field and recollections of past events, but also his life's narrative. In the face of the horror of the disease's progression, there were some beautiful aspects. His deep-seated gentleness and kindness, his innate sense of generosity and hospitality, and his unwavering love for my mother emerged as essential characteristics. At the same time, I was struck by how intimately memory and identity are connected, both for his own sense of self and for all of us who could no longer share memories of our common experiences. Dienstag's experiences with his group also resonated with my work on this book and reminded me of why memory matters. It is part of how we know who we are. It is essential to our sense of connectedness and to living in relationship with each other. It is a way that we recognize and respect each other's humanity. And when we are gone, the places and traces of our lives are ways in which communities continue to connect over time.

The California mission landscapes are important places for the construction of cultural memory that, at its essence, reveals who we think we are and how we understand our relationships to others. They are a material witness to the ideological potency of imagined pasts rendered in the media of gardens and aestheticized spaces. Specifically, these colonial sites are part of the ongoing American settler colonial project. Despite the missions' central place in the Spanish conquest of territory and subjugation of Native peoples, the landscape design presents a largely triumphalist view of the state's early history. And this celebratory narrative of colonialism conveyed in the mission gardens emanates through myriad forms of representation and cultural practices. Documented in the grand gestures of parades and the intimate renderings of postcards and miniatures, heritage practices have shaped the cultural memory of California's colonial past as beautiful, timeless, and sanctified.

But the evidence, like the sites themselves, is profoundly influenced by the authorship and authority of the archives that have preserved them. For the colonial period, archaeology offers an important avenue because, as Stephen Silliman has articulated, its "ability to study space and objects permits intervention in the historiography of colonialism by breaking silences."[2] As much as the missions were, and continue to be, part of an Indigenous landscape, those connections are often opaque. The vast majority of archival and material evidence related to the postcolonial landscapes privileges the perspectives of the dominant culture and reflects a systematic erasure of Indigenous people. And where Native peoples are represented, their presence rarely reflects Native voices or epistemologies.[3] The subaltern voices preserved in Indigenous archives (as Lisbeth Haas describes the "material made, represented, and/or saved by native communities")[4] are largely excluded from dominant narratives and popular heritage practices at the missions. Conversely, the few acres that comprise the contemporary mission properties are but a sliver of the broader social, legal, and political landscape California Native people occupied for millennia. As a result, much of the story of their ongoing resistance, activism, and survivance rarely intersects with the modern mission spaces.[5] The story of the construction of the missions landscapes as colonizing spaces is a powerful one, but as Jace Weaver has observed, while there is value in "exposing and deconstructing non-Native representations of Indians . . . , ultimately the story being told is about white people."[6] This study lies in that uncomfortable place, therefore, between deconstructing colonial spaces and understanding their importance within a Third Space of Sovereignty.[7]

The centuries of disenfranchisement and dispossession have created complicated and often fraught relationships among Indigenous people and the missions. Some Native Californians worship in mission churches and work on their staffs as historians, curators, and interpreters. Others eschew the sites as too painfully associated with historical traumas and injustice to set foot on. Native artists, scholars, and activists have challenged received dominant narratives for decades, but rarely have these critiques taken place at the missions or changed their interpretive practices. As a result, despite the fact that the missions are part of the Indigenous geography of California, the material explored in this book speaks largely to the production and reception of the missions as colonized spaces.

But the disjuncture need not be predictive of the future. The ultimate goal of this book is to influence how the mission landscapes are managed and interpreted and to open up their possibilities as decolonized spaces. Like the wide range of scholars working in critical race theory and settler colonial studies, *California Mission Landscapes* probes the relationships among race, racism, and power.[8] More specifically, like the members of the International Coalition of Sites of Conscience, the study uses the power of historicizing the origins and practices of injustice and of deploying historic sites to spur dialogue about human and civil rights issues. In addition to making transparent the profoundly political origins and meanings of seemingly benign gardens, this study also hopes to be a catalyst for conversation about the missions' role in shaping public memory, in the construction of Indigeneity, and in the exclusion of other marginalized peoples from California history. Maria Brave Heart-Jordan has written compellingly about the power of narrative to address historical trauma and grief among the Lakota.[9] In a similar vein, Renee Linklater's work on healing and wellness in Indigenous communities on Turtle Island identifies the "soul wound" of colonialism as a central issue and uses stories and strategies grounded in Indigenous worldviews and cultural knowledge as a path toward wellness for those who have experienced trauma.[10] Robben Island in Cape Town, South Africa's Table Bay was transformed from a prison for political detainees to a museum where the apparatus of apartheid became a space of reconciliation.[11] That the missions might similarly become a space for all people to engage with the painful issues of California's colonial legacy and racial and ethnic marginalization is the highest ambition of this project.

The most productive course to this end, I believe, is understanding the history of representation at the sites, not through the missions' highly didactic museum exhibits or scholarly tomes, but through their accessible, familiar, and seemingly natural settings. Tracing this rich, multivalent history of the mission landscapes recognizes their complex meanings to diverse constituencies, as well as names their consequences for contemporary peoples. It seeks not to blame but to understand the motivations, agency, and contexts of those who have shaped the land over the centuries. In a historiography that has tended to polarize and demand declarations of allegiance to a single version of past events, this account takes a decidedly wide-ranging approach to explore how those perspectives have been inscribed on the landscape and why. As Elizabeth Cook-Lynn has argued, Native Americans continue to be "the most colonized folks on the planet,"[12] and that remembrance of the colonial past and its ongoing policies is critical to moving toward a more just "postcolonial America." Mining the history of the mission landscapes to uncover and make explicit the origins and ideologies of the spaces is one small arena in the broader project of decolonizing American settler colonial history and its associated public heritage sites.[13] A critical history of the mission landscapes requires understanding them both as Indigenous landscapes and as powerful ideological naturalizations of western conquest and asserted racial superiority. Such revelations may not only spur dialogues about California's colonial past but also provoke changes in the management and interpretation of the missions as we move toward a decolonized future. This is the opportunity of heritage sites globally to claim, as Daniel Herwitz has written, this "moment of agency, poised between heritage practices of the past and the desire, need, or inevitability of breaking away from them to make something new."[14]

In the spirit of self-reflective cultural studies, I want to disclose that in many ways I come to this project as an outsider. Although I have long been fascinated with the history of California's Native peoples and the missions, I do not have a formal affiliation with any institutions in the state.[15] As a scholar working from a distance, I have missed out on the informal exchanges, relationships, and collegiality that proximity might have brought, and I have not had the opportunity to work in the Indigenous archives or closely with Native people in California. A small benefit of my working from a geographic distance, however, is that I have also generally avoided the entanglements concomitant with excavations on mission properties or extensive use of church-controlled archives that can subtly constrain published conclusions if the scholar wishes to maintain access to those resources. And while I have presented this material at a variety of professional conferences and publications, by fact of distance more than by choice I have worked largely outside the scholarly network, with its factions and frictions, of those who study California history and particularly mission history.

I also want to acknowledge that I am writing from a non-Native perspective. I come to these questions and this material with a background in anthropology, museum studies, landscape history, and heritage studies. I bring to the project great respect for the unique cultural perspectives of California's diverse Native peoples and yet also the sure knowledge that those experiences and epistemologies are beyond my reckoning. Where possible I build on the work of Native scholars, artists, and activists who have written so powerfully about California Indigenous experience, agency, and history. I look forward to the day when those voices and perspectives are more fully included in the interpretation at every mission.

Acknowledgments

One advantage of working on a project for decades is that you accumulate a long list of colleagues who have enriched the scholarship and the experience. Those who contributed to my thinking on the materiality of the past and its meanings for the present include Kevin Murphy, Norman Neuerburg, Ian W. Brown, Patricia Rubertone, Deana Dartt-Newton, John Moreland, Mark Tribe, Michael Sanchez, Steven Hackel, David Robinson, Barbara Voss, Chris Matthews, Therese O'Malley, Hank Millon, Helen Tangires, David Brownlee, Sally Promey, Anne Helmreich, Dianne Harris, Dell Upton, Mark Leone, Paul Shackel, Barbara Little, Parker Potter, Anne Pyburn, Elee Wood, Melissa Bingmann, Annie Coleman, Owen Dwyer, Rebecca Shrum, Susan Hyatt, Mario Caro, Jeremy Wilson, Jenny Mikulay, Modupe Labode, Holly Cusack-McVeigh, Laura Holzman, and Larry Zimmerman. In particular, Dede Ruggles helped me think through the conceptualization of the book at a critical stage and believed in the project throughout the extended process. Paul Mullins generously commented on multiple drafts, and his critiques have challenged my thinking and strengthened my argument, not to mention spurred me to finish the book.

The ideas in this book benefited greatly from the opportunity to present, publish, and teach them. I am grateful to the many discussants, session chairs, editors, and colleagues whose comments refined this work (full citations to those publications are in the bibliography). Similarly, the anonymous reviewers of the manuscript and of the articles in which I first developed some of these ideas offered cogent critiques. This kind of professional service is invaluable and is rarely rewarded. This project was also informed by my students, whose questions provoked me to consider new ideas and possibilities. I also benefited from conversations with participants in the National Council on Public History working groups "Imagined Places, Actual Spaces" and "Religion, Historic Sites, and Museums." I appreciate the opportunity to be in Kate Solomonson and Abby Van Slyck's series Architecture, Landscape, and American Culture at the University of

Minnesota Press. Kate's close reading of this manuscript and her insightful suggestions at several critical stages shaped and strengthened the book, just as her enthusiasm and encouragement sustained me during the vagaries of manuscript preparation.

This research would not have been possible without the assistance of many people. I owe a debt to the archivists, librarians, parish administrators and staff, and colleagues who helped locate and provide access to sources. I cannot begin to list all by name, but I'm particularly grateful for the assistance of Michael Hardwick in his introduction to La Huerta Historic Gardens (the Huerta project); Tina Foss and Monica Orozco for their help at the Santa Bárbara Mission Archive-Library; Susan Hector for sharing mission water system research; Father Jack Clark Robinson for the lead on the Malibu Tile Works history; Monsignor Francis J. Weber for his information on incense and liturgical practices; Lisa Rubens for guidance on the 1939 Golden Gate International Exposition records; Bradley Fogo on California curriculum history; Diane Mourgos and Nancy Butler at the California Missions Museum; Lara Eggleton for sharing her work on the Alhambra; Branislav Slantchev for his Mission San Gabriel photographs; and L. Frank, James Luna, David Avalos, Debra Small, and William Weeks for allowing me to publish their artwork. The staff and volunteers at several missions have been gracious in their hospitality and assistance: Ann Boggess at La Purísima; Sister Barbara Jackson at Pala; Megan Dukett, Jerry S. Nieblas, and Jan Sorensen at San Juan Capistrano; and Sheila Benedict at Santa Inés. Any errors or omissions are, of course, my own.

I am grateful for the institutional support that made this work possible. The Center for Advanced Study in the Visual Arts, National Gallery of Art, provided support for multiple research trips to archives and missions. The Huntington provided a Summer Research Fellowship, and the American Association of University Women provided a Publication Grant. The inclusion of color images was made possible by a David R. Coffin Publication Grant from the Foundation for Landscape Studies. The IU School of Liberal Arts, Indiana University–Purdue University Indianapolis (IUPUI), supported this project with two sabbatical leaves, technological assistance, and by providing a climate that supports public scholarship.

Finally, I am indebted to my family and friends for innumerable kindnesses, material support, and words of encouragement over the years. The Hughes–Combs family has provided a West Coast home away from home that made my California research trips both more fun and more productive. Katie Janssen shared her insights about writing and life–work balance. Dan Barden and Leigh Ann Hirschman gave wise counsel about writing and creativity. Grace Davis's gift of a santo watched over me and stood as a token of the many friends whose encouragement and interest helped sustain this project. My parents modeled the richness of a life of curiosity, learning, and teaching. Their love and their belief in me are gifts beyond words. My three daughters have grown up with the missions, and their part in this project has been formative, whether expressed as cynical commentary on "conspiracy theory gardens" or encouraging Post-it notes on my desk. Finally, my husband, Tom, has been a loving, supportive partner in life and stalwart companion on this journey.

INTRODUCTION

Missions, Memory, and Heritage

"There's Something about Them That Draws Me"

> I can't get over the fact that this place was first constructed the year the U.S. declared its independence. It seems unworldly. I love the rebuilding after the 1906 earthquake, and the baroque styles used. I love the fact that THIS is where S.F. started. And that freaks me out. It's a beautiful Mission, with its high walls, crumbling cemetery, and voices of a distant and unreachable past. I love it here, and I make it a point to stop in when I can. It takes me back to my love of history and context, and I'm glad to be there. (Teej T., review of Mission San Francisco, posted to Yelp, June 4, 2008)

> When I get something in my head, it usually doesn't leave until I take action. Such is the case in my quest to visit all 21 California missions. . . . Their sometimes bloody histories make me sad . . . and mad. But the beauty is undeniable. The missions are not grand and elaborate. But there's something about them that draws me. . . . When I was a child, my grandmother, who was an elementary teacher, told me stories about California and Mexican history. She brought it alive, and I loved it. So, it seemed right that my mom, sister and niece decided to join me on the first leg of my journey. We started in Sonoma and worked our way down the north coast of California to Carmel. All had gardens, some rather stark like Sonoma and San Jose; some towered over by palms and crawling with bougainvillea. (Kym Pokorny, blog posted October 16, 2008)

These posts capture the ineffable allure of the California missions. Their contradictory mix of beauty and bloody history, their evocation of another time, the embodied experience of space, and a sense of connection with the past have threaded descriptions of the missions for more than a century. In the foreword to his 1913 book, *The Old Franciscan Missions of California,* prolific chronicler of the missions George Wharton James wrote, "The story of the Old Missions of California is perennially new. The interest in the ancient and dilapidated buildings and their history increases with each year."[1] The California Missions Foundation, which funds mission preservation, asserts that "nothing defines California and our nation's heritage as significantly or emotionally as do the 21 missions that were founded along the coast from San Diego to Sonoma. Their beauty, stature and character underlie the formation of California."[2] James predicted that "hundreds of thousands will stand in their sacred precincts, and unconsciously absorb beautiful and unselfish lessons of life as they hear some part of their history recited,"[3] but even he could hardly have imagined the ways people experience and consume the missions. Mission memorabilia are sold in gift stores, and vintage mission material culture is regularly traded on eBay. Photos of the missions are shared virtually on sites such as Flickr and Google Earth. The missions are part of the formative fourth-grade California history curriculum and are popular attractions for tourists. You can have your bathroom tiled with scenes of a mission garden, or plant your own garden with heritage seeds from a mission.

These gardens gracing the twenty-one missions from San Diego to Sonoma are varied in their layout and plant material, but are still recognizable as a cohesive garden type. The typical mission garden is laid out in a courtyard setting either within the mission's central quadrangle or in its forecourt. The design centers on a fountain surrounded by geometric beds and intersecting paths, often edged with clipped hedges. The plant material varies but usually includes a variety of semitropical plantings of succulents and palms, and a mix of flowering annuals, perennials, vines, and roses that provide colorful accents. Some missions also include a specimen or demonstration garden of cacti, native plants, herbs, vegetables, or other species grown during mission times. Some of the gardens are extensive, such as at San Juan Capistrano, where the garden covers much of the mission property. Others, for example, at San José, are more modest. Some, such as the Santa Inés mission garden (Figure I.1), are meticulously maintained with closely clipped hedges, while others have been allowed to grow more naturalistically, as at Soledad, Solano, and La Purísima (Figure I.2). Dedicated to the pleasures of sight, smell, and sound, they are all designed to be attractive, inviting spaces. The gardens are also presented as appropriately historic, even authentic landscapes for the colonial mission buildings. And yet these gardens are relatively recent inventions, imagined heritage that has performed important cultural work and has shaped the cultural memory of the California past.[4]

California Mission Landscapes investigates the role of the California mission landscapes in the Spanish colonization of Alta California in the eighteenth century and their ongoing transformation to heritage sites through the late nineteenth and twentieth centuries. This study elucidates the deeply political nature of these landscapes that recast the missions from sites of colonial control to aestheticized,

FIGURE I.1. Mission Santa Inés Mission garden, 2008. Photograph by the author.

FIGURE I.2. La Purísima Mission garden, 2008. Photograph by the author.

nostalgia-drenched, sacred monasteries. It documents the history of the missions' designed landscape, and it investigates how they have been appropriated and mobilized in the constitution of social relationships, particularly in the contestation of social inequalities across boundaries such as gender, race, class, ethnicity, and religion. The study also reveals the role of landscape design in establishing hegemonic ways of seeing that were consumed in the colonial gaze at the mission sites and reproduced in the visual and material culture of the missions. By historicizing heritage practices associated with the mission landscapes, fourth graders' model making, marketing, collecting, and tourism, the book argues that the gardens planted in the mission courtyards are not merely anachronistic but have become potent ideological spaces that naturalize California's valorized settler colonial narratives. The transformation of these sites of colonial conquest into physical and metaphoric gardens has perpetuated the marginalization of Indigenous agency and avoided confronting the contemporary consequences of colonialism.[5]

These questions of the intersections of settler colonial politics and the uses of the past are particularly cogent because of the missions' enduring prominence as heritage sites. All twenty-one missions are open to the public and recognized as valued, historic places. At each of the sites stands some remnant or reproduction of the original colonial period architecture and some rendition of a mission garden added at some point in the past one hundred and forty years. The missions are not just colonial relics, however, and the story of their landscapes is not simply a matter of the accuracy or inaccuracy of restorations. They are colonial sites that have been mobilized in a postcolonial world for a variety of purposes. The crux of their ideological tension is that they are simultaneously exuberant celebrations of a romanticized Spanish past and sites of conquest. They are Indigenous landscapes that have been appropriated for the benefit of civic, commercial, and religious interests. They are memorials for the thousands of Native Americans as well as for the priests, parishioners, and mission supporters who also lie buried there.[6] The missions have been imbricated so intimately into cultural memory that they are inextricable from the fabric of California's and the United States' grand historical narrative and are complicit in its distortions and erasures.[7]

The mission landscapes also reveal the complex and intricate operations cultural productions have mobilized in daily life. As Michael Rothberg has observed, the investigation of "multidirectional memory," particularly among social groups with histories of victimization, has been a productive line of inquiry for Holocaust, African Diaspora, and Postemancipation studies, and other instances of cultural oppression and genocide that are part of postcolonial and critical heritage studies more broadly.[8] In the case of the California mission landscapes, the fine-grained analysis of material, textual, oral, and visual evidence traces the construction of the colonized gaze in the spaces, as well as the negotiation and contestation of memory in small acts of resistance. Archival evidence offers insight into the complexity of interests and the impact of individual agency associated with each garden's origins. It brings to light some of the lesser-known actors in the sites' history and reveals their strategic use of the past to promote their own interests. In addition, examining the history of the gardens' representation in forms as varied as photography, fiction, and miniatures highlights the specific discursive practices such as collecting, model making, tourism, and historic plant propagation through which the mission landscapes' meanings have been constituted. In this sense, the history of the landscapes is less about changing plants and pathways and more about how the spaces have been appropriated and transformed, and, in the process, have become instrumental in constructing a highly politicized representation of the mission past.

The detailed examination of the production and reception of the mission spaces reveals how they are performed as embodied experiences of a celebratory colonial heritage in their broadest narratives, but also how they were stages for the smaller dramas of local interests, personal piety, and individual agency. Just as the grand narratives of Indian extinction were written into the local histories of New England, as Jean M. O'Brien's exhaustive study documents, so too the transformation of the landscapes at the twenty-one missions inscribed a new epistemology of Western civilization signified by European horticulture and design that was written over both the ancestral Indigenous landscape and the austere, utilitarian spaces of the colonial sites.[9]

Despite the prevalence of the missions as emblems of a romanticized past, counternarratives have persisted from the critiques of visitors to the colonial missions during the colonial period through twentieth- and twenty-first-century protests of the canonization of the Franciscan leader Junípero Serra.[10] The agency and resilience of Native peoples throughout time are visible in the millennia-old diverse cultures throughout the coastal, mountain, and desert areas of western North America, and in the responses to the systematic dispossession and violence of colonization and the successive state-sponsored oppression.[11] These kinds of counternarratives are often obscured by settler colonial accounts, but they are crucial for deciphering the design of the mission landscapes. As Lisbeth Haas has argued, the colonial missions, despite being sites of disruption and death, were also places in which Native peoples "used Indigenous forms of authority, knowledge, and power to seek redress and to sustain the community."[12] The emergence of the missions as heritage sites over the past 150 years must similarly account for the absences and agency of native people in both the site-specific landscape history and broader geographies of power. In the 1830s, for example, Indigenous scholar Pablo Tac developed a grammar for his native Luiseño language and wrote an account of life at Mission San Luis Rey.[13] Connections between literacy and insurgency have been documented broadly.[14] In the face of systemic dispossession through legislative and judicial processes during the second half of the nineteenth century, Native people deployed legal, rhetorical, and political strategies to try to protect their rights and preserve access to resources.[15] Violence, whether at the hands of the first colonizers or U.S.-sponsored militias, was met with both armed resistance and strategic evasion.[16]

Another reason to investigate mission landscape history is that despite the wealth of scholarship on California history in general and the missions in particular, the mission landscapes have yet to be fully mined as an avenue into understanding the politics of the past as a continuum between the Spanish colonial period, emerging American nationalism, and the contemporary heritage industry. Archaeologists such as Barbara Voss and Stephen Silliman and historians such as Lisbeth Haas, Robert Jackson, Edward Castillo, and Steven Hackel have elucidated the operations of the colonial mission landscapes to subjugate the Native peoples.[17] Works by Kevin Starr, William Deverell, Phoebe Kropp, and many others have laid out California's dynamic social and political history and its complex construction of a "Spanish fantasy past," a term first coined by journalist Carey McWilliams.[18] *California Mission Landscapes* argues the connections between the colonial missions as "nodes in the Indigenous landscape," as Kent Lightfoot has described them, and the ongoing production of and resistance to the landscapes as colonizing spaces into the twenty-first century.[19]

At its most basic level, this study fills a gap in the scholarship on the California missions by tracing the history of their landscapes within California social and cultural history.[20] In spite of all the attention paid to the mission buildings and institutional history, their landscapes and gardens have largely been the visual fodder of coffee table books and calendars. Most mission and architectural histories either inaccurately attribute the cloister gardens to the colonial period, locate them vaguely as part of the mission restorations by groups such as the Landmarks Club of Southern California around the turn of the twentieth century, or neglect them altogether.[21] In fact, none of these approaches is correct. One contribution of this book, then, is to set the record straight on the origins of the gardens. More broadly, the interest in mission landscapes and in settler colonialism globally highlights the value of diverse perspectives that reframe colonialist histories to include indigenous perspectives.[22]

A final reason to investigate the history and significance of the California mission landscapes is their potential to create very different visitor experiences than they currently do. The scholarship of postcolonialism has made a compelling case for the importance of place in creating more inclusive narratives and in reconciliation and healing for communities that have suffered trauma.[23] Globally, heritage sites have proved the value of interpreting painful, marginalized, and contested histories in ways that encourage critical inquiry and support civil discourse about potentially divisive topics.[24] The mission gardens, seemingly so innocuous and pleasant, have the potential to be not only catalysts for discussions of California's colonial legacy and its consequences for all citizens, but also spaces for a more inclusive and critical representation of Indigeneity. But it would be naive to think this vision can be realized without profound changes and transformational relationships in the governance and curatorial authority currently in place at the missions. As Larry Zimmerman, Laurajane Smith, and others have made clear, the commemorations and representations of Indigenous peoples, indeed of any community, are complex transactions.[25] But the growing corpus of Indigenous-centered history and Indigenous scholarship, as well as examples of successful collaborations to construct inclusive narratives, are all hopeful signs.[26] To move toward this future for reinterpreted mission landscapes, however, we must understand how they got there in the first place.

An Overview of Mission History

The fountains, paths, and flower beds that fill the mission courtyards today were once dusty, bustling work and social spaces, and, prior to Spanish colonization, the homeland of Native peoples for millennia. Before European settlers arrived, an estimated three hundred thousand Native people lived in small villages throughout California.[27] They actively managed the natural resources of this abundant habitat through controlled burning, selective harvesting, and seed scattering.[28] As Kent Lightfoot and Otis Parrish characterize the geopolitical landscape of Native California prior to colonization, it was "a crowded landscape packed with many modest-sized, semiautonomous polities, each of which supported its own organization of elites, retainers, religious specialists, craft experts, and commoners."[29] Native Californians also had a complex cosmography that located realms of earth, sky, and sea within a spiritual belief system that collapses Western dichotomies of nature and culture.[30] It was these traditional tribal homelands that the Spanish Crown claimed as "Alta California" with the founding of Mission San Diego in 1769 as the first of what became by 1822 a chain of twenty-one missions stretched along the coast and inland valleys (Figure I.3).

Established in the name of Spain by Franciscans under the leadership of Junípero Serra to Christianize the Indigenous peoples of California, the missions varied in size and prosperity, but grew to house some 13,500 "neophytes" by 1800 and 81,000 by 1834.[31] The missions became part of the Mexican territory in 1822 following Mexico's War of Independence and were secularized by the government eleven years later.[32] Between 1769 and 1833 the missions were run by Franciscans with the assistance of a small number of soldiers at each mission and larger military forces housed in garrisons or presidios that could be called upon when needed.[33] The missions were intended to be self-sufficient plantations sustained by the labor of the neophytes. They often provided food and labor for the nearby presidios and pueblos, as well feeding those living at the missions. At their

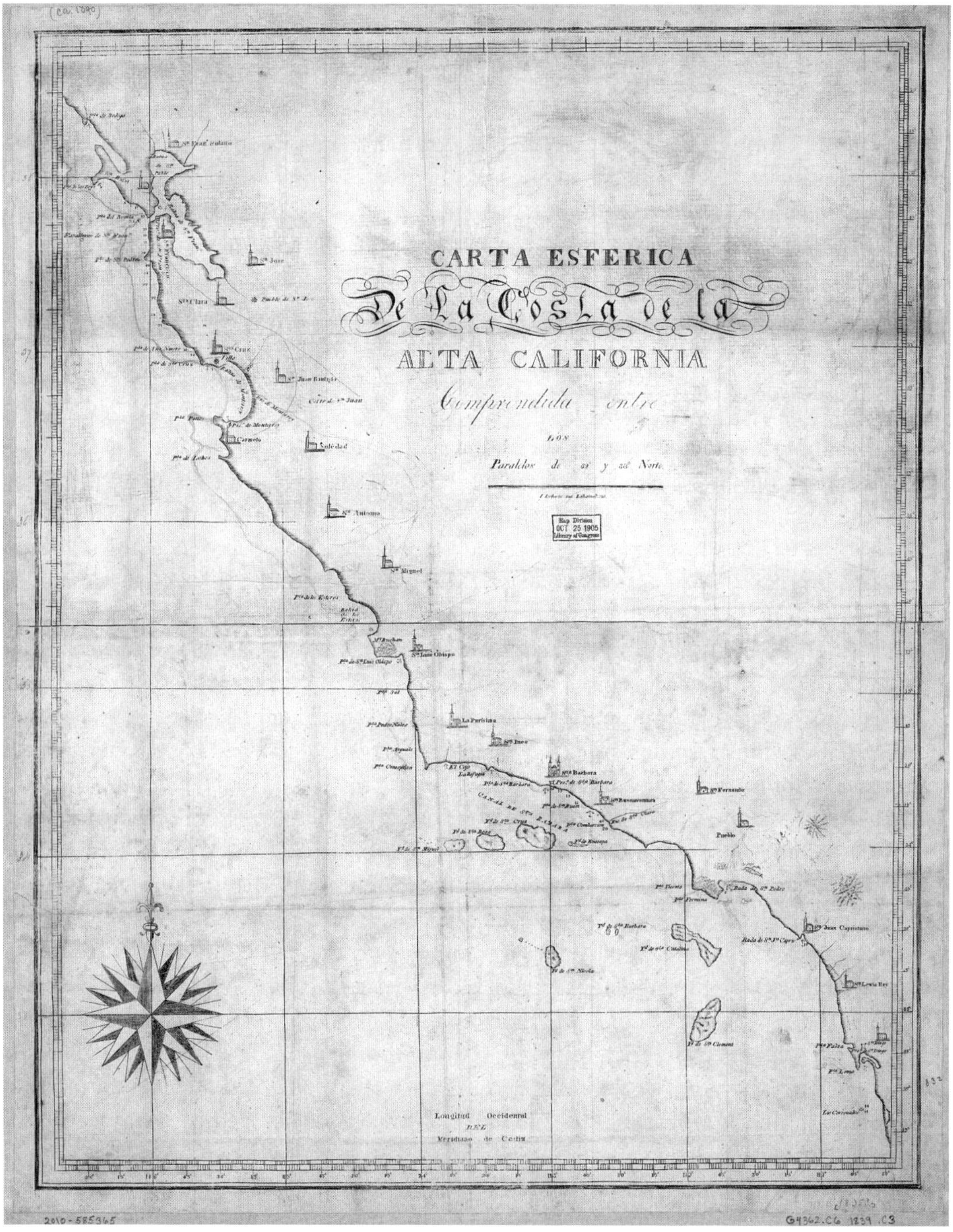

FIGURE I.3. Carta esférica de la costa de la Alta California: Comprendida entre los paralelos de 32° y 38° norte. Carl I. Wheat, 1839. Library of Congress.

peak, the larger missions eventually produced enough grain crops, hemp, olive oil, tallow, and hides to export.[34] The functions of the missions as productive farms and ranches and as institutions intended to convert and civilize the Native populations were effected through the design of their landscapes (Figure I.4). A visitor to a mission in the early nineteenth century would find a central compound with a church, cemetery, and attached buildings, often arranged in a quadrangle, which housed the priests, craftsmen, and, in some missions, the unmarried Native women.[35] The arrangement of the adobe structures in a quadrangle with an interior arcade followed centuries-old patterns of Franciscan monasteries, as seen in John Sykes's 1792 drawing of Mission San Carlos (Figure I.5). The landscape was designed for efficiency and control—both in the production of crops and goods and the oversight of the neophytes.[36]

Secularization decreed by Mexico in 1833 removed the missions from the missionary orders' control, and much of the former mission land or *patrias* was leased or granted to well-placed Mexican settlers for private ranching and farming.[37] For the Native Americans, the secularization of the missions was paralleled by a process of emancipation in which Indigenous people would be granted new political rights.[38] Some emancipated neophytes continued to work at the missions under the supervision of administrators, but with little to no compensation. Increasingly, the Native people withdrew their labor from the missions, went to live in Indian towns, work on ranches, or find work in the pueblos.[39] The promising initial prospects for full citizenship ceased, but Native people persisted in taking political action through legal petitions and labor stoppages, and, as Haas concludes, "their legal and social condition remained unsettled in Mexican California."[40]

In 1848 the missions were part of the treaty transfer of California to the United States following the Mexican–American War, and just two years later with the surging population of the Gold Rush boom it became the thirty-first state. The U.S. courts granted petitions during the 1850s and 1860s restoring the missions to the Catholic Church.[41] These mid-nineteenth-century events had a dramatic impact on the mission sites themselves. The land that was restored to the church was a far cry from the extensive agricultural enterprises of the mission days. A few of the missions became seminaries or schools, but most became parishes serving local communities. The properties conveyed back to the Church had deteriorated in private hands, and most of the groves and orchards had gone to ruin. As Henry Chapman Ford's 1883 drawing of Mission Soledad documents, many of the adobe buildings had begun to erode with exposure to rain, wind, vandals, and in some cases damage by earthquakes and floods (Figure I.6).

For Native Americans, Mexicans, and other marginalized groups, the injustices of Spanish and Mexican colonialism did not end with treaty transfer of the territory from Mexico to the United States in 1848.[42] In 1846 there were approximately

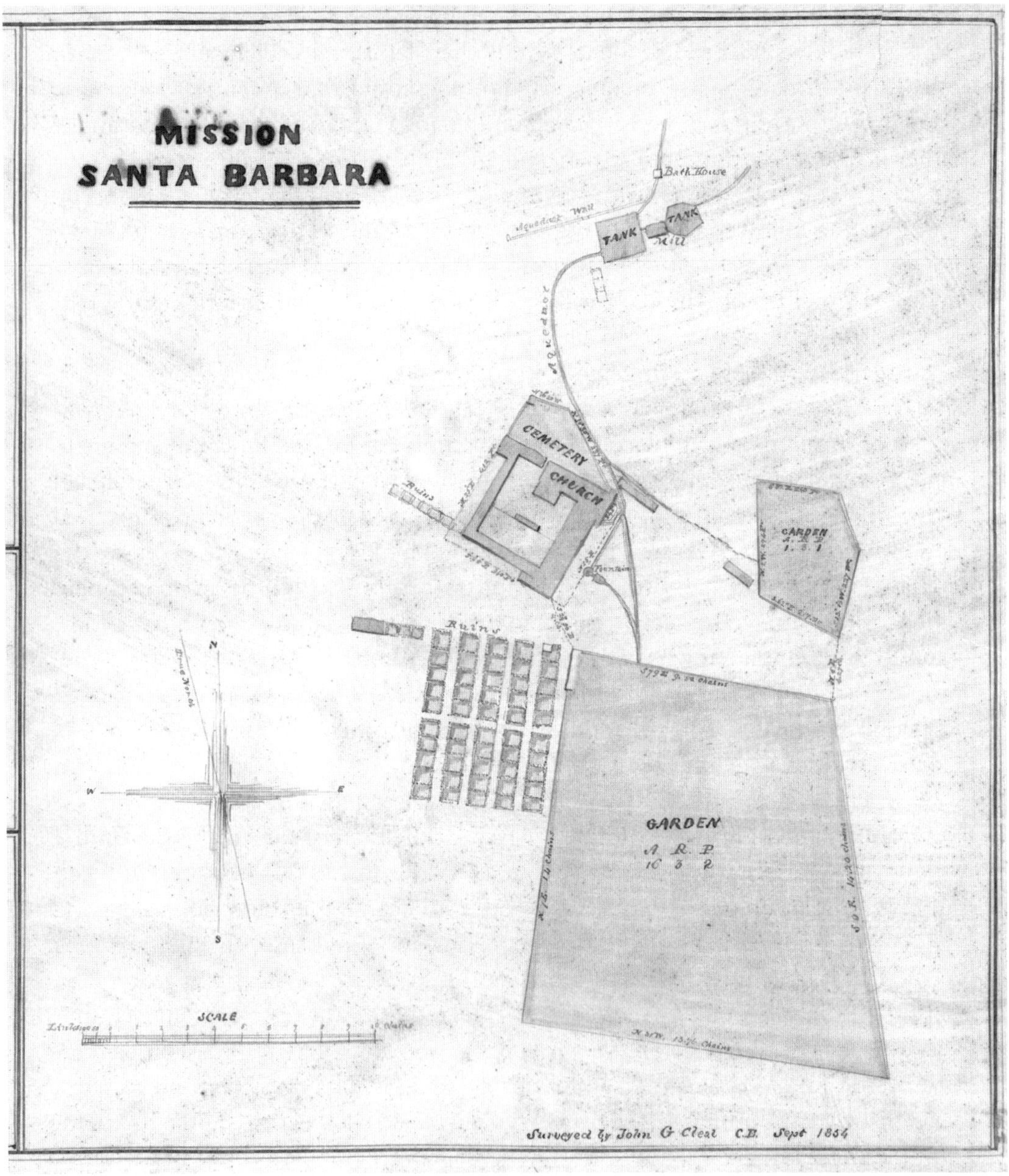

FIGURE I.4. Mission Santa Barbara, surveyed by John G. Cleal, C.E., September 1854. From U.S. District Court, California, Southern District, land case 388. Shows buildings, aqueduct, gardens; pen and ink and watercolor. Courtesy of The Bancroft Library University of California, Berkeley.

FIGURE I.5. John Sykes, view of Mission San Carlos Borromeo de Carmelo, November 1792. From *A Voyage of Discovery to the North Pacific Ocean, and Round the World.* Courtesy of the U.S. Department of Commerce, National Oceanic and Atmospheric Administration Collection.

100,000 Native people, and by 1870, just one-tenth of the eighteenth-century population, an estimated 30,000, remained in the state; most of those were on reservations without access to their traditional territories.[43] Factors such as disease, declining fertility rates, dislocation, habitat destruction, and policies such as forced removal to boarding schools and indentured servitude decimated the Native communities struggling to find a place in increasingly Anglo-dominated and racialized California (Figure I.7).[44] While there is ample evidence for acts of resistance, oppositional politics, and cultural survivance, systematic disenfranchisement and dispossession further dislocated and marginalized Native communities, as well as African Americans, recent immigrants and other non-Whites, well into the twentieth-century. These exclusionary politics were promulgated not only in legal and governmental spheres that denied the rights of full citizenship to these groups, but in the public discourse. As historian Linda Heidenreich has argued, "It was the dominant narratives of the nineteenth century that enabled Euro-Americans

FIGURE I.6. Henry Chapman Ford, view of Mission Soledad, 1883. Courtesy of The Bancroft Library University of California, Berkeley.

in the West . . . to practice violence and discrimination against racialized peoples on a daily basis in their everyday lives."[45]

This history of dislocation and disenfranchisement is critical to understanding the social and physical contexts of the missions when preservationists first began to take notice of their physical condition in the late nineteenth century. While local priests and parishioners had been doing their best to stabilize the buildings following secularization, many of the missions threatened to disappear altogether. In the 1880s and 1890s, the plight of the missions attracted the attention of artists, civic leaders, and promoters of California's burgeoning industries, as well as those interested in constructing a historical narrative for the origins of the state.[46] These mission preservation efforts were taking place at a time when California was seeing a growing Anglo-American influence in political and social circles, and the efforts to cast the missions as relics of a halcyon Hispanic era served both to romanticize and to distance that past.[47] A central part of that project was the invention of the mission garden (Figure I.8).

The missions, which the Franciscans established strategically near freshwater sources, arable lands, and Native communities, find themselves in a variety of settings in twenty-first-century California. Some are in the midst of dense urban areas (e.g., Mission San Gabriel near Los Angeles and Mission Dolores in San Francisco).[48] Others, such as Mission Soledad in the Salinas River valley, are more remote. Some have been catalysts for local tourism. San Juan Bautista's historic

FIGURE I.7. Carleton E. Watkins, *Indian Huts.* Watkins photographed the two thatched-roof structures on the Santa Anita Ranch owned by Elias Jackson "Lucky" Baldwin in San Gabriel, California, ca. 1877–80. The Huntington Library, San Marino, California.

FIGURE 1.8. Santa Barbara Mission garden, Keystone stereograph, cropped, ca. 1925. Keystone-Mast Collection, UCR/California Museum of Photography, University of California, Riverside.

plaza, for example, is a favorite locale for picnics and movie shoots, despite being directly over the San Andreas Fault. Santa Inés is part of the visitor package tour of the small and unlikely "Danish" town of Solvang, and Mission San Juan Capistrano, an hour south of Los Angeles, has become a vital engine of the town's tourist economy. Two of the missions, Mission Solano and La Purísima, are California State Park sites. The rest are owned by the Catholic Church in one form or another and continue to be active centers of worship, pastoral care, education, and outreach. Staffing and budgets vary widely. Funding at most missions comes from a mix of sources, including parish operating budgets, charitable contributions, grants for special projects, and earned income through admission, programs, rentals, and retail sales.

Whatever their particular context, all of the missions are also part of an Indigenous landscape. Not only are there vibrant reservation-based communities in the state or even, as in the case of Pala, surrounding the mission, but California, and the United States for that matter, is also an Indigenous landscape. This concept of Indigeneity in the land invokes both the historical claims to unceded territory that is an essential aspect of sovereignty, and also the enduring presence of what Native anthropologist Reyna Ramirez has called "Native hubs." These gathering spaces, both geographic and virtual, help sustain "senses of Native American culture, community, and identity" and help make connections across tribal boundaries, particularly for those living away from their land-based homelands.[49] While Paul Owns the Saber, a Lakota activist living in San Francisco, notes that the seventy thousand Indians in the Bay Area "are invisible," the city is nonetheless collectively known among Native Americans as "the urban rez," and it is redolent with Indigenous history, past and present.[50]

Similarly, the concepts of place and of Native cosmology continue to be central to contemporary understandings and experiences of Indigeneity and to producing Indigenous knowledge.[51] In this sense, the notions of private property and boundedness imposed by the Spanish have little relevance for enduring practices honoring sacred lands and enduring memories of the importance of place in Native histories. This is the "Third Space of Sovereignty," the space that, as Kevin Bruyneel has written, "refuses to accommodate itself to the political choices framed by the imperial binary: assimilation or secession, inside or outside, modern or traditional."[52] This space can be seen as exclusionary, as Bruyneel says, "inassimilable to the modern liberal democratic settler-state and nation." But as argued by Doreen Martinez in her proposal for retheorizing cultural tourism, the Third Space also holds the possibility for "Indigenous peoples [to] increase their involvement, means of production, and engagements with the consumer body . . . [and in the Third Space] . . . acts of authenticity take on a new narrative that includes the voices, positions, and understandings of Indigenous histories, terrains, and routes."[53] Just as images such as the photograph of Luiseños women at the rededication of

Mission San Luis Rey in 1893 (Figure I.9) offer a counterpoint to notions of the complete erasure of Native people from the mission landscapes in the late nineteenth century, so too reconceptualizing the place of the missions in the broader social and political landscape as Indigenous space brings the possibility of decolonizing their long-standing location in public discourse and in heritage practices.[54]

Thinking through Landscape, Meaning, Memory, and Heritage

Before probing more deeply into the history and significance of the mission landscapes, it is necessary to be explicit about the use of the key terms in this analysis, specifically *landscape, meaning, memory,* and *heritage.* Together these interconnected terms form the theoretical framework of this study.

Landscape

Denis Cosgrove has noted that the term *landscape* defies definition because it connotes everything from the surface of the earth to the pictorial practices of painting and poetic practices of literature. It is both space and idea, and therein

FIGURE I.9. Luiseños women at Mission San Luis Rey, 1893. The Huntington Library, San Marino, California.

lies its potency. Landscape, in Cosgrove's words, is a "way of seeing the world." It is "the external world mediated through subjective human experience. . . . Landscape is not merely the world we see, it is a construction, a composition of that world."[55] Significantly, landscape is both a tool for the imposition of power and a rich palimpsest recording its exercise over time. Heritage landscapes are both the material remnants of the past that inform our memory and give witness to what has come before, and they are the malleable and multivalent spaces we shape to forge our imagined pasts. Landscapes are therefore, as Richard Schein has noted, constitutive elements of societal ideas and ideals. We can study both the "materiality of the tangible, visible scene" and "the symbolic qualities they embed" to reveal the "duplicity of cultural landscapes."[56]

This study of the mission landscapes explores this duplicity by playing the histories of the mission landscapes as thing and as idea against each other to expose those histories' underlying ideologies and to tease apart their inherent tensions and ambiguities. The chapters that follow build a detailed social history of the spaces, including an examination of how the mission landscapes have shaped and been shaped by the generations who have lived, worked, and worshipped in them. That understanding of the origins of the designs is only a starting point, however. In his writings about the social practices of collective memory, Maurice Halbwachs has noted that for a belief of the past "to be settled in the memory of a group, it needs to be presented in the concrete form of an event, a personality, or a locality."[57] The missions are a compelling example of this kind of concretization of heritage and memory, and the history of their landscapes reveals the underlying ideologies of identity, power, and privilege that are encoded and enacted in the spaces. This study probes landscape as a verb, as W. J. T. Mitchell has phrased it, "as a process by which social and subjective identities are formed."[58]

This study also recognizes the role of landscape in colonialization globally and in the enduring structures and processes of settler colonialism. As Albert Memmi has noted, "Colonization is, above all, economic and political exploitation."[59] The institutions of colonialism are predicated on an ideology of land as property to be possessed by states and by individuals and a political economy in which land was a resource for extracting profit. In North American colonialism, the idea of landscape was also implicated in the "culture of conquest" through notions of Manifest Destiny, American exceptionalism, and, as Roxanne Dunbar-Ortiz has described, the "cult of the covenant" with its myth of the pristine wilderness and Calvinist notions of a preordained mandate to create a new society.[60] The political and ideological import of landscape is also an essential part of the contemporary discourses of sovereignty, Indigenism, and human rights.[61] In this sense the mission landscapes are both part of the physical dispossession of Native homeland and social spaces for narratives that assert and refute the complicated narratives of colonialism and resistance. Seeing how these ideologies of landscape play out in the particular histories of the California mission landscapes requires both an awareness of the larger political, economic, and ideological contexts and attention to the more minute changes of the built environment.

One premise of my approach is to eschew any distinction between garden and landscape at the contemporary sites.[62] While there are bounded spaces labeled on maps and described in guidebooks as "mission gardens," the mission properties in their entirety deploy a conceptual metaphor of "mission as garden." From their picturesque approaches to their foundation plantings, the mission landscapes invite visitors into a coherent postcolonial experience of a shared past by binding disparities of emotional resonance and ideological meanings through the construction of historic, beautiful, sacred spaces (Figure I.10). Similarly, imagery of the missions elides notions of landscape and garden as boundaries of walled garden, aestheticized ruins, and broader Edenic landscape are blurred and their metaphors enmeshed. For example, Union Pacific's 1922 "California Calls You" advertisement deploys the mission architecture, the citrus-laden tree, and the twin palms within the broader setting of a coastal landscape as an idealized setting for two adult tourists and a small child (Plate 1).

The mission landscapes are also places for the embodied experiences and the social performance of heritage in three-dimensional space.[63] In these spaces of manual labor, sensual pleasure, and spiritual pilgrimage, human contests of power

FIGURE I.10. Mission San Luis Rey, 2008. Photograph by the author.

and identity have been played out over the centuries, first in the colonial dynamics of the mission period and subsequently in the sites' nineteenth-century development as active parish communities and tourist destinations.[64] Anthropologist James Scott has argued that elites create public transcripts of apparent dominance in spheres of labor, rituals of hierarchy, speech practices, and punishment, as well as ideological justifications for the inequalities. At the same time, subordinate groups respond to the public transcripts of elites by creating hidden transcripts of resistance such as sabotage, rumor, vandalism, and other aspects of subversion and opposition.[65] The design of the California mission landscape is ripe for this reading of daily practices of domination as Native peoples not only participated in both the public and hidden transcripts but also experienced them in material and spatial ways. Describing this kind of close reading of landscapes, Ben Highmore has suggested that a "microgeography of daily life" is useful for understanding broader power dynamics because it "provides a way of pluralizing the self that a concentration on 'identity' in the singular would miss."[66]

As much as the missions are brought to life by the social actors as embodied experience, their history must also account for their materiality. The use of the landscape to position one's social standing is hardly a modern phenomenon. From cave painting to constructing new temples on plundered sacred sites, humans have, literally and figuratively, inscribed their claims to power on the landscape. They have used the built environment to legitimate political power through techniques such as ostentatious display, restricted access, privileged sight lines, links to previous regimes, and the other trappings of hierarchy conveyed in the landscape.[67] Physical space has the potential to be a disciplining force, to shape movements, organize bodies, and direct sight. As Michel Foucault has argued in his analysis of space and power, "A discipline fixes; it arrests or regulates movements; it clears up confusion; it dissipates compact groupings of individuals wandering about the country in unpredictable ways; it establishes calculated distributions."[68] The design of the mission landscapes, like that of plantations and prisons, is a disciplining landscape where individuals negotiated everyday experiences in this clash of Spanish and Native cultures and where tourists continue to participate in and resist messages of a romanticized colonial heritage. The organization of the space trains those who move through it, whether the neophyte following the Franciscans' daily regimen or the tourist following the audio guide.[69] In both colonial times and as contemporary tourist destination, the mission landscape fixes people in space and positions them to see and be seen, to experience the site in sequential and hierarchical ways. Space encodes power relationships and scripts the narratives of docile, obedient wayfarers. And yet, such disciplines are eminently resistible and subverted. So the history of the mission landscapes, as colonial and touristic spaces, reveals the perpetual dance between the disciplining expediency of space and the ever resourceful, creative agency of humans.

Meaning

I do not propose to define *meaning* or to argue a unified theory of the meaning of landscapes. Neither do I want to introduce a new concept of *metagarden,* along the lines of W. J. T. Mitchell's *metapicture.* Instead, I want to place this work alongside that of others who have sought to explain how, as Yi-Fu Tuan has phrased it, "the human person, who is animal, fantasist, and computer combined, experiences and understands the world,"[70] particularly through material histories and the ethnography of place. In this context, the mission landscapes are but one form of materiality implicated in the constitution of culturally constructed systems of signification, including gender, class, race, ethnicity, and religious identity (in this case breaking along both sacred/secular and Catholic/Protestant denominational lines). Furthermore, the study of landscape must reckon with the fact that these constructs are fluid, mutable, and dynamic, and they are forged in the contests of access to rights and resources, status and power. The material manifestations of commodified heritage and other forms of identity, such as dress, architecture, foodways, things, and gardens, are often "called on to prove that volatile and contingent social identities are stable and intrinsic personal ones."[71] Consequently, the mission landscapes' meanings are reducible to neither personally experienced spaces nor ideologically totalizing instruments. They are, instead, locations where this precarious mix of constituted meaning and power has been contested for centuries.

The quest to understand the multivalent mission landscapes is, therefore, a fraught but fascinating exploration of the interstices of socially constituted meaning forged through the tensions between subject and object, between the individual and the collective, the personal and the social, production and consumption, representation and reception. Here, too, I do not mean to imply a rigid, structuralist duality (despite this list of binary oppositions) or to suggest a systematic, discursive, semiotic logic that crosses time and cultures. But the evidence of the operations of the mission landscapes does suggest commonalities in the negotiation of power dynamics from the initial colonial encounters through the present realized in the opaque realm of the everyday. The work of Michel de Certeau, Ben Highmore, and others on the everyday is useful for understanding the production and negotiation of meaning in the mission landscapes because they embrace both the active agency of users as well as the efficacy of the materiality in which we exist. To apply Certeau's linguistic analogy distinguishing between the knowledge of language and the act of speaking, the inhabitation of the landscape involves individuals making "innumerable and infinitesimal transformations of and within the dominant cultural economy in order to adapt it to their own interests and their own rules."[72] People at the missions, whether living and laboring there or visiting them as tourists, are shaped by the ways in which the environment structures the movement of bodies and directs sight. But this power of landscapes to mold docile subjects is countered by the recognition that those same people produce meaning through the everyday practices or tactics of consuming the landscape—walking, gazing, digging, photographing. And this active appropriation extends to the consumption of landscape representations as well in acts such as reading texts and viewing art. All are part of the silent production of meaning or, as Certeau has argued, "the ingenious ways in which the weak make use of the strong, [and] thus lend a political dimension to everyday practices."[73]

The framework of everyday theory privileges the agency of individuals, whether Native Americans, marginalized mendicants, or tourists, to negotiate and resist those systems of signification and to reshape physically and ideologically the material world in which they live. The meaning of the landscapes can be interpreted, therefore, as evidence of both the public and hidden transcripts of oppression and resistance. By attending to the minute, such as the details of flower beds printed on cast porcelain miniatures, the gestures of statues, the framing of postcard views, and the plant selections of gardeners, this study weaves a thick description of these landscapes' social and political significance.[74] It seeks out not just the dominant narratives but also the subtle subtexts and manipulations as they are experienced in the everyday. Similarly, the narrow scale of material analysis and the mining of archival sources reveal the motivations, complexities, and contradictions complicit in the mobilization of enduring structures of privilege by some and the resistance to those strategies by others.

This attention to the hermeneutics of the production and reception of mission landscapes—how they were known and understood over time—builds on the scholarship of James Corner, John Dixon Hunt, W. J. T. Mitchell, and other landscape historians to trace the cumulative layers of cultural practices centered on the missions.[75] Just as reception theory accounts for the reader's role in literature, the examination of the "afterlife of gardens" considers the relationship between space and its occupants, that is, "how they are absorbed into the experiences of generations."[76]

Along with this attention to individual agency and the singularities of the experienced landscape, there is also a level of metaphorical meaning to be considered. As George Lakoff and Mark Johnson have argued, "Metaphor is pervasive in everyday life, not just in language but in thought and action. . . . The concepts that govern our thought are not just matters of intellect. They also govern our everyday functioning, down to the most mundane details."[77] The analysis of the mission landscapes across time and across media depicts the accumulated visual conventions and enduring tropes rooted in church, consumer, and state ideologies that can be traced over more than a century.[78] It seeks to interpret what Certeau has called "symbolizations that cannot be reduced to thought."[79] Specifically, the transformation of colonial outposts into Mediterranean-like gardens inscribed in the mission landscapes a conceptual metaphor that has endured for more than a century. Its persistence is testimony to the appropriation of the sites by enduring systems of power and privilege, as well as institutional interests invested in perpetuating the boundaries of class, gender, race, religion, and ethnicity.

Memory

A topic of interest to Greek philosophers and neuroscientists, memory has been a rich field of study for scholars across disciplines seeking to understand humans' cognitive capacities to retain information and reconstruct past experiences as well as the broader social constructions of the past often called "cultural memory."[80] While an exegesis on the semantic distinctions between the tangled and problematic terminology of memory studies is beyond the scope of this introduction, for the purposes of this study I share with Jeffrey Olick and Joyce Robbins the understanding of social memory studies to be a "general rubric for inquiry into the varieties of forms through which we are shaped by the past, conscious and unconscious, public and private, material and communicative, consensual and challenged." Furthermore, more useful for this study than the philosophical nature of memory or the qualities of "collective memory," if indeed such a thing exists, are the operations of memory—what Olick and Robbins call "the distinct sets of mnemonic practices in various social sites."[81] The more specific term *cultural memory* draws on Marita Sturken's definition: "Memory that is shared outside the avenues of formal historical discourse yet is entangled with cultural products and imbued with cultural meaning."[82] The flip side to this discursive notion of memory is that absence, erasure, and forgetting are equally potent.[83] Part of the reason the contemporary missions landscapes slip so seamlessly between venerated sites of nostalgia and detested sites of genocide is that their luxuriant gardens sit today where thousands of Native Americans once lived and worked under a Spanish colonial regime that consigned many to unmarked graves.[84] Sherry Turkle has argued that when "the objects of disciplinary society come to seem natural, what is most important is that what seems natural comes to seem right. We forget that objects have a history. They come to shape us in particular ways. We forget why or how they came to be. Yet 'naturalized' objects are historically specific."[85] Similarly, we forget that mission gardens, seemingly timeless and natural, have histories, distinct and purposeful.

This notion of cultural memory is also useful for theorizing touring, collecting, sketching, and other memory practices associated with the production of mission heritage. The result is that the triumphalist mission narrative is not merely a product of state propaganda, tourist marketing hyperbole, or even church apologetics. It is a widely dispersed narrative reflecting, as Turkle has observed, that "contemporary regimes of power have become capillary, in the sense that power is embodied in widely distributed institutions and objects."[86]

The concept of memory as a way of understanding the California mission landscapes is helpful for a number of reasons. First, more than merely old, the missions are perceived as relics or survivors of another age. They are origin sites in the historical narrative of the state, and the decisions of what to build, restore, plant, and excavate have been made in that context for at least the past 160 years.[87] Whether framed as "restoring," "re-creating," or planting an "old Spanish garden," the people landscaping the missions have done so with explicit reference to the past, whether imagined or factual. In sum, these sites are excellent examples of the construction of heritage. Second, as colonial sites, the missions are inherently tied to a painful legacy in which one group's will was imposed on another with devastating consequences for Native peoples. The sites have continued to symbolize that contested history, and therefore the politics of memory are inescapable. The choices of whose stories are told, whose voices are heard, and whose lives are commemorated or mourned are reflected in the postcolonial mission landscapes.[88] Similarly, the articulation of the motivations of the site administrators, landscape designers, fund-raisers, and others who have championed the mission garden projects illuminates the politics and ideologies informing their choices. Third, the missions and their landscapes have been materialized in various forms of popular culture, including fruit crate labels, souvenir pillows, magazine articles, decorative tiles, and clothing. This mission bricolage, though seemingly innocuous, extends the idea of the missions as gardens into classrooms, living rooms, storefront windows, and bodies. The consumption of this visual and material culture through quotidian practices of collecting, exhibiting, and shopping is as powerful a purveyor of structural inequalities over time as the sites themselves.[89] Fourth, as much as the mission gardens have evolved over time, they are a testimony to the persistence of memory. The image that the gardens convey of a past that was sacred, peaceful, and beautiful endures despite contradictory evidence. Even historians who note the gardens' modern origins still refer to the iconic image of the Franciscan padre in his sacred garden when in fact the colonial patio was a utilitarian workspace. Such narratives suggest that there is a broader discourse at play in both the popular and scholarly literature, one that is complicit in the systematic erasures that transform history into heritage.

Heritage

The term *heritage* connotes a specific perception and use of the past that imply connection or belonging and that are inextricable from structures of power and social inequalities. Essential to this understanding of heritage is that it is not the same as history. While history has its own subjectivities and politics, historians work under common assumptions of factual evidence, rigorous scholarship, transparency, and peer review. Heritage, in contrast, as David Lowenthal has argued, "restricts messages to an elect group whose private property it is. . . . Heritage passes on exclusive myths of origin and endurance, endowing us alone with prestige and purpose. It benefits us by being withheld from others. Sharing or even showing a legacy to outsiders vitiates its value and power. Heritage keeps outsiders at bay by baffling and offensive claims of superiority."[90] The mission landscapes as sites of heritage continually slip away from the past known through evidence to the realm of desire, indulging the pleasure of a sense of pride and belonging.

This notion that heritage is a political act has been recognized by scholars as a long-standing practice of invented traditions and imagined communities.[91] There is a growing interest in "critical heritage studies" that interrogates, as the manifesto for the inaugural Association of Critical Heritage Studies stated, that which "privileges old, grand, prestigious, expert approved sites, buildings and artefacts that sustain Western narratives of nation, class and science."[92] Of particular interest is how this heritage is deployed in the power dynamics of "nationalism, imperialism, colonialism, cultural elitism, Western triumphalism, social exclusion based on class and ethnicity, and the fetishising of expert knowledge"[93] The history of the mission landscapes offers an opportunity to investigate not only the narratives of constructed heritage inscribed over time at the sites, but also how those narratives have become part of everyday experiences through the complex intersections of formal and informal heritage practices. In the case of the missions, these practices both operate within the contexts of institutional sponsorship of curators and site managers and circulate outside the formal curatorship of heritage professionals in forms such as fourth graders' creation of mission models and the manufacture of collective miniatures. These objects, along with the vast visual culture of the missions, raise issues regarding community-curated heritage and how to balance one's right to "manage the story of one's past"[94] with the desire to promote an inclusive, reflective, and relevant stewardship of heritage.[95] The roles of heritage professionals are particularly complex given missions' contested history as monuments venerated by some and seen as sites of genocide by others. Interpreting their colonial history is further complicated given that the vast majority of the missions remain the property of the Catholic Church and under its administrative control. They therefore share many of the same concerns related to human rights and social justice found in other postcolonial heritage sites, particularly where former colonizers manage the interpretive program.[96]

The mission landscapes also offer evidence of how such dominant narratives of heritage can be resisted and challenge the monolithic notions of heritage. They highlight the creativity and agency of individuals such as nostalgic priests, wryly humorous gardeners, and critical cultural tourists who read and contest the scripted narratives of heritage, remaking the landscapes in their own image. Like studies of changing performances of race at Colonial Williamsburg and plantation sites in the American South, the missions are active arenas for the construction of heritage as a contested domain.[97] These examples nuance Lowenthal's claim that "loyalty and bonding demand uncritical endorsement and preclude dissent" and instead suggests that people are capable of navigating complex, often contradictory meanings in the landscape and producing their own interpretations.[98] The complexities of the mission landscape heritage multiply even more when one considers their diverse stakeholders. The labels applied variously to the mission landscapes—Spanish, Mediterranean, Native American, coyote, neophyte, Mexican, Anglo, Catholic, Californio, Californian, and American—suggest just how complicated these identities are. The mission landscapes are heritage sites for a variety of different faiths, descendant communities, civic groups, and economic interests. Heritage professionals have interests in promoting visitation, maintaining the reputations of their institutions, preserving their access to archaeological and archival resources controlled by private entities, and protecting their own professional reputations and allegiances.[99] There are tensions evident in local, state, and national narratives as well. The politics of memory implicated in the contests among these interest groups become visible in the mission landscape remade as a celebratory, heroic past and naturalized as timeless, sacred, and beautiful, but it is also evident in diverse religious iconography, the commemoration of the dead, and the celebration of agricultural, industrial, and preservation pioneers. The significance of the mission heritage to different interest groups is registered in markers as explicit as the statewide campaign to hang mission bells every mile along El Camino Real and as subtle as the Mission San Juan Capistrano profile on city trash cans.

Deploying heritage as an active tool in the construction of identity, particularly in postcolonial contexts, is not unique to the missions. Mitchell has noted that landscapes, due to their semiotic features and the historical narratives they generate, are "tailor-made for the discourse of imperialism, which conceives itself precisely . . . as an expansion of landscape understood as an inevitable, progressive development in history, an expansion of 'culture' and 'civilization' into a 'natural' space in a progress that is itself narrated as 'natural.'"[100] Heritage as it is framed at the missions is not simply about identity labels or even a sense of affiliation, connectedness, or cohesion. Instead, identity, as Rogers Brubaker and Frederick Cooper (2000) remind us, is a category of practice

> used by "lay" actors in . . . everyday settings to make sense of themselves, of their activities, of what they share with, and how they differ from, others. It is also used by political entrepreneurs to persuade people to understand themselves, their interests, and their predicaments in a certain way, to persuade certain people that they are (for certain purposes) "identical" with one another and at the same time different from others, and to organize and justify collective action along certain lines.[101]

Because this constitution of identity is socially constituted, its analysis offers the opportunity to explain "the processes and mechanisms through which what has been called the 'political fiction' of the 'nation'—or of the 'ethnic group,' 'race,' or other putative 'identity'—can crystallize, at certain moments, as a powerful, compelling reality."[102] This deeper reading of the mission landscapes exposes how heritage sites are deployed to mystify and naturalize inequities of the present as well as the contradictions of the past. American history has been intricately tied to a rapidly changing and diverse society, and California's historical narratives have contributed to emerging constructions of race, ethnicity, and nationalism.[103] While this broader discourse of identity and power does not reside uniquely at the missions, the landscapes reveal a subtle but telling perpetuation of inequalities as the colonial heritage has been rendered in a form palatable enough for consumption as public heritage.

One of the reasons the missions have become central to the construction of heritage in the western United States, perhaps more so than any other building or feature in the California landscape, is their potency as iconic symbols. Images of the mission garden, such as that advertising Patio Brand fruit (Figure I.11), have been reproduced, circulated, and consumed in so many ways that they have become referents for a codified and symbolic heritage. *Icon,* the ancient Greek word for "image," came to be used in early Christian times for images of saints and angels that graced the interiors of Orthodox churches. In that theology the icon was never the "real thing"; rather, it was a miniature pictogram, a diminutive window for "looking into" the real thing. In liturgical practice Eastern Christians did not pray to or worship icons, but viewed them as windows into the mysteries of the holy.

In this regard, the power of the California mission landscapes is like that of an icon with a reference not to the divine but to the past. The landscapes that became "mission gardens" function as windows into an imagined heritage. They are connected to a sense of time in which California's cultural origins reside and where that sense of past is quickened through the "experience of place and movement, memory and expectation."[104] They are iconic spaces in which connections to the past, experienced in actual or imagined visits, are framed in terms that were pleasurable and authentic. The landscapes reproduce the constructed historical narrative of California's heroic past and render it as an indelible part of the fabric of the sites. Like museum exhibits, the mission landscapes where "atmosphere," as curator Peter Bjerregaard has described "the in-betweenness of objects and subjects,"[105] creates affective spaces that can disturb or reinforce our everyday concepts of the world. This process of naturalizing the past into the present at the missions as a seemingly inevitable part of life goes beyond the marginalization of native and ethnic histories and the valorization of the priests' efforts during mission times. The issues of inequality and racism continue to be reproduced and power continues to be negotiated in the missions as tourist destinations and

FIGURE I.11. Patio Brand, San Fernando Fruit Growers Association. The Huntington Library, San Marino, California.

memorials today. A history of the mission gardens, therefore, is less a narrative written into the landscape by the people who lived there and subsequently decoded by historians and archaeologists who trail them than it is an active and complex set of ideas and negotiations in perpetual construction over time. In this sense the landscape history is always referential to the contexts of past and present, and always part of a negotiation of power and constitution of social relationships.

Organization of the Book

California Mission Landscapes is structured in four chapters. This Introduction establishes the basic research questions, thesis, and theoretical framework; the next two chapters lay out the colonial and postcolonial history of the landscapes.

Chapter 1, "Colonial Mission Landscapes," examines the history of the landscape during the mission period (1769–1833) and the ways in which space was mobilized in the contests of domination and resistance. It explores the ideology of landscape from both Spanish and Indigenous perspectives and accounts for those epistemologies in an analysis of the spatial practices of power relations and the changing social world of both colonizers and Native peoples. The chapter also establishes a baseline for the history of the mission landscapes as a fundamentally utilitarian design dedicated to labor and productivity, the control of docile subjects, and conforming to the Franciscans' expectations for practices of time, behavior, worship, and work.

Chapter 2, "Inventing Heritage: Time Binding in the Mission Landscape," extends the history of the landscapes from the end of the mission period following secularization in 1833 through the twentieth century. It traces the invention of the "mission garden" from its first iteration at Santa Barbara in 1872 through its replication in missions across the state in the twentieth century. This little-studied aspect of California landscape design challenges the standard chronology of Mission Revival architecture history and corrects the frequent attributions of the gardens to the colonial period. Six mission gardens developed in the twentieth century are profiled both to exemplify the import of Santa Barbara as an archetype and to investigate the ideological and political agendas informing their derivative designs. The history of these landscapes is all the more fascinating because it is also implicated in the construction of a romanticized vision of the colonial past and a broader expression of regional architecture and landscape design rendered variously as Mediterranean and Mission Revival. The unique stories of the five mission gardens also reveal the agency of their designers in exploiting vernacular garden design to serve their own interests and identities, as well as to negotiate systems of value and power in society.

Chapter 3, "Cultivating Heritage: Race, Identity, and the Politics of the Mission Landscape," traces the representation of the mission landscapes in texts, visual culture, and material culture. It analyzes the narratives, tropes, and conceptual metaphors that frame the construction of the past at and through the missions. It interrogates the connections of power, space, and visuality mobilized in the materiality of the landscape to signify a shared heritage that naturalized certain interests and marginalized others. While paying attention to their cultural contexts, a close reading of the mission landscapes representation lays bare their explicit narratives and implicit ideologies.

Chapter 4, "Consuming Heritage: The Embodied Experience of the California Missions," takes an ethnographic approach to the landscapes to explore the performative aspects of the mission landscapes as staged and embodied experience. It examines specific discursive practices, including tourism, gardening, and memorialization in historical and contemporary contexts. It also analyzes how the processional spaces are structured to create affective, multisensory visitor experiences that both reproduce the ideologies of the mission gardens and provide opportunities to contest, resist, and negotiate those meanings. The complexity of the production and reception of the missions as social stages exposes the recursive operations of meaning and the material activated by individual agency.

The Conclusion, "Third Spaces and the Future of Mission Memory Practices," returns to the initial questions about the contradictory role of the missions as shrine / memorial and colonial / Indigenous landscape in the construction of California heritage. It extends those questions by considering the stakes of remembrance and forgetting for the interpretation and stewardship of the mission landscapes and the possibilities of reinventing them as Third Spaces.[106] It poses the potential of transforming the interpretive programming at the missions and becoming part of the broader projects to decolonize American history and to mobilize heritage sites as places of critical inquiry, civic discourse, and reconciliation. It also champions recognition of the historic nature and value of the mission gardens with renewed attention to both their potential as teaching tools and their historic significance requiring a professional approach to historic landscape preservation and management. Several recent initiatives are examined as possible models for a more inclusive and collaborative approach to the presentation of the past at the missions.

A critical history of the mission landscapes is timely, even urgent, because the missions are such a prominent part of the public heritage practices of the state. They are also iconic sites in American history. By revealing the social relationships and ideologies encoded in the landscapes, the sites have the potential to instigate dialogue about the contested history of the missions and the human rights issues they raise.[107] The missions hold the promise for reimagining a different kind of interpretation of the past and, in particular, for presenting the landscapes of the missions in a way that reveals their ideological complexities and invites visitors' critical questions. Donald Fixico has made a compelling case for including Native epistemologies and experiences in American history. His "call for change" stems from the essential assertion that "it is necessary to attempt to 'see' things from the Native perspective of a tribal community's inside."[108] As historic sites, the California mission landscapes have the potential to enrich the public understanding of the past in both senses. They can encourage people to engage in the "infinitely subtle mediation" of the mission past, to reexamine their notions of California history, and to reflect on the experiences that have shaped their understandings of the past. They can also be spaces of inclusion and collaboration and even reconciliation. They can tell diverse stories through diverse voices and more fully engage their audiences with Indigenous knowledge and cosmologies, as well as with contemporary perspectives on the legacies of colonialism for Native peoples.

CHAPTER ONE

Colonial Mission Landscapes

Situating the Missions

The mission landscapes that survive today as popular heritage sites with their beautiful churches and courtyard gardens have deep histories that stretch back thousands of years. To comprehend the significance of the present landscapes it is necessary to examine the establishment of the missions at the end of the eighteenth century and understand their place within the ideological contexts of Indigenous cultures and of Spanish colonialism. From this perspective the missions were spaces where contrasting ideas of land converged and where the design of the landscape was one of the technologies employed in a daily contest of power. At the level of individual actions and in dwellings, sanctuaries, and plazas, we see the consequences of colonialism register in material and personal terms. The California mission landscapes reveal the drama of colonialism played out less in pitched battles and more in the spaces and habits of daily living, working, and worship. Recognizing the divergent ideologies of landscape converging in these mission spaces historicizes the deep-rooted metaphors of colonialism and horticulture as well as the role of the built environment in asserting and resisting social control. This history of the colonial period mission landscapes also highlights the agency of Indigenous people, and it helps challenge Western assumptions of implicit dualities of nature/culture, emotion/reason, practice/ideology, mundane/ritual, sacred/profane, cosmos/society. Finally, this analysis of the colonial missions establishes the idea of the spaces as Indigenous landscapes that have persisted through the centuries, before, during, and after colonization.

The missions were established at the end of the eighteenth century during a time of rapid and complicated change for California Native peoples. Environmental destruction, military oppression, and displacement took their toll, but most significant were the diseases to which the Native Americans had little resistance. The high mortality rates had devastating effects on every aspect of traditional lifeways, and the loss of human life had profound implications for the stability of Indigenous social, economic, and political structures. The impact of disease was compounded by the rapid environmental change brought on by the introduction of new, invasive plants as well as domesticated herd animals that disturbed critical hunting-and-gathering resources, particularly the rich shellfish and marine resources in the coastal plains.[1] Traditional Indigenous environmental management techniques were also thwarted by Spanish authorities. Intentional controlled burning, which had been a vital tool of the Indians for managing the risk of wildfires and for prompting growth of favored plants and basket-making materials, was banned.[2] As if these changes were not drastic enough, California was experiencing one of its cyclical periods of sustained drought that further stressed the Native peoples' capacity to sustain themselves as they had for millennia. In short, this was, as one archaeologist has put it, "a time of little choice."[3] To join the missions and become "neophytes" or *neófia/neófitos(as)* meant not only being added to the baptismal rolls but also entering the rules and restrictions of mission life. It meant residing within the mission confines, joining the labor force, and participating in the structured daily activities of the mission.[4] Many Native people stayed in autonomous villages beyond the central, northern, and eastern boundaries of the territories claimed by the missions, and some relocated to the interior and joined others in what are being identified as points of refuge or "colonial hinterlands" in response to the Spanish incursion in coastal areas.[5] Others became part of the Spanish *reducción* policy in which people living in outlying villages were brought to centralized locations within the mission system (which included missions, *asistencias* or sub-missions, and ranchos).

The missions have long been seen as oppressive, totalizing colonial institutions whose founding effectively en-slaved Indigenous people and transformed Alta California into Spanish territory and colonized space.[6] But scholarship over the past twenty years has situated the California missions as "nodes in an indigenous landscape," part of a web of interconnected social relationships, active economies, and enduring cosmologies.[7] Recent work has also recast interpretations of the oppressive regimes of the missions to account more fully for cultural pluralism at the missions, Native Americans' agency, and their active negotiation of the conditions of colonialism.[8] For example, excavations of shell mounds have yielded evidence that they were being utilized well into the mission period. Faunal and plant remains in neophyte housing contexts similarly indicate the persistent use of traditional foods, suggesting continued contact, exchange, and travel between those living at the missions and those in autonomous villages and hinterlands.[9] Evidence also indicates that various missionaries employed different *reducción* strategies depending on the Indigenous polities with which they were interacting.[10] Assemblages at the missions suggest those with access to new goods capitalized on opportunities to form new trade networks and take advantage of positions of privilege in the mission hierarchies.[11] Historian Lisbeth Haas has detailed how Indigenous interpreters and leaders helped to translate colonial constructs to their people, and similarly shared Indigenous knowledge in the missions.[12] Archaeologist Lee Panich's study of burials, grave goods, and shell and glass beads excavated at Mission Santa Clara suggests that Native people continued traditional mortuary practices and incorporated glass beads into local understandings of status and mourning, even as they continued to use shell beads throughout the mission period.[13] The picture that emerges is of a diverse landscape, rapid pace of social change, and complex social relationships as both the colonizers and Indigenous people navigated the changing conditions and constraints of colonialism.

These dynamics of California colonial domination and resistance are visible in individual activities of the everyday and in the larger episodes of coordinated revolt. In spite of the imposition of Spanish disciplines of time, space, and work, there is also wide-ranging evidence that Native peoples living within the missions persisted in aspects of their traditional lifeways, belief systems, and social relations. James Sandos has laid out a compelling case for "protective ingratiation" in which the neophytes participated in the Franciscan agenda of Christian, Western practices but did so selectively and consciously as acquiescence served their needs at the time. Sandos argues that Native peoples were overtly in compliance with Spanish expectations for behavior and willingly partook of the "knowledge power"[14] the missions offered, such as the ability to sow and harvest domesticated crops, weave woolen textiles, work metal, and other crafts. At the same time they persisted in their traditional knowledge power of the social and ideological relationships that bound their Native world together.[15] This dual participation is captured in objects such as a Chumash presentation basket (ca. 1822) made by María Marta, a neophyte at Mission San Buenaventura in Ventura County (Figure I.1). Marta made the basket to present to the visiting Mexican general José de la Cruz, and combined traditional Chumash basketry techniques and materials with geometric motifs and the Spanish iconography of royal insignia derived from a peso coin.[16] The basket is striking not only because it is one of the few surviving examples that includes the maker's name in the inscription but also because of the position of that text. Whereas on the peso, the inscription around the circumference names Spain's reigning king, Marta inscribes herself around the rim of the basket.[17] This kind of selective appropriation of symbols is also demonstrated by the Chumash who "routinely wore talismans under their shirts with the Christian rosary clearly visible on top."[18] And this negotiation of power through dual participation is also manifest through the materiality of the mission landscapes, where "intertwined concepts of power, belief, and politics structured the mission experience for both colonizers and indigenous peoples."[19]

FIGURE 1.1. Presentation basket made by Chumash María Marta (ca. 1766–1830) for presentation to the visiting general José de la Cruz, ca. 1822, Ventura County, San Buenaventura Mission. Using traditional Chumash techniques, Marta incorporated the Spanish royal coat of arms and the inscription "Me hizo An Maria Marta neofita de la mision de el serafico doctor San Buenaventura" ("I was made by Ana María Marta, neophyte of the mission of the Seraphic Doctor San Buenaventura"). The Phoebe A. Hearst Museum of Anthropology, University of California, Berkeley.

Colliding Landscapes: Ideology and the Spatial Practices of Colonial California

A visitor to California in 1750 would have described one of the most varied, diverse landscapes on the North American continent. Mountain ranges running parallel to the Pacific shore created rich coastal headlands, broad inland valleys, wooded hills, and deserts. Native Americans actively managed what M. Kat Anderson has called the "calculated abundance" of "California's cornucopia," transforming "roots, berries, shoots, bones, shells, and feathers into medicines, meals, bows, and baskets."[20] To sustain their communities Native people developed an intimate and symbiotic relationship with the land through controlled burning, weeding, sowing wild seeds, tending beds of wild tubers, and tending fruit- and seed-bearing shrubs. Settlement practices varied by region, but in general Native people along the coast were based in small villages and moved throughout their homelands, harvesting wild plants, game, and fish depending on seasonal availability. They were also skilled fishermen whose sophisticated watercraft and tools allowed them to harvest even the deep-sea mammals, as well as other oceanic, anadromous, and riverine fish species. For example, the Chumash created wooden plank canoes or *tomol* up to thirty feet long,[21] while Louis Choris's 1822 image from the San Francisco Bay depicts two men paddling a passenger in a reed or tule boat (Figure 1.2).

In contrast to Native settlement patterns, the missions were fixed in the landscape with permanent architecture, bounded and spatially segregated. The area within the quadrangle, sometimes called the patio or courtyard, provided protected and easily monitored areas for cooking and other work.[22] It was also the site of communal gatherings such as meals and assemblies, and it was the location of corporal punishment. Outbuildings for food processing and light industry were built around the central mission complex with features such as tanning vats, soap- and tallow-making facilities, baking ovens, iron forges, kilns, weaveries, threshing floors, and laundries. At several missions extensive water systems supplied water for irrigating gardens, washing laundry, and tanning hides.[23] The

FIGURE 1.2. Louis Choris, *Bateau du port de Sn. Francisco,* plate IX [9], 1822. Yale Collection of Western Americana, Beinecke Rare Book and Manuscript Library.

largest missions established satellite ranches (or ranchos) to oversee herds on distant grazing lands and a few founded asistencias such as Santa Ysabel established by Mission San Diego in 1818.[24] In addition to extensive agricultural fields and pastures, there were gardens of vegetables, herbs, and medicinal plants, fruit orchards, and olive groves closer to the central mission buildings. In warmer, drier areas, cactus hedges were effective barriers for livestock. Burial grounds were usually sited near the mission churches. The forecourts and patios of the buildings had scattered shade trees and possibly other informal plantings, but they were primarily utilitarian workspaces with scrubby grass or bare dirt, particularly in the drier climates.

The collision of landscapes in eighteenth-century California was not just a matter of competing claims for resources or of contrasting settlement and subsistence patterns; it was a clash of worldviews.[25] Two brief accounts of the landscape along California's Central Coast quoted at the beginning of the chapter illustrate two disparate ideologies of landscape. A little more than a hundred years ago, Maria Solares, a Chumash woman who had been born at Mission Santa Inés, told a story to John Harrington, an anthropologist who was collecting oral traditions from fluent Chumash speakers (Figure 1.3):[26]

> There is this world in which we live, but there is also one above us and one below us. . . . Here where we live is the center of our world—it is the biggest island. And there are two giant serpents . . . that hold our world up from below. When they are tired they move, and that causes earthquakes. The world above is sustained by the great Slo'w, who by stretching his wings causes the phases of the moon.[27]

Solares's account of the Chumash view of the world reveals a cosmology of the universe and an understanding of the landscape on which the Chumash resided that is quite different from a Western paradigm. Chumash stories map a concept of a closed universe composed of three flat circular worlds suspended in a great abyss and supported by powerful supernatural beings. The Chumash lived at the geographic center of the middle world, and moving from that center meant meeting increasing danger. The Chumash tales speak of a personalized universe where "plants, animals and birds, celestial bodies, and various natural forces are all part of the social universe," and where kinship was extended to creatures, plants, and supernatural beings.[28] It was a world in which objects and beings were mutable, where forms could change, and beings could be transformed. The negotiation or avoidance of those transformations was one of the challenges of existing in a dangerous universe. Navigating places of transformation such as passages, caves, bodies of water, and darkness required prudence, personal power, and fluency in the relationships that bound the world together. It is a worldview in which Cartesian dichotomies of mind/body and nature/culture seem to have little place.[29]

FIGURE 1.3. Maria Solares, photographed by John P. Harrington (detail), 1916. National Anthropological Archives, Smithsonian Institution (OPPS 91-31424).

The second account is a journal entry by a Spanish Franciscan, Father Juan Crespí, who landed in 1769 on the Santa Barbara coast, not far from Santa Inés:

> We went over land that was all of it level, dark and friable, well covered with fine grasses. . . . in sight of the shore, over some low rolling tablelands . . . [was] very good dark friable soil and fine dry grasses. . . . It was all flat land, excepting only some short descents into a few dry creeks. If it can be dry-farmed, all the soil could be cultivated.[30]

In Crespí's Catholic belief system the landscape was part of a natural world created by God for the purposes of mankind. Crespí's eighteenth-century education imbued him with the belief that observation and knowledge of the natural world were hallmarks of human civilization—the culture that set humans apart from nature.[31] Crespí also articulated the premise of his capitalist worldview that considered land "property" to be owned, presumably by the Spanish Crown, and a resource to be improved. That the soil was friable implied it could be farmed, potentially producing not only life-sustaining food but also surplus crops that could be sold at local markets or exported. Land, in this economic system, required labor to make it productive—to improve it—and in the Spanish colonial project that labor supply was solved by the premise that creating *gente de razón* (a label that connoted Spanish speaking and other markers of becoming a "civilized" and rational person) entailed training them in agriculture and husbandry practices, among other technologies.[32]

These contrasting landscape ideologies are evident in the Spanish and Native Americans' radically different ways of living on the land. The Spanish ordered the landscape into bounded zones of specialized functions, such as fields, pastures, gardens, orchards, vineyards, groves, and walled courtyards and patios.[33] For the Chumash, who had supported complex chiefdoms and semisedentary settlement patterns by harvesting the abundant and stable resources of the coastal waters and woodlands, subsistence meant mapping themselves onto the land, literally following migrating sea mammals or ripening acorns for seasonal harvesting and then returning to their historic villages.[34] The Indigenous California worldview stood in contrast to that of the Spanish in that land was something one lived in relationship with and used, but never "owned." The California Native worldview saw all of creation in relationship and animated with spirit. The Chumash, for example, saw creation as three layers with their people living in the middle layer, but passage between the layers was possible in life and in death. A person made his or her way in the world by maintaining those relationships with the community and with all of creation. This relationship with the earth was etched into the patterns of seasonal settlement shifts and in the layout of their houses.[35] For example, in the central California coast, one of the most densely populated areas, groups followed a seasonal round to traditional hunting, fishing, and gathering areas annually and returned to semipermanent village sites. In Native villages, houses were loosely grouped around open common space, and the architecture was fairly ephemeral. The bent-pole-and-thatch conical structures were used for a few years before they were burned to eradicate vermin and new dwellings constructed. Even communal structures such as sweat lodges and ceremonial buildings were relatively temporary, and could be constructed when a group decided to host a feast or specific ritual.

The mission layout was based on centuries-old monastic tradition as well as missions in Mexico and Baja California.[36] The first structures were simple wooden huts with thatched roofs, as depicted in José Cardero's 1791–92 view of Mission San Carlos, but these were quickly replaced by adobe and stone buildings, as materials and labor became available to construct them (Figure 1.4). These mission properties were far more extensive than the churches that now stand as the centerpieces of historic sites. Originally the mission landholdings were extensive agricultural plantations and ranches encompassing thousands of acres. The core of the mission complex was the most intensively developed. The padres' private and communal rooms, including separate quarters for unmarried girls, and the church formed a quadrangle. Its *corredors* facing the interior plaza served as the only passage between many of the rooms. The buildings' windows and doors opened mainly onto the interior courtyard, with restricted access to the outside only through the *convento,* the church, and one or two cart passages in the walls.[37] Near the quadrangle were quarters for the neophytes, either the traditional bent pole with bark or reed coverings or rectilinear adobe attached blocks of rooms or a combination of the two building types. Nearby were also specialized outbuildings such as tanneries, potteries, and mills. Many missions had elaborate water systems with dams, cisterns, reservoirs, and *lavanderías* (laundries); some missions, such as Santa Barbara and San Fernando, had aqueducts that conveyed water from distant sources (Figure 1.5).[38]

Surrounding the core buildings were kitchen gardens and orchards, pens and stables for horses and other livestock. Agricultural fields and grazing ranges were farther removed, sometimes encompassing thousands of acres. In 1828 José Bandini described a typical mission compound:

> The buildings in some of the missions are more extensive than in others, but they are almost alike in form. The structures are of adobe, with sections of whatever size they may be needed. In all of them there are comfortable living quarters for the ministers, warehouses for the storing of goods, granaries large enough for the grain, places for making soap, rooms for weaving, carpenter shops, forges, wine presses, cellars, large patios and corrals, separate apartments for the Indian youth of both sexes, and, finally, as many workrooms as the establishment may require. Adjoining these and connected with them are the churches, which form a part of the mission building.[39]

Some missions also had distant ranches or ranchos that operated almost as satellite missions with their own supervisors, labor forces, and sometimes chapels.[40] In the highly varied geography of California, with its valleys and ranges, the distance of even a few miles can make a large difference in temperature, rainfall, and the seasonal availability of resources. A *diseño,* or pictorial map, of Rancho San Miguelito of Mission San Antonio de Padua reveals the diverse catchment areas that were exploited at one of these outposts (Plate 2). The key to a map of the rancho identifies, among other features, land under cultivation, irrigable land, deer hills, sheepfolds, springs, as well as roads connecting the rancho to other missions and settlements.[41]

Given the premise that the California mission landscapes were instruments of both the imposition of and resistance to colonial rule, they reveal both public and hidden transcripts of colonial power dynamics and insight into the everyday at the California missions. As James Scott points out, the "social sites of the hidden transcript are those locations in which the unspoken riposte, stifled anger, and bitten tongues created by relations of domination find a vehement, full-throated expression." These landscapes of resistance therefore often operate in spaces "where the control, surveillance, and repression of the dominant are least able to reach, and . . . when this sequestered social milieu is composed entirely of close confidants who share similar experiences of domination."[42] Within this microgeography of the mission landscapes where individuals negotiated everyday experiences in this clash of Spanish and Native cultures, three specific elements are of particular interest: domestic architecture, workspaces, and worship spaces.

Domestic Landscapes

The dramatic contrast between Indigenous and Spanish architectural traditions is evident most starkly in the neophyte housing at the missions. For Spanish explorers, colonists, and missionaries, deeds and maps codified the land as property, while walls and fences reified that construct on the ground. Gardens and corrals were laid out and fenced to contain and protect the resources within them—whether

FIGURE 1.4. José Cardero, Mission San Carlos (Carmel) of Monterey, California, 1791–92. Courtesy of The Bancroft Library, University of California, Berkeley.

vegetable or animal. Similarly, the geometry of Spanish architecture introduced Native people to a whole new form of spatial order and sense of boundedness and interiority. Initially, baptized Indians were allowed to remain in their villages, which the Spanish called *rancherías,* until adequate housing and food could be provided.[43] Eventually the neophytes were confined to the missions, however, and required a pass if they wanted to leave periodically to attend rituals, harvest traditional food sources, or hunt.[44] The residential patterns at the missions were a heterogeneous mix of house forms, with a combination of conical Indigenous structures and rectilinear adobe houses.[45] Images document the presence of traditional Indigenous dwellings, for example, José Cardero's 1791 views of Mission San Carlos; the foreground of Ferdinand Deppe's view of Mission San Gabriel in 1832 and adobe dwellings on the left of the Deppe painting (Plate 3); and the "Indian village" to the left of the mission in Henry Chapman Ford's painting of Santa Barbara (Figure 1.6).[46] Alfred Robinson's description of San Juan Capistrano in 1829 details the typical layout of Indian dwellings at the mission:

> The arrangement of the mission of St. Juan is similar to that of St. Luis; in fact all these establishments are formed upon the same plan, and much resemble each other, varying only in their extent and population. In many villages the residences

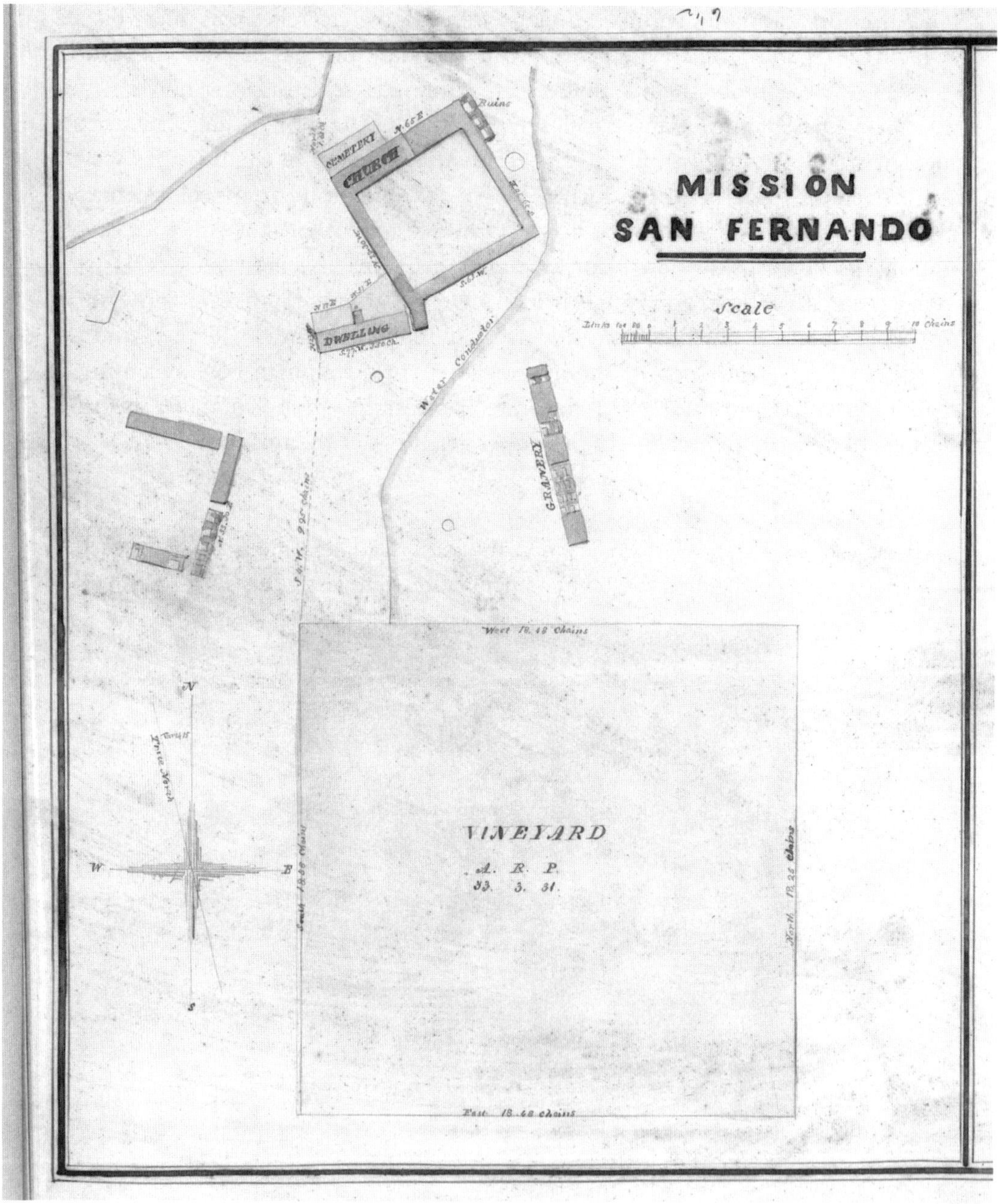

FIGURE 1.5. Mission San Fernando, surveyed by John G. Cleal, C.E., Sept. 1854. Courtesy of The Bancroft Library, University of California, Berkeley.

FIGURE 1.6. Henry Chapman Ford, Mission Santa Barbara, 188?. Courtesy of The Bancroft Library, University of California, Berkeley

> consist of straw huts of an oval form, which, when decayed, the Indians set on fire and erect new ones—here, however, they are built of unburnt brick, tiled and white-washed, forming five or six blocks, or streets, which present a neat and comfortable appearance.[47]

The "neat and comfortable appearance" belies the transformative impact of the adobe villages for their residents. The introduced building technologies of adobe structures, such as the example from Mission San Fernando photographed by C. C. Pierce in 1890 (Figure 1.7), represented a radical change in geometry, permanence, and the relationship of interior and exterior, as well as a changing social experience of space as expectations for Spanish moral and sexual behavior were imposed. As with most experiences of the everyday, the historical record contains no commentary on what it meant to live in one type of structure or the other, but visual and archaeological evidence of neophyte domestic architecture invites speculation nonetheless.[48] The change from traditional round or conical dwellings (which had different names, such as *kíicha, ewaa,* and *'ap,* depending on the tribal language) to square adobe houses in rows with streets created a shift in density of housing from freestanding to attached row houses with shared walls. The new architecture also encompassed a scale of interior space and a division between interior and exterior living space that was more demarcated, and visually

FIGURE 1.7. C. C. (Charles Chester) Pierce, *Two Old Indian Women at Mission San Fernando,* 1890. The Huntington Library, San Marino, California.

impenetrable, than the bent pole, reed, and bark traditional Indigenous building materials. This sense of boundedness did not end at the domestic sphere; at Santa Barbara a wall enclosed the entire housing complex (Figure 1.8).[49]

With new construction techniques also came new possibilities for confinement. Not only did the houses in the Indian village have doors and windows that closed, but in the central quadrangle new mechanisms, such as barred windows, keys, and locks, could be used to restrict access and restrain people.[50] This control was particularly relevant given that the Spanish notions of sexual behavior forbade same-sex couples, which were common in some central California societies, and they prohibited sexual relations outside marriage.[51] Unmarried girls over eight years of age were removed to the nunnery or *monjerío* to sleep and were locked in at night. Some have argued that the confinement was intended as much to protect the young women from the soldiers at the missions, but evidence of sexual violence by priests at some missions suggests that restricting freedom of movement may have made the girls vulnerable as well. Barbara Voss has argued that part of this redefinition of indoor domestic space was a relocation of sexual activity that "undoubtedly disrupted connections between sexual activity and a landscape marked by spiritual and mythical meanings."[52] Despite these expectations and precautions, reports suggest that such forbidden contact persisted as

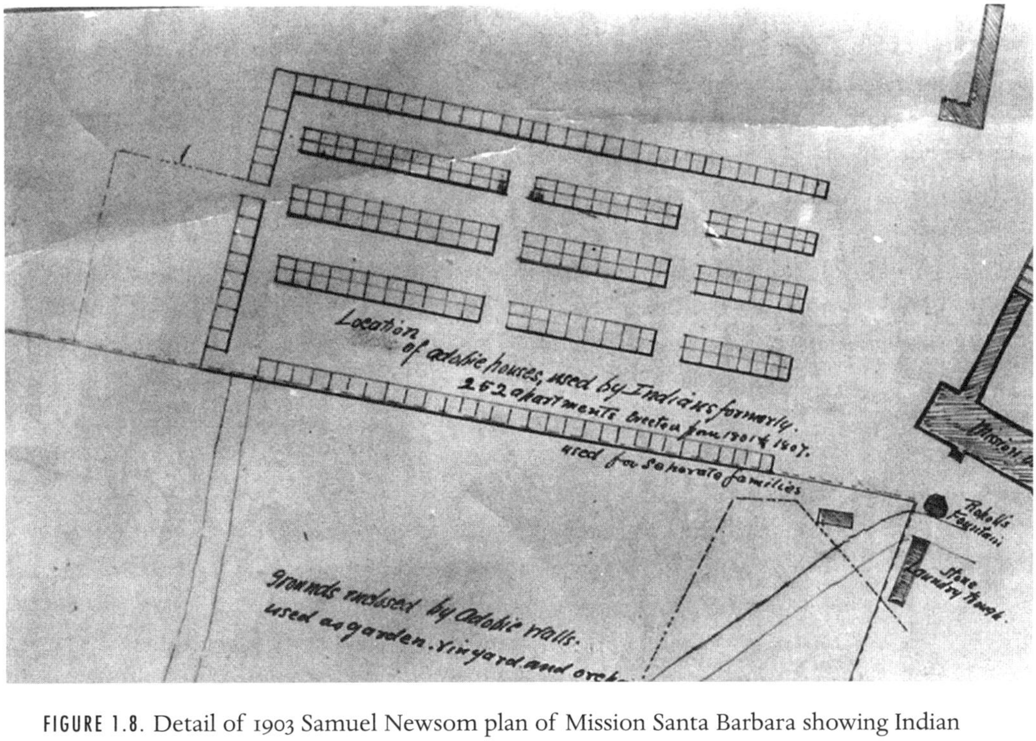

FIGURE 1.8. Detail of 1903 Samuel Newsom plan of Mission Santa Barbara showing Indian village adobe structures. Santa Bárbara Mission Archive-Library.

couples were found frequenting orchards and some of the less conspicuous parts of the mission grounds for their trysts.[53]

Living in these new kinds of mission dwellings entailed new habits and furnishing as well. Jean Baudrillard has argued for "the symbolic configuration known as home" where "objects take on a certain density, an emotional value."[54] In the Native tradition, the primary living space was what many today think of as "outdoors," unless, as Tongva and Acjachemen artist L. Frank has noted, there was inclement weather or a bear.[55] Native concepts of dwelling and relationship with the land were distinctly different from Spanish cultural practices, and houses were not used in the same manner to which the padres were accustomed. For Native Californians the flexibility of the house space, with its furs, mats, and blankets, accommodated shifting activities and social connections. The permeability of the layered thatch let through the light breezes and dappled light. In contrast, the Spanish-style houses contained less-mobile chairs, beds, and tables that raised their occupants off the floor, while the thick walls obscured the surroundings except through the perforations of windows and doors. Excavations at Mission Santa Cruz have yielded evidence that activities in the neophytes' quarters were a mix of Hispanic and Native traditions, leading archaeologist Rebecca Allen to conclude that while environment was "largely bounded by missionary dictates, . . . native value systems and ways of using space endured."[56] Rubén Mendoza's excavations at Mission Soledad similarly produced evidence of a hybridized material culture and foodways, suggesting, in his view, an incorporation of broader Indigenous Mesoamerican influences that Mendoza suggests represent the "Mexicanization" of the Indian community there.[57]

Landscapes of Labor

The mission production was reported in *fenegas* (a measure of volume equaling about 1.6 bushels for grain) of wheat grown and numbers of head of cattle raised, but the experience of work at the missions, spatially, bodily, and socially, is harder to reconstruct and even harder to compare to traditional Indigenous work practices. Clearly the need to feed, clothe, shelter, and heal community members was common to both mission and nonmission Indians, but there were dramatic differences in the specific skills, materials, and tasks, as well as new ways of organizing and thinking about work.[58] California's Native peoples had a long tradition of sophisticated subsistence strategies and complex technologies, such as Pomo basketry and Chumash plank canoe construction, and they had specialists who were masters of these technologies. But the padres introduced technologies that required new skills and new spatial and temporal practices of work, in addition to the fundamental coercion of the labor force. Visiting Mission San Luis Rey in 1829, Alfred Robinson described, for example,

> about three thousand Indians, who were all employed in various occupations. Some were engaged in agriculture, while others attended to the management of over sixty thousand head of cattle. Many were carpenters, masons, coopers, saddlers, shoemakers, weavers, &c. while the females were employed in spinning and preparing wool for their looms, which produced a sufficiency of blankets for their yearly consumption.[59]

Other accounts vary in the specific roles assigned and the amount of labor required. Observers were particularly sensitive to the work required of children and of pregnant women. In response to the critical reports of the strenuous work being performed by these groups, the padres offered the following response:

> The pregnant Indian women have never been, we repeat, have never been assigned to the *matate* for grinding *atole,* flour, and other arduous tasks. . . . They are employed in finishing wool, pounding oak bark for the tannery, and accompanied by other women who assist them, cleaning wheat on the threshing floor after threshing.[60]

Despite the varying accounts, it is clear that labor at the missions involved a dramatic departure from traditional practices. Prior to Spanish missionization, Indigenous social organization had been based on kinship, gender roles, and the political leadership of a chief and shaman; in the mission system, the Indians were partitioned into weavers, masons, carpenters, soap makers, blacksmiths, and tanners. These roles were also aligned with Spanish notions of gender-appropriate labor mediated by the pragmatics of seasonal agricultural demands that occasionally required everyone's efforts to bring in the harvest or process the crops. Spatially segmented landscapes of specialized working spaces such as mills and tanneries reinforced these social divisions.

A key objective of the control exerted at the missions was to impose restrictions and attempt to dilute the ties that bound Native people within their communities. One of the missionaries' strategies was to reproduce the hierarchy of Spanish society, particularly that of the military and church institutions that were the leading forces of colonization. Specifically, Indian "leaders," called *alcaldes* or *caciques,* were chosen and, according to one observer, their function was "like the overseers of a plantation."[61] The built environment further reinforced these social divisions as the alcaldes were given preferred housing and special access to the padres' area to report on the day's undertakings and to confer about future plans. These segmented spaces also created divisions. Discrete work areas with little visibility between them limited the opportunities to interact during the "workday," in contrast to the Native villages where multiple tasks were performed in the central communal areas and where the organization of work was less rigid and codified.

The mission labor also entailed a different scale and intensity, as the neophyte workforce sustained the hundreds or even thousands who now lived at the missions. The work of ranching, for example, was a radical departure from hunting and gathering subsistence and was a disciplining technology in its treatment of domesticated animals. Native people were certainly familiar with butchering and skinning prey and tanning the pelts, but to hunt was to participate in an animated web of relationships and in the mutual exchange of offerings of thanks and sustenance that was the fabric of Indigenous life. In contrast, the mission cattle industry was conducted on a whole new scale and utilized processes that were antithetical to the hunter–prey relationship. Slaughtering cattle was a production line in which a steady stream of cows were killed, skinned, and boiled down in tannery and soap vats, such as those documented at Mission Santa Inés in the 1930 Historic American Buildings Survey (Figure 1.9), to render fat or tallow for candles and hides for trade. The pristine ruins cannot begin to evoke the smells and sounds during the height of the butchering season. Spatially, the move to husbandry was also a dramatic change. Rather than stalking individual prey such as deer, bear, and elk, the mission Indians wrangled domesticated herd animals. In a parallel to the changing settlement patterns of the Native people who had previously moved among seasonally occupied villages, the animals had to be contained in rectilinear corrals and confined to pens awaiting slaughter.

FIGURE 1.9. View of tannery foundation toward the east, Mission Santa Inés, 1936. Library of Congress, Prints & Photographs Division (HABS, CAL,42-SOLV,1C—2).

But here, too, the hegemony of imposed colonial practices was met with active resistance. Evidence of faunal remains in excavated mission sites suggests that Indians chose to switch opportunistically between colonial and Indigenous subsistence practices.[62] The Native peoples assigned to processing hides or boiling cows were the same individuals who, when furloughed for up to two months to return to their homelands, picked up their bows and arrows to hunt and spears to fish.[63] Studies by archaeologists and geographers such as John Johnson, Julia Costello, and David Hornbeck suggest that the mission population changed seasonally as Indians took advantage of the stable rations and clothing supplies during certain times of the year while returning to their own settlements at other times to harvest traditional resources.[64] Evidence from excavations of neophyte barracks indicates that Indians at the missions continued to supplement mission diets with Native foods and to maintain long-standing trade networks. The more permeable boundaries presented by such reconstructions suggest that far from being the walled compounds of cloistered monastic communities or prisons with central exercise yards, the missions were, at least in some places and times, residential communities with relatively porous boundaries. The decision to join a mission was irrevocable from a Franciscan perspective, but the imposed strictures clearly could be negotiated and resisted. The landscapes that the mission Indians inhabited, therefore, were bounded by the walls, cactus hedges, and property lines of the Spanish, but also continued to include for Native peoples their traditional lands with all their sustenance and spiritual significance.

Like animal husbandry, the introduction of agriculture similarly changed the rhythm and scale of work. Traditional foodways involved intimate knowledge of the diverse botanical resources of the area with seasonal harvesting of acorns, wild grass seed, nuts, and berries, as well as grasses critical for sophisticated fiber arts and plants for medicinal purposes. Instead of a complex cycle of managing and harvesting wild plants across a rich patchwork of habitats, agricultural cycles involved large groups working intensively in orchards, groves, and fields in an endless cycle of plowing, planting, reaping—a cycle repeated three times a year in the temperate Central Coast. Robinson described at Mission San Buenaventura

> an abundance of fruits and vegetables. In their proper seasons they have apples, pears, peaches, pomegranates, tunas or prickly pears, and grapes. Along the margin of the river St. Buenaventura are many small gardens belonging to the Indians, where they raise fruit and vegetables, which are taken to town and disposed of.[65]

Processing fruits and grains is not unlike the work of leaching and grinding acorns for the staple meal, but the scale and repetition required for processing crops exceeded the traditional practices.[66] Father Lasuén observed resistance to the regimen: "The effort entailed in procuring a sustenance from the open spaces is incomparably greater than what is now enjoined on them so that they can sustain themselves; but the former is free and according to their liking, and the latter prescribed, and not according to their liking."[67]

In addition to its role in shaping social relations, the landscape was instrumental in enforcing compliance with the missionaries' expectations for an orderly, productive, docile labor force. Barbara Voss has argued that the entire California colonial enterprise was "fundamentally a transformation of spatial relations . . . : an appropriation of indigenous lands for colonial ends, and the ongoing movement of diverse human populations across both short and long distances as a means to accomplish these ends."[68] The design of the mission architecture was a fundamental strategy in the process of colonization, particularly as it reinforced compliance with expectations for orderly and productive behavior.[69] As Michel Foucault has noted, the efficacy of the panopticon is predicated less on constant surveillance than the constant possibility of surveillance. The mission architecture suggests the possibility of surveillance from a number of vantage points. The quadrangle plan has a long tradition within monastic, Mediterranean, and Roman architecture, and a number of its design principles have made it an effective architecture of surveillance in each case. For example, the quadrangle plan offered views into the central patio and along the interior corredors. The priests' quarters and work areas were ideally positioned, therefore, to monitor the conduct and productivity of the Indians working in the courtyard, as well as the girls' quarters. Furthermore, the mission bell towers and elevated campanile offered platforms for surveying the surrounding landscape, as illustrated in William Smyth's 1827 view of Mission San Carlos (Figure 1.10).

An account by the comte de La Pérouse, a member of the first French expedition to California, describes the significance of these central spaces in the daily regime of Mission San Carlos in 1786:

> The Indians . . . rise with the sun, and immediately go to prayers and mass, which last for an hour. During this time three large boilers are set on the fire for cooking a kind of soup, made of barley meal. . . . Each hut sends for the allowance of all its inhabitants. . . . There is neither confusion nor disorder in the distribution, and when the boilers are nearly emptied, the thicker portion at the bottom is distributed to those children who have said their catechism the best. . . . [After the meal] they all go to work, some to till the ground with oxen, some to dig in the garden, while others are employed in domestic occupations, all under the eye of one or two missionaries. . . . At noon the bells give notice of the time of dinner. . . . They return to work from two to four or five o'clock, when they repair to the evening prayer, which lasts nearly an hour and is followed by a distribution of the *atole,* the same as at breakfast.[70]

FIGURE 1.10. William Smyth, *San Carlos Mission near Monterey, California,* 1827, watercolor painting. Gift of the Estate of Belle J. Bushnell. Courtesy of the Peabody Museum of Archaeology and Ethnology, Harvard University (PM# 41–72–10/480; digital file# 60743089).

La Pérouse's description exemplifies the regimen of workers called to perform duties at specific points of the day and assembled in formations for communal activities all "under the eye" of their supervisors. The account also reinforces the relationship among the organization of space, patterns of behavior, and surveillance.

Another technique of social control at the missions was the organization of movement through the landscapes of labor. Certainly the introduction of the permanent, year-round mission complexes to groups who had seminomadic settlement patterns was discipline writ large. The Spanish introduced other forms of spatial control at a smaller scale as well. Two Franciscans, Estevan Tapis and Juan Cortés, replied to criticisms regarding oppressive labor practices, stating, "The customary hour for ringing the bell to go out to work is more than an hour after sunrise. At the stroke of the bell the people gather slowly in the quadrangle (with the exception of those doing piecework) and they jointly divide the duties of the day."[71] Images such as those by José Cardero of assemblies (Figure 1.11) and Louis Choris of forced marches (Figure 1.12) similarly depict the formations of ordered bodies and controlled movement that were essential to maintaining a compliant workforce.

FIGURE 1.11. José Cardero, *The Reception of Jean-François de la Pérouse at Mission Carmel in 1786.* Courtesy of The Bancroft Library, University of California, Berkeley.

As with the persistence of Indigenous foodways, resistance to this regulation and restriction of movement is also widely documented. The most dramatic examples are isolated but quite violent revolts, but there is also evidence of runaways and the neophytes' regular participation in kinship networks and traditional subsistence practices. There are also numerous references to the persistence of activities such as gambling and dancing at the missions, which the Franciscans did not condone.[72]

The social nature of the work also changed as some neophytes became skilled craftspeople or were assigned duties based on the Franciscans' notions of gender-appropriate labor.[73] Women, in particular, were given "domestic" duties that were far more restrictive than traditional Indigenous female roles, and the landscapes of women's mission labor appear to be implicated in the hidden transcripts of resistance. The Franciscan notions of appropriate work for women entailed a

FIGURE 1.12. Louis Choris, *Vue de Presidio Sn. Francisco* (San Francisco Presidio), 1822. Yale Collection of Western Americana, Beinecke Rare Book and Manuscript Library.

sphere of domesticity that encompassed a much smaller geographic range than the traditional foraging patterns. Gathering wood, cleaning, cooking, child care, and group activities such as weaving on looms and roasting and grinding corn for flour where all conducted within the vicinity of the mission core. Women and children worked, as needed, by making adobe bricks and transporting rocks.[74] As Ann Laura Stoler has argued, these expectations of social roles are potent political acts and central to imperial politics.[75] Spanish racialized and gendered notions of social identity differed radically from Indigenous epistemologies of body, sexuality, and relationships, and the imposition of new social roles and hierarchical power relations was an essential part of the colonial agenda.[76]

Despite the introduction of these new norms and hierarchies, there are suggestions in the documentary record and in the landscape that social cohesion among peer groups persisted among the mission Indians. A significant aspect of this resistance is the continued agency of Native women and continuity of Indigenous systems of gender and sexuality. As historian Antonia Castañeda has argued, these Indigenous constructs were "antithetical to a patriarchal ideology in which gender hierarchy, male domination, and heterosexuality were the exclusive organizing principles of desire, sexuality, marriage, and family."[77] While the Spanish efforts to "civilize" Native peoples required controlling their sexuality and imposing new gender roles, the records of punishments and repeated exhortations suggest that defiance of the rules persisted.[78]

Evidence also suggests that the spatial segregation along gender lines may actually have facilitated the solidarity of women's networks. For instance, segregation of unmarried young Native women in separate dormitories to protect their chastity, while devastating for formations of nuclear family bonds and also a contributing factor in the spread of disease,[79] may have reinforced women's agency and community. While new boundaries were created, a by-product of the Spanish-imposed gendered landscape of work was similarly an opportunity for unsupervised conversation, gossip, and carping—all the discourse one might imagine in the hidden transcripts of resistance. A prime opportunity for such unsupervised conversation was afforded by the myriad water features—fountains, lavanderías, and basins used for washing. While bathing and cleaning were obviously part of Native traditions, the introduction of woolen textiles and European-style clothes not only contributed to the process of cultural identity formation (or ethnogenesis), it also created a new burden of laundry.[80] Visiting Mission Santa Inés in 1829, Robinson described a "large brick enclosure" in front of the mission "where the females bathed and washed."[81] At Mission San Luis Rey, a marshy area was drained and turned into a lavandería, as described by Father Antonio Peyri, the mission's first guardian, "by hauling earth . . . little by little in forcing up so that it could be reached. By means of two dams the water was then collected so that it sufficed for the assembled Indians and for irrigating a garden."[82] The so-called sunken garden contained a series of pools and aqueducts that supplied water and irrigated an orchard "full of fruit trees, pears apples or *perones,* peaches, quinces, etc."[83] Reached by a wide stairway, the lavandería was out of sight of the main mission buildings. Thomas Farnham, a visitor in May 1840, described the lavandería and fountain in front of Mission Santa Barbara (Figure 1.13):

> Before the church they erected a series of concentric fountains, ten feet in height, from the top of which the pure liquid bursts, and falls from one to another till it reaches a large pool at the base; from this it is led off a short distance to the statue of a grisly bear, from whose mouth it is ejected into a reservoir of solid masonry, six feet wide and seventy feet long. From the pool at the base of the urn fountains water is taken for drinking and household use. The long reservoir is the theatre of the battling, plashing, laughing, and scolding of wash day.[84]

These baths and basins also yield hints of their import for the intersection of Spanish and Indigenous everyday living on the land. In the Native cosmology, the connections between layered spheres of the world were particularly resonant where water emerged from the earth or flowed into the ocean. Springs were sacred places of communion and power. It is of note, therefore, that several

FIGURE 1.13. Mission Santa Barbara lavandería, 2013. Photograph by the author.

Native-constructed lavanderías have waterspouts in the form of animal or spirit masks. An example from Mission Santa Barbara (Figure 1.14) has been described as a bear and a lion, while the San Luis Rey examples appear more human (Figure 1.15).[85] In each case, the waterspouts appear to transform the utilitarian landscape of laundry into a Native sphere of spiritual resonance. The conversations that took place at these lavanderías are lost to time, but the fact that in a number of the mission revolts, women were key conspirators suggests that the washday may have included hidden-transcript conversations as well as splashing, laughing, and scolding.

Sacred Spaces

The notion of sacred space was central to both the Indigenous ideology of landscape and the purpose of the mission to baptize and convert.[86] Religious beliefs and practices varied among the many California tribal traditions, and ideologies of landscape were similarly diverse. Some Indigenous cosmologies appear to privilege prominent peaks as symbolically charged locations, points at which the spheres of the world met, and places of sacred power.[87] For some groups, springs and locations where water flowed into the ocean were also potent spiritual places.

FIGURE 1.14. Mission Santa Barbara lavandería waterspout drawn by Raymond E. Noble for the Index of American Design, 1939. Courtesy National Gallery of Art, Washington, D.C.

Some California Native peoples, particularly those along the Central Coast, practiced their rituals in caves and rock shelters, such as the Chumash Painted Cave in the hills above Santa Barbara (Plate 4).[88] A significant aspect of the religious practices among the Chumash and other Southern California groups was the use of *toloache*, a hallucinogenic plant that was ingested to induce visions and dreams that they, in turn, interpreted as connections to the spirit world. Retreating to spiritually charged locales separated from the spaces of daily existence was intended to facilitate encounters with the divine both for those who ingested *toloache* and for worshippers in the mission churches, but entering into mother earth through the cave openings projected the experience literally into the geography of the divine.[89] For the Yurok in Northern California, ritual menstrual seclusion in sacred spaces for women in their "moon time," or *Apurowak*, created the opportunity for autonomous religious activity for Yurok women.[90]

FIGURE 1.15. Mission San Luis Rey lavandería waterspout drawn by Raymond E. Noble for the Index of American Design, 1939. Courtesy National Gallery of Art, Washington, D.C.

In addition to natural features, villages had central open plazas used for dancing, gambling, and other communal rites. Chumash ritual structures and areas, for example, included dance grounds, sacred enclosures, cemeteries, menstrual huts, male puberty huts, and sweat lodges.[91] Many groups also constructed specialized ceremonial structures for certain rituals. Father Gerónimo Boscana's account of the Juaneño of Mission San Juan Capistrano offers a description of a ceremonial *vanquech* for which, unfortunately, there are no known illustrations:

> The temples erected by command of the god, Chinigchinich . . . Ouiamot, were invariably erected in the center of their towns, and contiguous to the dwelling-place of the captain, or chief. They formed an enclosure of about four or five yards

> in circumference, not exactly round, but inclining to an oval. This they divided by drawing a line through the center, and built another [enclosure], consisting of the branches of trees, and mats to the height of about six feet, outside of which, in the other division, they formed another, of small stakes of wood driven into the ground. This was called the gate, or entrance, to the *vanquech*.[92]

Sacred space was also marked by raising tall wooden poles to honor deities and claim territories. Historian Steven Hackel has argued that the parallels between the practice of placing prayer poles and the Franciscans' practice of erecting crosses to mark the founding of a mission, as seen in Smyth and Cardero's views of Mission San Carlos and Choris's view of San Francisco, were not lost on either group. The Indians continued to associate traditional beliefs with the crosses and the Franciscans worked to replace the prayer poles with crosses, not just in front of the churches but along paths and roads in the broader landscape.[93]

In contrast to the sacred Indigenous spaces formed by the land in caves and peaks and inscribed with poles and mats, the Spanish mission churches were massive architectural statements that stood out in the landscape and announced their spiritual identity for miles. These churches shared similarities with the Spanish colonial churches in Mexico and were built by the neophytes, many under the supervision of craftsmen from colonial Mexico.[94] In them the Franciscans conducted daily Masses and a sung High Mass on Sundays and feast days. The monumental missions, with their imposing facades, *campanarios* (walls with niches or piercings for bells), *espadañas* (ornamental false fronts), and bell towers, represented a scale of architecture unlike any in Alta California before that time. John Stilgoe, historian of the American landscape, has noted the importance in early New England of *landschafts*—prominent features in the landscape such as steeples, lighthouses, and columns that created not only focal points visible at a distance but also features that marked a central place and signified a civilized locus in the midst of wilderness.[95] In the larger project of colonialism, this visible, permanent presence, which Thomas Bremer has called "the locative force of the colonial place,"[96] was a marker of power and stability. Travelers' accounts of approaches to the missions similarly note the impact of their profiles, which were visible for miles. For example, Robinson described Santa Clara as rising "far distant in the centre of a spacious plain."[97] Auguste Bernard Duhaut-Cilly described his visit to San Luis Rey in 1827 in the following way:

> After one and a half hours of travel, we descried before us, from the top of a slight eminence, the superb buildings of Mission San Luis Rey, whose brilliant whiteness was sent to us by the first light of the day. At a distance we were from it, and by the uncertain light of dawn, this edifice, of a very beautiful pattern, supported upon many pillars, had the look of a palace.[98]

The facades of the churches were of a scale for which there was no human-built precedent in Alta California. San Juan Capistrano's church, begun in 1796, was built of stone with a 180-foot-long nave, vault, seven masonry domes or *bovedas,* and a bell tower that was reportedly visible for ten miles. The facades of missions along the coast, such as Mission San Carlos and Mission Santa Barbara (Figure 1.16), were impressive sights for those entering the harbor. Not only were the buildings landschafts for mapmakers and artists, but for Native Americans they were of a scale surpassed only by natural forms such as mountain peaks and ranges. In contrast to the architectural traditions of Mayan stone temples, Mississippian earthen mounds, or the cliff dwellings of the Southwest United States, California Indigenous structures were no larger than the domed multifamily dwellings. The degree of transference of notions of the power of prominence between natural and architectural elements is not articulated in any written records, but the mission's presence in the landscape appears to go beyond merely a display of wealth (the "rule by ostentation" model) or technical prowess but introduced a new alignment of human and natural forces.[99]

FIGURE 1.16. Carleton E. Watkins, Mission Santa Barbara, 1876–80. Courtesy of The Bancroft Library, University of California, Berkeley.

The church interiors were also significant spaces in the landscape of colonialism and followed centuries of ecclesiastical tradition. The design of the naves was intended to teach the basic tenets of faith and also model Franciscan ideas of social organization. The dim, cavernous church naves may have mirrored some of the qualities of the sacred painted caves, but on a scale of interiority unknown before the Spanish arrived in California. Robinson, an American working for a hide- and tallow-trading company, toured the missions and his account, *Life in California,* published in 1846, offers some of the best descriptions of the physical layouts of the mission grounds at the end of the mission period under the Mexican Republic. Robinson described Mission San Luis Rey:

> The church is a large, stone edifice, whose exterior is not without some considerable ornament and tasteful finish; but the interior is richer, and the walls are adorned with a variety of pictures of saints and Scripture subjects, glaringly colored, and attractive to the eye. Around the altar are many images of the saints, and the tall and massive candelabras, lighted during mass, throw an imposing light upon the whole.[100]

The extent to which participation in Catholic liturgies was concomitant with religious conversion is an open question. Not only do scholars differ but observers' accounts vary tremendously regarding the degree of coercion and conversion.[101] Robinson reports at Mission San Luis Rey in 1829, "Mass is offered daily, and the greater portion of the Indians attend; but it not unusual to see numbers of them driven along by alcaldes, and under the whip's lash forced to the very doors of the sanctuary," but in the same year he visited Mission San Gabriel, where he described,

> The imposing ceremony, glittering ornaments, and illuminated walls, were well adapted to captivate the simple mind of the Indian, and I could not but admire the apparent devotion of the multitude, who seemed absorbed, heart and soul, in the scene before them. The solemn music of the mass was well selected, and the Indian voices accorded harmoniously with the flutes and violins that accompanied them.[102]

Regardless of the spiritual ramifications, the embodied experience of the liturgical space was a visible sign of the neophytes' status within the colonial social hierarchy. The neophytes were compelled to attend worship services, kneel and stand at appropriate points, and participate in processions and other liturgical movements. These formations of bodies enacted the communal relationships of a shared congregational experience. The position of the Franciscan priests leading the liturgy reinforced the subservient status of the neophytes receiving the words and sacraments. Acts such as kneeling for confession and venerating religious icons and santos (images of saints) reflected the Franciscans' view of the neophytes, expressed in texts and imagery, as obedient children. Expectations for veneration extended to the priest himself: neophytes attending Mass kissed the Franciscan's hand.[103]

The highly decorated interiors combining Christian iconography and Native motifs created rich sensory environments in the church naves, as well as in the interiors of some conventos such as at Mission San Fernando.[104] In addition to the prints that hung in the naves and were given to the neophytes, the Franciscans imported pigments for painting the interior walls. At some missions Mexican artisans produced the decorative programs, but particularly at the smaller missions, the Indigenous artisans did the painting.[105] In these colonial spaces designed to support cultural and religious indoctrination, the Franciscans' emotive and didactic agenda was clear. The images were intended not only to contribute nonverbal narrations of Christian stories and exemplars of Christian virtues but also to create "communities of viewers with a shared experience and fostered interpretive responses."[106]

But just as the physical landscapes of the mission are now understood as part of the broader Indigenous landscape, so too can the iconography be read within Indigenous knowledge systems.[107] From this perspective, rather than simply seeing them as motifs applied out of pattern books, scholars now recognize that the mission visual culture incorporated continuities of precontact visual systems and was received through the lens of Indigenous epistemologies.[108] There are numerous examples of the integration of Indigenous motifs, practices, and identity markers in the mission visual culture. The figure of the deity Tobet, venerated by the Tongva, Acjachemem, and Luiseño, was painted on the wall of the Serra Chapel at San Juan Capistrano.[109] At Mission San Fernando, a mural over the door of the convento depicts a deer being stalked by a hunter in deerskin camouflage (Figure 1.17). One of the most extraordinary examples is the Chumash painting, ca. 1825, of the Archangel Raphael at Mission Santa Inés. In this rare surviving example of a painting on canvas executed by an Indian at the missions, the archangel is depicted as a Chumash leader (Figure 1.18). In her close reading of the painting, Haas discusses how the Indian painter expressed cultural hybridity through the painting.[110] The image employs the standard Catholic representational conventions for the archangel, including the fish, wings, and humble dress. But it also incorporates Chumash iconographic elements such as the whale effigies that had been carved for centuries and served to guide shamans through rituals and the accessing of knowledge and power.[111] It also references the central place of deep-water fishing in Central Coast cultures.[112] Not only does the painting include Indigenous cultural objects and practices, but it had political import as well. Haas argues that the incorporation of Indigenous elements makes reference "to a specific leader and talisman" and to "a larger image of Chumash leadership and religious authority."[113]

FIGURE 1.17. Images of a hunt over a Mission San Fernando doorway, recorded by Geoffrey Holt for the Index of American Design, ca. 1937. Courtesy National Gallery of Art, Washington, D.C.

FIGURE 1.18. Chumash portrait of Archangel Raphael painted at Mission Santa Inés, ca. 1825. Santa Bárbara Mission Archive-Library.

This reading of the politics of mission imagery can be extended to the more ephemeral evidence of the multisensory experience of the architectural interiors. This line of investigation acknowledges that responses to images are inherently complex, particularly across cultural knowledge systems.[114] Even more challenging is recovering phenomenological experiences, but the investigation of the mission landscapes would be incomplete without at least attempting to attend to the embodied, multisensory experiences they offer.[115] For example, the formal similarities make plausible the associations between the gilding and the bright colors of the decorative programs and the Indigenous sacred spaces of polychrome cave paintings or even traditional practices of body painting and decoration of objects such as canoes and grave markers.[116] Similarly, the aroma of incense may have been a sensory reference to the traditional practice of smudging by burning aromatic plants such as white sage.[117]

Along with the sights and smells of the liturgical spaces, the churches also created a new landscape of sound. The introduction of polyphonic choral and instrumental music was an important part of the new sacred landscapes and also a radical departure from Indigenous music traditions.[118] Not only were the Western harmonic systems novel, but the practices of choral music also reinforced Spanish notions of order and space. Conversely, the incorporation of Indigenous practices such as drumming and vocalization produced an entirely unique sound.[119] The choir stood as a group and sang in stationary formation, in contrast to the dynamic movement associated with music-filled Indigenous dances and ceremonies. The mission choruses also learned their music visually with cues in the form of simplified chant coded onto vellum, a radical departure from the oral transmission of Native music and storytelling. Robinson reported at Mission San José in 1829 a feast day celebration with the visiting choir from Santa Clara:

> The music was well executed, for it had been practised daily for more than two months under the particular supervision of Father Narciso Duran. The number of the musicians was about thirty; the instruments performed upon were violins, flutes, trumpets, and drums; and so acute was the ear of the priest that he would detect a wrong note on the part of either instantly, and chide the erring performer.[120]

The Franciscan systems for "reading music" introduced a new relationship of sound and sight as well as new spatial practices of performance.

The significance of these multisensory practices and spaces within the Indigenous and colonial geographies is a complicated question. On the one hand, the participation and pageantry of the mission liturgy were seen as a validation of the progress of the colonial project. Eugène Duflot de Mofras's report of his 1841–42 travels includes the observation that Mission Santa Clara's "music was taught with marked success, and their neophyte orchestra was known throughout the land."[121]

Furthermore, according to Duflot de Mofras, thirty matching uniforms were purchased "from a French whaler," presenting a visual consistency and order that were the epitomized image of the "civilized" neophyte the Franciscans sought to create.[122] At the same time, the prospect of the multisensory experience of the liturgical spaces seen as part of a Native epistemology and system of knowledge raises the possibility that the churches were heterotopias of a sort—simultaneously physical and mental spaces that operated separately from the hegemonic forces of the mission's disciplinary regime.[123] In this sense, the meaning of the space is not a didactic narrative of Christian doctrine, but is constructed in movement and memory, encounter and association.[124] They are spaces referencing other geographies, both physical and epistemological. The naves are neither purely colonial nor Indigenous, but a juxtaposition of incompatible constructs. They fit Foucault's criteria of heterotopias and similar liminal spaces in that they function "as lenses or mirrors that reflect, distort and disturb our social and spatial worlds. They are a part, and yet apart, from all other spaces surrounding them."[125]

The liturgical space paralleled other spatial practices of power in trying to create a new social order in the mission Indian community.[126] The grouping of bodies in the churches reinforced Franciscan norms of sexual roles and hierarchies as men and women stood on either side of the aisle, and the younger members were seated nearest the altar.[127] Not only were men and women separated, but Sandos has identified specific symbolic elements in the decorative program whose placement suggests gendered target audiences. Specifically, certain santos were positioned so that those associated with them had privileged views. For example, women could see birth santos while men gazed upon cross santos, which accentuated the suffering and sacrifice of the crucified Christ. The lesson, Sandos argues, was "intended to teach male Indians their new role as head of a Christian family, the role of suffering for that family" while the women were expected to "model their behavior after the Virgin and to help maintain the integrity of the family."[128]

Mendoza has demonstrated the visual and cosmological expressions of colonial liturgical architecture, arguing that the didactics extended to what he has described as the "hidden traditions of sacred geometry and Franciscan cosmology" to produce a "Hispanicized Indian cosmos."[129] Specifically, the windows and altars at Mission San Miguel, the Santa Barbara Presidio Chapel, and Mission San Francisco de Asís (as well as other sites throughout the Southwest and northern Mexico) are aligned so that parts of the altar, including santos and the tabernacle enclosure, are illuminated at certain times of the year, such as the solstice and the equinox, as well as on the patronal feast day of Saint Francis (Figure 1.19). Mendoza makes the case that this "rise of solar Eucharistic worship and the solar Christ constitute a sanctified conflation, cultural accommodation, and spiritual reconciliation of both pre-Columbian and European cosmologies."[130]

FIGURE 1.19. View of the *bulto* of the Archangel and "Eye of God" atop the main altar reredos at Mission San Miguel Arcángel, 1934. Library of Congress, Prints & Photographs Division (HABS, CAL,40-SANMI.V7).

Another vivid image from the missions—a symbol known as the "All-Seeing Eye of God"—suggests a powerful convergence of both landmark and surveillance within the microgeography of the naves. In Christian doctrinal iconography this eye in a triangle represented the Trinity, and at the missions there are a number of examples of its incorporation into ecclesiastical architecture. In each instance the image was placed in a prominent, elevated position within the decorative program. At Santa Clara, the Eye of God was painted on the facade at the peak of the roofline. Descriptions of visitors approaching Santa Clara across a flat plain report it was visible for miles. At San Miguel the "All-Seeing Eye of God" has been restored as it was realized in three-dimensional form, jutting out above the altar, part of the elaborate interior decorative scheme designed by Estévan Munras and executed by neophyte assistants.[131] While this symbol is not unique, within the mission context it appears linked to the surveillance principles of mission architecture and the authority of the priests. Placed in its central, elevated position atop the reredos, this eye was a symbol of the omnipotence and omniscience of the All-Seeing God. Its location implies that the authority of the image was transferred in some way to the priests who commissioned the paintings, led the liturgy beneath them, and presented themselves as God's representatives on earth. The power of the imagery is even more credible given Mendoza's recent findings of the illumination of the altar and the Eye-of-God image above it at particular times of the year.[132]

Despite compulsory attendance, evidence suggests, however, that there was less than full participation and perhaps even active resistance to the missions' liturgical practices, as well as the persistence of traditional beliefs and ritual practices. A visitor to Santa Barbara reported that "priests or assistants rounded up stragglers, pinching their ears or striking their ears and heads with a long stick that was also used to awaken those who fell asleep during the service." Visiting Mission Dolores in 1816, Louis Choris noted an unusual reaction to the use of drums in the liturgy, which perhaps suggests some connection to traditional sacred drumming:

> On Sundays and holidays they celebrate divine service . . . which they also accompany with the sound of musical instruments. These are chiefly drums, trumpets, tabors, and other instruments of the same class. It is by means of their noise that they endeavour to stir the imagination of the Indians and to make men of these savages. It is, indeed, the only means of producing an effect upon them. When the drums begin to beat they fall to the ground as if they were half dead. None dares to move; all remain stretched upon the ground without making the slightest movement until the end of the service, and, even then, it is necessary to tell them several times that the mass is finished. Armed soldiers are stationed at each corner of the church.[133]

Other forms of resistance were literally inscribed in the architecture of the missions. Many of the mission churches had elaborately painted walls and ceilings. Norman Neuerburg, who studied mission church interiors and worked on several of their restorations, identified a number of the designers of the decorative programs and has also located portions of the wall paintings likely executed by mission Indians.[134] Significantly, Neuerburg identified several examples of "graffiti" by Native Americans. One was of a human form and the other an unidentified symbol found on the bottom portion of a column in the nave of San Miguel. The circumstances of these anonymous, presumably clandestine images is not known, but their direct contradiction of the European-derived, Christian imagery on which they were literally inscribed suggests the active practice of traditional iconography and faith systems or the fusion of Christian and Indigenous beliefs.[135]

The sacred spaces of the nave and the liturgies that were performed within them are examples of the role the mission landscape played in the imposition of Spanish power and its expectations for behavior, belief, and moral conduct. Sacred space was not limited to church architecture, however. For example, in the Chumash Revolt of 1824, some of the key instigators of the uprising were mission choristers, otherwise thought to be among the most integrated into the mission enterprise and loyal to the priests. After killing or wounding several people, the rebels fled into the interior with military forces from the Santa Barbara Presidio in pursuit. The padres negotiated a governor's pardon, and the fugitives agreed to return to the mission. The group's journey back to the mission happened to coincide with two feasts days on the liturgical calendar, and the entire party stopped to observe the holy days. According to one of the priests, the former choristers "cleared a space and built an arbor for a temporary chapel so that the priests could celebrate these feast days properly. In the wilderness, the Indians joined the priests in singing the High Masses and then returned to Santa Barbara."[136] The symbolic reintegration of the instigators through participation in a Catholic rite was materially registered in the landscape with an arbor marking it as a sacred space, distinct from what the Franciscans likely saw as "wilderness." For the Native Americans, however, not only was landscape infused with and inseparable from the divine, but the Chumash also built their own form of ritual enclosures or *siliyik* for dancing and bone whistle playing. Access to these sacred circular enclosures was restricted to the *'antap* or ritual specialists whose ceremonial activities were shielded from view by poles and mat screens.[137] There is no way to ascertain the meaning for the Chumash of the structure erected for the missionaries' worship services, but their creation of the temporary arbor and their participation in the rite suggest the integration of colonial practices within the context of Indigenous epistemologies.

The second example is a dance Choris witnessed and sketched at Mission Dolores in 1816 (Plate 5) that he described in great detail:

> On Sunday, when the service is ended, the Indians gather in the cemetery, which is in front of the mission house, and dance. Half of the men adorn themselves with feathers and with girdles ornamented with feathers and with bits of shell that pass for money among them, or they paint their bodies with regular lines of black, red, and white. Some have half their bodies (from the head downward) daubed with black, the other half red, and the whole crossed with white lines. Others sift the down from birds on their hair. The men commonly dance six or eight together, all making the same movements and all armed with spears. Their music consists of clapping the hands, singing, and the sound made by striking split sticks together which has a charm for their ears; this is finally followed by a horrible yell that greatly resembles the sound of a cough accompanied by a whistling noise. The women dance among themselves, but without making violent movements.[138]

The dance in San Francisco was only one among many that observers recorded in both public and clandestine settings.[139] Other traditional practices were performed in the mission landscape as well. Gambling, which had deep connections to the balance of the spiritual world, was also a common practice, although the Franciscans perceived it as a sign of moral weakness rather than a traditional religious practice. The archaeological finds of buried caches and objects placed beneath mission church tiles suggest the incorporation of traditional practices of burying ritually charged materials such as the practice recorded by Boscana's account of burying the afterbirth and Panich's interpretation of grave goods recovered at Mission Santa Clara.[140] Repeated instances of gambling, dances, construction of sacred structures for marriages and feasts, and ritual burying suggest not only the persistence of Native belief systems but also the co-optation of communal mission spaces for traditional practices. It seems likely that the continuity of such rituals indicates enduring Native belief systems as well as the concomitant bonding, exchange, and social debt that for millennia had bound people into a community of mutual social obligations. These practices and the use of mission spaces also indicate a continuity of the Native ideology of landscape in which there was no dichotomy between sacred and secular, and the physical settings of rituals were part of the very fabric of their belief system and daily lives. There is ample evidence, therefore, that sacred space, with its blending of Indigenous and European social structures and belief systems, was a malleable landscape constantly being negotiated to serve the interests of both Spanish and Native peoples.

Conclusion

In colonial contexts, where two distinct cultures were seeking dominance, the landscape was both a stage for that power struggle and a tool of control and resistance. The imposition of colonial power in Alta California entailed a complex mix of political goals, military objectives, ideological agendas, and economic imperatives, and the landscape was implicated in every regard. The prolonged drought that stressed traditional subsistence resources, the diseases and plants brought by Europeans, the introduction of new goods and their radical impact on Native trade and distribution networks—all these factors had a profound influence on the Spanish colonial incursion into California. It was a time of rapid and radical change, and yet on a daily basis the missions functioned with apparent stability and relatively minimal explicit violence, in the service either of Spanish domination or Native American resistance. Exploring the role of landscape in the everyday brings a humanist perspective to colonialism's broader theater of national and ideological agendas. It gives us a lens with which to view the individual human experience and personal impact of the missions. It invites us to consider, albeit obliquely, the realm of emotion—the tears, laughter, pain, joy, pleasure, tedium—so easily eclipsed by the dry facts of mission records and the mute objects of excavated assemblages.[141]

The examination of the missions as a space where two ideologies of landscape converged also reveals how mutable space and its meaning was for the Native peoples inhabiting the missions. The creative and subversive inhabitation of the landscape, in the face of rigid timetables, formations, and labor, makes tangible the complexity of interior colonization. The ways in which the mission Indians located themselves in the landscape also makes visible the agency of Native peoples in navigating the profound changes and dislocations in their lives.

Finally, this understanding of the hybridity of the space holds the possibility of theorizing these spaces as neither simply Indigenous nor colonial, but rather as heterotopias. The concept also presents the specter that these same spaces, currently interpreted as heritage sites in a narrowly construed and celebratory settler colonial paradigm, might be reimagined as Third Spaces where the dualisms of colonizer and colonized are brought into the "interstitial space of the witness."[142] In such a space, "paradoxical communities," whose lives intersect with, but are also disenfranchised by, the fictive histories at the mission, might begin to recognize their respective places in the sites' history and their geographies.[143] They might, as Homi Bhabha wistfully states, find a path toward "'being together' in the very act of recognition—of seeing oneself as another."[144]

CHAPTER TWO

Inventing Heritage

Time Binding in the Mission Landscape

The Treasures of Sentiment, the Charms of Romance, and the Riches of History

When William Henry Jackson published his 1894 collection of photographs of California's "ancient" missions and churches, he was documenting the crumbling remains of the state's colonial history. He lauded the missions for their picturesque architecture and "the treasures of sentiment, the charms of romance, and the riches of history which they possess."[1] He particularly noted the "sub-tropical loveliness" of the garden at the Santa Barbara Mission, "founded only ten years after the signing of the Declaration of Independence."[2] He claimed not only that it had "always been an object of admiration" but also that the "Mission Garden was, and still is, a place of peculiar beauty."[3] John Stoddard's publication of his popular traveling lecture series similarly presented the missions in a nostalgic light, cast the padres as "agèd pilgrims" from another era, and positioned the author as "the guest of an anachronism."[4] The illustrations in these volumes reinforced the authors' narratives with views of scenic landscape, mission ruins, and Native people, representative relics of a distant time and a vanished people. Within this visual trope of California's past, both authors included photographs of the "historic" mission garden at Santa Barbara. Jackson depicted a brown-robed Franciscan contemplating the beds of the central patio garden (Figure 2.1), while Stoddard's image of a friar gazing into the garden is captioned *Dreaming of Other Days.* Nowhere in these texts, however, is there any indication that the garden was less than thirty years old.

This chapter examines the "invention" of the mission garden, both the first patio garden constructed at Santa Barbara in 1872 and the subsequent construction of similar gardens at missions across California. Rather than a simple design genealogy, the history of mission gardens demonstrates the ways in which landscape design is mobilized in the politics of memory. This study traces the transformation

MISSION OF SANTA BARBARA.

FIGURE 2.1. William Henry Jackson, daguerreotype of Mission Santa Barbara Garden, 1885–90. The Huntington Library, San Marino, California.

of mission landscapes into ornamental gardens using a design vocabulary that materialized settler colonial narratives and helped to naturalize the complex discourses of race and power. The Manifest Destiny ideology of colonialism being inscribed into the narratives of public history throughout America was in California centered on the missions.

In a typically impassioned editorial championing mission preservation, Charles Lummis wrote in 1895 that California was rich not only in fruit, flowers, beauty, and money but also in "that much rarer heritage in America, a past of history and romance."[5] He further argued that its citizens should invest in the missions' preservation because, aside from the climate, the missions were "the best capital Southern California has."[6] To understand how that capital had been accrued at the turn of the century and to assess the significance of the invention of the mission garden in that transaction, one must fathom the pace of change in mid-nineteenth-century California. In less than thirty years it had gone from Spanish colonial outpost, to the northern frontier of a fledgling Mexican nation, to an American territory making the leap to statehood just two years later. Everything, from the changing fortunes of political and economic elites to the role of the church, the legal system, and the official language, was in flux. Social structures of colonial times were being dramatically altered with immigration sparked first by becoming an American territory and then ignited by the discovery of gold. During the 1850s and 1860s, racial lines were being remapped and class relationships realigned as Anglo-Americans came into power. Native peoples who had never joined the mission system, as well as those who had returned to traditional lifeways in California's interior after secularization, were subjected to some of the most atrocious campaigns of cultural genocide ever launched by the U.S. government. The former mission Indians who had left the missions to live and work in nearby towns were legally dispossessed, politically marginalized, and socially ostracized.[7] These exclusionary politics were promulgated not only in legal and governmental spheres that denied the rights of full citizenship to these nonwhites but also in the public discourse. As historian Linda Heidenreich has argued, "It was the dominant narratives of the nineteenth century that enabled Euro-Americans in the West . . . to practice violence and discrimination against racialized peoples on a daily basis in their everyday lives."[8]

The growing perception of the historical significance of the California missions in the second half of the nineteenth century is related to broader regional and national cultural currents as well as social and political trends in the state. The nation's centennial in 1876 ignited great interest in all things colonial, and the western Spanish colonial experience was held up as an equivalent to the East Coast legacy of the original thirteen British colonies. Mission San Juan Capistrano, founded in 1776, was a favorite example of a western parallel to Anglo-colonial origin stories. Popular interest in preserving colonial sites was also emerging nationally with efforts such as the establishment in 1850 of the country's first historic house museum at General George Washington's headquarters in Newburgh, New York, and soon afterward the rescue of his Virginia home by the Mount Vernon Ladies' Association in 1858.[9] Similar recognition of the value of historic sites was brewing in California as well, but it is the exact timing and sequence of these efforts that make the beginnings of the mission garden so significant.

Within an emerging ethos of historic preservation and Colonial Revival movements in the second half of the nineteenth century, the California missions stood at an intriguing crossroads in a number of ways. First, they stood at the juncture of church and state. In Alta California, the Franciscan order was given the primary responsibility for colonizing and converting the new territory. While there were increasing power struggles over time between the Franciscan leadership and the colonial governor regarding the control of the missions, the role of the

Catholic Church as the representative of the Spanish Crown meant that church and state were more closely integrated in the governance of colonial California than had been the case in the Anglo colonies of the East Coast.[10] Second, California's elite who traced their roots to a Spanish or Mexican Catholic past were facing increasing competition from newer arrivals whose lineage was broadly construed as Anglo and Protestant. There was a dramatic shift in locally elected officials as "old name" Hispanic families were voted out of office and a new political elite seized power.[11] The Catholic–Protestant tensions, which were echoed nationally in the Know-Nothing Party and other anti-Catholic and anti-immigrant movements, accentuated the delicate position of the missions as central monuments in California's early history and as sites of sectarian significance.[12] Finally, the evolving narratives of settler colonialism not only continued to legitimate the dispossession of Native territory and recast the colonial mission sites as national patrimony, but the missions also became didactic places of "Americanization" for inculcating immigrants and citizens alike in the ideologies of a racialized historical narrative.[13] It was in this dynamic political and social context that the first mission gardens came into being.

The development of first three mission gardens, Santa Barbara (1872), San Fernando (1920–22), and San Juan Capistrano (ca. 1910–33), marks significant landmarks in the invention of the genre. They established design templates, visual conventions, and ideological discourses for mission landscapes. Three later gardens, at Missions La Purísima (1935–42), San Gabriel (1930s), and San Antonio de Pala (1950s), reveal the various stakeholders, interests, adaptations, and appropriations of the mission garden form at each site. The histories of these slightly later gardens also demonstrate the influence of the earlier mission gardens, particularly Santa Barbara, and the ever more indelible connotations of the peaceful, sacred, and beautiful spaces for the construction of California's past.

Mission Santa Barbara

John S. McGroarty, author of *The Mission Play,* profiled the Santa Barbara Mission garden for *West Coast* magazine in 1909 and extolled, "There is no place in all California which clings to the past with an affection so noticeable as that which characterizes the Place of the Sacred Garden."[14] Founded as the tenth mission in December 1786, Mission Santa Barbara was sited near the relatively dense Chumash settlements along the Central Coast and close to the Santa Barbara Presidio (or fort), which had been established in 1782.[15] The first buildings were simple wooden structures that have been described as wattle and daub or log cabins chinked with mud and small stones and thatched with earth and *zacate* grass.[16] Adobe brick and tile soon replaced the wooden huts as labor and resources became available, and the first adobe church was built in 1789 with the first quadrangle completed in 1796. The mission continued to expand with the addition of outbuildings supporting agricultural and husbandry activities and, in 1798–1807, the construction of an "Indian village" that was home to more than seventeen hundred neophytes or baptized Indians. By the 1820s Santa Barbara had become one of the most intensively developed missions with a blacksmith shop, soap factory, tannery, pottery, and weavers' rooms. An extensive hydraulic system of reservoirs, aqueducts, and cisterns was constructed to supply both the daily water needs of the residents and the processing and manufacturing activities of the mission's light industries. Visitors to the mission prior to its secularization in 1833 described a rich agrarian landscape cultivated with fruit orchards, olive groves, fields of grain crops and vegetable gardens, as well as grazing land for sheep, cattle, and horses. Significantly, the areas that are today planted with lush lawns and ornamental gardens were in the mission period either unadorned workspaces or dedicated to subsistence farming. The central patio that today houses the quintessential "mission garden" was in the eighteenth and early nineteenth centuries primarily a workspace. A visitor in 1829 described the Santa Barbara mission courtyard as a place where "carpenters, saddlers, and shoemakers were at work, and young girls spinning and preparing wool for the loom."[17]

As at other missions, the years following secularization at Santa Barbara were turbulent. Despite the continuous presence of Franciscans, the mission saw sustained economic decline from the late 1830s through the 1860s, and the instability during this period is important for understanding the genesis of the mission garden.[18] The mid-nineteenth century marked not only a fundamental shift in the organization and purpose of the missions but also a combination of disrupted trade, transitions in state and ecclesiastical authority, declining Native American labor force, title disputes, and dwindling income that severely affected the mission's productivity and infrastructure. A separate parish church was founded to serve Santa Barbara's Catholics, and with neither a productive agricultural enterprise nor a parish for income, the Franciscans were left with high-maintenance historic buildings and few resources. Even if they had had the land and the labor force to sustain it, the bottom had dropped out of the area cattle industry, which was facing a series of devastating droughts and floods, as well as competition from Texas ranchers, who were raising a superior breed.[19] Father Antonio Jimeno pleaded the situation to Archbishop Joseph Alemany in 1857: "The lands . . . ceded to us are in such a deteriorated state that the yield in the past year does not amount to $100.00 worth. . . . Without a parish of white persons (what we have are Indians and everything is done for them gratis), . . . how can this college maintain itself? . . . The alms which we collect each month from the houses of the presidio are not sufficient to buy the bread we eat."[20]

There was little money at Santa Barbara for repairs, let alone improvements, and visitors commented on the dilapidated state of the orchards and fields. George Simpson, superintendent of the Hudson Bay Company who visited the mission in January 1842, observed: "In the [earlier] days of the priests, fruits were to be obtained here at every season. . . . But, ever since 1836, not only had the branches been left unpruned, but even their very produce had been allowed to fall to the ground; so that now most of the trees were in a deteriorated condition."[21] Henry Miller's 1856 drawing shows the intact church and quadrangle with the fountain and lavandería in front, but the outbuildings behind the mission and the Indian village to the left are missing their roofs and the walls are deteriorating (Figure 2.2).[22] By 1861, when the first geological survey of California visited Santa Barbara, the core buildings were in good shape, but the rest of the mission was in disrepair:

> The church is in good preservation, with the monastery alongside—all else is ruined. . . . I rode through the old town [the former neophyte residences]. Here were whole streets of buildings, built of *adobes,* their roofs gone, their walls tumbling, squirrels burrowing in them—all now desolate, ruined, deserted. Grass grows in the old streets and cattle feed in the gardens. . . . The old threshing floor is ruined, the weeds growing over its old pavement. The palm trees are dead, and the olive and fig trees are dilapidated and broken.[23]

The Franciscans' prospects began to brighten in 1868 when they opened the Colegio Franciscano or Boys' College for day students and boarders. The goal of the ambitious plan to teach primary grades through junior college was to generate tuition income and bring the mission back to self-sufficiency and prosperity. While student enrollment did not live up to expectations and the college was closed in 1877,[24] its greatest legacy may be that it gave rise to the first "mission garden." To lead this fledgling school, the Franciscans called upon Mexican-born Father José María Romo, who was at the time serving in Egypt to establish a hospice for Mexicans visiting the Holy Land. Upon receiving his orders in 1871 to go to Santa Barbara to be guardian of the college and superior of the mission, Romo began his journey traveling by way of Sicily, Naples, Rome, Marseilles, and Paris. Fortunately, his handwritten diary survives, and in it he recounts some of the sites he visited in each city, including monasteries, palaces, churches, convents, cemeteries, and seminaries. Of particular interest, he notes several "magnificent gardens" although he offers little detail.[25]

Upon arriving at Santa Barbara in 1872, Romo assessed the paltry economic support the bishop had provided and determined the place would need to generate more income if it was going to survive (Figure 2.3). If the Colegio was to attract tuition-paying students who were coming for a secular classical education rather than responding to a call to the priesthood, the facilities needed to be upgraded.[26] Under Romo the mission began extensive architectural renovations, including $1,455 in repairs to the church interior, expansion of the dormitories, and the creation of a cloister garden in the patio of the main mission quadrangle.[27]

FIGURE 2.2. Henry Miller, view of Santa Barbara, 1856. Courtesy of The Bancroft Library, University of California, Berkeley.

FIGURE 2.3. The Franciscan community at Santa Barbara in 1883. Father Romo is seated fourth from the left. In *Views from a Trip to California,* vol. 1. Courtesy of The Bancroft Library, University of California, Berkeley.

Correspondence between Romo and Bishop Thaddeus Amat documents the bishop's approval of Romo's request to connect the inner courtyard to the pressurized water system.[28] Romo's diary entry in January 1873 proudly reports the successful operation of the fountain.

The fountain was the centerpiece of the garden, which was composed of geometric beds and intersecting walks that over time became edged, but in the beginning were loosely defined as seen in one of the earliest views of the garden (Figure 2.4). The walks radiated from the circular fountain both on axis and diagonally within the quadrangle, creating a pattern of symmetrical parterre beds. The fountain in the garden today has a tiered basin, echoing the 1808 fountain in front of the mission, but it was originally a *jet d'eau* that when under pressure issued a single stream from the still surface of the water in the center of the basin. A photograph taken during President McKinley's visit in 1901 shows the effect of the fountain's single jet rising several feet and the 1902 stereographic view shows it issuing ten feet or more (Figure 2.5).[29] Henry Chapman Ford, who first visited the mission in 1875, noted, "The *patio* of this mission is now a well kept garden with walks, flowers, and shrubs, with a fountain occupying the center." He went on to add, as many others have, that "there, no female foot is allowed to tread."[30] There are no known drawings for Romo's original garden plan and his diary provides only scant detail, but photographs dating from the early 1880s show the garden layout with well-established plants, and a 1903 plan specifies plant species,

FIGURE 2.4. View of the "gray-frocked" padres in the Santa Barbara Mission courtyard. Undated but likely ca. 1880. Santa Bárbara Mission Archive-Library.

FIGURE 2.5. "A pleasant retreat from the World—Gardens of the old Santa Barbara Mission, California." Stereographic photograph, 1902. The Library of Congress, Prints and Photographs (LC-DIG-stereo-1s01717).

some of which, such as the "old orange tree" and the "Bishop's cypress," were likely part of Romo's plan[31] (see Figure 2.6 and the appendix). While the garden could have been reconfigured between 1872 and the mid-1880s, the maturity of plants in the photographs suggests that it is the same layout, albeit more neatly edged and more densely planted. The garden beds were planted with a mix of trees, succulents, ground cover, cacti, roses, perennials, and annuals.[32] The photos from the period also show two wooden structures suitable for supporting climbing

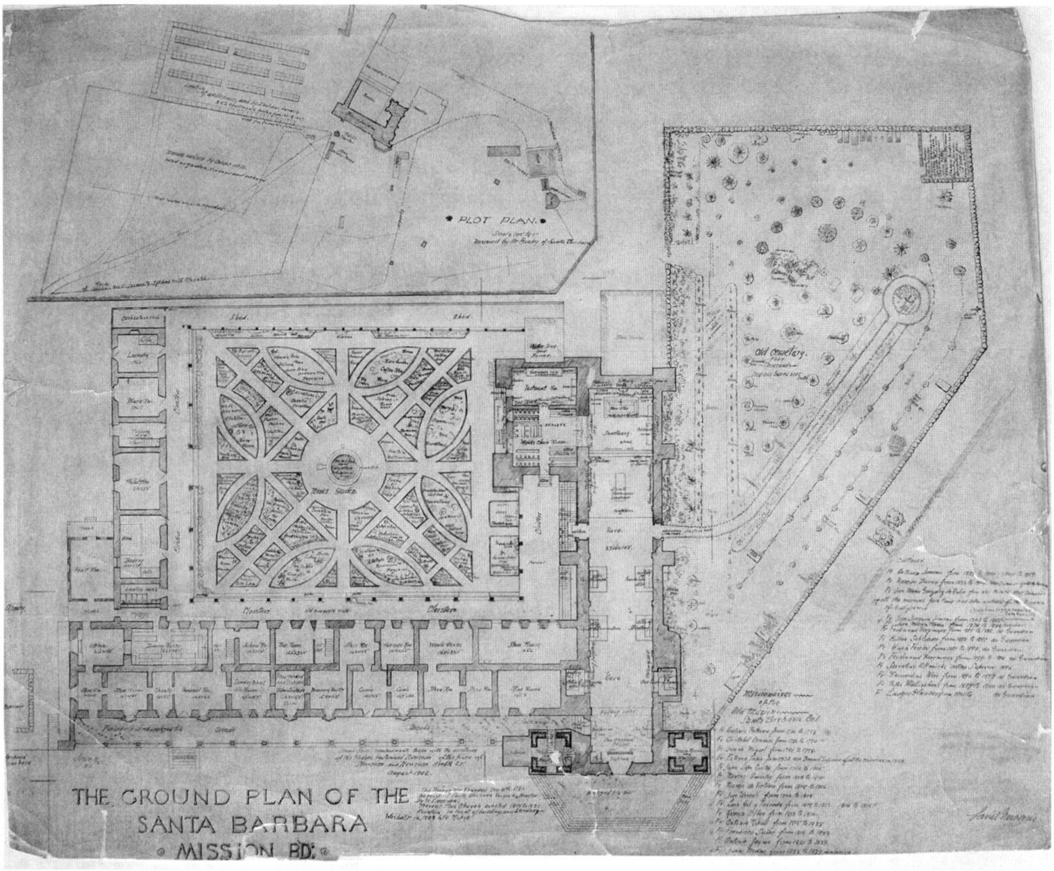

FIGURE 2.6. The ground plan of the Santa Barbara Mission. Samuel Newsom of the firm Newsom and Newsom Archts., San Francisco, August 1903. Santa Bárbara Mission Archive-Library.

vines: a rectangular arbor planted with grapes running parallel to the church and a lighter circular frame around the fountain that was removed by around 1890 (Figure 2.7).[33] There is no direct evidence of a specific source for Romo's design, but the layout of the garden is consistent with what he might have seen traveling around the Mediterranean in the early 1870s, particularly the kinds of designs he might have seen in quadrangles and courtyards of the convents and churches he visited.

More significant than Romo's inspiration for the design was its reception in the context of Santa Barbara's increasing "Americanization."[34] Prior to secularization, the civic leaders were a small elite group of governmental administrators, military officers, and mission fathers whose wealth, political influence, and claim to direct Spanish descent separated them from the majority mestizo population of soldiers and civilian colonists.[35] Following secularization and the resulting

FIGURE 2.7. Santa Barbara Mission garden ca. 1885–89. Taber Photo, San Francisco. Courtesy of The Bancroft Library, University of California, Berkeley.

redistribution of land and political power, Santa Barbara became a highly stratified and powerful community of wealthy ranchers, small-scale ranchers and subsistence farmers, and laborers and artisans. After statehood in 1850, Santa Barbara continued to be one of the largest Spanish-speaking settlements in the state, but that started to change during the 1860s as the slumping pastoral economy led to financial ruin for many Mexican ranchers while a real estate speculative bubble attracted an influx of Anglos. By 1870 Santa Barbara's population had become majority Anglo, and the 1873 local elections marked the transfer of political power as Californios lost all city and county offices except the county sheriff to Anglo candidates. The political change was accompanied by a parallel shift in the socioeconomic structure of the town as Anglos accumulated property and established themselves in higher occupational levels while the Mexican (both California- and Mexico-born) population experienced a downward economic trend.[36] These rising and fading fortunes were part of a broader process of increasing inequalities codified along racial lines. Historian Albert Camarillo has described this process of "barrioization" in Santa Barbara as one in which the "loss of land, decline of the pastoral economy, . . . the continuation of racial antagonism, . . . [and] the onset of political powerlessness began to create a new reality for Mexican people in Santa Barbara" that included the "formation of residentially and socially segregated Chicano barrios or neighborhoods."[37]

Whether Romo's work at Santa Barbara stemmed from his astute reading of the local context or was influenced by his Mediterranean travels, he created a garden that was perceived by those who saw it as a beautiful, sacred space descending from the long European tradition of courtyard gardens. At a time when status was inextricably tied to race and the fortunes of Santa Barbara's Mexican community were in decline, Romo's design rendered the space as an Iberian courtyard garden and tellingly bypassed references to Mexican design and even explicitly to Catholicism. For instance, while its setting in a Franciscan mission linked it to the contemplative tradition of monastic gardens, there were no crosses, statuary, or other religious iconography. The allusions to a European garden tradition associated the mission with a respected cultural legacy that transcended particular religious affiliation and was consonant with notions of white, Western civilization. Writing some years later, Charles Lummis made explicit Romo's implied design lineage when he wrote about the Andalusian origins of patio gardens, and lauded their benefits in a climate such as Southern California's, noting that "in the Spanish colonies of the New World [the patio garden] has become almost universal—so eminently lovable that neither tradition nor bigotry could hold out against it."[38] Romo's design not only served the interests of the mission administrators who were struggling to keep the mission solvent in the 1870s, but it also embedded their heritage in the more legitimate sphere of "Spanish" historical origins rather than Native American or Mexican heritage.

The cachet of the mission's garden was not lost on the administrators of the mission who succeeded Romo and continued to capitalize on the appealing image the garden created. In response to growing debt at the mission and increasing conflict with the bishop, leaders of the Franciscan order and the Catholic diocese decided in 1885 that the Santa Barbara friars should give up their identity as a separate Apostolic College and join the American province as a monastery.[39] The new stewards of the mission belonged to the Province of the Sacred Heart, an order of Franciscans with Germanic origins. The new brothers wore brown rather than gray robes, and they also brought a different sensibility and notion of order. Not only did they immediately embark on improvements such as landscaping the dilapidated cemetery, edging the garden beds, and plastering the facade of the mission, but they also reached out to the public in new ways. Particularly significant for the legacy of Romo's patio garden, these shrewd administrators managed to maintain both the mystique of a closed monastic community and publicly promote the "sacred garden" at the same time. In their first year the brothers inaugurated a formal guide program to lead visitors through the public parts of the mission.[40] The year 1886 was the centennial of the mission, and the friars partnered with the Santa Barbara Go-Ahead Club to organize festivities in celebration of the anniversary. They allowed professional photographers in the mission, cooperated with newspaper reporters doing stories on the mission, and posed in appropriately contemplative stances in corridors and standing by fountains (Figure 2.8).[41]

Published accounts convey a favorable reception of the garden. In addition to being admired for its beauty and peacefulness, the Santa Barbara garden was also quickly perceived as historic, despite persistent reports to the contrary, and its influence as a model of mission-style landscape architecture was significant. How a garden merely thirty years old in 1900 could have been so influential requires a close examination of the timing and context of the garden's creation. Not only does 1872 precede the generally accepted start of the Mission Revival style by almost three decades, but it also comes on the eve of the explosion of California's burgeoning leisure travel, the rise of photography, and the real estate boom that helped fuel Southern California's growth at the end of the nineteenth century.[42] Santa Barbara's first grand hotel, the Arlington, opened in 1875, and the Southern Pacific Railroad, linking San Francisco and Los Angeles, was completed in 1876. Santa Barbara became a convenient stop for rail and steamer travel, and, with the growing popularity of automobiles, traffic to the mission increased even more. It became one of the requisite stops for celebrity visitors, including Princess Louise (daughter of Queen Victoria) and her husband, the governor general of Canada in 1882, Mrs. Benjamin Harrison in 1891, President William McKinley in 1901, President Theodore Roosevelt in 1903 (Figure 2.9), and King Albert and Queen Elisabeth of Belgium in 1919.

Tourists who came to visit the mission at the turn of the twentieth century saw a colorful, well-established formal garden that resembled the images in widely circulated books about Spanish and Italian gardens.[43] Santa Barbara's garden was plausible, therefore, as what people imagined a surviving example of a Spanish-era monastery garden would look like, and its reputation grew. Santa Barbara was praised as one of the most picturesque along the mission trail, and the allure of the garden was only heightened by the fact that it was forbidden for women to enter it, although they might look in from the safety of the surrounding quadrangle. For those who saw published images of the garden, thanks to popular media such as magazines, postcards, and stereograph prints, the garden appeared to be a seamless part of the historical fabric of the mission and it was repeatedly characterized as timeless. While preservationists were just turning their attention to stabilizing walls and repairing roofs at San Juan Capistrano and San Antonio de Pala Asistencia in the 1880s, Santa Barbara and its garden stood as an example of a remarkably sound surviving specimen from the missions days and an excellent model for those seeking to bring other missions "back to life." This planting of a small garden in 1872 would have little significance were it not for its role in shaping perceptions of missions and their history. As it is, Romo's idiosyncratic garden

FIGURE 2.8. "Father Onesimus at Fountain. Santa Barbara, Cal." Postcard, ca. 1905. Collection of the author.

FIGURE 2.9. President Theodore Roosevelt and party at the Old Mission of the Franciscan Fathers, Santa Barbara, California, 1903. Underwood and Underwood stereographic print, cropped. The Library of Congress, Prints and Photographs (LC-DIG-stereo-1s02029).

in the monastery of a small town on the California coast became an iconic garden model for missions and Mission Revival landscape architecture throughout the state and beyond.

Mission San Fernando: Civic Memory Making

> We are "Time Binding" for we are taking the ideas and work of the early padres, developing and preserving things which were built more than a hundred years ago for our use and for the education and pleasure of future generations. . . . Some day

> when you feel the urge to get away from the "roaring town," drive out to the San Fernando Mission, have your luncheon under the pepper trees, wander around the Memory Garden; it will take you back hundreds of years, it will conjure up memories of the wonderful work of the padres who established, as an eastern park expert said, the first civilized gardens in America. (Martha Nelson McCan, "Mission Garden Restored," *Clubwoman,* 1924)

When Martha McCan reflected on her efforts to create a mission garden in front of Mission San Fernando, Rey de España in the early 1920s, she cited the philosophical writings of Count Alfred Korzybski. In *The Manhood of Humanity* Korzybski advanced the idea that human beings are "time-binders," carrying over from one generation to another special lines of human endeavor.[44] Not only did McCan's group of civic-minded women seek to block a citrus-packing plant from encroaching on the mission property, but they also envisioned a garden that would attract visitors, celebrate California's early heritage of "the first civilized gardens in America," and provide an oasis of pastoral beauty in the midst of Los Angeles's sprawl and in "this great rushing modern life of ours."[45] The garden McCan designed for the San Fernando public park in the 1920s was fabricated with no historical evidence of a garden on the site during colonial times, yet it was perceived as a preservation project. For those who designed, funded, and managed the San Fernando project, the garden was a re-creation of a historic relic, a "time-binder" that connected the present to the colonial past. They were bringing back to life a garden they believed had once been tended in or near the space. That impulse to create a historic mission garden is both the simple act of landscaping and a profoundly political act of embedding the present in an imagined past to serve particular interests.[46] Mission San Fernando was also the first mission garden instigated by a consortium of concerned citizens, rather than by parish priests or staff. It was one of the first instances in which mission preservation as a public cause focused exclusively on the landscape, rather than on the restoration of the buildings as the Landmarks Club had. It exemplifies the efforts of women in the early twentieth century to mobilize financial and political resources to accomplish civic improvements and to create visible monuments to a particular historical narrative. The imagined landscape they created brought discourses of the racialized geographies of suburban development to bear on the garden design of a single city block.

The mission lies in the eponymous San Fernando Valley, now a densely populated area of Los Angeles, but in the late 1910s it was still a relatively bucolic area with a small commercial downtown and modest neighborhoods surrounded by agricultural fields and orange groves. It was also an area where the spatial practices of race were manifested in a combination of rural and urban living envisioned as "gentlemen farming" and formed the "foundation of a middle-class white settler society."[47] The boosters promoting the area to transplants from the East and Midwest highlighted its climate and natural environment, as well as its unique cultural heritage, but framed the latter as safely removed to a distant past whose lingering influence flavored the town without contaminating its racial character. An 1883 promotional text celebrated the advantages of suburban Los Angeles communities, noting that "by a short and easy journey one can see the homes, orchards, vineyards, gardens, flowers, hedge-lined streets, live oak groves, the picturesque Arroyo, the Old Mission, a touch of the Mexican dominion, and the very best samples of Southern California."[48] The San Fernando Valley at the turn of the twentieth century was being settled by an ethnically diverse group, but the new arrivals were nearly unanimous in their "commitment to the ideals of suburban farming in a booming metropolis region"[49] and to becoming, as Paul Sandul has called them, "bourgeois horticulturalists in an agricultural wonderland."[50]

When rumors began circulating in 1920 that a citrus-packing warehouse was going to be built across from the "old Spanish mission," a number of women, including the formidable Mrs. Martha Nelson McCan, took up the cause of preserving the land in front of the mission as a "safety park."[51] These women approached the property owner, Mission Land Company president Mr. Leslie Coombs Brand, and persuaded him to donate the land. After moving the city to pass an ordinance to designate it as Brand Park, they launched a community-based fund-raising campaign to develop what was described initially as a "Memory Garden" and later as a "mission garden."[52] The project was ultimately funded by private contributions totaling $20,050, matched by a special allocation by the city council to the City of Los Angeles Park Department for the project.[53] McCan, a member and later president of the Park Commission, was "the originator of the scheme" and a primary advocate for its implementation. As an accomplished author, speaker, community leader, and politico, McCan had an extensive social and political network. She had been active in the suffrage movement, worked for the Federal Employment Bureau, and was the first woman appointed to the Los Angeles Civil Service Commission, eventually becoming its president. She held offices in numerous community groups, including president of the Southern California Woman's Press Club and the Friday Morning Club, and she worked on Meredith Snyder's campaign for mayor of Los Angeles. In addition to her local civic and political connections, she was well traveled internationally and had worked for a time in London, so she was familiar with European garden design traditions.[54] Described as a "committee of one" in the commission's records, McCan recalled the genesis of the idea: "When I became a member of the Park Commission, I made a tour of the parks. Brand Park with its historic surroundings gave me the thought that a most interesting garden in this park could be developed, carrying out as far as possible, the vision of the Mission Fathers."[55]

McCan's concept for the garden was based originally on the Mission Santa Barbara garden, which she described as the only mission garden "that has been continuously maintained,"[56] but she and the commission also sought historical evidence and other models for their project. The park commissioners requested Father Zephyrin Engelhardt's books on the missions from the Los Angeles Public Library, and they solicited advice and funds from prominent mission preservation advocates of the day, such as John McGroarty and Charles Lummis, president of the Landmarks Club.[57] After a trip to Mission Santa Barbara, McCan and some other park commissioners made a longer tour of public parks and missions north of San Fernando, where they talked with priests and collected plant cuttings.[58] One of the more helpful stops was at Monterey (presumably at the Presidio Chapel, since they had already visited the Carmel mission), where they met "Father Mestres, a Spaniard, and an authority on the Missions" who gave them "many valuable suggestions regarding the plans." The report of the tour notes that they saw a "beautiful garden" maintained at a girls' school at San José, but for the most part their visits confirmed their initial observations that Santa Barbara's was the only surviving garden from the mission period.[59]

Despite using terms such as *replica* and *restoration,* the garden design was clearly an amalgamation of features from multiple missions with a strong dose of European formal parterre garden influence. McCan described the garden in detail in an article submitted to the Native Sons' *Grizzly Bear* magazine, explaining that "the design of the garden reverts back to days in Europe when all gardenesque ideas were expressed in conventional and geometric design." McCan created a "formal landscape arrangement" with geometric flower beds intersected by "diagonal, right angle, semi circular and oval design gravel paths" (Figure 2.10). She noted that the planting plan incorporated both native plants and Old World imports because "history informs us that the Padres loved flowers and flora." McCan collected cuttings and seeds from the "descendants" of original plants at other missions with the goal of including representative plantings from each mission in the state, "thus symbolizing the chain of the twenty-one Missions in their geographical relation." The garden also incorporated tiles from other missions engraved with the missions' names, "inscribing the fact that the collection has been made to form a 'Memory Garden,' as, sad to relate, many of our Missions are now memories only." The garden was lined with pergolas supporting climbing plants such as jasmine, passion vines, and climbing roses, while other areas of the park were planted with pepper trees, olives, grapes, pomegranates, and other descendants of mission species, as well as favorites such as crape myrtle and oleander (Figure 2.11, Appendix).[60] The highlights of the garden were two water features, one of which was already on the lot and one of which was moved from a nearby location, a prodigious feat of engineering given the friable stone-and-tile construction (Figure 2.12).[61] The relocated water feature was transformed into a fountain

FIGURE 2.10. Brand Park, 1933. California Historical Society.

FIGURE 2.11. Pergola, west end of Brand Park, 1933. California Historical Society.

FIGURE 2.12. Moving the "star" fountain to Brand Park, 1922. California Historical Society.

with the addition of a central spout that pumped water into a tiered basin.[62] The incorporation of the two fountains as centerpieces of a mission garden further reinforced the template established at Santa Barbara, and these fountains, in turn, became models for the construction of other mission gardens.

In addition to preserving the land around the mission as a buffer, the garden was intended to serve other purposes as well. It was to be an "outdoor museum" with historic plant specimens and a restored tallow vat. The commission also proposed restoring a small adobe building to serve as a museum of "historical relics" that would be donated by local residents so that the public could study them and "realize the changes that have taken place even in the manufacture and design of domestic implements and utensils." They hoped to achieve the effect that "when you enter the room, . . . it has the appearance of having been recently vacated by someone who lived in the days of the padres."[63] The park was also intended to attract tourists to the area, and appeals during the fund-raising campaign touted the impact the park would have nationally and even internationally. In making the case for matching funds to the city council, McCan argued that "in no other state in the Union is there a city park with a Mission for a background, or, vice versa, a Mission before which a city park is maintained." With no small irony, she concluded that, if funded, the park and mission would become "a Mecca, unique in its picturesque, romantic and historic associations."[64] Other requests for sponsorships to business groups such as the Chamber of Commerce and the "Advertising Club" emphasized the economic advantages of creating a popular attraction, noting "the Park . . . will pay from the beginning."[65] As a public park funded in part by taxpayers' dollars and with ongoing maintenance provided by the Park Department, the park was also promoted for its contribution to civic life and recreational benefit to the local residents. The park had areas for picnics, ball games, musical performances, and other facilities "for the comfort and convenience of the public."[66] John McGroarty gave a speech at a fund-raiser for the park, proclaiming, "It is known among the local citizens that the park means more to this section than gaining many millions in industries of any kind."[67]

The public context of San Fernando's Brand Park mission garden required not only public accountability and transparency of goals in order to raise funds and develop community consensus, but also a delicate navigation of the tensions between church and state. When presenting the initial proposal to the city council and when unveiling plans to the public, McCan was very careful to point out that the garden was to be "purely historical in its intent and design and all reference to religion will be avoided."[68] She alleviated concerns about creating a "sacred garden" on public land by emphasizing the European origins of the garden design and the allegedly historic nature of the botanical materials, which were perceived as ideologically neutral and avoided sectarian iconography.

It is all the more remarkable, therefore, that within two years of its construction, the garden was "completed" with the addition of a statue of the founder of the missions, Junípero Serra. The statue was commissioned from New York sculptor Sally W. Farnham for ten thousand dollars (almost half the cost of the entire project at that point) and underwritten by Brand. The design proposed by Farnham was to depict "Junipero Serra as he made his pilgrimage from San Diego to San Francisco with his little Indian boy"[69] (Figure 2.13). It is not clear from the commission records who initiated the idea for the statue, but the Park Commission president commented in a letter to the Landmarks Committee, "I know that you will rejoice with me in the accomplishment of this achievement,"[70] suggesting that the commission was in favor of it. There were precedents at other sites, including a Serra statue at Mission San Juan Capistrano dedicated in 1914 and the heroic-scale Serra sculpture unveiled in San Francisco's Golden Gate Park in November 1907.[71] None of those specific models is cited in the Brand Park records, but it is possible to interpret the iconography of the statue as a reconciliation of the seemingly contradictory positions of being a "non-religious" reconstruction of a mission garden. Whether the project leaders were conscious of the fact or not, the statue represented the church's historical role in a way that was

FIGURE 2.13. Sally W. Farnham, *Serra and Indian Boy,* commissioned for Brand Park in 1923 (undated photo, ca. 1926). California Historical Society.

consonant with the rhetoric and conventional sculptural formulas of commemorative monuments. Serra's pose and gesture, with his arm draped protectively and comfortingly over the boy's shoulder as they walk in stride, evoked the image of the caring padre who sacrificed all to bring salvation to the California Natives. The statue of the frocked priest looking boldly ahead while the partially clothed child looks down parallels the paternalistic postures of Lincoln and slaves that were sculpted as public commemorations of Emancipation at the time of the Civil War.[72] The image of the innocent, "uncivilized" child subordinated to the kindly but dominant priest seems an obvious vehicle for colonialist justifications, but in the late 1920s it was praised as a perfect addition "to make the garden a complete unity." McCan argued that the Serra statue, when "placed beside the fountain, in the shade of the pepper trees," would continue "radiating peace, as did the good padre in his life time."[73] Still standing on its pedestal, albeit with a heavy patina, Serra continues to look out over the colorful flower beds and trickling fountains, a gentle, nurturing cultivator and the seeming antithesis of an oppressive colonial regime.

McCan's garden not only appropriated an imagined mission past as a suitable design for a public park but also invoked the discourses of California's Progressive and women's movements in the early twentieth century. McCan mobilized support for the project through women's organizations such as the Ebell Club, the Daughters of the American Revolution, the Women's Civic League, the Woman's City Club, and St. Simon's Episcopal Guild. McCan and her associates spoke at club meetings, published articles in club newsletters, and invited subscriptions from members as well as from the clubs themselves.[74] As historian Gayle Gullett has argued, following their success in winning the vote in California in 1911, female reformers in the 1920s found in the Americanization social movement sympathetic "ideologies of gender, class, and ethnicity to construct a new model of citizenship and thus answer a question posed by both social movements: Who is an American citizen?"[75] The Memory Garden project materialized the values and ethos of the "modern brand of Americanization" that was the concern not only of immigrants but also of "American citizens who need to be taught how to be the right kind of Americans for only in this way can the whole be leavened and the standard raised."[76] Being the "right kind of Americans" entailed identifying with Anglo-American values predicated on a white, Protestant, affluent, or middle-class positionality and embedded in historical narratives that supported this identity. In California, the Mediterranean Revival style, with its allusions to European garden precedents and its association as a regional style, suited these purposes.[77] The women leading the San Fernando garden project were also quick to point out that, unlike Santa Barbara's cloistered, all-male sanctuary, the Brand Park garden was to be "open to men and women at all seasons of the year."[78] For female reformers, these civic projects not only created spaces and narratives for inculcating American values but also were public displays of the women's social and political capital. Like other civic projects the women's clubs undertook, the public campaigns raised the profile of the women's leaders and demonstrated their abilities and influence. McCan observed that the project was a testimony to "the determination of women when they are aroused to action."[79]

The San Fernando garden exemplifies the influence of these early "restored" landscapes on other mission sites and the cumulative effect of the precedents each garden set for embedding the nineteenth- and twentieth-century gardens as "historic" in the public imagination and communal memory. The Santa Barbara Mission garden was taken by McCan and the commissioners as the premier example of a surviving mission garden, and early proposals emphasized that the memory garden was being "designed along the lines of a Mission Garden which we know to have been in existence since the days of the Padres."[80] The San Fernando rendition of the Spanish garden then became a model in its own right for other missions preparing to embark on landscape projects. The San Fernando fountains were copied in other mission gardens, such as the one constructed at La Purísima a decade later, and they helped reinforce the notion that the water features were ornamental elements rather than remnants of the more utilitarian settling tank, reservoir, and laundry functions they originally served.[81] Furthermore, when the Park Commission representatives came back from their tour of missions in 1922, they sent the San Fernando garden plan to a number of the rectors to request comments on the plans.[82] There is no record that they received any comments, but the circulation of the plan further spread the image of the mission garden as an appropriate historical setting for the mission buildings.[83]

Mission San Juan Capistrano: Aestheticized Ruins and Mission Marketing

Lying about two hours south of San Fernando is Mission San Juan Capistrano, one of the first missions to receive the restoration attentions of the Landmarks Club. Its garden history exemplifies the role of local priests, parishioners, and community members in using landscape design as an intentional promotional strategy to attract tourists. The mission's epithet, the "Jewel of the Missions," alludes both to the remarkable architecture of the original seven-domed chapel and to its reputation as one of the most picturesque missions. San Juan Capistrano's aestheticization of ruins not only has informed the design of other mission gardens but also has been a formative influence on the visual culture of the California missions.

Mission San Juan Capistrano's story, as told in popular accounts, is a tale of destruction and renewal. The highlights of the narrative are its founding in 1776 as the seventh Alta California mission, the completion of an elaborate chapel in 1806, and its destruction in a tragic earthquake six years later that took the lives of an estimated forty people who were worshipping in the church at the time. The mission's prosperous agricultural yield and productive hide and tallow trade declined after the 1812 earthquake and in the face of periodic drought, floods, and a disease that decimated the cattle herds. With secularization in 1833, salaried administrators were appointed to manage the remnants of the cattle herds and oversee the remaining Native Americans, while a lone Franciscan priest, José Maria de Zalvidea, continued to minister to the local parish that worshipped in the mission church. The mission was sold as private property to John Forster at a government auction for $710 in 1845, and he and his family lived in it for twenty years. His repairs to the buildings, which he used for his household as well for storing hay and stabling animals, helped halt the decay of the adobe structures. With the assistance of an Italian gardener, Forster also revived some of the mission's orchards and kitchen gardens. Judge Benjamin Hayes noted in his diary:

> By the industry of a little Italian, the old Mission garden, which three years ago I considered ruined, has been completely restored. Olives, pears that once administered to the enjoyment of the Fathers, are again productive. Many young peach trees have been planted. Corn, every species of vegetable, alfalfa, etc., etc., are growing luxuriantly. The Italian is trying an experiment with Russian wheat. . . . I would consider it almost a miracle, if this garden brings to maturity every thing that is planted there, yet the Italian and Mr. Forster are both sanguine.[84]

With the restoration of mission property to the Church in 1865, a diocesan priest, Father Joseph Mut, was assigned to San Juan Capistrano in 1866 and served for twenty years.[85] The parish's meager resources could not keep pace with the rate of deterioration, and images from the 1870s and 1880s, such as an early photo, depict the mission's barren forecourt and the ruined nave amidst piles of rubble (Figure 2.14).

Whether it was because of the prospect of attracting tourists with the opening of the new railroad depot in 1888, the arrival of a new Irish priest, Hugh Curran, in 1889, or the parishioners' desire to create a more picturesque setting for their parish home (Figure 2.15), restoration and gardening efforts gained momentum through the turn of the century. Photographs and drawings from the late 1880s show that small beds were planted at the base of the colonnade pillars in front of the mission, and vines were trained along the arches and small trees planted in the forecourt (Figure 2.16). As with Santa Barbara, the image of the frocked friar tending the garden was reproduced on postcards (Figure 2.17). In 1896 the mission was leased by the Landmarks Club to try to arrest the worst of the deterioration of the adobe buildings.[86]

As with other Landmarks Club restoration projects, the focus was on structural repairs to stabilize the buildings with little attention to the landscape. The San Juan Capistrano project took on a slightly different focus, however, with the arrival of Marah Ellis Ryan, author and preservation advocate.[87] With modest financial

FIGURE 2.14. Delores Yorba and George Lopez in the ruins of the stone church, Mission San Juan Capistrano, undated. San Juan Capistrano Historical Society.

FIGURE 2.15. Mission San Juan Capistrano, an unknown priest and parishioners, ca. 1895. San Juan Capistrano Historical Society.

FIGURE 2.16. Seth Jones, Mission San Juan Capistrano, 1889. Courtesy of The Bancroft Library, University of California, Berkeley.

support from the Landmarks Club, Ryan took up residence in the Capistrano mission in 1904. Critical of the Church's stewardship of the place and dismayed at the inadequate interpretation of the site to visitors, she lobbied Lummis to take greater control over the history of the site as well as its architecture. Writing to Lummis in September 1904, Ryan planted the seed of her scheme:

> If the Club grants a caretaker rooms, and the church grants the right to the keys so that we could get the tourist question placed on a business basis, instead of the desultory affair it is now, that alone would be a start in the right direction. . . . The present holders of the chapel key speak only broken English and have no knowledge whatever of the history of it beyond the fact that an earthquake once destroyed a portion of the building.[88]

Not only did Ryan plan to charge a fee to view the chapel, with the proceeds dedicated to the upkeep of the grounds and buildings, but she also seized on the

FIGURE 2.17. Padre watering the garden, Mission San Juan Capistrano, n.d. (early twentieth century). Postcard. Collection of the author.

grounds as a way to get local townspeople involved in the preservation of the mission (Plate 6):

> I am trying to interest the women of the parish to the extent that roses, Jasmine, and such permanent vines be planted around the inner court so far as water can reach them. . . . And I think the people can be persuaded to fall in line of improvement when they are made sure that this cleaning up is not meant as a merely transitory fancy.[89]

Although Ryan's efforts at the site were short lived and her proposal never fully realized, she identified key elements for ensuring the sustainability of the missions: provide informed historical interpretation, garner community support, and attract tourists. After Ryan's departure, the Landmarks Club, with the able leadership of local representative and mission restoration enthusiast Judge Richard Egan, continued to work on repair and stabilization of the mission property while the spiritual needs of the parish were tended to by visiting or part-time priests. None of the rapid succession of clerics took much interest in the preservation project, and some were even destructive. Judge Egan wrote to Lummis complaining about Fathers Joseph O'Reilly and John Reynolds, who "thought nothing of selling bricks and removing building materials from the ruins . . . selling whatever old things that remain to the highest-bidder and devoting the proceeds to compensating and maintaining the visiting padre."[90] While the ownership of the property was not in question, the competing claims of authority over its preservation exemplify the diverse and often conflicting interests in the mission.

In contrast to the Landmarks Club's goal of preserving the historic structures as civic monuments, the next steward of the mission saw his efforts in an entirely different light. In 1910 Father St. John O'Sullivan visited the mission to convalesce from tuberculosis and began to take an interest in the crumbling buildings. He set a lifelong goal of restoring the mission, eventually completing several major renovations of the buildings and constructing a garden (Figure 2.18). With support from the Landmarks Club, the bishop of Los Angeles, and local community leaders such as Judge Egan, O'Sullivan undertook a restoration program that stabilized fragile parts of the ruins, repaired damage from recurring floods, and eventually reconstructed much of the original quadrangle. In spite of the fact that his training was limited to theological studies, O'Sullivan was astute at identifying craftsmen with traditional building skills and at raising funds for the restorations.

O'Sullivan soon recognized that the ongoing support of the restoration effort was more likely to come from visitors than local parishioners.[91] O'Sullivan wrote to Monsignor John Cawley about the challenges of raising a requested diocesan assessment, complaining, "I have no hope of even ten per cent of this amount coming from the parish. It must come from the tourists. These Californians do

FIGURE 2.18. Father St. John O'Sullivan, pastor of Mission San Juan Capistrano, with Charles Lummis and Helen Stevens, May 1928. Courtesy of the Braun Research Library Collection, Autry National Center, Los Angeles (P33851).

next to nothing for their parish. . . . So far I have received the magnificent offering of one dollar from them for the restoration. . . . I mean a total of one dollar from the whole Spanish speaking community."[92]

His efforts were focused initially on the buildings, doing much of the work with his own hands, but he also recognized the need to attract and accommodate visitors to the site. He wrote a small guidebook in 1912 and was one of the first mission administrators to charge admission to visitors with a ten-cent entrance fee imposed in May 1916. In the following year he built an adobe wall along the front approach to the mission and remodeled one of the rooms to use as a museum.[93]

Part of O'Sullivan's vision for making the mission an attractive destination for visitors was to enhance the grounds by creating a park-like setting for the ruins. By 1917 O'Sullivan had created stone-lined paths leading from the entrance to the church and the quadrangle and had erected, at his own expense, a statue of Junípero Serra with an Indian boy (Figure 2.19).[94] The lack of a well on the property limited what could be grown, but that situation was rectified in 1918 when a new steel-cased well was drilled and planting beds expanded. The following year O'Sullivan embarked on a project that was reputed to be one of his favorite parts of the mission, a "Sacred Garden" he created by enclosing the area between the Serra Chapel and the stone church and adding a small circular fountain in the center (Figure 2.20). In 1924 a new well with larger-capacity pipes was completed, and O'Sullivan added a fountain near the front entrance.[95] With the tourist audience in mind, O'Sullivan also managed sight lines and placed focal points such as statues and fountains for dramatic visual effects. He used trailing vines to emphasize the lines of arched colonnades and gates. His paths created a sequenced, structured visitor experience as they invited visitors to meander the church ruins, discover the hidden Sacred Garden, and explore the reconstructed rooms.

FIGURE 2.19. Mission San Juan Capistrano, 1920. Keystone stereograph, cropped, showing the 1917 Serra statue in its original location and the edged walks of the early courtyard garden. Library of Congress, Prints & Photographs Division (LC-DIG-stereo-1s01709).

FIGURE 2.20. Father O'Sullivan's "Sacred Garden," constructed in 1919 at Mission San Juan Capistrano, photographed in 1936. Library of Congress, Prints & Photographs Division (HABS, CAL,30-SAJUC,1D—4).

O'Sullivan's efforts did not go unappreciated, and the reputation of the mission spread. Lummis's journal entry recording his visit to San Juan Capistrano in December 1915 noted that "the old Mission has never looked so well since 1812. He [O'Sullivan] has made the grounds attractive with flowers and neatness."[96] The diocesan newsletter, the *Tidings,* reported in 1928 that the mission "is certainly the most picturesque and . . . in a splendid state of preservation. . . . It has all been done with unusual taste and judgment."[97] The exuberant aesthetic has not been without critics, however. Architect-historian Rexford Newcomb wrote to restorers of another mission in 1936, "I do want to appeal to your committee to keep the gardens in the same spirit of the old mission buildings, and above all do not let the thing become the type of place that lovely old Capistrano (picturesque as it may be in some respects) has become."[98] Features such as the fountain in the forecourt, the bells hanging in the Sacred Garden, and the vine-draped arched corridor became favorite subjects for painters and photographers. The circulation of images such as Charles Rogers's *Mission Garden* (1913) (Plate 8), in turn, helped spread the reputation of the mission as one of the most picturesque. The popularity of the site's gardens only increased over time and fueled the further development of the grounds.

O'Sullivan also played on the theatricality of the setting. The site was used for movie shoots such as *The Two Brothers* (1910), directed by D. W. Griffith and starring Mary Pickford, who later renewed her wedding vows with then-husband Owen Moore at the mission and inspired a Charles Austin painting.[99] The inner patio, still a vacant, open area during the 1920s, was used for performances of *The Pageant of San Juan Capistrano* every Sunday beginning in the summer of 1924. O'Sullivan also selected guides who, according to a 1929 newspaper report, were not the typical "loud-voiced, matter-of-fact guide." Instead, "these pretty girls of Capistrano . . . tell the story in soft voices with a lingering Spanish accent. . . . A dozen times a day Senorita Odilla and the other girls, in their picturesque costumes of Spanish-California days, obligingly pose by the lily pool, gazing at the old sundial, smiling under the old Mission arches, silhouetted against the roses and the hollyhocks, or standing by the ruins of the ancient church."[100] In his theatrical productions, writings, promotion of the swallows, and selection of guides, O'Sullivan's presentation of the past romanticized the mission era and embedded it in a lush, colorful, Spanish "Old World" charm. Informing this aestheticized preservation ethic was O'Sullivan's earnest defense of the sanctity of the mission's purpose and the heroism of the padres. He created a landscape to glorify the past and to position the mission as a beautiful, romantic destination (Figure 2.21). His garden enhanced the picturesque, rustic beauty of the adobe and stone structures at the same time it shaped expectations for ways of seeing the mission. A newspaper report of his funeral summarized his accomplishments: "Out of ruin he made a garden."[101]

Father O'Sullivan's death in 1933 became an occasion for a concerted campaign to further develop the mission property in honor of the priest's work at the site. Local nurseryman Roger B. Sherman, who had designed the fountain for the inner quadrangle, completed the garden and underwrote a large part of the expense (Figure 2.22).[102] The continuing improvements to the grounds included a variety of projects that reflected the growing civic pride in the local landmark and the desire to increase tourism. The Brentwood Garden Club donated pipe for watering the mission garden as part of the effort to beautify all public places, particularly those of historic interest.[103] The plantings in the courtyard continued to mature, and an account of the jubilee celebration praised the "well kept gardens, a central fountain in the patio, and hundreds of gorgeous blossoms [that] add to the restful charm of the vine-covered arches, tile roofs, and adobe walls."[104] The 1936 Historic American Buildings Survey plan view shows the fully realized plan with the central patio and the entire front courtyard of the mission transformed into an enclosed garden (Figure 2.23).

Mission La Purísima: Government and Adjudication of Authenticity

As one of the best-documented chapters in the history of the mission garden, La Purísima Mission garden offers rare insight into the divergent preservation

FIGURE 2.21. Mission San Juan Capistrano, illustrating the axial view created by the fountain, walk, and relocated Serra sculpture. The reflected facade of the bell tower on the surface of the pool has been captured by generations of photographers. Postcard. Collection of the author.

FIGURE 2.22. View of the inner courtyard at Mission San Juan Capistrano, fountain constructed 1930–35. Postcard. Collection of the author.

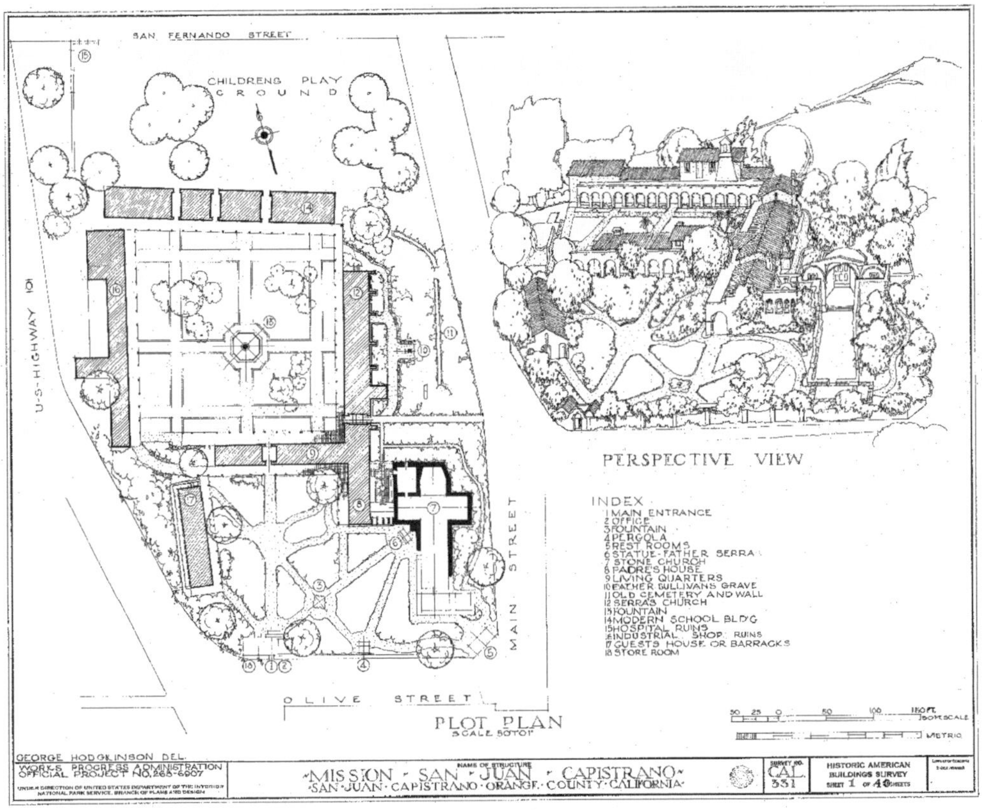

FIGURE 2.23. Mission San Juan Capistrano Plot Plan and Perspective View, 1936. Library of Congress, Prints & Photographs Division (HABS, CAL,30-SAJUC,1).

philosophies and priorities regarding the landscape design decisions and into debates about what it means to be "authentic."[105] In contrast to the earlier Church- and citizen-sponsored mission garden projects, the Civilian Conservation Corps's restoration of Purísima was a cooperative venture of a number of governmental agencies at county, state, and national levels.[106] With the labor of hundreds of CCC workers, La Purísima was also the most expansive reconstruction of a mission to date and the longest lasting of the CCC parks projects in the state (Figure 2.24).[107] The goal was to re-create an authentic mission setting as it looked in the early nineteenth century so that it could be interpreted to the public as a historical site. At issue, as the debates about the design document, were the definition of *historical* and the tension between balancing ideas of historical accuracy with perceived visitors' needs and expectations.

A critical part of reconstructing the early nineteenth-century mission was to develop a landscape plan that would serve three purposes: complement the buildings,

FIGURE 2.24. La Purísima Mission restoration by the Civilian Conservation Corps showing workers in the nursery, April 1937. The living quarters are partially complete and the chapel is under construction. California State Parks Photographic Archives (P1258).

convey to visitors a sense of a historical setting, and accommodate the public's logistical and recreational needs, such as parking, walkways, restrooms, and picnic and camping areas. One component of the landscape design was to be a garden to enhance the area in front of the mission. The gardens have been credited to National Park Service landscape architect Louis Brandt and horticulturalist Edwin Rowe, but theirs were only some of the many hands involved in the design, and particularly important was the input from an advisory committee of private citizens who brought historical, architectural, and community planning expertise to the project.[108] A preliminary proposal was approved in September 1935 calling for "a mission garden . . . located immediately in front of the main building . . . [that] should incorporate all the existing fountains, and its plantings and design should be an authentic example of the characteristic mission garden."[109] A February 1936 letter from Wallace Penfield to Newton B. Drury notes that a preliminary plan devised by "The Camp" (presumably a member of the CCC project team) "has not met with any great enthusiasm here."[110] In response, the Advisory Committee decided to bring in some outside expertise. With the approval of the chairman of the California Division of State Parks, they selected Harry Shepherd, an associate professor of landscape design at the University of California, Berkeley, who was to develop a draft plan for review by the National Park Service staff. Despite the official approval, Shepherd's plan seems to have caught the NPS staff assigned to the project by surprise, and a flurry of letters and meetings ensued to try to resolve varying ideas about what was authentic and historical.[111]

On one side of the debate stood NPS Regional Historian Russell Ewing, a recently minted Ph.D. from the University of California. He provided historical research to support restoration decisions about the buildings, and he was particularly skeptical of "so-called legends of recent fabrication."[112] In a memo to his regional officer, Ewing gave a candid assessment of Shepherd's plan, which he thought ignored the uniqueness of La Purísima's linear (as opposed to quadrangular) layout. He also criticized its attempt to fabricate a "type" restoration based on other mission gardens, despite the lack of evidence. Ewing concluded, with a phrase that was to rankle others working on the project, that to "lay out a garden for which there is neither historical nor archaeological evidence, would be doing violence to La Purisima's story."[113] The landscape engineers Emerson Knight

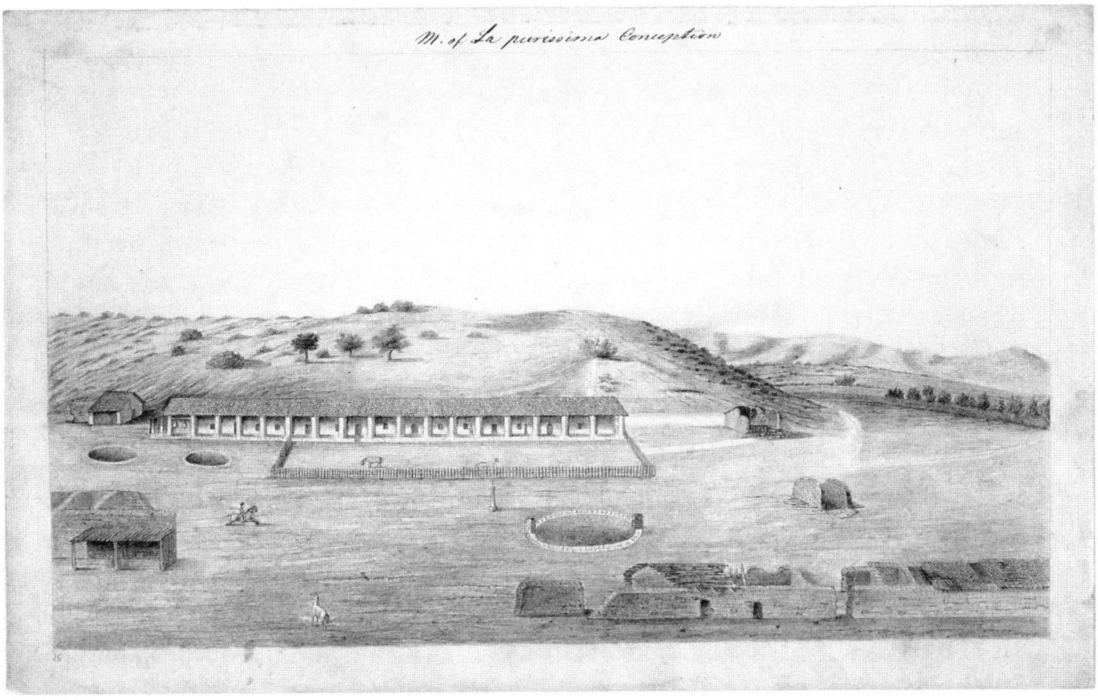

FIGURE 2.25. Henry Miller, view of La Purísima Mission, 1856. Courtesy of The Bancroft Library, University of California, Berkeley.

and Daniel R. Hull, at the NPS and the California Parks offices, respectively, were more sympathetic to the politics of the situation as well as to the pragmatics of accommodating crowds.

After a meeting of all the principal collaborators, the Park Service and the Advisory Committee agreed to develop a set of principles that would define key criteria for judging the appropriateness of a design and establishing a consensus regarding how to proceed. To help resolve the conflict, the design team looked to other mission gardens in California as models for La Purísima. One of La Purísima's unique challenges was the linear arrangement of the buildings that precluded a quadrangular patio garden. Instead, the broad open meadow in front of the mission with its three lavanderías, as seen in Henry Miller's 1856 drawing (Figure 2.25), was selected as the logical location for a garden.[114] Knight, charged with translating Ewing's historical principles into "landscaping principles and designs," proposed that the design should be "simple . . . and limited to fundamental elements," but that stipulation still left much open for debate.[115] It was noted that "in all known cloister gardens of California Missions, seclusion was effected through the use of walls, no less than six feet high." One solution proposed for La Purísima, therefore, was to build a low wall around the garden. Ewing, the historian, was adamantly opposed to "erect[ing] a wall where none formerly existed."[116] Knight's design principles tried to balance the contemporary desire for a picturesque setting with the lack of historical evidence. He noted that while "no record or traces exist of any former garden walls here," if such a wall were "justified" it should be straight and not curved. In one rare explicit reference to the Native Americans in the landscape, Knight also proposed a separation of the garden into segregated "portions used by the Mission Fathers and the Indians, respectively." Knight's choice of plants reflected an ambivalence about creating an ornamental garden in the midst of the California hills; he recommended that the plants be predominantly native, but added that "exotics are justified, with judgment and due restraint, in line with records of such trees, shrubs, vines, herbs and flowers as the Franciscan Fathers introduced."[117] Hull, writing for the State Parks, similarly proposed a compromise "since an ornamental garden probably never existed at La Purísima." His solution was to plant a few varieties in "small simple groups of plants with a broad plaza feeling between these as opposed to narrow walks and large masses of planting." He also proposed creating a sense of enclosure, which he argued was the measure of any garden's success, by planting a border of trees and large shrubs. Hull echoed Knight's assumption of a "use division between the various pools and fountains," and he suggested that the garden be made more rectangular by eliminating the southern fountain so that the garden "affords a more pleasing unit adjacent to the façade of the mission and . . . to give it proper scale while the views to be gained from within the garden, and toward the Mission would be fine."[118]

The Advisory Committee, for its part, took a diplomatic stance proclaiming that, in principle, the requirement of historical accuracy was paramount, and yet the committee simultaneously made a case for proceeding with the garden plan because it would enhance visitors' experience of the mission. For example, minutes of a meeting in 1936 of the La Purísima Advisory Committee summarized a discussion about an arbor in Shepherd's proposed garden plan:

> A discussion of the arbor . . . followed, particularly as to whether it would be too great a dividing line between the informal garden and the parking area. It was pointed out that, although there is no historical evidence of an arbor being present, it was a generally accepted practice in Spanish gardens to have an arbor or pergola of some type. Also, it was stated that the beauty of an arbor in the garden would be very pleasant and would attract visitors.[119]

The group also argued, quite forthrightly, that the notion of creating an authentic reconstruction was moot because there had been constant change since secularization and no amount of research would restore the broader landscape to its early nineteenth-century appearance. In a pointed refutation of Ewing's argument, Penfield drafted the Advisory Committee's own "Standards and Policies . . . Concerning the Grounds of the La Purisima Mission," emphatically stating, "It is realized that *any* landscape plan which is made to permit orderly present day uses of the area can be criticized on the ground that it does 'violence to the La Purisima story' . . . [but] modern conditions . . . *make impossible the recreation of an historic ideal* . . . . The RESTORATION . . . MUST NECESSARILY BE A COMPROMISE BETWEEN HISTORICAL AUTHENTICITY AND PRACTICIAL NECESSITIES OF A STATE PARK."[120] Furthermore, the committee argued that the option of inaction was not viable because the sandy soil was a poor walking surface and was vulnerable to erosion.

In response to the Parks staff's skepticism, the Advisory Committee cited mention of a "garden" in the mission's annual reports, although there appears no justification for assuming the references were to an ornamental garden rather than a more utilitarian kitchen garden or *huerta*. For the committee, the most persuasive evidence for the presence of an ornamental "mission garden" was the water features excavated in the front of the mission, which, they argued, invoking Newcomb and other "authorities on Mission and Spanish gardens," could be transformed into a "California mission garden" simply by connecting them with walkways.[121] Given that the plans in Newcomb's book were drawings of gardens planted in late nineteenth- and early twentieth-century gardens, it is not surprising that the team produced a garden design that looks strikingly like the 1872 garden in Santa Barbara's patio in its plan view and like the front courtyard at San Juan Capistrano in its use of fountains as focal points for axial paths

FIGURE 2.26. Aerial view of the newly completed La Purísima Mission restorations and garden construction, 1937. California State Parks Photographic Archives (#090–29717).

(Figure 2.26).[122] Those sites are not mentioned specifically, but Shepherd, the landscape designer hired by the committee, explicitly cited "a study of Mission layouts throughout California" as the basis for his recommendations.[123] The Advisory Committee's own set of principles rationalized the historical appropriateness of a mission garden by emphasizing the water features (which they called "reservoirs and fountains") and insisting on "authentic plant material." The committee was also particularly concerned about the visual effect of the garden on the architecture, insisting that it "must be of generous scale in accord with the building and outlying structures" and that it "should not obscure the building, but rather should provide a setting." Finally, with an eye to the maintenance of the garden, they required that the ongoing costs of tending the garden should be carefully considered in its design and planting choices.[124] The committee's report to the National Park Service concluded by noting that the decision to "establish the area for public use" had already been made and that the "time has passed for debate as to the propriety of these decisions." Its rather scathing condemnation of the historical purists' objections to the garden concluded that "a policy of inaction based upon the fear of committing historic sin will result in a weed-covered foreground which in itself will be a violation of the Purisima story."[125]

The wrangling and rhetoric of the local, state, and federal stakeholders reflected divisions concerning how to approach the re-creation of a historical landscape for the mission, but beneath the debate's surface was a shared assumption about the ultimate purpose of the space. Each group had its own ideas about the validity of the evidence, the definition of historical accuracy, and the appropriate balance of authenticity with visitors' needs, but all shared the vision of creating a landscape that celebrated early California history and conveyed nostalgia for the simple, peaceful life of the mission days.[126] Knight's principles articulated the key objective that the "design should be quiet, simple, well knit. . . . Creating a feeling of repose should be a major objective."[127] Intellectual gymnastics were required to reconcile minimal, even contradictory evidence of the mission-era landscape with the image of a garden that would, as Knight put it, "emanate peace as do old mission gardens in general and the traditions of this one in particular." So profound was the shared perspective of the group to create a celebratory monument, however, that no one questioned the reasoning. Penfield was able to argue emphatically, on the one hand, that it was "not conceivable that an intimate cloistered garden occupied any portion of this space, and a design which would contemplate the false creation of such a type would be an assumption not warranted by historical data, nor by any aesthetic requirement," yet on the very same page he also reasoned that "while it is impossible to plan an accurate interpretation on the type [of mission garden] . . . pardonable assumptions as to their arrangement may be made if carried out in the spirit of the Mission establishment."[128]

The inspiration for this "spirit" drew heavily on the precedent of gardens already constructed by this time at other missions. The excavated cisterns and basins were used as central design elements, but rather than restoring them as the still-water lavanderías or reservoirs they were historically, they were transformed into ornamental fountains with tiered basins fabricated by the Federal Art Project using fountains at San Luis Rey and Mission San Fernando as their models (Figure 2.27).[129] Edwin Rowe, a Santa Barbara horticulturalist who was brought in as foreman for the CCC garden crew to finish the planting phase of the project, went to great lengths to procure mature trees that would provide a canopy beneath which visitors would still have a clear view of the mission buildings.[130] Penfield's letter helping to broker the acquisition of the trees expresses qualities reminiscent of Santa Barbara: "It seems that he [Rowe] has his eye on same [trees] for the sheltered cloister of the Mission garden and has spotted these particular numbers as appropriate for his use in creating the atmosphere of peace, comfort, quite [*sic*], and serenity."[131] With qualms about historical accuracy seemingly resolved, Rowe later explained the garden's intent was to suggest "what might have happened if the mission period had continued and there had been a padre or succession of them there who were garden- and plan-minded."[132]

FIGURE 2.27. La Purísima Mission, unrestored "fountain," September 4, 1937. California Historical Society.

Pointedly missing from the plans for the garden are references to the religious significance of the mission, and the governmental agencies were very careful to keep a respectful distance from any connotations of promoting Catholic iconography, theology, or interests at the site in either their educational programs or their landscape reconstructions. While excavations revealed a small masonry circular feature that Frederick Hageman interpreted as the possible location of a cross, noting that it "was made exactly as though someone had planted a post, and filled around it with pieces of tile, rock and mortar to make it secure,"[133] the feature was not immediately reconstructed.[134] When a local Catholic parish proposed holding a midnight Christmas Mass in the newly restored church in 1936, the Advisory Committee and Park Service authorities scrambled for a response that would maintain cordial relations with the local church but preserve their separation of the state park from sectarian interests. Their last-minute diplomatic response denying permission to the priest cited the fact that the State Park Commission that would need to rule on such policy matters was not meeting until January and that "the Mission is not far enough completed for such as event."[135]

Similarly, the Advisory Committee recommended that educational plans for the mission downplay the religious history of the sites, stating that the "institutional side of Mission life is fully as interesting to the visitor as the religious, and should be more fully stressed." Even as various plans for a dedication ceremony for the restored mission were being debated, all agreed that whatever the specific program contained, it must be "kept entirely non-religious."[136] The site administrators' efforts to maintain separation of church and state had little effect, however, on the perceptions of the site by the public and other stakeholders. The Reverend Thomas Plassman, president of the Franciscan Educational Conference, was moved to write to Hageman to express his gratitude for his "promotion of historical research and the re-awakening of an interest in the life of the past." After visiting the mission Plassman effused, "You are not only unearthing the old ruins. . . . Your visitors are . . . people who wish to see the living past in the living present. They want to see the grand old monuments of the Padres as they really were."

In addition to marginalizing the religious history of the site, the design team debates, at least in the documentary record, are silent on the implications of the garden for interpreting lives of Indians at the mission. While those conversations may have been part of the interpretative program planning, the role of Native peoples does not appear to have been seen as relevant for landscape design decisions. Instead, European precedents, as well as models from other missions, legitimated a style that conformed to the image of an emphatically Spanish (rather than Native American or Mexican) past. Harry Shepherd's credentials, cited to the Park Service to support their selection of a designer, were his "considerable experience" and his "recent tour through Spain and France, where he made a particular study of mission gardens."[137] Consistent with the dominant narrative of the day and the precedents of the other mission gardens, the design cast the priests as gentle cultivators of a sacred garden, and it appropriated the idiom of elite and European garden traditions with its referents to Western civilization's ideals.

La Purísima provides an example of a mission garden developed not with the energy and devotion of an inspired priest but through a complex design process encompassing formal guidelines, advisory committees, and professional designers and historians, and all under the auspices of a governmental agency. And yet, the garden that the committee produced follows the general design template of Santa Barbara and San Juan Capistrano (Figure 2.28). It also reproduces the same ideological structures of an ornamental landscape supplanting the colonial utilitarian workspace and rendering invisible the Native people.

San Gabriel: Eclecticism and Heterogeneity

Mission San Gabriel's garden history highlights the evolution of a landscape design that has been adapted to accommodate the diverse community of the mission and reflect the practices of its stewards. Rather than the homogeneous parterre design organized around a central fountain, as at Santa Inés, the San Gabriel garden is an eclectic series of spaces that reflects the multivalence of the mission's

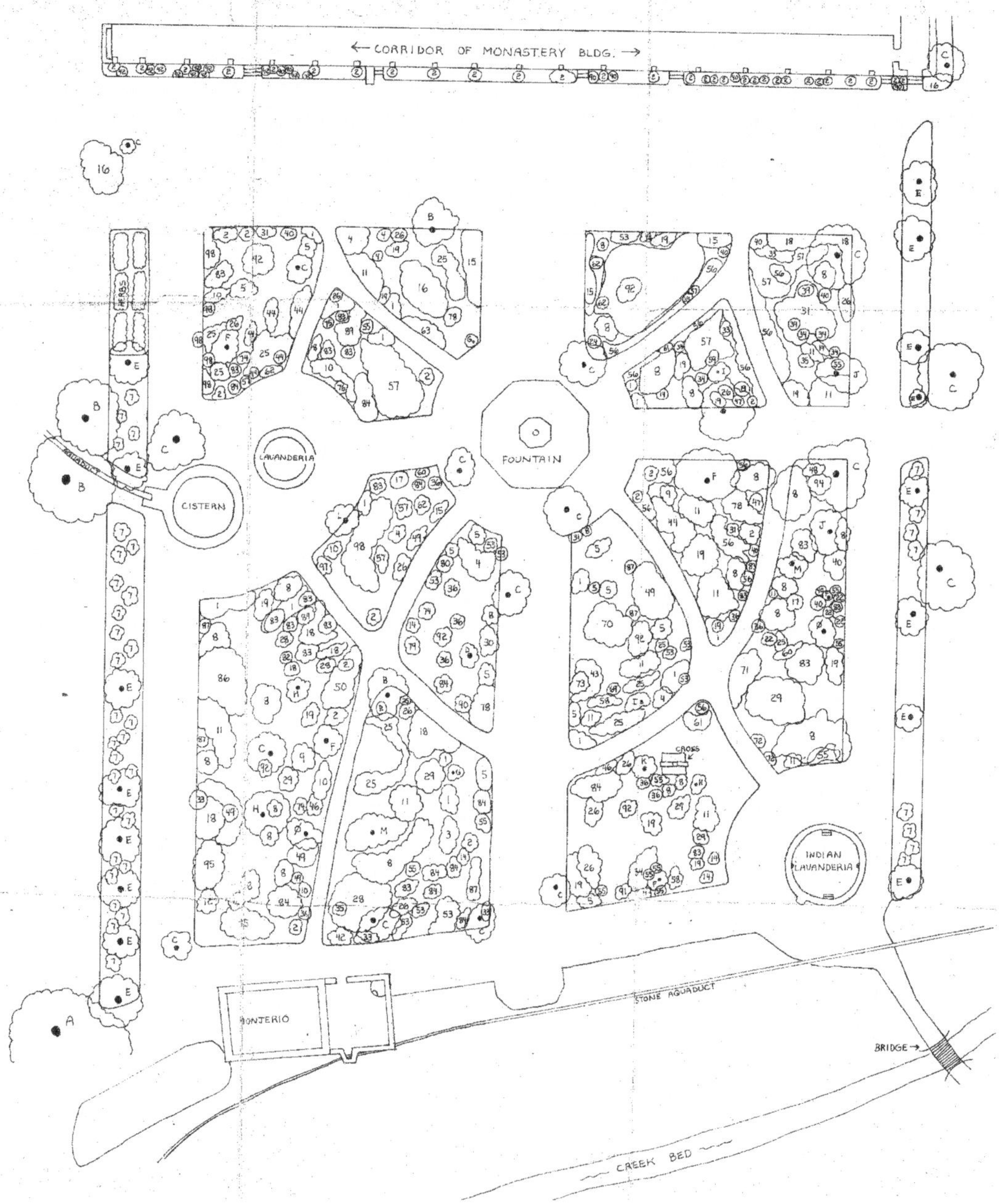

FIGURE 2.28. Plan of La Purísima Mission garden, 1977, with a plant inventory. La Purísima Mission Archives.

history and the social justice ministry of the Claretian Fathers, its administrators since 1908.

San Gabriel was one of the most successful of the colonial missions in its productivity, particularly cattle ranching and tallow production, with access to rich grazing lands in the foothills near modern-day Los Angeles and to reliable water sources. After secularization, San Gabriel's industrial features fell into disuse and the fields were largely abandoned. The church and outbuildings deteriorated, suffering from neglect and earthquake damage. Following the restoration of the property to the Church in 1862, the mission church was the subject of a number of restorations, including a Victorian-era renovation of the nave. Little attention was given to the grounds, however, and the outbuildings were mainly left to fall into ruin. Henry Chapman Ford, an artist who toured and sketched the missions in 1880–81, noted that San Gabriel's former mission vineyards and orchards had only "here and there remnants of the hedge, one large date palm and a few old pear trees."[138] In the location of the current mission garden, Ford recounted, "in the angle formed by the chapel and a wall extending from the front are a number of large elder trees under which are a colony of bees. Remains of the structure for rendering the tallow are to be seen north of the old cemetery, with cavities for 5 cauldrons and having two well preserved tanks near."[139] A C. C. Pierce photograph documents "the last of the Mission Indian settlements" in what is now the parking lot in front of the gardens (Figure 2.29).

The Claretians took over administration of the mission in 1908 and, like the new stewards at the other missions, began to tackle the task of stabilizing and repairing the mission buildings. At San Gabriel, where earthquake damage had taken a repeated toll, they excavated crumbling ruins, uncovering the remains of some of the early industrial features of the mission such as tanning vats and tile pipe. A *Los Angeles Times* article reported that one such attempt to correct poor drainage that was damaging the mission walls uncovered an unmarked vaulted grave identified in the church records as "the burial of the martyred Padres." The account continues in the valorized rhetoric of the day:

> So, stone by stone, Father Torrente built a monument himself, and planted the old wooden cross that was used in the provisional church. . . . And so it stands—a crude, but eloquent tribute to those great souls who have passed beyond, but whose dust and bones have mingled with the soil of San Gabriel where they lived and labored and died that civilizations might come to California and be ours today.[140]

The improvements to the grounds continued to celebrate the Franciscans even as they beautified the space to meet the expectations of the visiting public. The one hundred and fiftieth anniversary of the mission was commemorated in 1921 with the erection of a Serra statue. The following year the diocese approved the

FIGURE 2.29. C. C. (Charles Chester) Pierce, view of Mission San Gabriel with "the last of the Mission Indian settlements," 1885. The Huntington Library, San Marino, California.

establishment of a seminary, and the building, designed by A. B. Benton in 1922, included its own garden. An account published in the diocesan newspaper, the *Tidings,* describes the new building, visible on the left of a 1924 aerial view of the mission (Figure 2.30), as "typical Spanish Mission style . . . encircled by a large cloister, adorned by heavy arches in typical Mission style. The interior patio and fountain will be enclosed by an adobe wall thus separating the monastery from all worldly affairs. The patio and cloister will be exceedingly beautiful by the 'Old Grape Vine,' planted by the Franciscan Fathers."[141]

In 1930 the Los Angeles chapters of the Native Sons and Native Daughters of the Golden West planned a "restoration" of the mission garden with funds raised from performances of *The Mission Play* at the nearby Mission Playhouse. The designers of the garden are unknown, but a *Los Angeles Times* article notes that "many persons have donated all necessary materials and shrubbery, while the architects have provided the plans gratis."[142] Although it was described as a

FIGURE 2.30. Mission San Gabriel, 1937–38. California Historical Society, "Dick" Whittington Photography Collection, 1924–87 (DW-X6–24–10).

"restoration," the construction appears to have excavated the area, removing several feet of soil with the exception of the areas around existing grapevines and older trees to protect their root systems. A 1937 Historic American Buildings Survey photograph shows the new plantings interspersed with the exposed remains of the mission's former soap and tannery vats (Figure 2.31).

More intensive gardening efforts followed in the late 1930s (Figure 2.32), spurred on by Father Raymond Catalan (1906–87), whose memorial marker reads "Restorer of the mission gardens: The kiss of the sun for pardon, the song of the birds for mirth, one is nearer God's heart in a garden than anywhere else on earth." In 1940, the mission fathers partnered with the Native Sons and Native Daughters of the Golden West to erect a fountain dedicated "in the Memory of the Pioneer Mother and Father" (Figure 2.33). Like other descendant affinity groups nationally, such as the Daughters of the American Revolution, Colonial Dames of America, and the Sons of Confederate Veterans, the Native Sons and Native Daughters promoted

FIGURE 2.31. View of the Mission San Gabriel grounds, April 1937, showing the exposed industrial features and new plantings. Library of Congress, Prints & Photographs Division (HABS, CAL,19-SANGA,1A—3).

the preservation and interpretation of historical sites while simultaneously affirming their social standing through their affiliation with the sites and with fellow members meeting the same ancestral criteria.[143] The public recognition of their philanthropy through plaques commemorating their deeds registered the social value of their good works and proclaimed their status as patrons of a civic monument.

In addition to its partnerships with civic groups, San Gabriel exemplifies, like Santa Inés, the adaptation of the mission garden features to reflect the character of the parish and its setting. Mission San Gabriel lies in the midst of a diverse, urban neighborhood, and the parish leadership is committed to being active in social justice issues, working with recent immigrants, and ministering to the needs of the community. It is perhaps not surprising, therefore, that the layout of the garden is distinctive among the missions. Rather than the typical courtyard garden centered on a fountain with radiating walks and beds, San Gabriel has all the main mission garden elements but is arranged in distinct garden zones like separate galleries in a museum. The areas include a *campo santo* or cemetery, a cactus garden, a "court of the Missions," a shrine to Our Lady of Guadalupe, an area of historic plants (for example, an olive tree purported to have been planted in the 1860s and an orange tree planted in the 1980s to honor the area's citrus industry), a Peace Garden, and two "industrial" areas where the ruins of the

FIGURE 2.32. View into the Mission San Gabriel garden. Postcard. Collection of the author.

FIGURE 2.33. San Gabriel Mission fountain. Postcard. Collection of the author.

mission's soap making and tallow vats are incorporated into the garden design. Interspersed among these garden areas are sculptural ornaments, artifacts, potted plants, and folk art. The record of community collaborations is inscribed on numerous plaques and signs throughout the garden. The "court of the Missions" houses models of twenty-one missions constructed by Claretian seminarians in the early 1930s. In the spring of 2007 Girl Scout Troop 434 La Crescenta cleaned, repaired, and repainted the mission models.[144] The sundial was restored by the Los Californios Club for the mission's bicentennial in 1971. Most recently, the mission has collaborated with the local Gabrielino-Tongva Indian Tribe to develop a new "native plants" garden that was rededicated in a ceremony in June 2008.[145]

The San Gabriel garden also exemplifies the influence of those charged with maintaining the gardens on a daily and weekly basis. The impact of their design decisions, particularly when they have worked on the gardens for many years, is likely as profound as the decisions of those who laid out the paths and hardscape in the original garden designs. At San Gabriel two gentlemen, Manuel Ramirez and Bernardo Casas, a volunteer and a longtime employee of the parish, respectively, tended the garden and shaped its directions for more than two decades.[146] While the priests have oversight of the parish grounds and a curator must approve any major changes at the site, the daily decisions of what to transplant where, what to prune, and what to let grow were Casas's responsibility (Figure 2.34). The aesthetic of the garden, with whimsical touches such as a head-shaped planter filled with succulents in the place of hair, stands apart from the more meticulously groomed sites outsourced to landscaping crews.[147] The elements of the mission garden are present—the fountain, the walks, the geometric beds—but their idiosyncratic interpretation has resulted in a unique rendition of the type reflecting the heterogeneous community it serves.

San Antonio de Pala: Collaboration, Appropriation, and Shared Landscapes

The garden of San Antonio de Pala, technically an asistencia or sub-mission of Mission San Luis Rey, is unique among the missions in that it stands on a separate parcel of land in the middle of the Pala Band of Mission Indians' 12,273-acre reservation in northern San Diego County.[148] The transfer of the Pala Asistencia property after secularization followed the pattern of many of the missions. Civil authorities and other Mexicans confiscated tracts of mission lands to create private land holdings; more than twenty-five of these ranchos were created in San Diego County.[149] The Pala land was surrendered in 1835 to Pío Pico, who sold it to two private owners in 1846 in anticipation of the impending loss to the United States. The sale was voided, but the land was offered by patent to William Vale, who allowed the church, cemetery, and two rooms to be used by the local congregation. The Pala reservation was established in 1870 by an executive order

FIGURE 2.34. Bernardo Casas (*left*) has tended the San Gabriel garden for thirty-three years; Manuel Ramirez arrived at 4:30 a.m. every day to volunteer at the parish. Photograph by the author, 2008.

of President Ulysses S. Grant and further delineated through the transfer of some tracts to the public domain and a series of allotments in the 1890s.[150] Damage from an 1899 earthquake elicited the attention of the Landmarks Club, which helped to stabilize the building (Figure 2.35), and in 1902 the club purchased the remainder of the quadrangle. Following the forced removal of the Cupeños from their Cupa village (now Warner Springs) in 1903 in what is called the "Cupa Trail of Tears," the Luiseño and the Cupeño Indians shared the reservation and now, according to the website of the Pala Band of Mission Indians, "consider themselves to be one proud people—Pala."[151]

The particular iteration of the mission garden at Asistencia San Antonio de Pala reflects not only the proximity of the mission and the reservation but also the complex relationship between competing narratives and social practices on the landscape. Early twentieth-century photographs document landscaping improvements in the front of the mission, particularly along the front entrance (Figure 2.36). By 1936, when Henry F. Withey photographed the site for the Historic American Buildings Survey, a wall defined the forecourt, and a basin with a center fountain stood in front of a frequently photographed detached bell tower

FIGURE 2.35. Asistencia San Antonio de Pala, late nineteenth century. Courtesy of the Braun Research Library Collection, Autry National Center, Los Angeles (P19183).

(Figure 2.37). The HABS photographs are also evidence that the only landscaping of the "patio" or central courtyard was a stone-edged path. The Comboni Missionaries (commonly called the Verona Fathers) assumed responsibility for the mission in 1948 and, under the leadership of Father Januarius M. Carillo, renovated the buildings, including the 1954 restoration of the quadrangle and the planting of a patio garden.[152] In 1961 Congress removed the legal title to the two-thirds of an acre on which the mission sits from the Pala Reservation and conveyed it without compensation to the Diocese of San Diego Education and Welfare Corporation to be used for educational purposes.[153] In addition to the mission church, adjacent cemetery, and quadrangle, the mission houses an elementary school that was begun as a Catholic school by the Sisters of the Blessed Sacrament and the Sisters of the Precious Blood, and became a secular charter school in the Bonsall Union School District for which the Pala Band is listed as a community partner. In 2001 the Pala Band established a casino and resort hotel nearby, and there are currently four casinos in the area.[154]

Collaboration

Pala's history is reflected in the materiality of the mission landscape, particularly its iteration of the mission garden. As Pala was one of the last of the surviving

FIGURE 2.36. Children at Asistencia San Antonio de Pala. Courtesy of the Braun Research Library Collection, Autry National Center, Los Angeles (P1274).

FIGURE 2.37. Asistencia San Antonio de Pala. General view showing the garden planted in front of the bell tower, 1936. Library of Congress, Prints & Photographs Division (HABS, CAL,37-PALA,1—1).

missions to begin a courtyard garden project, the influences and referents were well established. But unlike the well-funded projects at Purísima and San Fernando, or the strong community settings of well-established parishes, the Comboni Fathers struggled to find resources to fund their restoration project in the 1950s. For monetary support, the mission leaders looked to outside philanthropic assistance. During the 1950s the Friends of Pala Mission was formed to raise funds for the restoration, and plaques at the site attest to the financial contributions of local leaders such as Carl T. Burkhard and Hollywood personalities like Ramón Novarro.[155] Fund-raising for the project was advanced by the publication of a *Los Angeles Times* article about the mission in 1955 by Edward Ainsworth and by the release of *The Man Who Shot the Devil*, a film based on a script by Ainsworth. The Pala Indians had few resources to contribute to the project, but according to Father Carillo, "On week-ends the Mission became a beehive of activity. Men and women, Indian and white alike, worked side by side."[156]

Dedicated in 1959, the garden exemplified the "typical" mission garden design of walks and geometric beds edged by hedges and planted with flowers and fruit trees. A fountain with mosaic tile risers and a number of shrines in niches offered focal points. Not only did the Pala design follow the mission garden template, but Carillo's description also echoes the typical rhetoric of the day:

> The garden with its humble cacti and beautiful flowers, the soft murmur of the dripping water in the fountain, the shrines inviting to prayer and meditation, add a soothing and inspirational touch to the quadrangle, so that immediately you feel an appeal to peace as you enter the patio.[157]

According to parish archivist and administrator Sister Barbara Jackson, the 1950s garden plan was not fully executed when it was dedicated. Father Carillo and others continued to add to the garden over the years, doing much of the construction themselves. While they struggled to keep pace with the repairs, they contributed their own unique touches, including an aviary in the garden.[158]

Appropriation

The Pala garden exemplifies the appropriation of landscape design with its attendant conceptual and political ideologies, as well as its associations with the growing sense of cohesion as destinations along the mission trail (more on this topic in chapter 4). Romo's 1872 design for Santa Barbara, which established the mission garden template, had been informed by his experiences in Egypt and travels around the Mediterranean. The Pala garden similarly was designed by priests with reference both to the other mission gardens and to their ethnic origins. As the name suggests, the Comboni Fathers are an Italian order, and they have maintained close connections to their hometown of Verona since first coming to the United States in 1939. The Pala priests regularly visit Italy and have occasionally returned with ornaments for the garden, such as an Ave Maria fountain (Figure 2.38).

Both gardens were conceived at a time when the missions were trying to rebuild with few financial resources. Both were seeking to present a refreshed public face that allied the missions with sophisticated, European-derived design traditions. Both designs also played on the association of their stylistic precedents. Romo's design recast Santa Barbara's courtyard as a European patio garden and monastery. Pala's garden allied it with the rest of the mission "chain," as well as with the taste for the Mediterranean Revival–style gardens still popular in the 1950s. Of particular note is the appropriation of colorful tiles in the Pala masonry, such as on the risers of the steps to the Ave Maria fountain and at the base of the circular fountain.

These polychrome, glazed terracotta tiles, reminiscent of Mediterranean garden architecture, were manufactured by the Malibu Tile Works and in a serendipitous twist of events ended up in missions throughout California in the 1940s. The Malibu Tile Works had suffered a fire in 1931 and, with the collapse of the construction industry during the Great Depression, never fully rebounded. May Rindge, the owner of the tile works, was forced to stop construction on her massive house in the Malibu hills, although she continued to use it as a storehouse for her tile inventory. Following Rindge's death in 1942, the house, including the collection of Malibu tile, was sold to the Franciscan Order for fifty thousand dollars. Not only did the Franciscans incorporate the tile into the house's interior and garden as they finished construction, but they also distributed tile to other Franciscan properties, including Santa Barbara Mission, Mission San Miguel, and the Saint Francis Retreat in San Juan Bautista.[159] Today those tiles can be seen in garden elements such as an interior courtyard fountain at the Santa Barbara Retreat Center.[160]

This serendipitous gift of tile to the missions reflects the recursive influences of the mission gardens in broadly dispersed heritage practices. Romo's original 1872 courtyard garden at Santa Barbara had no tile and little ornamentation. While it was influential in the reception of Mediterranean Revival as a regionally appropriate style, it was the incorporation of polychrome tiles in the landscapes of elite estates such as El Fureidis in Montecito, California, that helped spread its popularity. The incorporation of the colorful accents of Malibu tile in later mission gardens of Pala and San Miguel helped to elide the associations. Today "Spanish style" tile is available from manufacturers such as the California Pottery Company, and home improvement stores reference the missions in their marketing as historic precedents. For example, Avente Tile offers a hand-painted "California tile": "Inspired by historic California missions, these tiles use the Spanish technique of Cuerda Seca, a centuries old process used to separate the different glazes on the tiles."[161]

FIGURE 2.38. Ave Maria fountain in the San Antonio de Pala Mission garden imported by the Comboni Fathers. Photograph by the author.

Hybridity

Pala has long operated in the interstices of colonial and Indigenous space. The Pala Band's account of the 1903 removal registers the persistence of Indigenous knowledge and belief systems (Figure 2.39):

> The Cupeño were finally moved to a small reservation at the Luiseño village of Pala in May of 1903. There were no houses there for the new residents, and the Cupeños remember sleeping in the open, tortured by the insects and dampness of the unfamiliar coastal valley. Furthermore, the new reservation lacked the rich religious associations and traditions of clan ownership that the old lands had held. For a people who had invested so much spiritual importance in their relationship to the land, the removal was devastating.[162]

More than fifty years later, when the transfer from the Franciscans to the Comboni was being negotiated, a report from the pastor at Santa Ysabel stated that "the greater part of the native population is still addicted to paganism in varying

FIGURE 2.39. Removal of the Cupeños from Cupa to the Pala reservation, 1903. Courtesy of the Braun Research Library Collection, Autry National Center, Los Angeles (P1295).

degrees . . . to eradicate gradually what is harmful in the old system, and to incorporate what is good in the Catholics' scheme of things is the fundamental duty of the missionary."[163] At the same time, the Pala Asistencia, under the auspices variously of Franciscans, Comboni Fathers, Barnabite Fathers, and diocesan priests, has been providing services, spiritual and material, to the people of the area for well over a century. The Pala website proudly claims the status of being "the only surviving Asistencia in the mission system and the only mission-related structure still ministering to an Indian population."[164] Like the other missions, Pala is a space where different systems of knowledge and epistemologies continue to coexist in varying degrees of friction, ignorance, prejudice, and resolution, but the proximity of reservation and Catholic property heightens the sense of tension wrought by their contested histories. In these and many other respects, the landscape of the Pala Asistencia has always been a shared landscape.[165]

Scholars have noted that the terms *colonial* and *postcolonial* are problematic because there is not a distinct termination of social relations and material conditions, regardless of changing legal status. The legacies of dislocation, trauma, and injustice at Pala Asistencia endure, as do the solace and support of spiritual beliefs and practices. The specific "archaeologies of attachment"—that is, those relationships between the material traces of the past and their significance to contemporary Indigenous and non-Indigenous communities—are rarely visible in the material and documentary archives.[166] But occasional glimpses capture moments of shared understanding and mutual respect that point to the possibilities of the missions becoming Third Spaces. In this light, I share a rather lengthy quote from an account by Father Herman Manuel, a Filipino priest and member of the Divine Word Missionaries (Societas Verbi Divini, SVD) who began serving at Pala in 2011:

> On June 15, 2011, I moved to San Antonio Mission Church in Pala, CA, as a Parochial Vicar. When I first set foot at the mission, I could not wait to see the Indians. Fr. Rey Manahan, the Pastor, told me that in order to meet a bunch of Indians, eat breakfast or lunch over at that little store, *Pala Store,* in front of the Mission Church. . . .
>
> True enough, the first time I went with Fr. Rey, the store was full of Indians eating breakfast. However, because of what TV shows and movies have created in my mind, that Indians are people to be feared, I was quite hesitant and nervous to talk to anybody looking dark-skinned, strong, and having long hair. However, eventually, the tension within me broke when suddenly one of them commented, "O-ow here comes the trouble maker and he brought another one with him." And we all laughed together. After having introduced myself to them, I befriended them right away. . . .
>
> In addition to meeting the Indians in the Pala Store, we also share stories with them. A good source of their history is to hear the stories from the elders. It seems

> that they are more reliable than the books written by foreign authors. They shared how "whites" treated them badly. It makes me remember my own Filipino history of how we were also treated badly by the Spaniards for so many years. Some of their rituals were removed because they were branded as "pagans," causing more pain to them.
>
> One ritual retained is what they do during Indian funerals that make the funerals more solemn. They show great respect to their dead by not allowing anybody to take pictures and it should be in complete silence. When I presided at my first Indian funeral, one of the things that connected me right away to our Filipino custom was the turning of the casket clockwise and counterclockwise before entering the cemetery. The reason is that nobody will follow the deceased right away. Then there are bird singers who sing several chants for the dead. The burial ends with the priest throwing a handful of dirt onto the casket followed by the members of the family, relatives and friends of the deceased. The funeral lasts for about 3 to 4 hours.[167]

The Pala mission courtyard garden continues to attract tourists who make it up the winding road from the coast or perhaps are taking a break from the casino. The graves in the cemetery beside the church, with its bare earth and spreading pepper tree, continue to be decorated with flowers and other offerings. The Corpus Christi Fiesta (celebrated for the 198th time at Pala in June 2014) includes a Mass at the bell tower, Native drummers, and a procession through the town, as well as a bouncy slide, food, and a talent show. It is described in the local newspaper as "a historic and spiritual event in the life of the Mission and in the life of the reservations."[168] The two are recognized as distinct places, and yet images of the procession are visual reminders of the possibility of finding commonality in these shared landscapes.

"An Integral Part of the Picture"

The mission landscapes in their postcolonial "restored" iterations do not just include or contain gardens, they have become gardens. The most iconic element of the landscape has become the central cloister garden that links the sites to the centuries-old tradition of monastic courtyard gardens and to the contemporary fashion for patio gardens in Mediterranean Revival residences. While the cloister gardens were styled as the centerpieces, the entire grounds became ornamental landscapes for the building jewels they framed. During the restoration at Purísima, for example, aesthetic effect ultimately held sway over historical authenticity. The advisers to the CCC project argued that

> it is particularly important that the relationship of the garden to the Mission structures should be established—in such a ways that the buildings will be enhanced and

> not concealed; and the garden itself will be an integral part of the picture, without dominating the scene. . . . The propriety of having a few plants for shadow and contrast against the wall of the Church and cemetery, must be discussed.[169]

These park-like spaces not only created beautiful settings for the ancient buildings but also suited the missions' emerging twentieth-century functions as parishes, schools, and tourist destinations. Site administrators, whether Park Service staff, parish rectors and administrators, or volunteers and affiliated friends groups, have developed the sites to serve their modern purposes, which often included both the needs of local parishioners, students, and staff and the requirements of tourists. The contemporary mission sites include features such as playgrounds for parish schools, retreat centers, restrooms, and parking for those attending worship services, concerts, and parish festivals as well as for tourist buses. Some missions include parish cemeteries, columbaria, Stations of the Cross, and other spaces essential for active faith communities, and all have some form of exhibit, museum, or interpretative space for visitors.

Along with these modern amenities, mission administrators have continued to create attractive spaces for the historic missions that meet the expectations of visitors. They have added foundation plantings to soften the austere facades, landscaped drives and walks to create more picturesque approaches, and designed attractive vantage points to create photogenic views. For example, at Mission Santa Barbara a row of palms was planted in 1901–2 along the front colonnade, and an understory of yucca and other plantings was added soon after to further soften the foundation. The vineyard in front of the church was replaced by a lawn on which a large concrete cross was erected in 1913 to honor the bicentennial anniversary of Junípero Serra's birth. The appealing setting for the mission was extended when in a series of transactions the Franciscans deeded adjacent lots to the town for use as a park in 1948, with the condition that the colonial outbuilding ruins be preserved and nothing permanent be built. As the local newspaper reported, the effect was both natural and historic: "Every resident of Santa Barbara, everyone who becomes a resident of Santa Barbara, and every visitor in Santa Barbara from now on will see the Old Mission in its natural setting with and against which the first Padres in California planned their building's beauty."[170] The notion that the mission had been returned to its original natural setting belied the fact that the park's manicured lawn was only possible with irrigation, that it was planted with modern hybrid roses surrounding a historical marker, and that it was bounded by an expanse of asphalt parking suitable for coach tours.

In addition to creating park-like settings, mission administrators also continue to plant and redevelop formal mission gardens that privilege the jewel-box settings of the mission buildings and to shape the viewer's gaze. Mission San

Buenaventura redeveloped its garden in the 1990s. At the same time, Mission San Rafael was seeking funds to redo the plaza next to the replica mission church, which was built in 1941 after a fire destroyed the original mission. Mission San Luis Rey announced in 2003 a multi-million-dollar master plan that will include public and private gardens as part of efforts to create a sustainable business model for the historic landmark.[171]

An important part of the invention of the mission garden is the enduring presence and involvement of Native people in the mission landscapes. For example, C. C. Pierce photographed a group of Indians at the rededication of San Luis Rey in 1893 (Figure 2.40). A photo of Doña Perfecta Encinal and her family taken at Mission San Antonio de Padua in 1903 similarly attests to the continued involvement of Native peoples in the mission restorations (Figure 2.41). In a letter to Franciscan historian Zephyrin Engelhardt, accompanying the San Antonio photograph, Joseph Knowland wrote, "The picture of Doña Perfecta Encinal and her family taken at the mission during the restoration, shows her sons, and daughters and grandchildren. . . . She brought her sons every week to labor at the mission during the restoration. No one was more keenly interested in the work as it progressed than this old Indian woman"[172] Similarly, Juaneño José de Garcia Cruz, also known as "Acu," assisted Father O'Sullivan in the early restorations at Mission San Juan Capistrano.[173]

FIGURE 2.40. C. C. (Charles Chester) Pierce, Indians at rededication of San Luis Rey, 1893. The Huntington Library, San Marino, California.

FIGURE 2.41. Doña Perfecta Encinal and her family at Mission San Antonio de Padua during its 1903 restoration. California Historical Society.

While Native people built the missions and have been involved in their ongoing development, the narratives promulgated in the mission gardens and their representation in texts, images, and objects largely exclude the Native presence, voices, and agency. Martha Nelson McCan's notion of time binding extolled the creation of a "replica of a garden such as was planned and developed by the Mission Fathers in conjunction with their spiritual and educational work" so that it would be available "for the education and pleasure of future generations."[174] McCan's recognition of the connection between past and present makes explicit her use of historic precedent but it also leaves other significant embedded ideologies unspoken. Instead of recognizing the realities of colonial oppression or ongoing presence of Native California people, the mission gardens reduce them to an Indian boy standing in the protective embrace of Father Serra, pristine tallow vats, and scattered manos and metates appropriated as garden ornaments. The (re)creations of mission gardens embedded the sites in a mythic past and served both to naturalize and legitimate the hegemonic interests of the present. But while the endeavor was part of a broader discourse that marginalized Native peoples and constructed a "Spanish fantasy past," the particular potency of the spaces was that they naturalized this ideology legitimating White, Anglo superiority and privilege in a medium that was seen as "just a garden." By creating spaces reminiscent of formal European gardens that were also perceived to be remnants or re-creations of California's early landscapes, the designers were constructing a communal heritage that was acceptable to the public and palatable as part of the mainstream historical narrative.

CHAPTER THREE

Cultivating Heritage

Race, Identity, and the Politics of the Mission Landscape

"Our Common Inheritance of Romance and History"

An editorial published in 1948 in the *Santa Barbara News Press* declared that "the people of every California city would like to have Santa Barbara's Old Mission, but it sits here where it belongs in time and place and public understanding."[1] This statement of local pride and ownership reflects the fact that the transformation of the missions from sites of colonial conquest to celebrated sites of California heritage was not just a result of physical changes at the missions but involved a complex set of ideas, as well as formal and informal heritage practices. The identification of the missions with California's dominant historical narrative was, in turn, part of the widespread appropriation of Indian, Spanish, and Mexican pasts that, as Phoebe Kropp has observed, is "so forceful that to disentangle romance and history, one would have to unravel race and nation itself."[2] And yet the fabric of settler colonial ideologies is woven one thread at a time, and the history of the representation of the mission landscapes in images, words, and objects reveals how they became lodged so subtly yet inextricably in "public understanding."

From the earliest restoration efforts in the late nineteenth century, the missions were deployed to convey a sense of belonging to a uniquely Californian heritage. Writing on behalf of the Landmarks Club of Los Angeles in 1896, Frank Dyer urged the populace to claim the sites as "part of our common inheritance of romance and history."[3] Dyer's assertion that the conservation of the missions would "depend largely upon public intelligence and public spirit" was predicated on the assumption that the "public" saw the missions as a valued part of the state's patrimony and its colonial legacies. When the promoters of the 1915 Panama-California Exposition wanted an image that conveyed the essence of California, they evoked both the ruins of an arched colonnade and the garden elements of climbing vines, a flowing fountain, colorful blossoms, and a frocked padre lost in his book (Plate 7). These mission gardens were described variously as "Spanish," "Andalusian," and even "Moorish," but this was not Spanish heritage translated through Mexico-born padres or those born in Mexico-era California, and certainly not traced to the more recent immigrants of Spain's former colonies. This was the Spanish garden of a romanticized Castilian past with all the connotations of a centuries-old Mediterranean horticultural tradition. Not coincidentally, this was also a garden type consistent with the taste and cultural referents of the upper class (or aspiring) Mediterranean Revival villas and California estate owners. Scholars have detailed how California's cultural landscape was mobilized in the first half of the twentieth century to legitimate the interests of social and political elite through the evocation of California's "Spanish fantasy past."[4] As Kropp has argued, the resulting "racialized understanding of regional identity and belonging" was promoted through a spatial and a temporal segregation whereby Mexican and Indian Californians resided in the past and were rendered in the Anglo-American present only as materialized objects.[5] Linda Heidenreich has similarly argued that linear historical narratives in Northern California media such as the local press and school readers naturalized social inequalities and promoted hegemonic racial ideologies even as marginalized nonwhites strenuously resisted them.[6] Clearly, the stylistic expressions of the Spanish fantasy past were inextricable from the early twentieth-century politics of privilege and racial superiority.

By the mid-twentieth century the missions had become must-see destinations for tourists seeking to experience a uniquely Californian past and were scripted as celebratory origin sites into California's mainstream historical narrative across every medium imaginable. For example, after covering the "prehistory" of California Native peoples, the missions were the first chapter of the state "history" in state-sponsored textbooks, and their characterization of colonialization was benign, to say the least. A 1949 California history textbook introduced the chapter on missions with the statement: "The mission fathers were happy. Father Serra was the happiest of all. To build missions in California and teach the Indians were what he had dreamed of doing for many years. The mission fathers made friends with the Indians."[7] Mission images appeared on postcards and fruit crate labels where they helped sell the state as a "New Eden" with a perfect climate and abundant produce. Figuring in popular songs and movies such as Alfred Hitchcock's *Vertigo,* the missions conveyed a distinctive California setting. Integral to this reception of the missions as historic places signifying the beginning of "civilization" was the fact that their gardens had become an immutable part of the sites and their narratives. In this regard, the mission landscapes are not only symbolically charged but also spaces where the social relationships were negotiated through the politics of the past on a daily basis.[8]

These kinds of relationships of the past, narrative, and politics are endemic to heritage sites around the world. Romanticized sites of national origins such as Colonial Williamsburg, Virginia, and Skansen in Sweden, and sites of the contested histories of incarceration, oppression, and tragedy such as Robben Island, where political prisoners were held in South Africa under apartheid, Australian Convict Sites, German concentration camps, the Kigali Genocide Memorial in Rwanda, and the Museum of the History of the Gulag in Moscow, create stages for powerful narratives and places for visitors to perform particular heritage scripts. Sites associated with histories of colonization bear a particular burden as their narratives are both witness to and complicit in the legacies of colonial dispossession and displacement. They are also often the symbolic birthplaces of the Western nation-states that emerged as victors in colonial contests. These "geographies of postcolonialism" hold in common the same dichotomies of Western vs. non-Western constructs applied to historical narratives (mind/body, reason/passion, culture/nature, white/black, adult/child).[9]

Like other heritage sites around the world, the California missions are living, evolving monuments with multivalent and often contested meanings.[10] In some regards they have become essentialized, that is, reduced to a simplified, codified, idealized materiality that references the purportedly natural, essential characteristics of a culturally defined group or construct, in this case a dominant-culture narrative of "California." In other respects these sites remain as complex as any constructed and contested history. The California mission landscapes traverse the formal and informal heritage practices of work and leisure, celebration and contestation, group and individual, pilgrimage and protest. The sites invoke the grand narratives of state and national identity and serve as houses of worship for local faith communities. They are part of the broad cultural practices of the tourist and heritage industries, and they encompass the quotidian habits of parishioners, staff, laborers, students, and visitors. The dynamic interplay of materiality and representation is particularly compelling in the case of the mission landscapes because like all gardens, they have evolved over time and yet their place in cultural memory has remained remarkably unchanged for more than a century. This history reveals an emerging notion of the mission garden, not just as a feature of the mission landscape, but as an idea and symbol. The gardens' production and reception as iconic heritage sites claim an ownership of the past that invokes certain lineages and affiliations as it distances others. This chapter explores the complex ideas, objects, and images that have circulated for decades and traces the meanings evoked and invoked through the mission gardens. Specifically, it explores the construction of an idealized mission materiality with connotations of beauty, timelessness, and sacredness that has been produced through formal and informal heritage practices. It argues that this notion of the "mission as garden" remains integral to the missions' cultural work as heritage sites.

"Venerable Monuments of Architecture and Art and Faith and Heroism"

The transformation of the mission landscapes to garden settings reveals the deepening sense of a uniquely Californian or regional identity connected with the spaces. The architecture of the missions had long been associated with a distinctive Californian identity. For example, the committee appointed by the campaign to raise funds for repairing Santa Barbara following a 1925 earthquake was composed of Charles Lummis, John S. McGroarty, and Mrs. A. S. C. Forbes, three public figures active in mission preservation and promotion. The authors' case for public support argued the public benefit of the missions: "If you had to define California in a single word what would it be—oranges, oil, gold, climate? No! The only other name for California is 'Romance.' . . . Why? Many elements have entered into the making of this indefinable but irresistible glamor. It is essentially Spanish—of the most romantic nation in history." The authors argued further that the missions could attract tourists in ways no modern construction could. The missions, they proclaimed, were "venerable monuments of architecture and art and faith and heroism, builded in the wilderness by men vowed to chastity and poverty [that] outweigh in their grip upon the imagination and interest of the world the greatest achievements even of our mighty day." In contrast to Chicago, they asserted, "all the brains, all the brawn, all the money in America cannot build a century-old Franciscan mission."[11]

Not only was mission architecture embraced as distinctly Californian, but the mission gardens planted throughout the first half of the twentieth century also mirrored current design trends of an increasingly distinctive California regional gardening style. The mission gardens, like their Mediterranean Revival counterparts being created on elite estates and imitated on a smaller scale in more modest residences, simultaneously connected the site to the particular heritage of California and to European precedents. Elements such as flowering vines, cacti, agave, and yucca identified in Belle Sumner Angier's *The Garden Book of California* (1906) were incorporated in the planting schemes of missions and Mediterranean-style residences alike, such as the array of cacti and succulents planted near the driveway entrance to Mission Santa Barbara and frequently used as a foreground in views of the mission (Figure 3.1). The aesthetic of the columnar *Cereus* contrasting with the stark white of stucco walls was appreciated at E. W. Scripps's country residence at Miramar just as the effect of Italian cypresses was admired repeatedly in Santa Barbara's courtyard and planted in the Mission San Antonio de Padua garden.[12] Angier praised a circle of palms, such as was planted in San Luis Rey's and Santa Barbara's grassed courtyards, for its "exquisite blue-gray coloring" and recommended it as a lawn ornamentation, particularly "for the small enclosed courts which belong to many of our fine homes of the early mission type."[13]

FIGURE 3.1. Mission Santa Barbara, view of the church and front convento, 1936. Library of Congress, Prints & Photographs Division (HABS, CAL,42-SANBA,5-1).

Similarly, a pairing of palm and pine at Mission San Gabriel echoes Angier's illustration with the caption "The Palm and the Pine Lords of the mountain and the plain in fraternal embrace in a California garden." Such allusions to California's diverse habitats were also reflected in the growing interest in private cacti collections, such as that of C. R. Orcott and the public cacti display gardens in Golden Gate Park and in Riverside. Despite the fact that many of the specimens being planted at the missions were being imported from Australia, their adoption as part of the quintessentially California "historic" gardens helped spread the acceptance of these nonnative plants as appropriate for the region.

The missions' formative influence on California landscape design, particularly the role of the Santa Barbara Mission garden, has generally been overlooked in the standard telling of the history of the Mediterranean Revival style.[14] California's elites planning horticultural counterparts for their new Mediterranean-style estates in the early twentieth century followed the fashion for Mediterranean gardens seen elsewhere in America. Such was their passion that the style has been described as "almost obligatory in California."[15] The taste was fueled in part by the similarity of Mediterranean and Californian coastal climates, which allowed groups such as the Southern California Acclimatizing Association to import from southern Europe, Australia, and other semitropical locales a wide range of plants that expanded California gardeners' palettes.[16]

In addition to this climatic parallel, many estate owners had toured the gardens of Italy, Spain, and Persia, and even those who had not were familiar with the pan-Mediterranean garden aesthetic through publications such as Edith Wharton's *Italian Villas and Their Gardens* (1903), Charles Latham's *The Gardens of Italy* (two volumes; 1905, 1909), Constance Villiers-Stuart's *Spanish Gardens* (1929), Helen Fox's *Patio Gardens* (1929), and Mildred Stapley Byne and Arthur Byne's *Spanish Gardens and Patios* (1924). These books were filled with romantic descriptions and richly illustrated not only with photographs of sites but also with plans and other details readily applied to one's own backyard (Figure 3.2).[17] The images in these volumes reinforced the Mediterranean design aesthetic, while the texts argued for its suitability for California. Villiers-Stuart, for example, reproduced plans, sketches, and photographs of iconic Spanish sites such as the Alhambra and the Alcázar. Her illustrations, such as views down a garden axis and oblique perspectives into a courtyard garden through an arch, employed conventions of the gaze that resonated with representations of the missions. Prolific editor and

FIGURE 3.2. Ralph L. Reaser, illustrator, plan of the Garden of the Prince, Aranjuez. From Helen Morgenthau Fox, *Patio Gardens* (New York: Macmillan, 1929), facing 161.

journalist Charles Dudley Warner wrote an account of the climate and resources of Southern California based on his travels and rooted the region's Mediterranean parallels firmly with the title *Our Italy* (1891). He noted the climatic and topographical similarities, and promoted California as a garden "in perpetual bloom and fruitage, where semi-tropical fruits mature in perfection, and the most delicate flowers dazzle the eye with color the winter through."[18] If the analogy were not persuasive enough, Warner strengthened it by including an image showing the classic pose of the monk beside the fountain with the mission towers looming in the background (Figure 3.3). The Santa Barbara garden was the embodiment of Old World heritage transplanted to the new Eden.

These connections between the missions and the garden traditions of the Mediterranean were particularly appreciated in the Santa Barbara area. Designers such as Lockwood de Forest and Bertram Goodhue gave their clients exotic oases with playing water and intricate colored tilework that echoed both the gardens shown in travel books and Santa Barbara Mission's storied garden. Many such clients were not only readers of garden literature and veteran travelers, but Californians who built houses in the Santa Barbara area where a view of the mission was a prominent and highly sought-after local landmark. A 1908 *Sunset* magazine article noted with some humor, "If a property owner here can not build his house so that he may see the mission towers he considers life a failure and moves away. Neighbors quarrel over which has the view. . . . Oak trees are felled, rocks are blasted, houses are razed, that a new vision of those two towers and their bells may be secured as part of one's realty holding."[19] For owners of Santa Barbara estates, a "Mediterranean" garden style offered not only the allure of European antecedents but also an association with a prominent local historical site and the charm of its romanticized past.[20] Despite its 1872 construction, the Mission Santa Barbara garden was popularly perceived as a colonial relic that referenced European garden tradition in a uniquely Californian idiom. For California's recent transplants from the East Coast and Midwest looking for a distinctive garden style adapted to the climate and sympathetic to their idea of living in the "land of sunshine," the appeal of the Santa Barbara Mission garden in its historic, authentic setting was undeniable—a precedent for landscapes that celebrated California's origins as a beautiful and cultured new Eden.

These discourses that touted the salubrious, productive California climate were not simply promoting agriculture, tourism, and relocation from the East Coast and other regions of the United States. The mission gardens were such potent political landscapes because the correlation of horticulture and progress was a fundamental premise of social evolution invoked to legitimate social and racialized inequalities.[21] For example, at a horticultural fair in 1878 Dr. Ezra Carr expounded, "Love of country could not exist till cave and wigwam were supplanted by the hut, the permanent abode around which the vine might clamber, and the

IN THE GARDEN AT SANTA BARBARA MISSION.

FIGURE 3.3. Charles Dudley Warner, "In the Garden at Santa Barbara Mission, 1891." From *Our Italy* (31).

gentler races of animals gather for protection. The sour bog had to be reclaimed by the labor of the husbandman, who reclaimed the wildness of his own nature in the process."[22] The mission gardens, as the symbolic primogenitor gardens of California's new Eden, became a quintessential setting where the rhetoric of the Spanish fantasy past could be registered in the landscape. In his appeal for preserving the missions, published in the *San Francisco Chronicle* in 1896, Frank Dyer invited his readers to consider the import of the missions:

> Long after the paisano, with his riata and silver-decked saddle and bridle, has forever passed into history, and the black-eyed senorita, with fan and mantilla, has ceased to be aught but a tradition, the noble piles that their forefathers erected amid deserts peopled with savages may exist with proper care, to excite in the stranger a curiosity to know the story of the people who wrested this fair domain from its wild condition and made it to blossom and become fruitful.[23]

From the turn of the twentieth century onward, those responsible for caring for the missions, including preservationists, Franciscans, Catholic parish administrators, and State Parks employees, capitalized on the synergy between these residential gardens of the elite and the reconstructed gardens of the missions. Allegedly introduced by the learned and noble mission fathers who came to save heathens and tame the wilderness, the gardens stood as an enduring legitimation of the hegemony distilled as "civilization" and "progress."

"A Place of Peculiar Beauty"

As popular as visiting missions was becoming in the early twentieth century, it was the visual representation of the sites that helped spread their reputation broadly and establish a typology and terminology for the missions. Fundamental to the reception of the missions as beautiful, peaceful, sacred spaces was the aestheticization of the mission landscapes in both their design and their representation in visual and material culture. Informed by deeper structural and ideological dynamics of historical narratives, the visual consumption of this mission imagery was also part of the broader construction of the touristic gaze and its associated practices of photography that emerged at the end of the nineteenth century.[24] Historian of photography Jennifer Watts has traced how civic boosters in Southern California used photography to construct a "strikingly fixed visual narrative."[25] This corpus of mission imagery also offers a body of work through which we can see the intricate relationships of site, image, and viewer/visitor/consumer that were formative in securing the privileged position of the missions and their landscapes as esteemed sites of California heritage.

While sketches and engravings of the missions from the colonial period exist, it was the broadly circulated imagery of the postsecularized missions that helped bring them more prominently into public consciousness in the second half of the nineteenth century. These images highlighted the architectural features, often focusing on their striking facades set amidst the landscape or views through ruins of abandoned colonnades. Sketches such those by Henry Miller and the photographs of William Henry Jackson and Carleton Watkins presented the missions in splendid isolation, almost entirely devoid of human occupants.[26] The composition of Watkins's mission images, such as Mission San Luis Rey (Figure 3.4), is similar to his photographs of the natural landscapes of the West. He privileged the texture of the buildings and the undulating mounds of eroded and collapsed adobe, recalling the textures, patterns, and forms of his better-known photographs of arresting geological formations. In many of his mission images, both the original Native occupants and the contemporaneous settlers were erased from the scenes, and only the muted tones, eroding surfaces, and repeating patterns of arches of the buildings' shells remained.[27] The missions' timelessness and their faded glory signified the nostalgic romanticism surrounding these remnants of another era at the same time they conveniently dispossessed, or at least bypassed, those who continued to lay claim to the properties.

FIGURE 3.4. Carleton E. Watkins, Mission San Luis Rey, ca. 1876–80. Courtesy of The Bancroft Library, University of California, Berkeley.

PLATE 1. California Calls You, Union Pacific Railroad Company, 1922. Travel brochure, back cover. Courtesy of the California History Room, California State Library, Sacramento, California.

PLATE 2. A *diseño*, or pictorial map, of Rancho San Miguelito, Monterey County, of Mission San Antonio de Padua [1841?]. Courtesy of The Bancroft Library, University of California, Berkeley.

PLATE 3. Ferdinand Deppe, *San Gabriel Mission,* 1832. Laguna Art Museum Collection. Gift of Nancy Dustin Wall Moure.

PLATE 4. Chumash Painted Cave. Carol M. Highsmith, photographer. Library of Congress, Prints and Photographs Division (LC-DIG-highsm-24389).

PLATE 5. Louis Choris, *Danse des habitans de Californie à la mission de St. Francisco,* plate III, 1822. Hand-colored engraving. Yale Collection of Western Americana, Beinecke Rare Book and Manuscript Library.

PLATE 6. Mission San Juan Capistrano, ca. 1910. Postcard. Early landscaping efforts complement the Landmarks Club's restoration of the colonnade. Courtesy of the Orange County Archives.

PLATE 7. Panama-California Exposition, San Diego, 1915. Postcard. San Diego History Center.

PLATE 8. Charles Rogers, *Mission Garden,* 1913. Photograph courtesy of Bonhams.

PLATE 9. Amédée Joullin, *In the Garden of Santa Barbara Mission,* 1889. Encore Editions.

PLATE 10. Standard-size Mission San Buenaventura porcelain miniature model on display at the Mission San Fernando gift shop. Mission de Oro Collection, Cameo Guild. Photograph by the author.

PLATE 11. Mission Trails Building, Golden Gate International Exposition, San Francisco, 1939. Postcard. Collection of the author.

PLATE 12. Buckley McGurrin, *Christ Teaching,* 1939. Mural in the San Gabriel Mission garden, 2008. Photograph courtesy of Branislav L. Slantchev.

PLATE 13. *California Mission Daze,* mixed media installation created by David Avalos, James Luna, Deborah Small, and William Weeks at Installation Gallery, 1988. Printed with permission of the artists.

In contrast to images of romanticized ruins, the images of the California missions and their gardens marked a distinctive shift in mission representation beginning in the mid-1880s that is tied to the growing recognition of the missions as important heritage sites and to the changing administration of Mission Santa Barbara. Rather than focusing solely on the mission facades, distinctive architectural features, and the buildings' place in the broader landscape, artists and photographers also began to depict the interiors, courtyard gardens, and the Franciscans within them.[28] This new visual vocabulary finds its origins at Santa Barbara, particularly after 1885, when the new order of Franciscan caretakers opened the mission's doors to professional photographers. Isaiah West Taber (1830–1912) was one of the first to offer pictures of the mission commercially, publishing a collection of forty-one photographic prints titled "California Scenery" in about 1885 that included an image of the Santa Barbara garden.[29] A few years later Henry Chapman Ford (1828–94), who settled in Santa Barbara in 1875 and made extensive sketches and paintings of the missions, produced a series of etchings featuring all twenty-one mission sites, including an engraving of the Mission Santa Barbara garden that was published in 1888 (Figure 3.5).[30] The Santa Barbara garden was

FIGURE 3.5. Henry Chapman Ford, Mission Santa Barbara, 1888. The composition appears to be based on a photograph of the garden (see Figure 2.4). Photograph courtesy of Sullivan-Goss.

also sketched by Seth Jones, painted by Amédée Joiullin in 1889, and by Chris Jorgensen during his horse-and-buggy tour of the missions in 1903–4.[31] Ford's images, in particular, have been credited with kindling an interest in California's Spanish heritage, but they were only a small, albeit significant, part of the rich and varied mission visual culture of the late nineteenth century as those images began to be copied and circulated widely.

The representation of the mission gardens in paintings intersects with many aspects of the developing artistic practice in the state, including plein air painting and California Impressionism, that go beyond the scope of this book.[32] It is significant to note, however, that the imagery in these paintings both informed the ongoing creation of gardens at the missions and helped to codify and disseminate certain visual representations. For example, in many of the paintings the confluence of garden and site is rendered literally; the architecture and plantings are inseparable. Charles A. Rogers's 1913 painting titled simply *Mission Garden* depicts Mission San Juan Capistrano arches with drifts of blossom-laden climbing vines (Plate 8), and Joullin's 1889 view of the Santa Barbara garden marries the warm terra-cotta colors of the roses, the tile roof, and the flowerpots by the fountain (Plate 9). These images helped establish the modern "colorization" of the mission landscapes with signature palettes that were subsequently replicated in tinted postcards and painted porcelain miniatures. The trope of melding building and colorful vegetation in a unified aestheticized composition was also used in backdrops for performances and historical pageantry in the West.[33] For example, the vine-covered arches of San Juan Capistrano served as a backdrop for McGroarty's *The Mission Play,* as seen in the "Finding of the Jeweled Chalice" scene in act 3 that was reproduced in postcards of the play (Figure 3.6). Paintings inspired by the play, such as Guy Rose's 1915 *The Leading Lady,* similarly used the background convention of the vine-draped arch.[34] This imagery of missions as architectural fragments being both reclaimed by nature and incorporated as garden ornaments was not merely an aesthetic conceit. As Chelsea Vaughn has noted, these tropes reinforced one of the common "constructions of the Spanish fantasy past, the idea that the Anglo rather than the Mexican residents of California were the rightful inheritors of the area's Spanish legacy, and that this legacy persisted in the form of ruined buildings rather than through actual living persons."[35]

The mission imagery not only provided a visual schema but also, when associated with text, conveyed an even more explicit conceptual framework. William Henry Jackson, for example, published an image of the Mission Santa Barbara garden in his monumental photographic survey *Ancient Missions and Churches of America* (1894). The depiction of the garden alongside other "ancient" settings registered it as a historic landscape. Even if it occurred to readers to question the garden's date, they were reassured by Jackson's accompanying statement that "the sub-tropical loviliness [*sic*] of the Santa Barbara Mission garden has always

FIGURE 3.6. *The Mission Play,* act 3, "Finding of the Jeweled Chalice." Postcard. Collection of the author.

been an object of admiration. The Mission was founded only ten years after the signing of the Declaration of Independence, and its founder died in 1793. . . . The Mission Garden was, and still is, a place of peculiar beauty."[36]

Harry Fenn's illustration of Santa Barbara's courtyard garden, "Garden of the Mission," which accompanied a short story in *Harper's* (discussed later in this chapter), similarly exemplifies the visual representation of the garden as an exotic place of mystery and sanctity (Figure 3.7).[37] Fenn employed the same conventions of depicting the "mission garden" typically seen in photographs (likely his model), with appropriately painterly effects one would expect from a contributing illustrator to *Picturesque America* (1872), *Picturesque Europe* (1875–79), and *Picturesque Palestine, Sinai and Egypt* (1881–84). The perspective shows the garden looking from the west toward the northeast corner of the garden with the mission towers in the background. The central fountain anchors the foreground, and two friars working in the garden offer scale and the symbolic resonance of robed figures. The contrasts of light and dark are played out in shadow and direct light on the foliage and the architecture. The repeated rhythms of the arched colonnade, piers, and windows provide the backdrop for the plane of walks and geometric beds. The textures—the dense cedar evergreen, spiky tropical succulents, delicate-leaved

FIGURE 3.7. Harry Fenn, "Garden of the Mission," Santa Barbara, *Harper's New Monthly* magazine, November 1887.

fruit trees, and thick mats of ground cover—highlight the lush and varied plantings even in the black-and-white engraving.[38] Fenn's images also demonstrate the importance of photography informing engraved and lithographic illustrations and the resulting multiplier effect as the images derived from photographs circulated broadly.

A clear watershed in the emergence of photography as the prime purveyor of mission visual culture was the advent of postcards. Although the postcard was copyrighted as early as 1861, it was not until the approval of privately produced postcards and the introduction of a lower postal rate in 1898 that their use became widespread.[39] Their popularity exploded between 1905 and 1915, when as many as 677 million postcards were mailed in a single year, at a time when the U.S. population was only 88 million. Mission garden images were reproduced as stereographs, hand-tinted, and eventually real photos. Frequently visited Santa Barbara and San Juan Capistrano are the most commonly encountered in the expansive offerings of "vintage" postcard dealers, but all of the missions are represented. Tinted postcards, such as the axial view of San Juan Capistrano's forecourt, promulgated the aesthetic of bright floral accents amidst contrasting green foliage and blue pools of water (Figure 3.8). A sampling of postcard publishers—Keystone View Company, Adolph Selige Publishers (St. Louis), Edward H. Mitchell (San Francisco), Osborne's (Santa Barbara), M. Rieder (Los Angeles), Newman (Los Angeles), Souvenir Publishing Co. (San Francisco), Standard Oil, and Southern Pacific Railroad—is indicative of the industries promoting the sites. For example, the Southern Pacific published a postcard view in 1911 titled "Forbidden Garden, Mission Santa Barbara, California. Road of a Thousand Wonders" (Figure 3.9).

"A Long Found Place"

Another aspect of the representation of the mission gardens is that even as they were an important influence on an emerging California landscape design they were also seen as relics from the past, offering a seemingly timeless experience distinct from contemporary life. As Martha Nelson McCan's invocation of time binding reflected, the mission representation often elided past and present and authenticated the anachronistic gardens.[40] In his paean to the mission garden, McGroarty makes the deceptively simple statement, "The place of the Sacred Garden is a long found place."[41] Over the years, generations have projected their aspirations and desires onto the missions, both as a constructed past and as an exoticized other.[42] The gardens have been perceived as spaces apart, removed in time or by cultural affiliation. They were sacred spaces in a secular society, peaceful oases in a harried existence, timeless monuments in an ever changing world, and authentic sites in a miasma of suburban banality. And yet, in their distinctiveness they were also seen as touchstones of the conditions and qualities for which society yearns. The mediation of these tensions in these long-found places is revealed in their representation and reception across multiple media.

The sensory landscape figures prominently in the gardens' reception as places apart. Visitors comment on how the walls exclude views to the wider landscape and buffer outside sounds as well.[43] Bird and insect noises in the garden are cited as evidence of the peaceful, pastoral oases created at the mission, especially in their courtyard gardens. The meaning of silence is also evident in comments on the absence of the din of modernity when one enters the thick-walled buildings. In her account of a visit to San Antonio de Padua for the *Los Angeles Times* travel

FIGURE 3.8. View from the Mission San Juan Capistrano entrance toward the stone church ruins and the Serra sculpture, ca. 1940. Postcard. Collection of the author.

FIGURE 3.9. E. H. Mitchell, "Forbidden Garden, Mission Santa Barbara, California. Road of a Thousand Wonders Southern Pacific," ca. 1908. Postcard. Collection of the author.

section, Jane Engle mused that "to drift to sleep here amid silence, except for a soft chorus of crickets, was like disappearing into a dream of Old California."[44] On their trip to Santa Barbara, the Boucher family discovered the sanctuary of the courtyard where "we couldn't hear any traffic in this hemmed-in space, just the mission's modern-day congregation singing."[45] Similarly, visitors cite the colors and textures, the dramatic contrasts of lush plantings against pale walls, and the enticing, cooling play of water as sensory effects that transport them to the sense of another era. Pamela Hallan-Gibson, credited with being one of the "foremost authorities on the history of the California missions," wrote in 1995 of Mission San Juan Capistrano:

> Behind the walls are the colorful gardens and time-worn pathways that lead to peaceful fountains, the lights and shadows of pillars and corridors still musty with age. If you look over your shoulder, perhaps you'll see the skirts of some long-departed Franciscan disappearing around a corner. If you listen intently, you might hear the laughter of Indian children playing in the quadrangle. If you sit on a bench in the rear of Serra's chapel, you can easily transport yourself back into another era when life was regulated by the sound of a mission bell and cares were left in the hands of God.[46]

These design principles of light and shadow, the effect of water, and the textures of plant and masonry have been central to the aesthetic of the gardens and link them stylistically to their Mediterranean, Moorish, and Persian antecedents. But in the California context this sensory experience takes on an ideological significance for these postcolonial sites. The gardens have been praised repeatedly as places of peace and quiet, whether in opposition to the bustle of modern life or to the violence and threat of war. For example, with World War I raging, the *San Francisco Chronicle* published a full-page story including photos of Missions San Carlos, Dolores, San Juan Capistrano, and San Gabriel along with the headline "Old Spanish Missions Standing as Silent Symbols of Peace amid Tumult of World at Arms to Be Preserved as Monument to Christian Brotherhood."[47] On the eve of World War II, Maude Gunthorp invoked the power of the missions to transcend time to an imagined peaceful past:

> There we may dream awhile in that fragrant, sun-filled garden beneath the beautiful bell tower where it is hard to remember that there are battles to wage, livings to be made, and struggles to be had on every hand; there, where the peace of the Carmel Valley seems to settle like a benediction upon our hearts. For this is not tomorrow nor even today; it is yesterday, and it is California chanting her *pax vobiscum.*[48]

Part of this ability to conflate time—to be both timeless and historic—is that the gardens are framed as sensory spaces connected to the past by the continuity of their faithful Franciscan stewards and the perpetual lushness of their garden settings. For example, Harry Downie's 1938 guide to Mission San Carlos describes the scene as one that invites visitors to another time, aided by the sensory effects of the garden:

> As the traveler enters the gate of the courtyard, formerly the plaza, where the people would gather to make fiesta, a garden springs up in all its grandeur terraced with stones gathered from the bottom of Rio Carmelo by the neophytes of yesteryear. The trees, shrubs and flowers form a riot of color against the ancient walls of the Mission buildings. A fountain murmurs the peace of a by-gone day.[49]

Another strategy that perpetuated the notion of the missions' timelessness was their presentation as isolated artifacts in the form of floats, models, and miniatures. For example, in 1911 the Panama-California International Exposition celebrated its groundbreaking with a four-day festival of parades, demonstrations, banquets, balls, and speeches. For the final day's parade, thousands lined the streets of San Diego in the area of what was to become Balboa Park. Included in the procession were reduced-scale replicas of the state's twenty-one missions. Gliding down the parade route, the missions were flanked by costumed representatives of California's past. Leading each mission's float was a volunteer dressed as the saint after whom the mission was named, accompanied by a boy holding a canopy over his or her head and girls scattering flowers. Other historical characters were personified by nearly one thousand volunteers costumed as Franciscan friars, Native Americans, soldiers, and settlers who marched alongside the floats (Figure 3.10).[50] Bertram Grosvenor Goodhue, writing in 1916, described the spectacle as one designed "to recall to mind the glamour and mystery and poetry of the old Spanish days."[51] The mission floats were simplified in form, but with enough of their distinctive signature architectural features to identify each one.[52] Placing the mission buildings on rectangular platforms disembodied them from their landscapes, but their natural surroundings were alluded to by potted shrubs and palm fronds.

This imagery of the missions as timeless, vacant, "long found" places is realized compellingly in the material culture of the Mission de Oro Collection, a series of cast porcelain miniatures produced by the Camarillo, California–based Cameo Guild beginning in 1994.[53] Innocent in appearance yet potent in ideology, reproductions of the twenty-one missions are displayed in Cameo Guild's showroom in eye-catching, sleek glass-and-wood cases with mirrored glass shelves and soft, golden-toned lighting. They come in two sizes, the standard and the cameo, and currently retail for fifty-eight and twenty-six dollars, respectively.[54] The miniatures

FIGURE 3.10. San Diego Mission float in the 1911 groundbreaking parade to celebrate construction of Balboa Park to host the 1915 Panama-California International Exposition. Postcard. San Diego History Center.

replicate the colonial-era mission churches and adjacent buildings within their twentieth-century garden settings. While architectural detail is their hallmark, the landscaping is clearly part of their appeal. San Buenaventura (Plate 10) and Santa Barbara feature detailed formal courtyard gardens. San Luis Obispo, Carmel, San Rafael, and San Juan Capistrano (cameo size only) include fountains. Vines trail over the walls of Mission San Francisco and are trained along the arcade of Santa Cruz, while flowers edge the paths of Soledad. All of the missions have verdant lawns, and their rounded bases are accented with soft blue drifts of flowers.

As a representation of California colonial heritage, the Mission de Oro miniatures both collapse past and present and cater to nostalgic yearnings. Each mission is a timeless illustration rendered in three-dimensional form. Pretty and tidy, with a soft, warm palette, each hand-painted sculpture is a perfect setting for a tale of simpler, slower times. The manufacturer's literature reflects the interplay of past and present implicated in the objects. The product brochure highlights a romanticized history of the missions and celebrates their continuing popularity with tourists from around the world, drawing "more travelers to their pleasant grounds than any other historical attraction in the state." The text states that the "tiny buildings are seen as they look today," but each replica is also "a reflection of the heritage and tradition that has defined the missions . . . [and they] evoke a nostalgic look back at the missions in their early days."[55] Michael Harley, director of creative services for Cameo Guild Studios, commented, "People who collect our missions come away with pieces of history."[56]

The manufacturer's description clearly locates the aesthetic in a romanticized iteration of the past: "Painstakingly sculpted by hand, then reproduced in cold-cast porcelain, each Mission de Oro collectible contains the minute details that remind us of their pastoral history. Towering palm trees shelter colorful gardens while red-tiled roofs keep the rain off white stucco walls—each mission tells a warm story of California history."[57] The promotional brochure praises the "warm Mediterranean colors of the garden" and notes that the fountains bring the sculptures "to life." The brochure also notes that "whether embraced by a concrete cityscape, or still beautifying the open valleys, the missions today continue to remind us of the pastoral charm that was once their setting."[58] These bucolic miniature landscapes share the sensibilities of Lilliput Lane collectible miniature cottages and Thomas Kincaid prints (both owned by international conglomerate Enesco), but the mission miniatures' colonial legacy distinguishes them from other nostalgia-drenched representations.[59] The Mission de Oro sculptures erase not only the historical agents, native and Franciscan alike, but also those whom the product brochure describes as the "fiercely loyal townspeople, who use them as parish churches, chapels, and active community centers."[60] They are vacant, mute landscapes whose aesthetic sanitizes any associations with the struggles and injustices of mission history.

The Cameo Guild's marketing of the Mission de Oro collection miniatures reveals yet another layer of discursive media that reinforces the mission-as-garden aesthetic appeal. Both the Cameo Guild Mission de Oro website and product brochure feature alluring close-ups of each mission photographed at oblique angles that enhance the contours of the building facades set against a background of pink and purple, as if silhouetted by a brilliant sunset. The missions seem to float in space and time. They are lit so that each Mission de Oro "signature" gold bell sparkles and the warm colors of the red tile roofs, white walls, and colorful flowers glow. The store displays similarly enhance the visual appeal of the miniatures as precious objects and as a collection. Standing on their mirrored, glass shelves, the missions bask in the LED spotlights that make the soft colors come alive. The irrefutable and seemingly innocuous nostalgia of the Mission de Oro miniatures exemplifies the production of a fine-grained materiality of an ideology that celebrates a benign colonial past referenced in the patina of adobe and drifts of blossoms. Their representations both reinforce the paradigm of mission as garden and shape the expectations of visitors to the sites.[61]

"The Whole Scene . . . Incarnated"

The meaning of the mission landscape has been its construction not just as a beautiful garden or even a historic garden but also as a sacred garden. This notion of sanctity is a complicated trope in the mission discourse because it intersects with mission historiography in a number of quite distinct ways. First is the obvious association with the original Franciscan padres who founded the missions both to claim the land for Spain and to bring salvation to the Indigenous people by baptizing them, educating them in the tenets of the faith, and instructing them in Christian practices. This image of the missions as a legacy of the colonial-era Franciscans' evangelical purpose is evident in descriptions and visual representations. For example, Jackson's introduction to *Ancient Missions* (1894) praised them as places where "the padres planted the cross of Christian faith, where they taught the gentle arts to wild and savage men; there we may see the shrines they builded, and there can be learned the legends of a past filled with the spirit of self-sacrifice tinged with the romantic color which time bestows on all things that emanate from the heart or hand of man."[62] The image of Serra and other Franciscans as self-sacrificing heroes of their faith is present throughout much of the mission literature, particularly in texts authored by Catholic scholars such as Father Zephyrin Engelhardt and Monsignor Francis J. Weber. Researchers have argued about the historiography of the missions, and scholars associated with the Catholic Church have pursued a "Christophilic" focus, but for this exploration of the representation of the mission landscapes it is important to note that their perspectives have also been disseminated through secular journals such as *Boletín,* published by the California Mission Studies Association, and other historical publications and that the landscapes are implicated in their triumphalist narratives.[63] For example, Weber wrote in Mission San Fernando's "bicentennial tribute" volume published by the Historical Society of Southern California the following description of the mission's gardens:

> The grounds at the Old Mission convey a sense of permanence and beauty that no building and no monument could portray. They confirm and epitomize the fable landscape celebrated in books and portrayed on television. By the early 1800s the garden at San Fernando had already become a center of agricultural productivity and ornamental delight. . . . Mission San Fernando is regarded as one of the most attractive and yet authentic windows to California's past. Those walking through its gardens, gazing at its buildings and looking at its displays truly have a glimpse of paradise.[64]

Furthermore, the perspectives of those closely associated with the Church and the sites have informed public interpretation at the missions. For example, around 1940 Harry Downie, who was a prominent figure in the restoration of the missions, particularly Mission San Carlos, wrote a visitor brochure for the site in which he stated, "Carmel Mission stands today as a monument to the great conquistador of the Cross who left his home and the comforts of conventional life to come to our Western wilderness to preach the Gospel of Christ and to teach the better way of life to a pagan race."[65]

Representations have also portrayed the mission landscapes as idealized monastic cloister gardens. Despite the fact that Franciscans are not a formally cloistered order, the monks within the missions were depicted as living in consecrated places with associations both ancient and eternal. The connotations resonated in the late nineteenth- and twentieth-century imagery of the priests and brothers in their newly created, yet seemingly timeless gardens. For example, early twentieth-century postcards often reinforced the sanctity of Santa Barbara's cloistered garden with titles such as "Sacred Garden," "Holy Garden," "Flowers for the Altar," and "Forbidden Garden." One commercial postcard of a brother reading in the cemetery beneath a flowering datura tree is captioned "Waiting for the Angel's Trumpet" (Figure 3.11). While the brothers themselves called this space the "private garden," the images lend credibility to the publishers' descriptive texts.[66] The poses of monks contemplating a bunch of lilies for the altar, reading scripture, or gazing into a fountain's reflective surface conveyed their faithful service, while their robes, little changed for centuries, and the "historic" garden setting invoked an imagined colonial past of similarly peaceful, holy lives (Figure 3.12). The sanctity of cloister gardens was also perpetuated in travel writing and other popular accounts. Dorothy Reynolds, for instance, recounted the story of the mission gardens for *Pacific Discovery* in 1956 in ways that both highlighted their spiritual significance and elided contemporary and historic periods:

> Mission gardens were a deep source of comfort to the Franciscans who brought civilization to the strange, heathen land of California. In them, the padres paced softly back and forth, telling their beads in the light shade of rustling palms or gray-green olive trees, reading the office beneath the fruit trees which showered them with fragrant petals or temptingly offered delicious peaches, pears, and apples as symbols of the goodness of God.[67]

But the notion that the mission gardens are sacred spaces goes beyond their particular historical and religious origins and includes a more diffuse sense of reverence and sanctification that was part of the consumption of the sites as well. The descriptive rhetoric appropriates religious imagery, such as "shrines" and "rosaries of the roadside," but translated to a secular heritage context where the devotional liturgies have taken the form of pageants and fiestas, and the worshippers are tourists making their historical pilgrimages.[68] For example, *In the Path of the Padres,* a 1934 book of mission photographs, opens with an editor's note advising readers that "with two exceptions, each Franciscan monument is easily reached by motorbus or railway."[69] It is also the title of hikes currently offered by the California State Parks staff at the San Luis Reservoir State Recreation Area. The listing for the hikes on the California State Parks website invites members of the public to join a "Path of the Padres" hike, so called "because it was the path through the Diablo Mountain Range taken by the padres as they came from Mission San Juan Bautista 35 miles along Los Banos Creek and into the Central Valley in the early 1800s. . . . You will find clues that tell you that Native American Indians lived along the creek. Later came the Spanish missionaries, the Californios, the miners, the ranchers and now, you can walk in their foot steps."[70]

The cloister garden also played into notions of a gendered, celibate, contemplative community. Commentators on the Santa Barbara Mission garden frequently recounted that women were not permitted to enter it, and this exclusive maleness of the space seems to have added to its sense of romance. For example, in 1887 the widely read *Harper's New Monthly* magazine published "A Santa Barbara Holiday," the story of a group of Easterners who winter in Santa Barbara for the city's healthful qualities. In the story's text and images the mission gardens, like the state itself, represented for the sojourners an oasis of perpetual warmth and beauty away from the cares of the gray and weary life of eastern city dwellers. The story includes several passages describing the Santa Barbara mission garden and three engraved illustrations of the mission by Harry Fenn.[71] In the story, the serious, thoughtful sister, Edith, goes daily to the mission, where she sits "on the rim of the fountain basin dreamily gazing."[72] One day she is invited

FIGURE 3.11. "Waiting for the Angel's Trumpet. A Study at the Santa Barbara Mission." Postcard. Collection of the author.

FIGURE 3.12. "Flowers for the Altar, Santa Barbara, Cal." Postcard. Collection of the author.

by one of the frocked fathers to tour the mission. Although as a woman she is not permitted to enter the garden, Edith looks at it through the sacristy doorway and later recalled to her companions, "There was perfect quiet, and the sunlight made beautiful shadow patches on the walks. . . . Some of the fathers were seated in its shade. I wish I could have painted it, but fear I couldn't give the true coloring, it was so varied and deep."[73] The story continues:

> On returning from his devotions the father found Edith still looking upon the scene, and was greatly pleased at her enjoyment.
>
> "It is beautiful?" he asked at length.
>
> "It is more than that, father; I never saw so lovely a place. How happy you must all be, having such a garden!"
>
> "So we are, child. It is our home, and some of us couldn't live without it now."[74]

Perhaps the best-known representation of the mission garden as monastic cloister has been reproduced as the trope of the solitary figure of a monk in contemplative repose or carefully tending his plants. For example, the frontispiece of James Steele's *Old Californian Days* (1889) is an engraving of the garden with a friar standing next to the fountain, and he published a photograph captioned *Fountain and Inner Court* as well.[75] Alice Hare, an active historic preservationist and amateur photographer who turned professional in the early 1900s, collected material for her short history of the missions and shot a classic view at Santa Barbara (ca. 1905) of a brother, standing in front of the central basin ringed with flowerpots, garden tools at the ready (Figure 3.13).[76] Engelhardt's San Juan Capistrano volume in his series on mission history included a photograph of Father St. John O'Sullivan standing next to a fountain. The friar in the garden was such a common image that it became an anticipated part of the mission experience. Writing in 1897, the Reverend Ernest Warburton Shurtleff alerted travelers to be on the lookout for such an encounter at Santa Barbara:

> If the tourist chance to come upon the scene in the hour when the white-haired padre stands in the garden with folded hands and reverent mien, the picture presents its highest charm, for in that solitary figure the worshipful spirit of the whole scene seems incarnated and humanized.[77]

The simple images have rich connotations. They reinforced not only the spaces as monastic gardens but also the characterization of the missions as cradles of civilization where husbandry and horticulture transformed the wild landscape and the brothers domesticated the heathens. The imagery echoed a common device of depicting an exotic figure as a symbolic construction of the Oriental other. At the Alhambra, for example, mid-nineteenth-century visitors could photograph

FIGURE 3.13. Alice Hare, Santa Barbara Mission garden, ca. 1905. Courtesy of The Bancroft Library, University of California, Berkeley.

the site with "gitanos" or Spanish Roma posing in the shots. Lara Eggleton has argued that the inclusion of these figures, like the Alhambra architecture itself, "placed the ruin and the gypsy in the same picture, so that the materiality of the monument was once again re-envisioned as a relic of the past."[78] Closer to home, Jennifer Watts has traced photography's role in the construction of Southern California identity in the late nineteenth and early twentieth centuries. The visual tropes of the era, she argues, "centered on a salubrious climate that gave rise to a peculiarly fecund, even exotic landscape; a graceful antiquity characterized by architectural relics (particularly missions); and the quaint appeal of the 'ethnic other.'"[79]

The imagery and ideology of the mission landscapes as sacred spaces that circulated in photographs, paintings, and other two-dimensional media were reproduced in the material culture as well. For example, a set of models was commissioned for the Mission Trails Building at the 1939 Golden Gate International Exposition in San Francisco by the building's architects, Harold A. Edmondson and Robert Stanton. Thirty German cabinetmakers at Miniature Fabricators Inc. of Pasadena, under the direction of an Italian artist named Leon Bayard de Volo, constructed the models.[80] Fabricated from a mix of wood, clay, and "molded paperboard," the models included replica cast metal bells, and several re-created mission gardens in their courtyards (Figure 3.14). The models reinforced romanticized and sanctified representations of the missions by including gardens and frocked monks in poses of contemplation, study, and worship.[81] For example, in the Santa Barbara model two monks kneel before a wooden cross (Figure 3.15), while at Mission San Francisco a monk walks through the cemetery garden with book in hand. At San Fernando, three monks are seated on benches that surround the fountains while two others gaze contemplatively into the garden.

The models' presentation of the landscapes around the missions as all-male, cloistered, monastic gardens reiterated the conventions of mission visual culture. The models also add to the understanding of the mission landscapes' role in shaping cultural memory through their unique history in the public display of discursive objects. Not only have they passed through numerous hands and been on display in settings as varied as a San Francisco high school, a roadhouse restaurant, and, their current repository, the California Missions Museum, they also evoke the same celebratory impulses seen in text, images, and objects over the past hundred years.[82] The museum's supporting foundation states its purpose: "To preserve, restore, and display the California Mission Models and other historical items in an educational environment, which promotes appreciation of the ingenuity, commitment, and perseverance of the early California missionaries and pioneers."[83] The dedicatory plaque at the entrance, erected by the Native Sons of the Golden West in June 2006, declares, "This museum hopes to impart to all who visit it a sense of awe at the ingenuity, dedication, and tenacity of those who have

FIGURE 3.14. Mission San Fernando Model, commissioned for the 1936 Golden Gate Exposition, on display in the California Missions Museum. Photograph courtesy of the California Mission Museum.

gone before us." The conventions of representation in the 1939 models and in the fourth-grade mission models are so pervasive that a made-in-China miniature of Mission San Luis Rey includes a padre gazing into a fountain (Figure 3.16).

The idea of the mission gardens' sacredness belies the more complicated relationships of sectarian and secular politics implicated in their religious associations. One conflict is the tension between Catholic and Protestant interests. Anti-Catholic sentiments run deep in American history, and, as Philip Jenkins has noted, it is not easy to "disentangle hatred for the Church as an institution from the popular contempt for Catholics as a community, though the two types of prejudice were expressed somewhat differently."[84] In the late nineteenth and early twentieth centuries, anti-Catholic social and political movements were integrally connected with theories of nationalism and regional identity formation.[85] Similar politics and prejudices are played out in representations of the California mission landscapes, particularly after Anglo-Protestants ascended to political power in the last quarter of the nineteenth century. For example, these tensions are evident in a 1915 story by Charles Francis Saunders and J. Smeaton Chase in a compilation of "historical facts . . . discursively woven into a personal narrative . . . designed to

FIGURE 3.15. Detail of two Franciscans kneeling before a cross in the garden of the Mission Santa Barbara model, California Missions Museum. Photograph by the author.

portray some feature of mission life or history."[86] The story tells the tale of two young lovers, Dick and Kitty, who steal into the Santa Barbara Mission garden on a lark. The story describes their admiration of the "sacred" garden and the thrill of trespassing this male-only enclave. Dick recounts, "The garden is laid out in beds of shrubs and flowers, with winding walks between. We kept in the shade as much as we could, as there were several windows that look on the garden. . . . But there were lots of trees, and we skirmished about from one to another and had no end of a good time. Kitty was enjoying it immensely, and it did seem a

FIGURE 3.16. Mission San Luis Rey miniature, made in China. Collection of the author.

pretty good joke to be dodging about in the old garden right under their noses." Having strolled the garden, posted a "votes for women" placard on a tree, and proposed marriage, the couple forget themselves in the throes of the moonlit night and are discovered. "I heard the Father, or Brother or whatever they call themselves, coming after us: we could hear his skirts flapping about and I think he must have been a fat man from the way he puffed."[87] After much drama the couple finally escape back over the garden wall where they hid and "listened to the chaps inside calling us awful names in Spanish, Irish, German, and about everything else."[88] The fictional account presumably played into readers' pejorative associations of Catholicism and recent immigrants and was consistent with prejudices and political movements such as the Know-Nothing Party.

Another aspect of the complexity of the notion of the mission gardens as sacred spaces is the implicit tensions between state heritage and being Catholic in a country where church and state are ostensibly separate and yet interests have been closely allied with Protestant doctrines and traditions. Thomas Bremer has argued that this conflict is evident in the preservation efforts of the missions at the turn of the twentieth century that was led primarily by Protestant civic leaders.[89] He suggests that the relatively minimal presence of Catholic motifs and iconography in the San Juan Capistrano gardens is related to the preservationists' desire to distinguish the missions as central to the state's historical narrative rather than the Church's. Kevin Starr similarly argues that restorations of the missions by the Landmarks Club were led by Protestant civic leaders interested in celebrating the Protestant virtues of piety, productivity, and a strong work ethic.[90] But, as noted, Romo's garden in Santa Barbara avoided explicit religious references as well.

At times this tension between sectarian and secular heritage has been openly addressed. The recent canonization process for Junípero Serra brought to the surface much debate about the role of the Church in California history, but the tensions date back to the early restorations of the missions. For example, the press coverage of the campaign to restore Mission Santa Barbara after damage in the 1925 earthquake argued that saving the building was "a task above church or creed."[91] Iconography in the fund-raising campaign deployed a Lady Liberty–like figure variously holding a banner or wearing a crown inscribed with the word *California*. An appeal titled "Will you help restore California landmark?" argued that the "California institution" is "dear to the hearts of all Californians and everyone interested in that which is picturesque and historical."[92]

The conflict between Catholic ownership and secular heritage has been articulated more recently in objections to government support for the missions as a violation of the First Amendment's Establishment Clause separating church and state, for example, protests and lawsuits following the passage of the 2004 federal California Missions Preservation Act (S.1306).[93] The legislation's purpose is "to support the efforts of the California Missions Foundation to restore and repair the Spanish colonial and mission-era missions in the State of California and to preserve the artworks and artifacts of these missions, and for other purposes." The lawsuit challenging the act represented the first case law addressing federal funding for the historic preservation of resources with both religious and historical significance.[94] It was ultimately dismissed and the funding for the legislation was approved, but the discourse the suit spurred exemplifies the tensions of the missions' multivalence. Tellingly, the legislation leads with the finding that "the California missions represent some of our Nation's oldest historical treasures," and they "contribute greatly to the rich historical, cultural, and architectural heritage of California and the American West." Nowhere in the bill is there any reference to the Franciscans, the Catholic Church, or any other aspect of the sites' religious association. Senator Barbara Boxer, one of the two authors of the bill, posted an introduction on her website making an argument that mirrors almost exactly Lummis, McGroarty, and Forbes's rationale for repairing Mission Santa Barbara in 1925. Boxer noted: "Aside from being a source of historical and cultural significance to their communities, the missions also provide income to local businesses. Tourists from all over the world visit Mission San Juan Capistrano to observe the migration of the swallows, and nearly half a million 4th graders visit the Mission each year . . . to learn about California's rich history. The California Missions Preservation Act will protect these great symbols of California's cultural and historical heritage for future generations."[95] Debate in the House of Representatives similarly emphasized the importance of the missions in the state's history, and the representatives from various California districts repeatedly articulated their significance as "symbols of Western exploration and settlement" and as "an important part of the State's cultural fabric."[96] In contrast, a letter filed by the Americans United group argued that the legislation would provide funding "to maintain or restore religious artifacts and icons associated with devotional and worship activities at the missions" and asserted that the legislation was unconstitutional because nineteen of the missions "are churches, not just museums, and are still used for religious services."[97] The argument for the secular value of the missions prevailed, but the careful distribution of the funds for physical preservation and security projects continually requires navigating this apparent conflict of secular and sacred functions of the spaces.

Consuming the Past

The missions are not represented merely as isolated images and objects. They are part of discursive practices, such as photography, collecting, and pageantry, which are, in turn, predicated on cultural patterns of behavior and ways of seeing that are inextricably bound to social relationships and structures of power. From Renaissance painting through the introduction of the camera obscura, Claude Lorrain's landscapes, and the expectations of the Grand Tour, ways of seeing and representing the landscape were expressions of ownership and power.[98] Even more specifically, as Denis Cosgrove has noted, "the pictorial dimension of landscape has been charged with duplicity [with] landscape's capacity to 'naturalize' social or environmental inequities through an aesthetic of visual harmony."[99] For example, Stephen Daniels has demonstrated how Georgian landscape design and painting practices glossed over the displacement of local communities wrought by landed gentry consolidating their land holdings.[100] Mark Edmonds has argued that romantic representations of the landscape of Britain's Lake District created "ways of seeing" that often overlook local communities and activities that fall outside the scripted grand narrative of the iconic landscape.[101] Similarly, Susan Sutton and Anna Stroulia have traced how Greek archaeological sites and their visual representations have systematically erased histories that were not associated with the classical period or were inconsistent with other notions essential to Greek nationalist narratives.[102]

While visual culture's representation of the missions as beautiful, timeless, and sacred spaces was an important way in which the sites were absorbed in the dominant narrative, the missions' potency in the production of cultural memory was animated in the discursive practices associated with that visual and material culture. For example, postcards did not simply represent an idealized mission materiality; tourists mailed postcards that documented their visits and wrote messages on them that conveyed to friends and family their experiences at the sites. Photo albums were not simply collections of mission images; they were created by people who arranged and pasted photographs on the pages (Figure 3.17).[103]

FIGURE 3.17. Page from an unidentified photo album labeled "San Fernando, Aug 14, 1928" showing the fountain at Brand Park. Collection of the author.

They were both personal memory markers and ways to share the experiences with others when the albums were shown to friends and family.[104] These artifacts extended the mission experience into the future as, over time, the pages were turned, the images shared, and the stories told.[105]

Souvenirs offer another avenue into the discursive practices of mission representation. As Susan Stewart has argued, a souvenir is a narrative device that locates the story of the visit in a tangible object and "reduces the public, the monumental, and the three-dimensional into the miniature . . . [and] temporally . . . moves history into private time."[106] A 1916 essay suggests that the trade in mission memorabilia dates to the early twentieth century and notes that "the influence of the outburst of admiration for the missions has affected even the business world. . . . Curio dealers, too, have also taken advantage of this feeling, and as a consequence have stocked their shops with all sorts of souvenirs of the old missions. Photographers, as well as postal card and calendar dealers, likewise have reaped a golden harvest."[107] Father O'Sullivan at San Juan Capistrano was one of the first to recognize the profit potential of souvenir sales, and he produced small guidebooks for sale at the mission in the 1910s. Another early example of mission merchandising was the production of miniature mission bells in 1914 as part of the larger effort to place a mission-bell guidepost every mile along the six-hundred-mile El Camino Real.[108] The trade in mission material culture continues, and mission aficionados can purchase in gift shops and boutiques, and from online retail sites, items such as mission miniatures, tiles, thimbles, spoons, and plates that depict individual missions. It is significant to note that the gift shops in Catholic-owned missions also carry merchandise associated with spiritual practices, such as rosaries, charms related to saints, votives, and religious texts. These objects are spatially segregated from the secular heritage objects in gift shop displays, suggesting that people engaging with the sites as part of their religious heritage and practices also have a different involvement with the material consumption of the missions.[109]

The evidence for the reception of mission souvenirs is anecdotal but seems consistent with other touristic consumption patterns, particularly with regard to "sets" of heritage sites such as historic baseball parks, national parks, or Underground Railroad sites. Many of these items are issued in serial form, and assembling a complete set mirrors the practice of "collecting" visits to every mission. For example, one tourist shared his experiences in a public blog, noting, "We have been collecting cheap refrigerator magnets as souvenirs of our travels, and have been diligent about getting one from each mission."[110] His confession that he had "cheated" by buying a magnet from a mission he had not yet visited suggests the magnets were as much scorecards as mementos.

These souvenirs operate like other commodities in that they provide consumers the emotional pleasures of collecting, or, as Walter Benjamin has described it, the "most profound enchantment."[111] The critical transaction is not the purchase but how consumers turn these commodities into meaningful collections, a system of objects that poses some reconfiguration of the social world and, in turn, shapes their very subjectivity.[112] For example, the particular meaning of the collection such as the Mission de Oro miniatures may be for some a wistful nostalgia for a pastoral landscape in the face of suburban banality and for others a form of veneration for early heroes of the faith. Whatever their personal meanings, the objects reinforce the imagery of the mission as an architectural jewel set in a garden landscape, heritage divorced from history and recast as a charming collectible. Collections then become guides, ways of seeing, ordering, and knowing, shaping us even as we shape them. As Susan Pearce and Paul Martin have argued, collecting is "the human activity, above all, which aspires to control time . . . [and] much collecting energy is put into the effort to gather material which by catching time passing in tangible form will turn it into a kind of eternity."[113] In miniature form, the living landscape of each Mission de Oro is frozen in time and rendered as dainty, immaculate grounds in a perpetual state of perfect preservation.

In an abstract but potent way, this traffic of mission material culture similarly takes elements of the landscape and reconfigures them in the domestic and private space of personal collections.[114] For example, miniature replicas of the mission bells that were installed along California's El Camino Real are sold in mission gift shops and on eBay.[115] The opportunity to bring these miniature landmarks into the home helps create a link between the domestic sphere and the broader cultural landscape. Furthermore, mission bell miniatures continue to be incorporated into the material heritage of the sites as artifacts displayed at mission museums such as Mission San Fernando, where they function as garden ornaments marking entrances and edging paths. The minimal representation of mission-as-garden inscribed on a linen tea towel, lapel pin, or tile reduces the complex mission history to a logo or brand consumed and displayed like memorabilia for Coca-Cola, Route 66, or other objects of desire for nostalgia collectors.

Crafting the Past

One of the most prevalent and long-standing practices reproducing the mission-as-garden imagery has been the practice of making and displaying models.[116] These models also exemplify the reification of the idea of the missions as beautiful, timeless, sacred spaces reproduced through widely dispersed informal heritage practices. Although there is little documentary record in official archives, we know that mission models have been produced by hobbyists and artisans since the 1930s and for at least fifty years by fourth graders as part of their study of California history.[117] These school mission model projects, while never mandated by state educational standards, are such a pervasive part of the California elementary school experience that they have been described as "rites of passage" and the "highlight of every California student's fourth grade experience."[118] A 1949 textbook includes in its list of "suggested activities" having students make "facsimiles" of Indian "tools, weapons, clothing and homes" or create "an imaginary tour of the missions . . . by illustrated reports or soap sculpture or clay modeling."[119]

There have long been objections to the California history curriculum, including a public protest in 1965 launched by the American Indian Historical Society and a lawsuit filed in 1972 by the Mexican American Education Commission and a coalition of ethnic groups. Nicole Myers-Lim (Pomo), executive director of the California Indian Museum and Cultural Center, prefaced her critique of elementary schools' presentation of the missions by recalling the "traumas that I experienced as a fourth grade student" after her daughter encountered much the same curriculum thirty years later.[120] Despite such persistent critiques and protests, model making has spanned generations and continues to be a prominent part of many classrooms and communities.[121] For example, the public programs coordinator of the San Francisco Presidio, which hosted an exhibit of fourth graders' models in 2010, commented, "This project is a fun hands-on opportunity to rebuild history in a creative way. . . . [It's] a chance for San Franciscans to celebrate the creativity of our students and reminisce about their own elementary school days."[122] In another example, the author expressed an emotional connection with mission models:

> My eldest offspring is a fourth-grader.
>
> In addition to capturing giggles from the girls and frowns from the teachers, this means it's time for that annual rite of passage: *the California mission project.*
>
> This is a project very close to my heart. I never got a chance to do a mission in my fourth grade—either because I'm basically ancient or because my school district skipped it.
>
> So I've been wanting to "help" with this project for years.
>
> My son wasn't quite so ambitious. His first goal was to do a PowerPoint presentation. But with just a little urging from me *(C'mon, Julian, do the model, do the model, do the model, pleeeeasseee . . .),* he decided to do a model.[123]

Model making has been so closely associated with the heritage of the missions that the California Missions Foundation, a not-for-profit organization supporting the historic preservation of the missions, made its case for the importance of the missions, noting that they have "become synonymous with the state's fourth grade curriculum: Students famously build mission models and write research reports as part of California history lessons."[124]

Making models is interesting as a multigenerational, informal heritage practice, but the models' role as cultural productions is amplified by their public display at schools, local libraries, museums, and at the missions themselves. For example, *The Mission Play,* itself an ideologically indulgent paean to the Spanish fantasy past, was accompanied by a set of mission models in the Theatre Garden in San Gabriel (Figure 3.18). This seemingly innocuous and beloved tradition of model making and displaying is a complex social and ideological practice that has been a powerful force in constructing a specific, codified ideal mission materiality. As Jean Baudrillard has argued, these historical objects, like antiques, exotics, and folkloric artifacts, play roles in modernity as markers of "historicalness" and purveyors of the symbolic value of origins and belonging.[125] The models are objects "where history is transformed into space, into property . . . [where] history itself appears as a commodity."[126] In public display contexts the hand-built models are transformed from private markers of personal experience into publicly accepted memorials.[127] The models act as what John Bodnar has called "memory symbols," and they contribute to the public perception of the missions as central to the dominant historical narrative.[128]

The mission models are, therefore, a point of intersection between formal and informal heritage practices, a critical juncture for understanding the production of cultural memory. A closer look at the production of models in the context of fourth-grade curriculum offers insights into the relationship between state-sponsored educational goals and the influence of the models as purveyors of an

FIGURE 3.18. *Mission Play,* Theatre Garden, San Gabriel Mission Playhouse, San Gabriel, California. Postcard. Collection of the author.

idealized materiality that serves a settler-colonial narrative. The California State Educational Standards currently mandate that fourth graders should be able to "describe the social, political, cultural, and economic life and interactions among people of California from the pre-Columbian societies to the Spanish mission and Mexican rancho periods." Under this general rubric, students specifically should also be able to:

> Describe the Spanish exploration and colonization of California, including the relationships among soldiers, missionaries, and Indians. . . . Describe the mapping of, geographic basis of, and economic factors in the placement and function of the Spanish missions. . . . Describe the daily lives of the people, native and nonnative, who occupied the presidios, missions, ranchos, and pueblos. . . . Discuss the role of the Franciscans in changing the economy of California from a hunter-gatherer economy to an agricultural economy.[129]

As historian Zevi Gutfreund has documented, the current standards are the result of activists, primarily Native Americans and Chicanos, who challenged the socially constructed myths purveyed by the curriculum.[130] The articulation of the state's learning objectives, while far more inclusive than earlier textbooks, echoes some of the same polarities of the broader discourse of California colonial history. Specifically, the inquiry into the human cost and contemporary social justice issues of colonialism's consequences is framed as an investigation of quotidian details, infrastructure, and economics.

While students are asked to describe "relationships" among soldiers, missionaries, and Indians, the evidence of the models produced suggests that students focus primarily on the built environment, rarely including figures in the landscape. Furthermore, they frequently echo the tropes and conventions of the mission-as-garden imagery rather than the more historically accurate agricultural and industrial colonial landscape, let alone the features of control, confinement, surveillance, and punishment. For example, a sampling of the models created by fourth graders available on display in missions and posted on school and newspaper websites illustrates that students commonly include mission gardens in their mission models. For all their research on architectural details, founding dates, and crop yields, children's models still often include representations of a lush, colorful mission garden in the forecourt or inner patio. Some, such as a model of Mission Santa Inés, reproduce full gardens, with a fountain, walks, and flower beds that replicate the aesthetic of red tile roof, white adobe walls, and green plantings with vibrant colorful accents (Figure 3.19). Others represent the ornamental spaces more abstractly, with items such as out-of-scale plastic flowers, birdbaths, and colorful tiled fountains (Figure 3.20). The mission model gardens are not simply sanitized, romanticized, or even aestheticized. They present an

FIGURE 3.19. Model of Mission Santa Inés created by an unnamed fourth grader on display in the Mission Santa Inés garden, 2008. Photograph by the author.

FIGURE 3.20. Detail of a child's model of San Gabriel Mission depicting a colorful mosaic tile fountain with animals on display in the mission's garden, 2008. Photograph by the author.

idea about what the colonial landscape might have looked like if, indeed, the Spanish frontier in Alta California had been vacant and settled by close-knit communities of contemplative, peaceful monks who conquered the "New World" by assuming devout poses, gazing into fountains, meditating on scripture, and doing a little gardening on the side.

Not only are the models informed by the mission gardens and the conventions of mission visual culture, but they also are increasingly shaped by a model-building industry developed specifically for fourth-grade mission projects. While generations of California fourth graders have built missions from household items such as Popsicle sticks and sugar cubes, students can now purchase model-building kits, instructions, accessories, and plans. These products perpetuate many of the romanticized tropes of the classic mission garden.[131] At the Create-A-Mission website, for instance, one can purchase not only a "rustic cross made from 2 wooden twigs nailed together" and "gold metal bells to hang in your tower," but also a plastic water fountain and a wishing well.[132] While one would not expect a fourth grader to have the capacity to critically represent colonial history, the replication of the mission-as-garden aesthetic is revealing of both how formative the garden setting is for shaping the understanding of mission history and how heritage practices such as model making perpetuate the narrative of a valorized colonial past.

As with most expressions of the Spanish fantasy past, the mission models curriculum has not gone unchallenged. Some educators have offered alternative assignments that emphasize more experiential learning (such as site visits) and information literacy (library research). Commentators have expressed concern in newspapers and blogs, wondering if it "is time to burn down the mission" and describing the assignment as "loved and hated by teachers and parents . . . steeped in nostalgia and controversy."[133] But the most pointed critique has come from Native Americans and other proponents of critical pedagogy. Edward Castillo (Luiseño-Cahuilla), for instance, has long criticized the California curriculum: "For years, California schoolchildren have been presented with a nostalgic, rose-tinted picture of gentle, brown-robed Franciscans bringing deprived and primitive Indians to the missions to learn an orderly, wholesome, agricultural way of life . . . completely overlooking the suffering of Indian people, and oblivious to the soundness and validity of Indian ways of life."[134]

Rupert Costo (Cahuilla) was one of the most active critics, writing reviews of history textbooks, advocating for curriculum reform, and authoring along with his wife, Jeanette Costo, a pointed counternarrative, *The Missions of California: A Legacy of Genocide* (1987). In 1970 Rupert Costo proposed an alternative lesson plan for engaging students in critical approaches to California colonial history that is worth sharing in detail.[135] His 1970 role-playing lesson, titled "It Happened in California: You Are There," presented students with three historical settings.

Two were at the missions and the third was an inland village near Mission San Diego. In the scenario the students were asked to take on the role of the Indians living in the village. As Gutfreund summarizes Costo's instructions, students were reminded that "in addition to demanding, backbreaking work, the padres would separate Indians from their families and many would be vulnerable to disease."[136] The students were then instructed to choose from among the following courses of actions:

1. You could run away, because the guards are not always watching.
2. You could organize a revolt to overthrow the people who are controlling you.
3. You could accept what has happened to you and try to do the best you can.
4. You could poison the missionary.
   REMEMBER: You are not armed. The Spanish have guns. Discuss among your group.

As Gutfreund observes, "All four choices had sad outcomes, especially the option to submit. The 'revolt' and 'poison-the-missionary' options did not significantly change the student-neophyte experience. The only way to achieve freedom was to run away, and that involved risk."[137]

These more critical approaches have also addressed the issues of reproducing mythologized landscapes through models. One particularly telling commentary by writer and activist Deborah Miranda (Ohlone-Costanoan Esselen Nation of California) offered an instructive thought experiment in which the mission model assignment is repeated but with the substitution first of a slavery plantation as the reconstructed environment and then a German concentration camp.[138] Miranda described her own education about California Indian history when she learned from her Esselen and Chumash father "the real deal—the blessings and the genocide. . . . California Indian history is brutal" in contrast to the "typical California Fourth Grade curriculum, that lovely mythology about happy Indians, gentle Padres and the nobility of sacrificing yourself to build missions out of adobe bricks for future tourists to visit."[139]

Despite these critical perspectives, making and displaying mission models remains a common undertaking in many classrooms and living rooms across the state. School websites post pictures of smiling, proud fourth graders standing beside their creations. Local historical societies, museums, libraries, and the missions put the children's creative output on exhibit for public viewing. News programs cover the annual undertaking, and class projects are profiled for local public television documentaries.[140] The coverage often nostalgically frames the event as an annual rite of passage that adults who grew up in California can invariably recall. The perpetuation of the tradition suggests, despite the complaints, that some find enduring value in the practice. Whether it is a form of veneration for symbols of California's origins, an exercise intended to involve students in a deeper understanding of the complexities of colonial history, or some other outcome altogether, participation in the annual production and consumption of mission models has become a secular ritual and a shared performance of heritage. The models reinforce the missions as central sites in the public memory of yet another generation of California schoolchildren, and, for some at least, reinforce the codified images of the mission garden as a central element of the landscape.

"A Perfect Index"

Architectural historian Rexford Newcomb has written, "Architecture is a perfect index to its backgrounds, material or spiritual, and expresses, as can no other art, the life and thought of a race or an age."[141] The California mission gardens may be seen as indexes, not so much to "life and thought" as to the political ideology and mythologized identity inscribed in the landscape. As the history of the romanticized reinvention of the missions as gardens has demonstrated, the dominant narrative of the mission landscape confirmed the key tropes of the Spanish fantasy past, and it encouraged affirmation of values celebrated in Church, state, and national discourses. The contemporary sites are in many ways the antithesis of their colonial era predecessors: stylized twentieth-century fantasies of a Spanish monastery transplanted in California's new Eden.

From the turn of the twentieth century onward, those responsible for caring for the missions, including preservationists, Franciscans, Catholic parish administrators, and State Parks employees, capitalized on the synergy between the reconstructed gardens of the missions and the political objectives and ideologies of the Anglo elite. Allegedly created by the learned and noble founding mission fathers who came to save heathens and tame the wilderness, the gardens stood as an enduring legitimation of "civilization" and "progress." These mission gardens could be read conveniently as both the legacy of colonial victors and the heritage of elite white society. They were, as Tomás Almaguer argues, witness to the "domination of civilization over nature, Christianity over heathenism, progress over backwardness and, most importantly, of white Americans over the Mexican and Indian populations that stood in their path."[142] The cumulative accretion of the significance of the mission gardens, represented in a range of media across multiple generations, begins to explain why they remain so resistant to the critical inquiry that has penetrated many other aspects of postcolonial narratives. Discursive practices such as collecting miniatures, making and displaying models, buying souvenirs, viewing paintings, reading travel literature, and sending postcards embed these representations of, and ideas about, the missions into cultural memory.

CHAPTER FOUR

Consuming Heritage

The Embodied Experience of the California Missions

Destinations

The missions were destinations in design and in practice long before they became popular tourist sites. Beginning in 1769, crosses were erected and bells hung to announce the missionaries' arrival to the local natives. The colonial mission churches were self-consciously public buildings; their architecture invested heavily in facades, bell towers, campanarios, and other highly visible features that proclaimed their presence for miles. The landscape similarly had a public face. The placement of the few ornamental elements in the landscape, such as the fountains in front of Missions Santa Barbara and San Luis Rey, suggest that the Franciscans desired to create a favorable impression on those viewing the missions from the outside. As the missions were restored in the last quarter of the nineteenth century, they began to be visited as self-styled historic destinations. Today, as U.S. Representative Samuel Farr has stated in congressional debate, "The missions help drive tourism, the State's third largest industry. These iconic symbols of California are the most visited historic attractions in the State, attracting over 5.3 million visitors a year. They account for a sizable contribution to the State's economy from millions of tourists."[1] This chapter explores spatial practices and embodied experiences at the missions, along with their associated visual and discursive conventions in the touristic landscape.

The history of California mission tourism is distinctive in its particular narratives and associations, and it is also part of a larger context of tourism in the West, both spatially and chronologically.[2] The missions were some of the first sites in the West actively marketed as rustic retreats appealing both to eastern and midwestern tourists and to Californians seeking to escape from the increasing crowds of burgeoning cities like Los Angeles. The notion of the missions as a series of destinations aligned with the interests of the emerging transportation industries in California, and travel to the missions was spurred in part by the growth of railroad and automobile transportation.[3] For example, the Inyo Roads Club sponsored tours of the missions and simultaneously argued for improved roads and transportation infrastructure. Car dealers sponsored mission junkets that were reported in news stories with the names of the dealers and cars featured prominently.[4] Popular magazines such as *Land of Sunshine* and *Sunset* published articles on the missions with titles like "Motoring among the Missions: A Real Joy Ride through the Cathedral Towns of California" that emphasized the freedom and adventure of touring by car.[5] Marketing the missions served early twentieth-century ideological as well as economic interests.[6] The writers and artists who saw the missions' crumbling walls and decaying roofs as picturesque ruins of a romanticized past perpetuated those images in articles and artwork in magazines and popular literature, further cementing the missions in the popular imagination and feeding readers' appetites for similar experiences.[7] If the roadside mission bell markers were not enough, guidebooks, marketing materials, and maps (Figure 4.1) created by oil companies and auto clubs inscribed the historical route so that tourists could travel the El Camino Real, as Charles Moore did, "in the footsteps of the padres."[8]

It is clear that the practice of visiting the missions has become its own invented tradition that has been instrumental in their construction as symbolically charged heritage sites.[9] As Thomas Bremer has argued, travel involves visiting "distinct places in the human itineraries that experience the landscapes they transverse and then narrate those experiences to themselves and to others."[10] To understand how the missions work in material and ideological ways as tourist destinations and cultural productions, this chapter looks at the staging of visitor experiences in terms of movement, narrative, and multisensory impressions.[11] This analysis of the mission spaces identifies the structures, conceptual metaphors, and underlying ideologies that inform visitor engagement, and the ways in which they produce narratives through the embodied experience of the landscape.

Before exploring the embodied experience of the missions, it is important to consider the institutional and operational aspects of their contemporary management. One important factor is that the people making the decisions about the landscape designs—the mission administrators—are embedded in institutional hierarchies with their own respective histories, cultures, and purposes. The majority of missions are to some extent under the authority of the broader Catholic Church. Some are independent parishes led by a rector under a bishop. Others are part of Catholic educational institutions, such as Mission Santa Clara, which is part of Santa Clara University. The administration of San Juan Capistrano has been delegated to an independent nonprofit, but the property is still owned by the Diocese of Orange and has close ties to the adjacent parish. Two sites, La Purísima in Lompoc and Mission Solano in Sonoma, are owned and managed by the California Department of Parks and Recreation. Each mission's administration has some combination of staff, contracted laborers, volunteers, and friends groups who help to design and maintain the grounds.[12]

A second point to keep in mind is that the missions have been used by multiple audiences over the years, and that the landscapes have long been important parts of their engagement with the missions. For example, visual evidence documents all manner of interactions, including photography clubs with their tripods and painting groups with their easels focusing on the aesthetic qualities of the missions; Native people posing in front of the missions for a staged anniversary celebration; school groups dutifully trailing a guide who is trying to hold their

FIGURE 4.1. Gerald A. Eddy for the California Mission Trails Association Ltd., expanding map of California's Mission Trails, "Travel with California's scenic coast highways, America's most beautiful 400 miles," 1939. Collection of the author.

wandering attention; parishioners assembled for an Easter sunrise service; wedding parties posing in the garden; heritage plant enthusiasts propagating historic species; celebrities and politicians making public appearances; as well as an endless stream of tourists (Figure 4.2). As varied as these constituencies have been, the contemporary sites are designed for two primary audiences: tourists and those connected with the faith communities.[13] The sites' designs have been informed by the cultural practices of both groups since the late nineteenth century.[14] Part of the power of touristic cultural productions is that they represent engagement on a larger scale and with a sensitivity distinct from the mundane routine of the everyday.[15] The same may be argued for worship spaces where members of a faith community participate in corporate liturgies as part of their personal devotional exercises and spiritual lives.[16] Each of these is an individual, personal, embodied experience and yet part of a broader social activity. Each engages the senses and the imagination in a way that "can carry the individual to the frontiers of his being where his emotions may enter into communion with the emotions of others."[17]

A third important point to bear in mind is that people experience the California mission landscapes as intentionally constructed heritage sites through which the past is mobilized in the interests of the political present. The mission landscapes, as we have seen, are neither restored to a pure reconstruction of their colonial forms nor interpreted as twentieth-century Colonial Revival gardens. They are,

FIGURE 4.2. Tour group at Mission San Juan Capistrano. Postcard. Collection of the author.

as Mary-Catherine Garden has called them, "heritagescapes," bounded, cohesive, and visible landscapes that are as much concept as materiality and that must "create a sense of the past . . . [and] an experience of a past place which is (ideally) both vivid and credible to those who visit the site."[18] As such, the California mission landscapes are not forgeries or fakes, but complex, ideologically resonant spaces that continue to be adapted for each setting. The mission landscapes, with their complicated history of restaging spaces of colonialism, perpetuate the reproduction of the past where the specific landscape history of an individual mission is largely subsumed by the replication of a recognizable and even beloved garden type. Significantly, this familiar, repeated form has been part of the gardens' appeal for visitors and designers alike. The gardens help to locate the buildings, even the modern reconstructions, in historic settings and to elide them with what Representative Samuel Farr has called the "historic vein running through our State from south to north."[19] Heritage as it is framed at the missions, however, is not simply about identity labels or even a sense of belonging, affiliation, connectedness, or cohesion. They are spaces where "identity" is not a concretized thing but a set of processes used both by political entrepreneurs to mobilize perceived sets of shared interests in order to "organize and justify collective action along certain lines." Identity is also perpetually constituted and deployed by lay actors in "everyday settings to make sense of themselves, of their activities, of what they share with, and how they differ from, others."[20] The mission landscapes are complex places whose meaning, scholars have noted, resides "in a multiplicity of often contradictory perspectives, . . . symbols of the heritage of California's Native American, Spanish, Mexican, and Anglo-American peoples, [and they] resist any simple, single interpretation."[21]

As heritagescapes the mission landscapes are animated by the complex interplay of representation, site design, and visitor experiences. In this nexus, people construct their own meanings of the spaces within the context of the ideological messages of the missions and the performance of social identities. These contexts, while not deterministic, are a significant part of the construction of cultural memory. For example, the embodied experience of the mission landscape, although framed by the highly individualized, idiosyncratic confluence of what the person brings to the experience, is also almost always preceded by some prior contact with representations that prepared the visitor for the experience before it actually transpired.[22] These representations in turn influence the reception of the sites and result in what Dean MacCannell has called "constructed recognition."[23] For example, the visual tropes and conventions of representing the missions (e.g., reflected facades in the still pools of fountains, the sole figure of the padre in the garden, visitors holding birds at San Juan Capistrano) are repeated in tourists' photographs. As described in chapter 3, late nineteenth- and twentieth-century imagery of the mission landscapes circulated through illustrated lectures, published albums, stereographs, and postcards, generating a widely recognized visual culture that similarly informed visitors' experiences. Today's technology offers multimedia options such as television, Google maps, Flickr, and YouTube, which provide an endless array of mission images and commentary, in addition to traditional media and even View-Master slides (Figure 4.3).[24] The commercial enterprise Virtual Video Tours offers downloadable thirty-minute podcasts with photos and audio tours of La Purísima in which "experienced guides . . . walk you through your destination as you simultaneously see seventy-five or more photos of the featured locales." You can view the tour to prepare for your visit or use it as a digital guide while at the mission, and after the tour "you can relive and share it again, expanded with your own stories and photos, with your friends, grandkids, or grandparents!" The developer suggests that podcasts can even substitute for the visit itself, so that you can "travel the world without leaving your desk or armchair!"[25] The new media now also offer the possibility of critique and even exchange as websites from Yelp to Virtual Tourist post reviews of the missions and some sites provide space for others to comment.[26] Despite the radical changes in media format, this meta-experience of the mission destinations reproduces the century-old narratives of heritage as both preface and epilogue to an actual visit.

This kind of constructed recognition applies to conceptual constructs as well as visual conventions. For example, an enduring trope of visiting the missions is conceiving of them as a series or a collection of experiences. Descriptions of the missions are replete with statements that they were "founded to be a day's ride apart," even though the first four missions (San Diego, San Carlos in Carmel, San Antonio de Padua, and San Gabriel) spanned much of the length of Alta California.[27] While site selection was dependent on a variety of factors (the location of potable water and arable fields, concentration of Native population, access to a harbor, and so on), the enduring premise that their arrangement across the state was defined by the needs of travelers is telling. The notion of the missions as a series of stops along a route was central to Alfred Robinson's 1846 tour and to guides produced by the California Mission Trails Association in the 1940s, and it is perpetuated in contemporary tourist package promotions. The same impulse to collect the complete set of Cameo Guild miniatures and to sketch all the missions is captured in the use by a mission staff member of the term *mission fever* to describe the ambition to visit every mission.[28] Writers of nineteenth-century journals and twentieth-century travelogues described their journeys along the mission trail variously as "tracing the footsteps of the padres" and visiting the "chain," "garland," or, more devoutly, the "mission rosary."

Finally, exploring the embodied experience of heritage requires recognizing the complex interplay of space and bodies at the nexus of the mission experience.[29] Part of the power of the mission landscapes, as with any landscape, lies in their mutability. Their significance is constructed, not inherent. It is created in the

FIGURE 4.3. View-Master 3-D tour of the California missions. Collection of the author.

performance of the spaces by those who live on, work in, and move through them. In this sense, the mission landscape and visitors cocurate their engagement with the landscape. The meaning of the mission sites is perpetually constructed and reified by this interplay of people and spaces, and yet it is also part of and informed by the cultural production of California mission heritage as it has accrued over time. The sites are activated by bodies' movement through them and made meaningful through embodied experience. Yet landscapes also guide that movement, structure the sequence, and spur the emotional arcs of narrative that are themselves informed by received notions of California history. They are environments for kinesthetic, multisensory experiences, amplifying or muffling sound, directing the gaze, encouraging or repelling touch, and even inviting taste. Outside of the formal museum exhibits there is minimal interpretive text so that while brochures and signage may indicate an intended path, for the most part the architecture, landscape, artifacts, and plants structure the visitor's experience.[30] The lack of didactic interpretation at the missions increases the power of the narrative because visitors are rarely conscious of the subtle use of stagecraft to create atmosphere, set symbols, and guide them through the spaces. Visitors move along routes that establish a sequence, rhythm, and flow of the experience of space in time. Paths, doorways, gates, and corridors guide and constrain movement while the placement of objects and seating invites bodies to pause and assume the classic gestures and poses of dutiful observers (Figure 4.4). The space directs the gaze, hiding some elements and accentuating others, framing distant views and encouraging close inspection. The senses of hearing, touch, taste, and smell are stimulated to accentuate the connection with another time, a space apart.

The complex interplay of space and body must also account for individual agency. As cultural geographers Nicky Gregson and Gillian Rose have argued, performances and performed spaces are complex and uncertain. Because they are mediated by particular social and citational practices and by the performative power of the spaces themselves, landscapes are essential to the construction of social identity, difference, and power relations.[31] Just as the landscapes once operated in the mission era, the techniques of controlling movement, registering time, framing vision, and stimulating senses shape the tourist experience. And, as in the colonial landscape, visitors resist, negotiate, and subvert the structured, disciplining aspects of the landscape to create their own personal, mediated experiences. For example, almost as soon as the Brand Park Memory Garden was completed and dedicated, the Park Commission secretary acknowledged receipt of a letter "regarding the trouble you are having with the man at the Mission who persists in washing his dogs in the fountain."[32] A short story reveling in the romantic imagery of the Sacred Garden at Santa Barbara included a young couple trespassing and mocking the immigrant priests.[33] Vandals, graffiti, and neglect plague the more public gardens, and Native Americans activists have staged protests against

FIGURE 4.4. Two visitors pause before a sculpture of Junípero Serra at Mission San Francisco de Asís, 2008. Photograph by the author.

the canonization of Junípero Serra on the same mission landscapes where statues honor his legacy.

Senses and the Embodied Landscape

An easily overlooked aspect of the embodied consumption of the missions is the multisensory immersive nature of the experience that makes them such potent cultural productions.[34] Landscape historians and theorists have repeatedly pointed out that the efficacy of landscapes is in the experience of three-dimensional space, with all its attributes, as perceived through the human senses.[35] And yet, the study of the landscape reduced to the pallid media of text and printed photographs inherently minimizes what in reality is the primary experience of space. These multisensory experiences of light, sound, smell, textures, and taste are part of the central drama of the missions where the stage design is brought to life with the entrance of the actors/tourists and the embodied experiences of the sites (Figure 4.5). Even more pointedly, the sensory experience of the spaces can engage visitors with the missions' contested legacy as memorials and shrines in ways that transcend ideological divisions and sanitize potentially disturbing encounters with their history of trauma. Affective and physiological responses to dark or violent heritage, such as Tim Cole has described regarding the experiences of visitors to Auschwitz, demonstrate that landscapes are not inert but act "on the body in often unexpected and unwelcome multisensory ways," and the result is a "symbolic and material multisensory landscape that enters into the 'muscular consciousness.'"[36] Visitors to the mission landscapes, in contrast, generally describe pleasurable experiences in which the sights and sounds delight the senses.

Paramount among the sensory experience of landscape is vision, and the control of sight has been a conscious part of the missions' design since their founding. The elevated settings of sites such as San Diego and Santa Barbara lend them to more dramatic approaches than missions in dense urban environments or flat plains, as at Solano and San Antonio de Padua, but each mission has a carefully landscaped visitor path. San Diego's hillside between the parking area and the mission entrance is planted in thick beds of green succulents accented with palm trees, the colonnade has elaborate foundation plantings, and in front of the church is an artfully placed crucifix and sculpture in a small garden designed to foreground photographs of the famous campanario and facade. At San Luis Rey the mission is approached by a drive that wends through a green lawn. The impressive vista of the mission's stark white facade seen across the horizontal greensward is framed by a middle ground of ancient branches spreading over a fountain, creating a painterly effect for the vibrant bougainvillea cascading across the colonnade. At Santa Barbara, the similar viewshed across the front lawn is accented with a cross, a bed of cacti, a fountain, and a bed of roses, an effect not lost on photographers

FIGURE 4.5. Tourists with white pigeons at Mission San Juan Capistrano in 1935. Orange County Archives.

who stop to capture the mission's imposing facade framed by a foreground of colorful blossoms.

The management of sight is also apparent in the arrangement of viewing platforms and plantings in the courtyard gardens. Both San Luis Rey and Santa Barbara restrict access to the inner courtyard, but visitors are more than welcome to take pictures subtly staged with roses in the foreground at Santa Barbara. In San Luis Rey's inner quadrangle a bell hanging in an arch is placed at a perfect angle to foreground the patio's central fountain. The mission's renowned pepper tree stands in another courtyard that is open only to retreat participants. There is a small fenced viewing area for tourists, however, where the pepper tree is visible through a single standing arch remnant planted with a bed of colorful flowers at its base (Figure 4.6). San Carlos's forecourt garden similarly provides a colorful, picturesque setting for the approach to the mission and creates a view that has become a favorite of painters and photographers. At San Juan Capistrano, the Serra statue was moved nearer the stone church and a walkway added to link it to a circular fountain by the front entrance. The sight lines from the arabesque fountain down the walk with the statue and famed ruins as the backdrop create a dramatic effect (Figure 4.7). The vista is not only frequently photographed but also is the signature image for a series of mission tiles sold in many

FIGURE 4.6. Mission San Luis Rey, 2008. Visitors are restricted from entering the area, but may view what is thought to be the oldest pepper tree in California through the arch, which has been planted with colorful flowers. Photograph by the author.

FIGURE 4.7. Mission San Juan Capistrano, 2008. View from the fountain to the stone church ruins and the Serra sculpture focal point at the terminus of the walk. Photograph by the author.

mission gift shops. The landscaping at the missions not only directs the gaze of visitors but also stages photo opportunities that reproduce the visual conventions of mission representations promulgated, as we have seen, over the past century.

In addition to the management of sight lines, the mission landscape experience is also shaped by the quality and intensity of light. Although not as overt as the lighting at sites such as the Alamo, illumination is an important element of the drama of the landscape experience, particularly in the contrast between interior and exterior created by the passage into subdued, dimly lit museum and church spaces. Visitors entering the churches must become accustomed to the darkened naves with their votive candles flickering prayer offerings at the back of the church and the subtle glow of the hanging sanctuary candle. Leaving the church and moving back into the dazzling California sunlight accentuates the bright verdure of the gardens and enhances the sense of entering a living landscape of the present. The contrast of dark and light, the massed adobe walls and delicate foliage, the static stillness of the naves, and the animated play of water and wind in the gardens all serve to reinforce the sense of time transport between interior and exterior spaces.

Less obvious than the management of vision is the soundscape of the mission, which provides a subtle but critical element of the mission drama played out by visitors. Travelogues note both the sounds visitors hear and those they do not. The sounds of singing coming from the nave during services bring alive the churches as houses of worship. Some of the missions with more developed tours incorporate formal audio programming into visitors' experiences. At Mission Santa Inés a speaker hidden in a rock in the garden can play recorded music or project recorded text, thus serving as an interpretive guide. At San Juan Capistrano visitors can rent handheld devices that are cued to listening stations around the site. The curious visitor may also imagine the sounds of the mission era: Native Americans of all ages, living and working in close proximity; conversation, laughter, cries, shouts, and moans; hammers striking anvils and the heaving bellows of the blacksmiths and iron smelters. These long-silenced sounds are now replaced by the conversations among visitors sharing their experiences and the distant modern soundscape of passing traffic.

Other sensory experiences of the mission landscapes are even subtler than sight and sound, and yet these ephemeral aspects are the essence of the grounds as living spaces—touch, smell, and taste cannot be replicated in virtual tours or captured in books. Richard Rodriguez's tour of the missions included an encounter at La Purísima with a multigenerational Spanish-speaking family, and he described how "young fingers tear herbaceous leaves, then hold them up for Grandmother to test with the force of her bony jaw."[37] At San Gabriel a school group was being walked past the fountain when a child reached out to dip her fingers into the irresistibly cool wetness of the fountain. Travel writer Geoff Boucher's descriptions of his family's vacation tour of the missions conveys the significance of textures and surfaces: "Maybe it was the dusty rock floors and the walls with bits of twig and earth still visible, but I had had the impression of a drab and muted past."[38] Visitors experience the wafting scents released as the sun warms the earth and plants. Hands brush the softness of a petal or feel the prick of a cactus needle. Lucky visitors to the huerta might be offered a taste of an early lemon species. While rarely mentioned in accounts of the missions, these sensory impressions comprise an ineffable part of the experience of heritage in and through the landscape.

Embodied Heritage

Since the return of the missions to the Catholic Church in the 1860s, mission administrators, volunteers, and preservationists have created aesthetic, processual spaces for people to experience the sites. José María Romo spruced up Santa Barbara's courtyard when he was trying to recruit students. Marah Ryan and later Father St. John O'Sullivan planted flowers in the forecourt of San Juan Capistrano to attract the touring public. Mamie Goulet Abbott kept potted plants on the front colonnade of Mission Santa Inés that served as the porch of the mission residence (Figure 4.8).[39] The impetus for the Memory Garden at San Fernando was the prospect that the view of the mission would be spoiled if a packing plant were built across the street, and the solution was to create a public garden that would evoke and continue to celebrate the accomplishments of the mission padres. Furthermore, these postcolonial landscapes were not just about presenting an attractive facade to the world; their designs embedded the missions in a larger field of referents of key tropes of the Spanish fantasy past, and encouraged the affirmation of values celebrated in church, state, and national discourses. This complex interplay of space, narrative, and the visitor experience is the crux of how the missions operate as embodied experiences.

The landscape design continues to shape how visitors see and experience the missions. While there is no single pattern or sequence of a mission tour, the main elements are fairly uniform across the twenty-one sites: the approach, orientation/admissions, museum, gift shop, garden (either in a courtyard or forecourt setting or both), cemetery, church, padres' quarters, reconstructed traditional Native American dwellings (usually only a single example), and the ruins or reconstructions of industrial features (e.g., tallow vats, furnaces, mill wheels, and floors). In some missions other rooms are also interpreted, such as the soldiers' barracks,

FIGURE 4.8. Santa Inés, front colonnade, n.d. The Huntington Library, San Marino, California.

infirmary, padres' library, and kitchen. The serial presentation of the mission story unfolds in procession through discrete architectural spaces along a structured route that leads visitors to key purveyors of the narrative—the didactic museum, the hallowed nave, the spartan padres' quarters, the melancholy cemetery, and the beautiful courtyard gardens.

The walk-through of Mission San Juan Capistrano is typical of the scripted, mediated experience of visiting a mission.[40] While visitors come with their own goals, needs, and preconceptions, administrators, both secular and religious, have constructed narratives and anticipated visitors' expectations as they developed the sites for public presentation (Figure 4.9).

The mission website offers information targeted to Catholic and international visitors, as well as general information for tourists. In these interstices of the performance of the space and of visitors lie some revealing aspects of how heritage is performed at the missions. Even more particularly, the performance of heritage helps to negotiate the contested aspects of the missions' colonial past so that they are palatable within a settler colonial discourse. For example, the missions are historic sites whose maintenance requires tremendous resources, but this historiography of their restorations and changing interpretation over time can be at odds with the messages of the timelessness of the mission-as-garden imagery. Similarly, the landscapes create a beautiful setting for the presentation of the peaceful, sacred history of the missions, but this impression is predicated on the notion that the spaces are ornamental, in contrast to their utilitarian colonial uses. For this benign, ornamental landscape to seem natural, it must appear effortless and self-propagating. Furthermore, the missions are sites of both conquest and memorialization. They operate as celebratory origins of civilization as well as memorials to those buried at the missions. The mission landscapes are implicated in the discursive practices of gardening, particularly the complex ideas concerning native plants and heritage species. Finally, the missions are devotional landscapes that local parishioners, visiting Catholics, and others use as part of their own spiritual practices. The performance and performativity of these six, often contradictory aspects of mission landscapes—philanthropy, labor, Indigeneity, time, gardening, and devotion—are therefore productive avenues for interrogating the embodied experience of contested heritage in the mission landscapes. To help convey a sense of visiting the mission, I offer the following walk-through of Mission San Juan Capistrano based on a visit I made in 2013:

I'm excited for my visit to Mission San Juan Capistrano on this sunny southern California summer day. I feel amply prepared, having consulted my guidebooks and the website for directions and information. As I pull into a shady spot in a lot near the mission just before 9 a.m., I'm glad for my early start since it's already starting to warm up. I walk toward the entrance gate at the intersection of Ortega

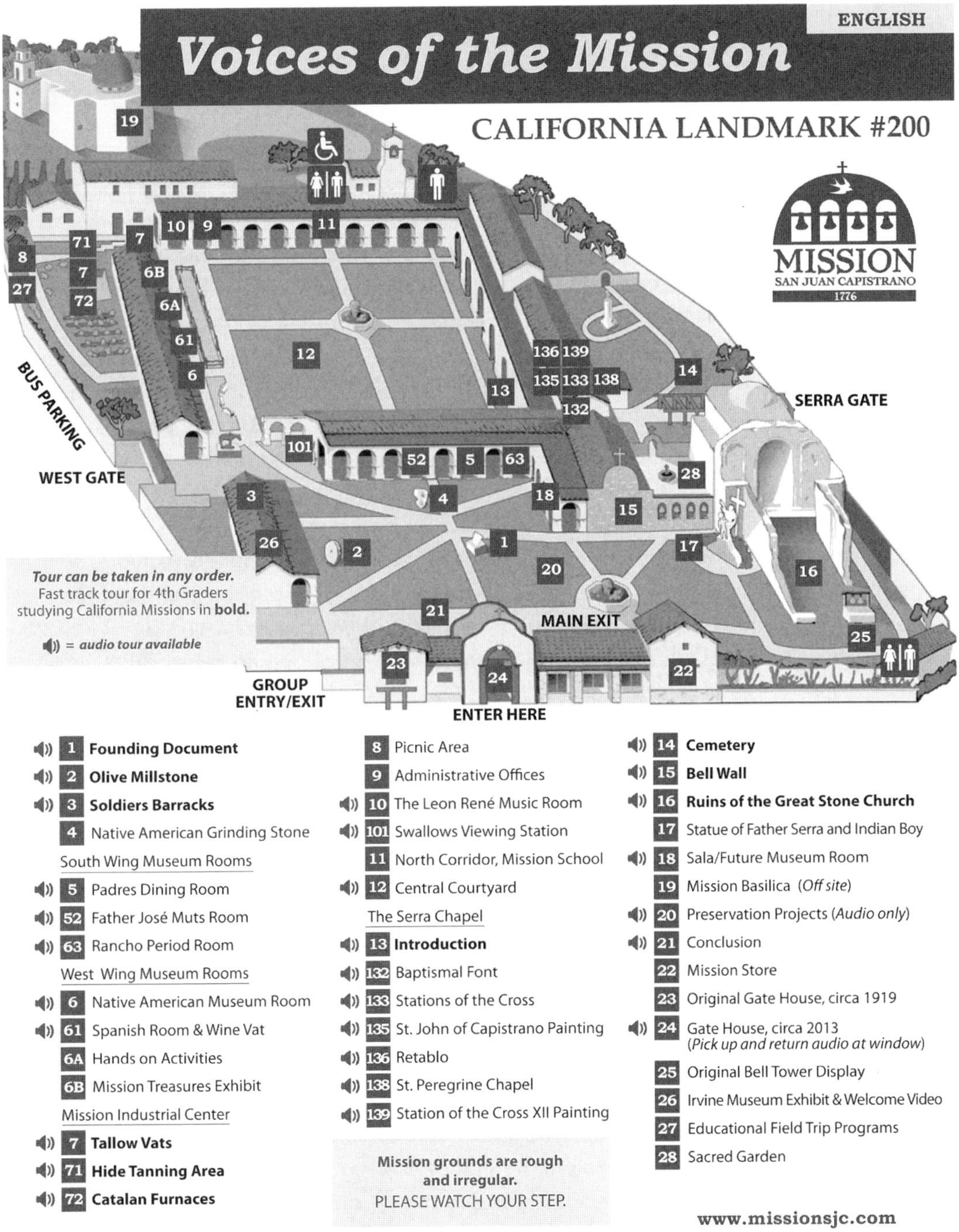

FIGURE 4.9. Mission San Juan Capistrano, "Voices of the Mission" audio tour map. Courtesy of Mission San Juan Capistrano.

Highway and Camino Capistrano—streets whose names mirror the historic feel of this town. A quick stop at the Starbucks opposite the mission entrance gives me the chance to study the mission across the intersection's bustling traffic. The smooth adobe walls that surround the property are almost completely covered by the lush bougainvillea vines draping over them, their red flowers set off by the silver-gray spikey cactus planted along the wall. There is a different entrance since the last time I visited that is adjacent to a slick new museum store.[41] I miss the quaint old arched entrance since this corner of the mission is now indistinguishable from the other modernist Spanish-style retail shops. Bypassing the store, I head through the arched passageway to the ticket window, where I purchase my nine-dollar ticket and pick up my audio guide and map.

Emerging from the dim light of the ticketing area, I enter into the mission's forecourt created by the arched colonnades to my left and in front of me, and the stone church ruins to my right. Even knowing the mission well through pictures and previous visits, I'm struck anew by the contrast of the colorful flowers and the textures of the adobe and stone. As my eyes adjust to the brightness, a soft breeze carries the fragrance of the June roses warming in the morning sun. In front of me, the smooth surface of the water in the arabesque-shaped fountain reflects the curving shapes of the stone ruins. I am drawn down the path from the fountain toward the Serra sculpture at its terminus. There is a small group assembling to witness the recently established tradition of ringing a bell daily seven times to honor the mission's founder, Friar Junípero Serra.[42] The bell's deep, sonorous tones echo across the grounds, and there is a sense of solemnity in the moment. In spite of the intent to honor Serra, I'm struck by the similarity of the sound to a tolling bell at a funeral, and the sense of loss in the place overwhelms me for a moment. As the group disperses to explore the mission, I turn toward the church ruins, where I read the text panel describing the 1812 earthquake when the building collapsed during morning Mass. I plug in the number to the audio guide and hold the slim, black handset to my ear. The recording starts with the re-created sounds of the earthquake, and I'm instantly imagining the panic as the earth started to shake and the great stone domed ceiling rained down. Suddenly the forty deaths I'd read about hit home even more poignantly. The surviving ruins with patches of smooth protective coatings where the adobe portions of the walls have been stabilized seem ancient and yet somehow sanitized, so far removed from the wood, paint, and people who animated them during that service. On the audio tour voices of experts explain the history and significance of the restoration of the stone church and tell me that these are ruins that won't be restored because "you don't rebuild Stonehenge."[43]

I walk back into the center of the forecourt, past the Serra sculpture where a school group in matching navy and khaki uniforms is being cajoled to stand tightly together for a picture. I stop into what is called the Sacred Garden, which

I know from my postcard collecting was St. John O'Sullivan's favorite part of the mission while he restored it in the 1910s and '20s. I pause to listen to the audio guide, which starts with the sound of the ringing bells. The narrator, Ms. Romero, and other local residents recount how important the bells were for those growing up in the town because they marked the passage of the day as well as the parishioners' deaths.

I leave the enclosed Sacred Garden to wander back through the garden beds, admiring the blend of colors and fragrances of the interplanted roses and lavender. The main paths have been paved with rust-colored pavers since I was last here, and it lends a formality to the garden, despite the unstructured arrangement of plantings. On the opposite side of the forecourt from the stone church are the soldiers' barracks, which I glance into before heading back out into the garden toward the kíicha. There I plug in the code on the audio guide and listen to Teeter Maria Romero, a member of the Juaneño Band of Mission Indians, Acjachemen Nation, talk about grinding acorns and other traditional practices of her people. She is charming and funny, and seems to take delight in the interpretation of her people's ways of living. I wonder what she thinks of the juxtaposition of the kíicha and roses, but the audio tour is a frustratingly one-way conversation.

The sun is getting intense and a large group is coming through the ticketing area, so I head into the restored rooms along the south wing of the central quadrangle. I peep into the cool, dimly lit padres' dining room and a room that's been furnished to re-create the rancho period. They are quiet and empty, and I find them oddly sterile. I had hoped to see the mud nests of the famed swallows, but they have stopped nesting at the mission in recent years, supposedly because mature trees are crowding their preferred open terrain. The Swallows Day festivals continue, nonetheless, and I hear a docent explaining to a tour group that they are experimenting with a mobile wall of plaster nests to try to lure the cliff swallows to return.

I next head into the central courtyard where the central fountain draws me toward its cooling burble and colorful flowers, centering the intersecting walks that divide the lawn into quadrants. The map indicates the interpretive exhibits are around the perimeter of the quadrangle, so I dutifully head clockwise around the quadrangle, visiting the Native American Museum Room, the Spanish Room, and the exhibit of "mission treasures." In what is called the "Mission Industrial Center" to the west of the quadrangle, I check out the tannery and furnace where the labels give only minor technical details. I also glimpse the field trip students laughing and talking while having their sack lunches in the picnic area and feel both relieved not to be on chaperone duty and somewhat lonely on my solo tour.

Working my way around the north and east sides of the quadrangle, I get to the Serra Chapel. It is disconcerting to be a voyeur in this worship space, with its lit prayer candles and liturgical schedule posted at the entrance. When another person enters and kneels in the front pew, my sense of being an intruder compels me outside. This part of the mission grounds contains the mission cemetery, and here, too, the newly paved walkways create a more directed sense of moving through the space than on my previous visits and the plantings are sparer. The bare dirt is punctuated by simple wooden crosses, stone-edged plots, and the occasional granite memorial marker. A sign informs me that it is believed that approximately two thousand people were buried here. Again I have the odd sensation of trespassing, a tourist unsure how to navigate this landscape of loss.

Staging Philanthropy

A fundamental premise of the missions is that their preservation and interpretation require resources. The relationship between those who have supported the missions and those who have shaped their narratives reveals the politics of preservation. Philanthropy has become part of the embodied experience of the missions through the positions of privilege inscribed in the landscape in the form of markers. Since the first restoration efforts of the late nineteenth century, contributions have been registered in a variety of ways. Bronze plaques honor major donors while more modest contributors are recognized in "buy a brick" or "plant an olive tree" programs. Other signs publicly acknowledge the years of service of staff and volunteers who gave of their time. Throughout the missions, the staging of philanthropy conveys several messages. It provides and reinforces the notion that the missions have been preserved because of the benevolence of donors. This public recognition of charitable acts conveys a notion that the missions are of value. It demonstrates that people have cared enough to commit their time and treasure for their upkeep, and it models that generosity for others. The staging of philanthropy is also a public record of support that also confers a certain social standing on the donors. Gifts from affinity groups such as the Gardening Angels, who help support San Juan Capistrano's restoration projects with the proceeds from their annual Flower, Garden, and Fine Art show, help create group cohesion and identity. For descendant groups such as Native Sons and Native Daughters of the Golden West, who gave the fountain at Mission San Gabriel, being recognized in markers registers a public acknowledgment of the connections between their ancestral genealogy and the heritage sites. Finally, the public donor recognition is testimony to the breadth of support for the sites across religious and secular groups. At San Juan Capistrano an "Empty Saddles" sculpture and memorial plaque is dedicated to the "fallen compadres" of the El Viaje de Portolá (the Portolá Riders), an invitation-only equestrian group that raises money for the mission. The reason for the memorial's placement at the mission is not made explicit, but the connection between the colonial heritage of the site and the philanthropic capacity and social standing of the group implies a symbiotic relationship.

Volunteers who give of their time and talent to tend the gardens similarly engage in the landscapes through the physicality of cultivating the soil and tending the plants, and their donated efforts are often acknowledged in annual reports, newsletters, and signage at the sites. An interview with a member of the Gardening Angels, the volunteer group that maintains the San Juan Capistrano gardens, reveals a similar understanding for the purpose and meaning of the landscapes by those tending them today. Jan Sorensen, who codirected the group in 2008 and also holds an MA in landscape architecture, commented that people see San Juan Capistrano as an "ideal garden." When they see the setting they say, "My God" and think it is beautiful. Sorensen reflected:

> Seeing how much people enjoy them [the gardens] is what has kept me going. All the Angels feel so good about being able to give people this experience. The gardens feel so calm and peaceful. People love it. It keeps the Gardening Angels going. . . . Most people feel this is how it always was. It has evolved into a haven, as it should. . . . It's a learning citadel. . . . I feel attached. I feel a part. I'm just a stranger from Wisconsin, but I don't feel a stranger. We're bringing out that Franciscan hospitality. It's a welcoming beauty.[44]

Performing Labor

While much of the evidence of the infrastructure required to support extensive agricultural and industrial operations at the colonial mission sites was destroyed by encroaching development of the original landholdings, some features, particularly those associated with the padres near the main church, were preserved or reconstructed. In contrast, those more closely associated with neophyte life and housing were usually demolished or their crumbling adobe ruins plowed under or paved over. As Mark Pedelty has pointed out, this selective reconstruction has resulted from the choices of mission restorers and administrators to preserve those aspects of the mission system that related to their own interests, while "destroying or neglecting those elements not considered to be part of their own heritage (e.g., Indian burial grounds and living quarters) or not compatible with their view of mission history (e.g., soldiers' barracks)."[45] This selective preservation has resulted in some telling treatments of industrial features that are integral to the history of Native labor and the industrial production at the missions. In some cases, such as the tanning vats at San Gabriel, the features were incorporated into the general garden plan, and at other missions, such as San Luis Rey and La Purísima, the lavanderías became the focal points for new gardens. A mural above a doorway in San Fernando's restored convento offers an interesting example of the incorporation of Native American labor into the mission aesthetic.[46] It depicts Native workers harvesting grapes from trailing vines (Figure 4.10). The

FIGURE 4.10. Grape harvest mural painted above a door in the Mission San Fernando convento, recorded by Geoffrey Holt for the Index of American Design, ca. 1935. National Gallery of Art, Washington, D.C.

biblical allusion to the parable of the workers in the vineyard (Matthew 20:1–16) could be read at a number of levels and may indeed in colonial times have had a didactic purpose, but in the contemporary context in which visitors see the mural as they tour the padres' quarters, an image of neophyte labor is transformed into a decorative wall treatment.

The aestheticization of labor has a long tradition in mission garden visual culture. The garden constructed in front of the Mission Trails Building at the 1939 Golden Gate Exposition included a *carreta* as an ornamental accent amidst the edged beds (Plate 11). A postcard of Mission Santa Barbara similarly evokes historic charm with a carreta parked near the fountain where frocked padres gather (Figure 4.11). This incorporation of utilitarian features into the mission garden persists in contemporary designs as well. Specifically, historic objects and industrial remains in the landscape are deployed as ways that reposition notions of labor by transforming them into decorative ornaments.[47] For example, at San Buenaventura the well is hung with potted ferns and the barred windows decorated with colorful window boxes. Portable artifacts are placed as in the gardens, such as mill grinding stones at San Diego (Figure 4.12) and metates at San Luis Rey (Figure 4.13). The

FIGURE 4.11. "The Old Mission, Santa Barbara, California," n.d. Postcard showing iconic elements of the mission visual culture: Franciscans posed by the fountain, colorful vines and peppertree, palms, and a carreta in the foreground. Photograph by Obert (3A-H607). Collection of the author.

FIGURE 4.12. Mill stones in the garden cemetery at Mission San Diego, 2008. Photograph by the author.

FIGURE 4.13. Display of metates at Mission San Luis Rey, 2008. Photograph by the author.

translation of these industrial features and tools of the colonial era into decorative garden elements is a ubiquitous practice, and yet it generally escapes comment either by garden interpreters or by visitors. The interpretive sign at the lavandería at Santa Barbara, for example, includes the following request: "Please treat this historic structure with respect as the achievement of the Chumash people who lived and worked here in Mission time. Landscaping around this lavandería features native and colonial period plant varieties. . . . Historic rose varieties are found interspersed with mission period cacti and perrenials [*sic*]."[48] At San Juan Capistrano, gardeners placed a reconstructed carreta laden with barrels as a focal point in a flower bed while using another as a planter (Figure 4.14). A well used as a decoration on a suburban lawn might seem merely banal, but in the former colonial setting of a mission its ornamentation contradicts its former role as an essential source of water and evidence of the labor it took to draw and carry that water. Bells that signaled the call to work, meals, and rest during the missions' early days grace the gardens today as if they were oversized wind chimes. Similarly, an olive press at San Buenaventura bedecked with pots of hanging ferns seems to trivialize both its historic function and the labor its intended use required. The distortion of the structure's aestheticization is amplified by a verse hanging from the roof: "Only one life / 'Twill soon be past / Only what's

FIGURE 4.14. A reconstructed carreta used as a container garden in the forecourt garden at Mission San Juan Capistrano, 2008. Photograph by the author.

done / for Christ will last." In these symbols, the forced labor system on which the missions were predicated is materialized as artifacts, both fake and real, and those objects are then repurposed as garden ornaments.

The labor it takes to maintain the contemporary landscapes is similarly rendered invisible. The tools, work sheds, irrigation systems, and hoses required to maintain the gardens are hidden from public view. Upon close inspection, an observant visitor can see the spigots and nozzles for irrigation systems, and on certain days, crews can be seen trimming vines or cleaning fountains, but for the most part the gardens appear to exist effortlessly in the rich soil and bountiful sunshine. While today's landscaping crews are not subjected to the same conditions or circumstances as the Native American neophytes of the colonial period, there is a similar entanglement of landscape, race, and social inequalities, particularly in how that work is made visible to the mission visitor. The same aesthetic that marginalizes the neophytes who worked in the fields historically also removes laborers who maintain the luxuriant gardens today. Several of the more prosperous missions, such as Santa Barbara and San Diego, have hired commercial landscape crews to maintain their grounds. The workers trim, weed, edge, and water, and then move on to their next job. The seduction of landscape implicit in these garden spaces is that they are timeless and effortless, removed from the human hands that produce them. The "lie of the land," as Don Mitchell has argued, is that the beauty of California's Edenic imagery has been possible only because of generations of migrant laborers.[49] The fertile productiveness and beauty of the missions' miniature Edens are predicated, like the broader agricultural landscape of California, on the invisibility of the labor that is indispensable to its very existence.

Performing Indigeneity

The story of the Native American past is conveyed at the missions explicitly in formal museum exhibits and implicitly in the landscape, and the main message is that at the missions two cultures became one.[50] The mission museum exhibits vary in how they account for that eventuality. Whether the Native American "other" dies off or simply disappears from the historical time line, the overall plotline is consistent. As Deana Dartt-Newton has established in her comparative analysis of mission, natural history, and tribal museums, mission interpretation celebrates the achievements of the Franciscans and objectifies the Native past.[51] Chelsea Vaughn has argued that the interpretation also marginalizes the lives of women, and particularly the issue of their confinement in monjeríos.[52] The broader conceptual paradigm of the mission interpretation is that its history is rooted in bringing civilization, with all its associated qualities of progress, reason, culture, and technology, to California. It was victorious over what was formerly called "primitive" and is now more obliquely associated with that which is static, emotional, wild, and natural. The distinctions between the European and Indigenous cultures are exaggerated and commodified in the exhibits' presentation of artifacts signifying, ostensibly, their contrasting technologies, languages, and lifeways. The exhibit narratives celebrate the achievements of illustrious persons associated with the missions, and the typical protagonists are the mission founders, those who led the preservation efforts, local notables, and occasionally one or two high-profile Native people associated with the mission. The history of the missions through time is presented as the inevitable course of civilization, the growth of faith communities, and restoration of buildings. It is the story of progress and it is good.

These messages are communicated through exhibits executed with varying degrees of professionalism, but all have similar artifacts associated with Native American "prehistory," colonial mission history, and the more recent restoration and parish growth. The key themes are the courage and sanctity of the founding padres, the success and productivity of the missions at their height, and the valiant efforts of the church over the years to maintain and restore the sites. The raw ingredients of the Native American story (stone tools, plants, and baskets) stand in contrast to the story of new technology (olive presses and firearms), new skills (books and musical manuscripts), and new belief systems (religious artifacts). Pedelty's analysis of the exhibit at Mission San José summarizes the typical celebratory interpretation and their presentation of Spanish–Indian relations as a teacher–student or "benevolent mentor" paradigm in which the Indians "sanctioned their own subordination as willing catechists and hungry students."[53]

The staging of Indigeneity in the landscape is much subtler, but carries many of the same messages as the exhibits. Some of the more pointed examples are the reconstructed Native dwellings or kíichas that have been built at six missions: San Juan Capistrano, La Purísima, San Gabriel, San Antonio de Padua, San Francisco, and Santa Barbara. As participatory heritage in collaboration with California Native people, the dwellings are significant both as indications of shared authority at the missions and as steps toward a more inclusive history. At San Juan Capistrano, for example, visitors can read that the kíicha was built "by the local tribe under the leadership of Tribal Chairman, Anthony Rivera, as a recent project celebrating those with ancestral ties to the Mission."[54] The audio tour description includes Teeter Maria Romero, a member of the Juaneño Band of Mission Indians, Acjachemen Nation, who describes how willows were used to make the bentwood structure and how the branches of the elderberry near the kíicha were carved into flutes. At Santa Barbara, the dwelling is accompanied by a hand-lettered sign that reads, "This Chumash traditional house was built May, 1997 by Chumash Indian descendants Joaqun Robles Whiteoak and Nashun Hoate. It depicts the type of house originally built by local Indians. By the early 1800s a village of larger adobe houses was built (over 200 homes) where the parking lot is currently located."

But these bent-pole and reed- or bark-covered structures are also problematic in that they register Native peoples in the landscape only in limited ways. The dwellings have minimal interpretive signage and little associated domestic material culture. Where signage is present, as at La Purísima and San Juan Capistrano, it focuses on the dwellings' construction and materials, describes accommodations for inclement weather, and explains that the stones positioned in front of the kíicha were used to grind acorns for food preparation. At San Gabriel the sign installed in conjunction with the *kiiy* constructed in 2008 is titled "Tongva and Where They Lived." It describes the "marvelous houses" they built of willows and reeds and acknowledges that after seven thousand years "their culture was almost wiped out in 1773 by the arrival of the Spanish." The relationship of the Native people, the Franciscans, and the current Claretian administrators of the site is somewhat ambiguously framed in the interpretive sign that states the Tongva were "used to build the San Gabriel Mission" and that their descendants built the kiiy in 2008, when it was dedicated "during the Claretian Missionaries Centennial Celebration of serving 100 years" at the mission.[55]

In some instances, the juxtaposition of the dwellings with other elements of the landscape creates uneasy visual relationships. At San Francisco, for example, the dwelling stands in the densely planted cemetery, near the statue of Junípero Serra. At Santa Barbara, the short-lived reconstructed dwelling stood in the corner of a parking lot (Figure 4.15). According to the director of the Santa Barbara Mission Museum, the Chumash who built the dwelling wanted to locate it there because of the proximity to the razed Indian dwellings and for security reasons, but its position behind the chain link fence also conveyed visual messages of confinement and marginalization.[56] At sites where the dwellings are incorporated into gardens, as at San Juan Capistrano, San Gabriel (Figure 4.16), and San Francisco, the landscaping around the kíicha or kiiy creates an ornamental edging and frames the dwelling as yet another focal point in the garden. At sites such as San Antonio de Padua, where it stands in the dry grass in the front of the mission near the ruins of outbuildings and the Indian cemetery, the isolated, empty structure gives little sense of the people who lived there or their circumstances. For people touring the missions, the interpretation of these dwellings is also limited in that they represent the domestic sphere and "daily life" rather than the institutional scale of the missions' agricultural and herding operations. As single, isolated structures, these reconstructions also give little sense of the scale of Native populations living at the colonial missions.

Another aspect of representing Native people in the mission landscapes has been the practice started at some sites in the late 1980s and 1990s of establishing "native plant" gardens and preserving "heritage plants." Like the kíicha, these gardens register the presence of Native Americans in the landscape in important ways, and they also raise some of the same issues of objectifying Native peoples,

FIGURE 4.15. Chumash traditional house reconstructed at Mission Santa Barbara in 1997 by Chumash Joaqun Robles Whiteoak and Nashun Hoate. Photograph by the author.

FIGURE 4.16. A kiiy constructed by members of the Gabrielino-Tongva Tribe in the Mission San Gabriel garden in 2008. Photograph by the author.

marginalizing the politics and power dynamics of colonialism, and absorbing their Indigenous cultural practices into the aesthetic of a western garden tradition. In emphasizing the potential of Native plants to reflect Indigenous heritage in the mission landscapes, Chief Anthony Morales Sr. stated during the Gabrielino-Tongva ceremony rededicating the Mission San Gabriel garden, "Here we are with the descendants of the ancestors for whom this memorial was dedicated. . . . Our parents, our grandparents inherited the mission cemetery. It's very meaningful, because now this garden here has our own native plants, our sages, our medicine plants"[57] (Figure 4.17).

While the native plant gardens, such as those in the front border at Santa Barbara (no longer under cultivation) and in the central courtyard of San Francisco Solano in Sonoma, were similarly intended to register the Native peoples in the landscape, they can create misleading impressions for visitors (Figure 4.18). Limited signage identifies the plant names and explains some of their traditional uses for cooking, utilitarian, or medicinal purposes, but the arrangement of the plants in beds with edging, intersecting paths, and labels follows standard gardening

FIGURE 4.17. Gabrielino-Tongva ceremony at Mission San Gabriel rededicating the garden, June 27, 2008. Photograph by Ellie Hidalgo, the *Tidings*.

FIGURE 4.18. Native plants garden at Mission Santa Barbara, 1997. Photograph by the author.

conventions. This presentation mirrors the metaphor of domesticating the wild Indian that pervades the dominant mission narrative and is illustrated graphically in the 1855 publication *The Annals of San Francisco* (Figure 4.19). The lithograph depicts the California Indian classified in three stages: wild on the right, partly civilized in the center, and "civilized and employed" on the left. Telling in the social evolutionary paradigm is the parallel between the domestication of plants and the "civilization" of the Indian. Within the minimalist setting of the three figures, the ground treatment is significant. Native plants grow at the feet of the uncivilized Indian while the civilized Indian is separated by a ridge of soil suggestive of a garden furrow. In a similar way, the representation of Native people through "native plant" gardens within the context of cultivated, bounded garden plots frames Indigenous peoples' traditional plant use in the paradigm of settler colonial narratives.

While these horticultural efforts relate to contemporary interests in heirloom varieties and local food movements, the symbolism of the plants in the context of the mission landscapes is more complex. One such ideologically charged aspect is the presentation of historic specimens as artifacts from or survivors of an earlier time but ascribed to non-Native historic actors or divorced from human agency altogether. These specimens, such as the historic grapevine at San Gabriel,

FIGURE 4.19. The equation of "savagery" with wild "nature" is illustrated in this engraving of "3 stages of civilization," published in Frank Soulé, John H. Gihon, and James Nisbet, *The Annals of San Francisco* (New York: Appleton, 1855).

the pepper tree at San Luis Rey, and the olive tree at San Antonio de Padua, are interpreted with signage identifying the species, the estimated age, and notes such as "planted by the padres," "the first pepper tree in California," or, as at San Gabriel, naming it the "Ramona Grape Vine, 1774" (Figure 4.20).[58] By highlighting and interpreting these specimens as ancient relics, the plants are presented as paeans to the padres for bringing horticulture to the state, and they locate the sites as the symbolic birthplaces of California's agricultural industry.[59] Largely absent from the interpretations are connections to the labors and lives of the Native people who tended the plants and harvested their fruits.

A third example of staging Indigeneity in the landscape is the representation of Native peoples as figures in the landscape, a practice that has been part of the mission garden designs since their creation in the early twentieth century and has expanded ever since. Numerous examples exist of statuary in the missions, and

FIGURE 4.20. The "Ramona Grape Vine" at Mission San Gabriel, 2013. Photograph by the author.

almost all of it depicts saints and historical figures; Saint Francis is the most popular of the saints, as befits the Franciscan order, and Junípero Serra is the most heavily represented historical figure.[60] Two statues in particular, Serra at San Juan Capistrano (1914) and in the Memory Garden at Mission San Fernando (1925), both incorporating young Indian males, inform the embodied experience of the landscapes through their representation of the relationships of Native people and the Franciscan missionaries. As was typical in the imagery of the 1920s and 1930s, the statues replicated the ideologies of social hierarchy through paternalistic representations of the adult Serra and Indian boys and the central civilized/wild construct contrasting the frocked monk and the minimally clothed youths (Figure 4.21).[61] They conveyed the benevolent view of missionization through Serra's protective stance and, at San Juan Capistrano, his gesture pointing to the cross.[62]

Such representative conventions were typical of imagery of California Native peoples that codified constructed markers of race and other social relations.[63] They also mirrored narratives of Father Serra's founding of the missions that highlight his trek into Alta California in other media. Specifically, these texts and images highlight the act of walking as an essential part of the establishment of the missions. For example, a 1949 fourth-grade textbook titles the chapter introducing the missions as "Father Serra Walks to California." It also includes the passage, "Father Serra was very, very happy to be going to California . . . [but he] was no longer young. He had a sore leg which hurt him all the time. . . . But he wanted to go to California. And he wanted to walk! He did walk all the way. Sometimes his leg hurt so much that he could not walk as fast as the others. Portolá wanted him to ride on a mule. But Father Serra said, 'No.'"[64] It is telling that in the 2008–9 restoration of the San Juan Capistrano sculpture, the bow that the Indian boy had been holding in the original 1913 sculpture was replaced with a walking stick.[65] For visitors to the mission gardens, the notion of "following in the footsteps of the padres" is both a common trope in mission narratives and an inalienable part of the experience. The performance of the space through the movement of bodies along the intersecting paths and the visual consumption of historical actors similarly striding across the landscape suggest the subtle but pervasive ways in which social relationships with the Franciscans are privileged in the experience of the gardens.

Memorialization, Time, and the Embodied Landscape

The dichotomy of wild versus civilized operates as a deep conceptual paradigm in the gardens, but it does not entirely account for their complex presentation of California's colonial legacy or how visitors negotiate this mediated landscape. While visitors experience the narratives through sequenced encounters with spaces and objects, an equally significant part of the embodied experience of the missions is the staging of time, both physically and metaphorically.[66] These time

FIGURE 4.21. Mission San Fernando, *Serra and Indian Boy,* by Sally Farnham, 1925. Photograph by the author.

markers take a variety of forms, including artifacts, plants, architectural features, sundials, inscriptions, memorials, and ruins, and they register time in different ways. Some materialize time literally. For example, a plaque at Mission San José commemorates the bicentennial of explorer Juan Bautista de Anza's 1775 expedition, while other markers recognize donors and honor seminal figures in the life of a parish. Other time markers are more symbolic. Historic specimens of heritage plants, such as grapevines, olive trees, and pepper trees, are labeled with their dates. At several missions architectural features, such as "the original nineteenth arch" at Santa Inés and the earthquake-damaged nave at San Juan Capistrano, have been stabilized and preserved as ruins in the landscape, visible artifacts of the former life of the missions in frozen testimony to their destruction and loss.[67] In contrast to the authenticity of historic plant material and original architectural elements, some time markers are fabricated. At Mission San Miguel, for example, the patina of age is implied by a failing-stucco-over-adobe treatment not only on the mid-twentieth-century fountain and entrance gate but also on the modern restrooms.

Other time markers metaphorically register the relationship between past and present, particularly in the gardens' operations as both shrine and memorial. At some point in their tour of the mission grounds, visitors encounter memorials or grave markers. Some are in formal cemeteries adjacent to the church, as at San Luis Rey, Santa Inés, San Miguel, and Santa Barbara, while at other missions, such as San Francisco, San Gabriel, and San Diego, graves and gardens are melded in the same space. Some have recently erected markers and others have headstones so eroded that the names are illegible. The cemeteries contain crypts and graves with individuals' identities and dates as well as memorials dedicated to the thousands of nameless Native Americans whose remains lie in unmarked or displaced graves. The sheer volume of deceased in such a short time required extreme solutions, as Alfred Robinson's 1829 and Thomas Farnham's 1840 descriptions of Santa Barbara attest. Robinson described the "charnel house, crowded with a ghastly array of skulls and bones."[68] Farnham's account makes clear the reason for the "ghastly array": "in order . . . that no Christian Indian may be buried in a less holy place, the bones, after the flesh had decayed, are exhumed and deposited in a little building in the corner of the premises."[69]

The missions reckon with the loss of Indigenous life differently, but most include some sort of memorial markers. The cemeteries are often commented upon by visitors as the part of the tour in which the past is made strongly personal through the mortal remains of those who died at the missions. For example, an engraved stone in the Mission San Diego garden reads "Memorial to Indians—California's First Cemetery—Mission San Diego," and embedded in the fountain base at Mission San Antonio de Pala is an engraved stone stating, "In this holy place lie the bodies of those who built the mission. May their souls rest in Peace.

Erected 1924." The cemeteries locate in powerful ways the tensions of the past and present, and convey the essence of the missions' contested history. They fix in visible and material terms both the human tragedy of Native American history and the final resting place of priests and brothers who left their own homelands to serve their church. The skull and crossed femurs above the passage between the cemetery and the church at Santa Barbara is vividly poignant and is one of the most photographed features of the site. It references not only the death that is part of the human condition but also the loss, anonymity, and pain that are the legacy of these colonial outposts. Its use of human bones is also particularly disturbing given Native American beliefs about the sacredness of human remains and requirements for burial. At Mission Santa Inés, the campo santo (cemetery; literally "holy ground") is dedicated to the "memory of over two thousand Chumash neophytes who built, lived, and died here" but contains only the marked headstones of those buried since secularization.

Critical to understanding the visitor experience of the mission gardens is understanding how time markers produce both victors and vanquished in the visual and ideological logic of the gardens. By materializing temporality in literal, symbolic, and metaphysical constructs of time, the markers perpetuate an ideology that naturalizes and legitimates California's colonial legacies.

Although each mission has its unique rendering of the mission garden template, a closer examination of one site, Mission San Gabriel, exemplifies the interplay of ideology and the materiality of time in the narrative and structure of visitor experiences. The contemporary Mission San Gabriel garden stands in a rectangular courtyard created by the stone mission church to the south, the new parish church on the north, the school and priests' residence to the west, and the parking lot to the east. The design contains elements of the classic mission garden template—edged walks, geometric beds, and splashing fountains—but it is divided into sections or garden rooms, rather than the more common pattern of a patio garden organized around a central fountain. Roughly characterized, these sections are the cemetery and memorial garden on the south third, the fountain and Peace Garden leading to the "Court of the Missions" in the center, and a cactus garden along the north third.

The aesthetic is an amalgamation of classic mission garden elements combined with the vernacular traditions of Mexican-influenced gardens such as folk art and specimen cacti and succulents. There are also elements of Catholic iconography such as a small shrine to the Virgin of Guadalupe. The eclectic landscape also includes a demonstration kitchen, an old winery, and the ruins of large tanning vats.[70] The San Gabriel Mission garden's spatial logic and visual aesthetics reflect both the design tradition of California mission gardens and a distinctive expression of the mission's local community and caretakers. Similarly, the underlying ideology implicated in the materiality of time at Mission San Gabriel can be read as participating both in the dominant narrative of California's colonial history and in the unique iteration of the mission's particular story.

Examining the materiality of time at the San Gabriel Mission requires first accounting for its contemporary context. Like most of the missions, it is owned and administered as a Catholic parish, yet also designed and experienced as a touristic landscape. Visitors from a wide range of backgrounds and beliefs systems make the trek to the mission as part of secular and sacred pilgrimages, parish festivals and tribal ceremonies, field trips, coach tours, and casual visits. School groups, tourists, parishioners, and members of the local Gabrielino Tongva Tribe all bring distinct perspectives to their experiences of the space.[71]

Mission San Gabriel's time markers at their most literal level inscribe time in the form of dates and other chronological signifiers that historicize and naturalize the twentieth-century garden as part of the mission era. Dedicatory plaques not only record the specific dates but also imply that the garden is a restoration of an earlier garden to its former glory. Father Raymond Catalan's memorial plaque, for example, calls him a "Restorer of the mission gardens." The inscriptions associate the garden space primarily with a distinctly western rather than Indigenous heritage, as the 1940 fountain dedication "in the Memory of the Pioneer Mother and Father" exemplifies. These markers conflate chronologies so that the colonial past, the restoration history, and the contemporary landscape are elided.

Time is also registered literally through didactic, interpretive panels placed throughout the garden that cite dates and quote historic sources. They also marginalize Native history and its contemporary consequences, while highlighting the agency of the padres.[72] For example, a panel quotes Governor Don Pedro Fages's 1787 report: "It cannot be denied that the activity and efforts of the mission fathers have equaled the fertility of the field cultivated by them. . . . In this way they have been able to provide abundantly for the maintenance of its Indians."[73] The narrative also presents Indian labor in a positive light and, by using passive voice, minimizes the arduous and unpleasant nature of tasks such as hide processing. For example, one sign notes that the quadrangle was used for "trades" taught to the Indians. Another interpretive panel for tallow rendering positions the cauldron as the historic actor and completely avoids mention of those performing the labor (Figure 4.22): "The enormous cauldron is one of seven used in the early days . . . which would receive fat taken from the slaughtered cattle, then wheeled by 'careta' to the fire pits . . . to be rendered. Then the hot cauldrons, one by one were lifted out by pulley and wheeled to their respective workshops for candle making and soap making."[74] This benign description conveys little of the intense heat, noxious smell, arduous labor, and constant risk involved in boiling down cattle for their fat. And nowhere in the interpretive text is there any reference to the systems of coercion and punishment for those who did not comply. As Father Zephyrin Engelhardt's defense of the treatment of the neophytes argues, while

FIGURE 4.22. Mission San Gabriel tallow cauldron, 2008. Photograph by the author.

Spanish law "restricted the application of the lash to twenty-five stripes," the missionaries "like true fathers who love their children . . . were loath to inflict corporal punishments, wherefore the whole dose of twenty-five lashes was seldom applied, save in the cases of concubinage, repeated stealing of valuables, refusal to work, etc."[75] These historical sources alongside contemporary presentations of artifacts disrupt connections between past and present by marginalizing native peoples and emphasizing the Franciscans' agency. The effect of this representation of Indians as "frozen in time" in a "historic" garden that is simultaneously living and growing creates a colonial apologetics narrative that resists critique.[76] By presenting the Native peoples as residing in the past only, the mission landscapes minimize or altogether exclude contemporary Native peoples, their dynamic cultures, and their ongoing struggles for rights and recognition.

Another set of literal time markers consists of the memorials that reference the presence of untold dead buried around the mission property but identify time in distinctly different ways, depending on whose deaths are being commemorated. While the priests' graves are individually identified with birth and death dates, the memorials to Native Americans are anonymous and corporate. A marker at the base of the 1935 cross, for example, dedicates it "in memory of the

6,000 Shoshone–Gabrieleño Indians buried within the confines of the stone walls R.I.P."[77] As at other missions, at San Gabriel the circumstances of the deaths of the colonizers and the colonized are generally ignored. There are no indications of the mortality rates due to diseases introduced during colonization, no mention of the sexually transmitted diseases that decimated birthrates. There are no oppressors and oppressed, no colonizers and colonized, merely the markers indicating the common status of those who are long departed.

Another category of marker registers the passage of time and the relations of past and present symbolically. A sign at the entrance to the garden, for example, reminds visitors that they are standing on "sacred ground" where are "treasured the riches of two civilizations blended together." The rhetoric of a valorized mission history impregnated in the fabric of the sites echoes an account in the *Los Angeles Times* of Father Camilo Torrente's 1921 exhumation of the padres at San Gabriel when he evoked the imagery of "holy men who spilled their life blood on the soil of California." The reporter continued: "So, stone by stone, Father Torrente built a monument himself, and planted the old wooden cross that was used in the provisional church. . . . And so it stands—a crude, but eloquent tribute to those great souls who have passed beyond, but whose dust and bones have mingled with the soil of San Gabriel where they lived and labored and died that civilization might come to California and be ours today."[78] The idea of becoming one with the earth is a common trope, but the image of "dust and bones . . . mingled with the soil" so that California might be civilized is performed in the garden space in a way that transcends a mere "ashes to ashes" allusion to mortality. The embodied experience of the San Gabriel garden is tactile and visceral. The dust clings to one's shoes and the scent of roses fills one's nose. The visitor's encounter is with the commingled heritage of colonialism rendered in the lush beauty of a garden, and the seduction of the garden design makes the two aspects of the mission not only inseparable but indistinguishable.

A third set of time markers mediates the tension of monument and memorial by materializing time in a metaphysical sense. These time markers acknowledge the pain and loss of the Native peoples, but at the same time they elide that cost with the existential human questions of mortality and the afterlife. They embed the Native American dead within the context of fleeting human existence, both owning up to the consequences of missionization and also diluting its implications for admission of guilt by framing the issue as a universal one. Some of these metaphysical time markers are literal; for example, the sundial in the center of San Gabriel's Court of the Missions bears the Latin inscription "Horae omnes vulnerant. Ultima Nect," which translates as, "Every hour wounds. The last one kills."[79] Similarly, the scripture passage on the cemetery entrance, crowned with a skull and crossbones, literally marries the mortality of the flesh with the promise of eternal life in the Lord: "I know that my Redeemer liveth. . . . I also am to rise again—from the earth and dust . . . and in my flesh I shall see God" (quoting Job 19:25).

One of the most powerful metaphysical time markers is a mural painted in 1939 at the rear or western boundary of the garden.[80] In the painting, titled *Christ Teaching,* three arches frame a triptych in which an angel and the Queen of Heaven, attended by an acolyte and a choirboy, respectively, look toward the center image of nuns teaching schoolchildren with the figure of Christ standing over them, his hands raised in a gesture of blessing (plate 12). The entire scene is set in a colorful garden with the distinctive San Gabriel bell tower in the distance. The marriage of the earthly and heavenly worlds invoked obliquely in the rest of the garden is rendered in vivid color. The mural is positioned so that it can be seen through one of the garden's few axial views down the grape arbor in the campo santo.

In the San Gabriel Mission context, the faith-based message of the mural not only resonates with the Claretian Fathers' mission of service but also creates an image of life and afterlife merged in a mission garden.[81] Past, present, and future are united in the promise of salvation. The mural's fair-skinned figures and contemporary dress are far removed from the neophytes who lived and worked at the mission, but the conflation of time brings their deaths into the same fate we all face and their mortality into the theological realm of eternal life. The colonial conundrum of conquest is resolved in the materialization of eternal salvation, the very promise that drew the Franciscans to baptize the Indians to begin with. In this mural, the materialization of temporality becomes the most profoundly ideological in its allusion to the immaterial.

The oasis of artillery, foliage, and blossoms in the Peace Garden reveals the conflicts implicit in this valorized postcolonial site, but time markers placed throughout the garden provide a unifying narrative (Figure 4.23). Markers commemorating garden "restorations" celebrate and naturalize the 1930s transformation of a utilitarian workspace and burial ground into a romanticized Mediterranean Revival garden. Other interpretive markers distance the colonial legacy, privilege the Franciscan padres, and present Native peoples as a vanished race. Still other time markers elide past, present, and afterlife so that the culpability of the colonial legacy of San Gabriel is made visible in the acknowledgment of lives lost, but redeemed through the claims of eternal reward. The political and ideological implications of time in the San Gabriel garden might seem a rather obvious reading of the landscape from a twenty-first-century critical perspective and a redundant exercise in an age when postmodernist sensibilities to injustice and the politics of memory seem so heightened. And yet the fact remains that the mission continues to be a prominent landmark in the California heritage landscape. Thousands of visitors, including numerous school groups, tour the garden annually and are greeted by the following welcoming text:

> Saludos Amigos
>
> We witness here the beginning of a new civilization wherein Christianity was introduced to a pagan sphere some 190 years ago. For nearly two centuries this garden of peace has been a haven for the weary travelers, adventurous pioneers and builders of the magical desert. Here trod the daring Redskin, the blithe spirited Mexican, the valiant Spanish soldier, and the venturesome "Americano."
>
> Here you are welcome—forget your cares and troubles as you re-live the early days of the western world.[82]

The Discursive Practices of Gardening

While less visually prominent, an important aspect of the embodied experience of the mission landscape is gardening itself. As noted in the discussion of labor in the garden, the work of gardening is done by a mix of staff, volunteers, and contracted workers, but the practice of engaging with the missions through gardening is a long-standing one. When the king and queen of Belgium traveled to Santa Barbara in 1919, a report of their visit to the mission in the *New York Times* noted, "After mass, the party filed into the mission church yard, where the king planted a cypress and an orange tree to memorialize his visit there."[83] Clearly,

FIGURE 4.23. Peace Garden at Mission San Gabriel, 2008. Photograph by the author.

the act of planting resonates at a number of levels. It is a way to participate in the lineage of cultivators who have gone before and to leave a behind a legacy that will continue to flourish amidst the other plants, becoming a part of the garden to be enjoyed for years to come. And the power of planting to create bonds extends beyond the sites themselves. For example, mission administrators make plants available both as a way to raise funds and to engage visitors with the spaces. When Mission San Juan Capistrano offered seeds from the gardens for sale in the shops, they sold well and a staff member commented that "people liked the idea of planting something that had come from the mission in their own gardens."[84] At Mission San Antonio de Padua one of the four main annual fund-raising events is the Annual Cutting of the Roses in which for a donation visitors receive rose cuttings from the Mission Padre's Garden to take home and propagate.[85]

A particularly interesting gardening practice at the missions in recent years has been the creation of heritage species gardens. A leader in this effort has been the Huerta Project at Mission Santa Barbara. In a partnership between the mission and Santa Barbara City College's Career Horticultural Program, volunteers have been identifying surviving "refugee" plants from mission days and propagating them in a huerta (garden) on the mission grounds. Since December 1998 this group of Hispanic, Chumash, and Anglo volunteers has collected cuttings and stone fruits from surviving species such as olive, mission-era grape varieties, apricot, plum, and lilac.[86] By rooting cuttings of plants such as pomegranate, rose, and grape and grafting the stone fruit species onto mature modern cultivar trees, the huerta now boasts more than four hundred historic-era plants (Figure 4.24).

As with the native plants gardens, however, the huerta volunteers focus on propagating and preserving historic species, but they do not conceive of their work as political. And when the historical significance of the horticultural experiments is raised, they continue to privilege the Spanish colonizers. In his summary of the heritage plants program, Jerry Sortomme concludes, "Imagine re-growing plants genetically identical to those raised by the mission padres."[87] Coverage in a local newspaper, the *Santa Barbara Independent,* similarly notes, "A project is underway . . . to recreate the huerta, or garden, where the friars cultivated the food and utilitarian crops they relied on."[88] While the article elsewhere acknowledges the labor of Native Americans in constructing the missions, the notion of the padres tending their gardens continues to be a powerful image. In the huerta, as in the other landscapes of the mission, the lives of the Native Americans at the missions are minimized in deference to the colonizers' experiences. The planting plan and interpretation of the huerta garden at Santa Barbara are predicated on prevailing winds and sun to create microclimates against the hillside. The fact that the mission is located in the area of the former neophyte adobe residences, or that the specimens such as the orange tree planted in the mission's courtyard from which huerta volunteers are taking grafts is part of a 140-year-old landscape

FIGURE 4.24. The Huerta Project, Mission Santa Barbara, 2013. Photograph by the author.

design history in its own right, is not germane to the organizers' conception of their work. Just as the kíicha dwellings and the manos and metates are divorced from their historical context and repositioned in the ornamental settings of the gardens, so too are these historic plant specimens objectified as botanical material relevant for their lineage, but not their associations with colonialism's imposition of agrarian subsistence and labor practices.

Embodied Devotion

As we have seen, the mission landscapes have always had distinct audiences, and those audiences have always exercised social agency. Just as in colonial times the neophytes moved through and perceived the landscape in very different ways than did the colonizing explorers, soldiers, and priests, so too do contemporary audiences have different perceptions and practices. Like "dual economies" that operate as parallel systems in the same country, the mission landscapes operate very differently for their constituencies, particularly for members of local faith communities, those who visit the sites on pilgrimage or retreat, or come as a part of their spiritual practice or religious heritage.[89] These multivalent, layered landscapes are not spatially distinct, but are instead defined by the needs, desires, and behaviors of those moving within them. Recognizing the interests of these contemporary constituents is vital to understanding the evolution of the contemporary missions as devotional landscapes as well as their classic "mission garden" heritagescape.

Many of the missions serve as the spiritual home for the faith communities associated with the parishes and institutions that own and administer the mission sites.[90] These uses are reflected spatially in the form of active cemeteries, spaces and facilities for parish social gatherings and fiestas, and the Stations of the Cross for spiritual meditations (Figure 4.25). Parishioners engage with the sites in ways that are distinct from those of tourist visitors. They live locally, attend regularly (albeit with varying frequency), have friendships with each other, and pastoral relationships with the active clergy. The mission landscape for these people is the place of their faith community, their church home. For missions that serve as parish churches, the congregants' performances of the mission spaces follow the patterns of the liturgical and social life of the parish. Rather than the wondering gaze of the tourist, parishioners move in and through the familiar spaces with specific purposes, whether in liturgical processions, posing for family wedding photos, walking the Stations of the Cross, grilling meat for parish fiestas, or visiting the graves of loved ones. These contemporary concerns do not negate the significance of the missions as historic sites, however. Many parishioners contribute to

FIGURE 4.25. Stations of the Cross, Mission Santa Inés, 2008. Photograph by the author.

the preservation efforts and volunteer as docents. At the same time, however, sharing their parish home with visiting tourists can lead to conflicts. For example, Richard Rodriguez's memoir includes an account of his visit to San Juan Capistrano. Rodriguez writes of how, after he entered the Serra Chapel, he knelt "to say a prayer for Nancy—a prayer that should plead like a scalpel." His meditation was soon interrupted by "camera flashes at the rear of the church. . . . A group of tourists has entered the sanctuary to examine the crucifix; one of them laughs. I cross myself ostentatiously, I genuflect, I leave the chapel."[91]

At the missions the resident religious and parishioners move in a different way about the landscape than do tourists.[92] Barrier, chains, gates, and signs, such as the one guarding the "Sacred Garden" at Mission San Luis Rey, explicitly restrict access to private areas while other divisions are more subtly managed. For example, the modern Stations of the Cross at Santa Barbara and Santa Inés are off to the side of the missions and out of the direct path of most visitors, but they are available for the personal piety practices of the parishioners who can maintain some semblance of privacy away from the tour buses and school groups. The devotional landscape is managed through temporal control as well as spatial segregation. For example, churches are closed to tourists during services, and at San Juan Capistrano religious processions take place in the garden after public hours.[93]

Devotional landscapes are created not only by spatial and temporal control but also by the performance of the spaces by those who understand them and engage with them as part of their spiritual lives. The shrine to the Virgin of Guadalupe at San Gabriel may appear to some to be a display of colorful tile, but to others it is a sanctified place of prayer and solace. Murals, such as those painted on the convento walls at San Gabriel, are loaded with religious imagery and references to local people and landmarks that are inscrutable to an outsider. There are also variations on the inclusion of religious iconography distinct to the traditions of the particular order at each mission. For the Verona Fathers at Mission San Antonio de Pala, the Italian statuary they collected during their visits home bring a flavor of the "old country" to their Southern California mission garden, while a mural depicts the local Pala Indians and their homeland with features that are likely recognizable to tribal members.[94] In imagery and in practice, these embellishments created not just a pleasing aesthetic but a home that speaks to ways of being and belonging to those who live, work, and worship there.

This distinction between the tourist and the devotional landscape is recognized locally and mapped virtually. Most missions structure their websites into distinct parish-related or historic-mission-related information, either as separate pages tabbed on the main page or completely distinct sites. For example, the San Carlos Borroméo de Carmelo Mission website home page in 2013 welcomed visitors to "a place of worship, education, history and art" and invites people to "choose a destination below to start your journey" by clicking a tab for either "Parish," "School," "Museum," or "Store."[95] San Juan Capistrano's website similarly recognized this distinction with a separate page for "Catholic Visitors" acknowledging that the mission's purpose was "to spread the Catholic faith and tradition to the Native Americans." It describes the Serra Chapel as the mission's "heart, or spiritual center" where "generations and generations of Catholics have celebrated mass, attended weddings, baptisms, and funerals. The Serra Chapel houses memories generations past, and future."[96] And this virtual sacred landscape extends beyond parish websites. For example, the Franciscan Pilgrimage Program offered California mission pilgrimages and provided a wiki page for former pilgrims where they can share their ongoing reflections and spiritual journeys following a mission pilgrimage, as well as continue the fellowship formed during the tour.[97]

Perhaps nowhere is this duality of the secular and the sacred meaning of mission materiality more evident than in the consumption of the Serra statues at the missions. The convention of the figure of the lone priest in the garden that is prominent in the mission visual culture has been perpetuated in the contemporary mission gardens with an initiative to place a statue of Junípero Serra at every mission. Serra statues were erected in several of the early twentieth-century mission garden designs, such as the San Juan Capistrano and San Fernando examples, but the effort became more systematic in 1991, when William H. Hannon, a Southern California real estate developer, launched a campaign to place statues of Serra at every mission and at other associated sites. Hannon's intent in commissioning the sculpture was to "promote the spirit and contributions of Father Serra."[98] The bronze sculptures stand in various positions in the mission landscapes. At Missions Santa Inés, San Gabriel, San Rafael, San Antonio de Padua, and Santa Barbara, the Serra statue is positioned near the main entrance (Figure 4.26). At other missions the statue is in the garden, as at Santa Cruz, San Buenaventura, Carmel, San Diego, and Mission Dolores. The statues are typically blessed and dedicated when they are placed at a mission.

Hannon was a proponent of Serra's canonization and held his Catholic allegiances openly, but in other respects the figures reflect the multivalences of mission heritage more broadly. Hannon, for example, articulated a connection between his own profession and Serra's: "The man was the first real estate developer in Los Angeles if you think about it. Serra helped to settle what is now the Valley. It's important to remember where we came from."[99] The sculptures' contexts suggest a certain symbolic complexity. In the front of missions they stand as welcoming doorman and sentry. As marker and signal at the approach to the missions they also appear to lay claim to Serra's role as valorized founder, regardless of the controversy surrounding his legacy and canonization process.[100] Within the gardens, the figures become both ornament and owner, referencing the same visual tradition as the frocked friars in the postcards. They stand as silent, static,

FIGURE 4.26. Serra statue at Mission Santa Barbara with flowers placed at the feet, 2013. Photograph by the author.

costumed interpreters performing the presence of the sites' principal historical actors. Within the context of the touristic consumption of the sites, the sculptures can also be seen as part of the construction of the exotic other representing the frocked figure from another time or religion.

The meaning of the reception of these statues is difficult to assess, but they are highly visible markers. In some respects they are consistent with other religious art in that people engage with them as devotional objects. At Mission Santa Barbara, for example, an offering of flowers was laid at Serra's feet.[101] Other examples are more idiosyncratic. The Hannon Foundation website recounts the placement of statues in schools: "At dedication ceremonies, where a school's student body often was assembled, William would encourage the children to rub Father Serra's toe for good luck. He would tell the children, 'After all, he walked all across California, so those toes are lucky; maybe rubbing his toe will help on your next big test.'"[102] At the missions it is not uncommon to see tourists posing for photographs as they stand next to Serra (Figure 4.27), suggesting that the sculptures have become their own hyperreality and an anticipated part of the mission experience. They, like the gardens, mediate the sacred and the secular, and they perform the work their distinct audiences require of them. They also mask the contested history of Serra and the missions, fixing that meaning instead in his presentation as a classic, figural sculpture, part of the long tradition of valorizing portraiture.[103] Finally, the Serra statues stand along with the tourist and

FIGURE 4.27. Couple posing for a photograph in front of the Serra and Indian Boy sculpture in the Mission San Fernando Memorial Garden, Brand Park, 2008. Photograph by the author.

parishioner alike as a performer of the space, inhabiting the beautiful, peaceful landscape, with walking staff in hand, a fellow wayfarer on the journey.[104]

Handmaidens of Amnesia

William Henry Hudson eulogized the affective experience of visiting the missions, arguing that "these things have a subtle and peculiar power—a magic not to be resisted by any one who turns from the highways of the modern world to dream among the scenes where the old padres toiled and died."[105] The complexity of the spaces and their reception by diverse audiences reveal the contestations and collusions of interests that both resist and perpetuate the postcolonial fictions of the sites. In his description of the "Protestant" restorations of La Purísima and their marginalization of Catholic history in which preservationists have "become handmaidens of amnesia," Rodriguez noted that "a secular altar guild that will not distinguish between a flatiron and a chalice, between a log cabin and a mission church, preserves only strangeness."[106] But a similar criticism can be applied to all the missions that transform spaces of colonization into gardens and historical objects into ornaments.

The overwhelming material witness of the landscapes is clear testimony to a highly politicized historical narrative inscribed in the missions, but the embodied experience of the landscape presents a much more complex view of their operations. In addition to their metaphorical and ideological transposition of colonial history, the missions are also active, living landscapes where stakeholders have sought resources and status within the shifting power relations of California's political and social structures. The subtle and peculiar power of the spaces is not so much that they resist critique but that they embrace and neutralize it. Boucher prefaced his account of his family's mission tour vacation with the comment, "And what a history it is—framed by both the holy and the horrible, marked by moments of individual altruism and mass greed." He embarked on the trip acknowledging the subjectivity of the mission story in which "fourth-grade teachers filter out many of the harshest details and, at the missions themselves, the Roman Catholic Church emphasizes the good works and California achievements."[107] But as clearly as Boucher acknowledges the ambiguity and amnesia of the mission experience, in the end he recommends that others take the same journey, reflecting that the trip yielded not only "enough answers to get our daughter that good grade, but we also found out more about the place we call home."[108]

CONCLUSION

Third Spaces and the Future of Mission Memory Practices

Critical Spatial Memory Practices

The California missions have been and continue to be many things to many people. They are monuments to the origins and accomplishments of California's western civilization. They are memorials commemorating the lives of those who lie buried there. They are faith communities and field trip destinations. They are workplaces and retreat centers. They are sites on the National Register and attractions on motel tourist information displays. They are beloved and despised. They have been called sites of genocide, sites of conscience, and holy pilgrimage sites.[1] In spite of this multivocality and contestation, mission landscape design has remained remarkably static over much of the past century. The exclusionary, triumphalist rhetoric of California boosters in the late nineteenth and early twentieth centuries can be understood in the context of social and political discourse when marginalization of the subaltern was the norm, but why does it persist in the twenty-first century?

In contrast, other forms of representing California colonial and Indigenous pasts, such as scholarly literature, public exhibits, and school curricula, have begun to invoke a more critical examination of California's colonial past and its implications for diverse constituencies, particularly for Native peoples.[2] For example, during the 1992 Quincentennial Edward Castillo (Cahuilla), who was at the time chair of the Department of Native American Studies at Sonoma State University, countered the celebrations of Columbus's "discovery" by observing instead that the anniversary

> will underscore the profound loss of our beloved homeland and the cruel dismemberment of our native cultures. For years, California schoolchildren have been presented with a nostalgic, rose-tinted picture of gentle, brown-robed Franciscans bringing deprived and primitive Indians to the missions to learn an orderly,

> wholesome, agricultural way of life . . . completely overlooking the suffering of Indian people, and oblivious to the soundness and validity of Indian ways of life.[3]

Native scholars have not only critiqued dominant narratives and heritage practices, but also presented alternative paradigms for understanding the complex hybridity and political entanglements of settler colonial contexts. For example, Indigenous studies scholar Doreen Martinez (Mescalero Apache, Mexican, and Dutch lineage) has described her works' intent to disrupt "modernity's reliance on *Indians as others.* This disruption forces the development and recognition of new maps, that is, new ways of understanding locations of culture, identity representations, interpretations of cultural commodities, and the *intelligence of participation* in the third space."[4]

In addition to decolonizing academic methodologies and advancing Indigenous scholarship, these forums often disrupt the celebratory narratives and homogeneous stories of erasure in creative ways.[5] Native American artists have for decades created work intended, as artist Frank LaPena (Wintu) wrote following the exhibition of his *Diaspora: California Indians* at the Venice Biennale in 1999, "to let the world know what happened in California to the indigenous population and to point out that survival issues are still of concern."[6] For example, in 1988 three Native artists, David Avalos, James Luna, and Deborah Small, along with historian William Weeks, collaborated on *California Mission Daze* at the Installation Gallery in San Diego.[7] According to LaPena, the mixed-media installation combined video, audio, objects, texts, and images in order to "offer new perspectives and to challenge conventional viewpoints of history"[8] at a time when Junípero Serra was being proposed for beatification. The installation appropriated elements from California mission architecture and landscapes. By layering objects, names, and iconography drawn from Native cultures, the artists repositioned familiar mission forms in ways that provoked closer examination.[9] In one work re-creating a small cemetery, the artists combined crosses and headstones with shells, white pebbles, and dripping wax candles to assemble a miniature landscape that evokes the colliding practices of funerary rituals and the universal of grief (Plate 13). The goal of the exhibit was, as Luna explained, to get people to "stop for a minute and think about the information that they're getting."[10] For Small, the exhibit was also a chance to challenge the received imagery of the missions and how they shape memory. The critical issue, she argued, is "knowing *how* we should remember these things. Whose interpretations are we going to look at and whose are we going to present? What kinds of images are going to be in textbooks?"[11]

L. Frank, a Tongva-Acjachemen artist, writer, activist, and self-described "decolonizationist,"[12] has similarly used art to offer ironic and often sharply humorous critiques from a Native perspective. Her artistic production includes single-panel graphics or cartoons regularly contributed to *News from Native California,* a selection of which has been published in her book *Acorn Soup.*[13] These drawings offer stinging commentary on a variety of topics related to Native history, including the missions. The text on the drawings is always written backward and requires careful attention to decipher, an intervention that, as Susan Bernardin points out, not only befits the contrarian intent of the art but also "draws sharp attention to other kinds of redirections and reversals, namely in point of view and place of viewer-readers" by decentering and defamiliarizing the English text.[14] For example, one image depicts the entrance to what might be a mission colonnade or a campo santo mausoleum with her trademark mirror image writing on a sign next to it reading "Franciscan Showers" (Figure C.1). Her image of her recurring protagonist Coyote dressing a scarecrow in Franciscan garb amidst the furrows of a tilled field has the caption "Be Afraid. Be Very Afraid"[15] (Figure C.2). After years of working largely within the Native arts and cultural revival circles, Frank is now also presenting her work in dominant-culture institutions. For example, her oral history is part of *California Indians: Making a Difference,* the California Museum's first collaborative exhibition including Native voices from one hundred groups across the state.[16]

Along with other Native artists, Frank also contributed to an exhibition at the Huntington Library on the life and legacy of Junípero Serra. The curators' goal for the exhibition and symposium coinciding with the three-hundredth anniversary of Serra's birth was to take a holistic approach to the range of perspectives

FIGURE C.1. L. Frank, "Franciscan Showers," *The Outcome of Culture Clash. Mission Times* series, *Acorn Soup,* 26. Used with permission of the artist.

FIGURE C.2. L. Frank, "Be Afraid. Be Very Afraid." *Mission Times* series, *Acorn Soup,* 32. Used with permission of the artist.

on his historical import.[17] Native artists, including James Luna, L. Frank, Linda Yamane, and Gerald Clarke, created works that conveyed decolonizing views of the mission past. Luna's video piece included a montage of images from archival sources, the mission records, and family photographs that makes tangible the enduring presence of Native peoples. Cocurator Steven Hackel noted that the exhibition sought to present "a story of conflicting, blending, and overlapping cultures, of imperial expansion and human drama and loss, and then, finally, of the perseverance and survival of not only European institutions in California, but the California Indians who were the focus of Serra's missions."[18] While these alternative narratives challenge the unyielding insistence of the mission-as-garden imagery, they also introduce possibilities for what the mission landscapes might become.

Heritage Sites as Third Spaces

Building on the formative work of Edward Soja, who promoted translating spatial theory into active political practice, archaeologists, preservationists, historians, and geographers have not only theorized such critical heritage practices but also implemented the ideas.[19] In a related argument, Dell Upton has pointed out that scholars working in various ways on historic sites are part of "the mechanism that manufactures heritage" and should seek to "understand heritage, tradition, and modernity as strategic political positions, rather than as fixed or essential qualities of sites or cultural practices, much less of individual identities."[20] To fail to address social inequalities is to be complicit in the dominant narratives that perpetuate those injustices. Recent attention to the entanglements of archaeologists in absences, omissions, and erasures similarly demonstrates that "archaeology can also be a discipline of forgetting" as well as recovery and preservation.[21] Critical heritage scholars have been pursuing more equitable and inclusive approaches by recognizing the diverse values, relationships, and epistemologies of heritage contexts around the world. For instance, in *Counterheritage* Denis Byrne investigated people-object relationships in Asian societies and posits the need for entirely different heritage practices in response to their beliefs of objects' spiritual potency and their assimilation in local economies.

Museums and other cultural organizations in communities with contested histories around the world have likewise used juxtaposition, community curation, and other collaborative approaches to democratize and diversify interpretation at heritage sites. Whether using the term or not, they have created "Third Spaces" in which perspectives of colonizers and the colonized are brought into conversation.[22] There are powerful examples of the potential of this Third Space model. Fred Wilson's *Mining the Museum* exhibition at the Maryland Historical Society in 1992 included an installation of objects from the permanent collection to reveal the systematic marginalization of African Americans and Native Americans. The exhibition was effective not only in deconstructing the history of persecution and oppression masked in the museum's interpretive program but also in spurring conversation among visitors, docents, and museum administrators.[23] Historian David Thelen, who has studied the uses of history in U.S. museums, observed that "the most thought provoking dialogues seemed to arise when the situation combined familiarity and safety with the intriguing potential of differences in such a way that individuals did not feel compelled to identify with a single role or group."[24] These kinds of interventions are particularly resonant at heritage sites where the cultural landscapes and built environments of oppression, terrorism, or tragedy become didactic spaces.[25] For example, the District Six Museum in Cape Town has transformed a church on the edge of the neighborhood razed in South Africa's campaign of apartheid into a site of public memory. A series of exhibitions, such as the "memory cloth," oral histories, and forums have created an international model for using heritage sites to address injustice and to support healing and reconciliation.[26] These kinds of projects usually embrace collaboration and shared authority. Community-based archaeology projects are burgeoning around the United States with work such as Paul Mullins's African American community archaeology project in Indianapolis, Carol McDavid's Levi Jordan Plantation project in Brazoria, Texas, and Christopher Matthews's investigation of Setauket's historic Native and African American community on Long Island, New York.[27] Museums and historians are similarly embracing a shared-authority model of cultural curation, as evidenced in the case studies in Bill Adair, Benjamin Filene, and Laura Koloski's *Letting Go?* and in Paul Shackel and Erve Chambers's *Places in Mind*. These projects not only recognize the power relations in historical memory practices, they also embrace the productive outcomes of sharing authority with descendant communities for the richness of the interpretation as well as the engagement of broader audiences.

The idea of using history as a way to address social justice issues has been embraced by heritage sites around the world as a form of professional practice identified as "sites of conscience." There are more than two hundred members of the International Coalition of Sites of Conscience whose mission is to activate "the power of places of memory to engage the public in connecting past and present in order to envision and shape a more just and humane future."[28] Numerous sites of conscience have been recognized with World Heritage designations.[29] In addition to addressing issues of human rights and social justice, this concept for the role of heritage sites seeks to democratize heritage sites so that "memories belong to us all."[30] The contested colonial and postcolonial history of the missions suggests that they are well positioned to join the existing two hundred–plus sites of conscience that interpret the past in a way that reveals its complexities and conflicts.[31] By naming those tensions, exploring their contemporary cost, and honoring the cultural legacy of California's Native peoples over the centuries and today, the missions have the potential to realize more fully their role as "a living link to our past"[32] and as sites of meaningful discourse and reconciliation.[33]

The California missions incite emotions of all kinds. They elicit, as we have seen, feelings associated with nostalgia and patriotism in the face of romanticized, triumphalist colonial rhetoric, as well as pain, loss, and trauma ensuing from systematic dispossession and erasure.[34] These emotionally charged responses also make them ripe for destabilizing the dominant narratives, for new ways of telling the story of California's past. Deana Dartt-Newton (Chumash, California, Mayo) has called for mission museums to acknowledge their ethical responsibility and radically alter their interpretations to engage more diverse perspectives and present more inclusive narratives, but there seems to be little will to change the interpretation at many of the missions.[35] Nicole Myers-Lim (Pomo) has similarly argued that for the "framework of genocide" of the mission narratives to be dismantled, they must reflect Native voices.[36]

The call for more inclusive interpretation is not coming from just academics and Native American activists. During the debate over the California Missions

Preservation Act, James Gibbons, a Republican representative from Nevada, addressed the missions' contested history. He supported the legislation, but also urged his colleagues

> to remember that we are preserving buildings and structures that bring up uneasy memories for many who live today in California. . . . It is estimated that California's Indian population was about 310,000 at the beginning of Spanish rule. At the close of the 19th century, their population shrunk to approximately 100,000, largely due to the inhumane conditions under which the Indians were forced to live while serving as slaves.[37]

Gibbons added, even more pointedly, "I believe it is important that when the missions are refurbished that it is not just the bricks and mortar which are restored, but also the truth. These facilities are deserving of our help, but they also must be restored with the acknowledgment of all those who suffered so that the missions themselves could survive." Lois Capps, U.S. representative for California's Twenty-Fourth Congressional District, which includes the Santa Barbara Mission, agreed with Gibbons and noted that "preserving the missions gives us an opportunity to preserve that sorry chapter of our Nation's history and to learn from those lessons so that we do not repeat them."[38] While preserving a "sorry chapter" doesn't necessarily recognize those who were oppressed or address the ongoing struggles of Native peoples for equal rights, it is significant that even elected representatives understand the contested nature of the mission history.

This transformation of mission interpretation faces strong barriers, however. One challenge is that the alternatives to racist or demeaning representation can be complicated. For example, in Buckley McGurrin's *Christ Teaching* mural at Mission San Gabriel, the child standing in front of Christ was originally depicted holding a Native American doll (Figure C.3). The doll was recently overpainted with the image of a teddy bear (Figure C.4).[39] It is not hard to understand, particularly given the Claretians' work with the Tongva, why they wanted to remove a stereotyping and problematic image of a white schoolchild holding an Indian doll with a feathered headband. At the same time, the addition of the bear simply removes the only representation of a Native person in the heavenly vision set in a mission garden. Removing a racist image is a positive step, but the enduring messages of the mural, indeed of the entire garden, persist.

Another potential barrier to changing presentation of the past is that the missions are largely under the control of the Catholic Church, which has vested interests in aspects of the current historical narrative. Compounding this institutional resistance to change is the fact that the missions are also perceived as iconic monuments in the broader cultural discourse. Kirk Savage notes that monuments "are the most conservative of commemorative forms precisely because they are

FIGURE C.3. Detail of Buckley McGurrin, *Christ Teaching,* mural, 1939. San Gabriel Mission garden, 2008. Photograph courtesy of Branislav L. Slantchev.

FIGURE C.4. Detail of Buckley McGurrin, *Christ Teaching*, mural, 1939. San Gabriel Mission garden, 2013. Photograph by the author.

meant to last, unchanged, forever. While other things come and go, are lost and forgotten, the monument is supposed to remain a fixed point, stabilizing both the physical and the cognitive landscape."[40] But even the fixed points of monuments are not impervious to cultural critique. For example, in 1994 a statue of Juan de Oñate was dedicated in Alcalde, New Mexico.[41] Oñate was a Spanish conquistador who, like Serra, has been both lauded as the leader of the first Spanish expedition in the area and vilified for his brutal treatment of the people of the Acoma Pueblo, where after razing the buildings the Spanish punished Acoma warriors by amputating their right feet. Four years after the dedication, Native American protesters severed the right foot of the Oñate statue and sent a message to the *Albuquerque Journal* explaining their actions:

> We took the liberty of removing Oñate's right foot on behalf of our brothers and sisters of Acoma Pueblo. This was done in commemoration of his 400th year anniversary acknowledging his unasked for exploitation of our land. We see no glory in celebrating Oñate's fourth centennial, and we do not want our faces rubbed in it. If you must speak of his expedition, speak the truth in all its entirety.[42]

Historian Erica Doss has argued that the contentious debates about memorials such as the Oñate sculpture are understandable when such reminders are seen "as the public symbols of disputed narratives of American ownership, legitimacy, belonging, and control."[43]

The mission landscapes offer similar potential. In spite of the fact that the missions are often described as monuments, their landscapes are neither fixed nor immutable. Their origins are traceable to the actions of individuals who had very explicit reasons and particular conditions for shaping the spaces. They are susceptible to perceptions of being self-evident and self-sufficient, but, as we have seen, what may be thought of as "natural" in the mission landscape is the result of extensive intervention. The mission gardens are also spaces with profound political implications. The potential for reinterpreting these sites is, therefore, first, to invite those who consume the landscapes to think about how and why the spaces look the way they do. Second, stewards of the sites can consider new strategies to present more complex, inclusive interpretations of the landscapes and the historical narratives conveyed through them.

An alternate vision for the California mission landscapes is that they might become productive Third Spaces.[44] The premise of mobilizing Homi Bhabha's and Edward Soja's theoretical constructs in the interpretive programs at the missions is that this kind of intervention, as Bhabha writes, "challenges our sense of the historical identity of culture as a homogenizing, unifying force, authenticated by the originary Past, kept alive in the national tradition of the People . . . the narrative of the Western nation."[45] Instead, Third Spaces are places of hybridity and enunciation, where those who have been divided by historical and structural inequalities are able to come together, shedding the roles of oppressed and oppressor.[46] For this to happen, the languages and constructs of representation must be revealed and new ideas must disrupt dominant paradigms so that conversations can take place where all voices are truly heard. This vision is not simply to include diverse perspectives, but to acknowledge and create understanding across cultural differences.

So what might the intervention of Third Space look like at the missions? Most significantly, they must recognize the missions as residing in Indigenous landscapes as well as settler-colonial geographies. There are excellent examples of Native people already leading these efforts. Andrew Galvan (Ohlone/Miwok) has been the curator at Mission Dolores in San Francisco since 2004, and Jacque Tahuka Nunez is the first Acjachemen tribal member contracted at Mission San Juan Capistrano to present Native storytelling.[47] At other missions, Indigenous people must continue to be involved, not just as drummers at fiestas or guests to bless the gardens, but as cocurators of the interpretive programs at the sites. Indigenous knowledge systems and archives must be presented with equal respect and weight. The missions must be spaces for open dialogue about even the most contentious issues—the enduring consequences of colonial trauma and the ongoing controversies over tribal recognition, sovereignty, and enrollments. Research programs must include Indigenous people not only as informants or consultants but also as cocreators and collaborators. This collaboration is challenging in what archaeologists Martin Nakata and Bruno David have called "the muddied entanglements in the intersections between Indigenous and Western ways of 'knowing.'"[48] Archaeologists, curators, and other heritage professionals must be willing to acknowledge and critically assess their roles in the contemporary political contests for Indigenous peoples' access to rights and resources.[49] Lightfoot, Panich, and others are working to expand this discourse, but much work remains.[50]

A productive starting place is exposing the "mirror of representation in which cultural knowledge is continuously revealed as an integrated, open, expanding code"[51] by looking at the ways in which the mission gardens have been represented. For example, the aestheticization of the landscape could be unpacked with a straightforward sequence of photographs of a site such as Mission San Diego over the past century and a half. The sanctification of the landscape could be explored by examining the language describing Mission San Carlos in Carmel or looking at the Serra sculptures in the gardens. Conversations about the representation of Native people could be provoked by looking at the presentation of domed traditional dwellings and the artifacts of food production.

Similarly, exploring the history of the gardens could be an entrée into the deep social divides that continue to be reproduced in the spaces. As Nunez has described the multicultural spaces of the missions, "Mission San Juan Capistrano was built by my ancestors and preserved by many different cultures. Today our Acjachemen voice is respected and heard. My heart says, 'Thank you, Creator. Om'paloov. Thank. You.'"[52] Not all would agree with her, and the same cannot be said of many of the missions, but conversations about whose voices have been included and why could help identify and challenge the ongoing structures of exclusion and privilege at the missions and in the community. For example, texts written about the missions over time using terms such as *Spanish, Hispanic, Mexican, Latino, Brown, Chicano, Moorish, Andalusian, Mediterranean, Native American,* and *Indian* could be used to investigate the construction of ethnicities and their places in the mission narratives. The spaces are also ripe for probing issues of American exceptionalism, Manifest Destiny, sovereignty, and other broader narratives that have resonated at the missions. These discussions could help reveal the entanglements of local, tribal, ethnic, regional, and national narratives and the ways they subvert, reinforce, or contest social relationships and power dynamics. These Third Spaces could also be places for conversation about the relationship of religious and secular heritage at sites so clearly important to both church and state. Specifically, they might explore how a state-sponsored heritage site such as La Purísima can interpret the religious history, or how school curriculum and preservation funding can account for the premise of the Establishment Clause of the First Amendment separating church and state. Just as students are taught to use primary source material from the colonial period, they could be invited to analyze critically the promotional rhetoric of early twentieth-century mission preservation efforts or analyze the newspaper coverage of the fund-raising campaign following the Santa Barbara earthquake in 1925. Similarly, visual culture could form the basis of an educational program that starts with the historical imagery of fruit crate labels and automobile advertisements and then invites comparisons with the current marketing of the missions. Conversations could consider notions of authenticity in the landscape. Exploring ideas about different notions of authenticity might lead to dialogue about what is inauthentic and for whom.

The missions' rich botanical and material culture collections could similarly support public dialogue in ways that unpack the polarized colonial narratives and make connections through common contemporary concerns. For example, heirloom plant breeding projects offer the opportunity to probe connections among "heritage species." The spaces could be forums for contemporary concerns about sustainable food systems by inviting people into a conversation about Indigenous and mission subsistence practices. As at the Kuaua Pueblo, where naming and performance practices reveal underlying assumptions of privilege, a study of maps and place-names associated with the missions could start conversations about the constructs of territory, property, eminent domain, cultural commons, and cultural patrimony.[53] Community-curated exhibits recognizing the diverse stakeholders of the missions might be catalysts for conversations about the complexity of these sites and could, in turn, generate new ideas for more inclusive and multivocal interpretation. Finally, art has long provided a compelling critique of the missions. Pieces such as James Luna's 2005 Venice Biennale work *Emendatio* could be mobilized to provoke and disrupt the embedded visual conventions of the mission landscapes.[54] *Emendatio,* a performance and installation project, includes *Chapel for Pablo Tac,* which was inspired by the experiences of the California Luiseño Indian sent to Italy in 1834 (Figure C.5). Its themes offer many possible entries into conversations about the agency of Native people and their treatment as the subjects of study. *Emendatio* also includes the installation *Past and Present Apparitions* in which Luna "contests the popular notion that there is a discontinuity between the Indigenous world of the past and that of the present."[55] As Luna has stated, his work not only brings a critical lens to historical interpretation but also "addresses the mythology of what it means to be 'Indian' in contemporary American society and exposes the hypocrisy of the dominant society, which trivializes Indian people as romantic stereotypes."[56] These pieces are just a few examples of the rich and varied activist art that both critiques California history and challenges ongoing stereotyping and dehumanizing representations

FIGURE C.5. James Luna, view of *Chapel for Pablo Tac,* including the altar; an installation in *Emendatio,* sponsored by the National Museum of the American Indian and exhibited at the Biennale de Venezia (2005) and the George Gostav Heye Center in New York City (2008). Printed with permission of the artist.

of Native peoples.[57] Such artwork could raise questions about how the mission landscapes work in similar ways.

In conceiving of the missions as Third Spaces, the ultimate goal is not merely to be inclusive and create a space for mutual understanding, recognition, and respect—for, as Bhabha puts it, "seeing oneself as another"—but to establish the fundamental humanism of these places. In this sense, the missions can be a crucible for what has been debated as "post-Indian."[58] This new paradigm, as art historian Mark Watson has argued, "explores possibilities for framing histories and relationships outside the largely United States–centered 'Indian' paradigm. The work . . . asserts the freedom to define these connections through transnational styles and subjects, concepts of counterhistory, and a performance of interconnectedness and dialogue that directly challenges preconceived ideas of ethnic identity in visual art."[59] The missions could similarly go beyond the narrow confines of "mission history" or even "Native history" to address critical issues underlying much cultural heritage internationally, including those identified in the founding document of the Association of Critical Heritage Studies in 2012: "nationalism, imperialism, colonialism, cultural elitism, Western triumphalism, social exclusion based on class and ethnicity."[60] At an even more fundamental level the missions can be spaces for a humanist approach to history that seeks to transcend divisions. As C. S. Lewis has written, "The man who is contented to be only himself, and therefore less a self, is in prison. My own eyes are not enough for me, I will see through those of others . . . and in knowing, I transcend myself; and am never more myself than when I do."[61]

A critical history of the mission landscapes also raises an oddly perverse possibility for the future of the sites as well—namely, the interpretive potential and preservation ethics of mission gardens that are of value in the history of California landscape design. In fact, it can be argued that Mission Santa Barbara's central patio garden laid out by Father Romo in 1872 is the oldest extant and continuously cultivated designed landscape in the state and perhaps in the western half of the country. Despite their significance, the planting plans and maintenance of the gardens at many of the missions are outsourced to landscaping crews and loyal volunteers who are not trained in the care of historic gardens. Frequently landscape management decisions are informed by contemporary aesthetics and cost considerations, rather than by historical evidence or other criteria for managing historic landscapes.[62] Newer plantings, such as the herbs trimmed into a cruciform at San Juan Capistrano (Figure C.6) or the charming herb garden at La Purísima (Figure C.7), could provoke discussion about the role of gardens in the interpretation of the missions. There is much to be gained from a critical interpretation of the ideologies informing the landscape design at the missions, but if the story of the gardens is to be told, it also requires a sensitivity to preserving that historic fabric. The decision to let the plantings grow in a more naturalistic way, as has

FIGURE C.6. Shrubbery in the Mission San Juan Capistrano "demonstration garden" planted and trimmed in a cruciform, 2008. Photograph by the author.

FIGURE C.7. Mission La Purísima Herb Garden, 2008. Photograph by the author.

been done at Solano and La Purísima, is neither a satisfactory interpretation of the colonial landscapes nor the 1930s Colonial Revival gardens (Figure C.8). In these instances, benign neglect becomes its own form of selective amnesia.

This book has made the case that the California mission landscapes have been appropriated and mobilized in the constitution of social relationships, particularly the perpetuation of inequalities across lines of gender, race, and ethnicity. Through complex representational forms and practices and through embodied experiences, the mission landscapes helped establish hegemonic ways of seeing that have reproduced the colonial gaze and created in cultural memory an indelible image of the mission as a garden. But in this same notion of memory and place as socially constituted lies the potential of the mission landscapes to be reimagined. In their study of official history and the private memories of visitors at Colonial Williamsburg Eric Gable and Richard Handler note that "official history erases messy or unpleasant truths in order to make useful propaganda out of the past. Memory, by contrast, is the weed that grows through the cracks in a public monument's foundations. . . . Memory contests and resists official history. . . . Memory is what we can recover in order to give voice to the disenfranchised, the oppressed, and the silenced."[63]

FIGURE C.8. Mission La Purísima, beds of the 1930s Civilian Conservation Corps–constructed gardens. Photograph by the author.

Empowering and including the memories of all people opens up the possibilities for creative and dynamic ways to critique and rewrite the dominant narrative of the mission past. Tongva / Acjachemen artist L. Frank, in her oral history recorded for the California Museum, stated:

> To have survived and to still call yourself indigenous to a place, belonging to a place, . . . that's pretty strong. . . . And even though we people have been so obliterated and this is now our reality, we still know that. . . . This is our place and we know how to talk to it. Even if we don't use the language, we still know how to talk to it. And even beyond that we know how to listen to it, and in that listening to it, it's in the doing or the making where there's the power.[64]

The power of place and the potency of memory are socially constituted. This means that with intention, they can be deployed to effect change. They can be used for telling more complete stories and for creating forums for dialogue. The missions can be used as material witnesses to call attention to the structures of privilege and diversity of perspectives that are negotiated in the public sphere. They might even become sites of conscience and places of healing and reconciliation. But realizing that potential requires action. As Frank says, "It's in the doing or the making where there's the power."

APPENDIX

Plant Lists

Santa Barbara Mission Garden, 1903

Drawn from measurements taken with the assistance of the Padres by Samuel Newsom of the firm Newsom and Newsom Architects, San Francisco, August 1903. [Newsom's spellings of plant names have been preserved.]

Abutiton
Agave
Althea
Amaryllis
Anemone
Arbutilons [?]
Aurelia
Bamboo [?]
Banana
Begonia
Bottle tree
Bouganvillea
Box border
Bulbs
Cacti (labeled "Cacti bed")
Caladium
Calla lily
Calyanthus
Cannas
Carnation
Chinese shaker tree (along church)
Cig plant
Coffee tree
Coprosma [?]
Custard tree (large)
Cypress ("The Bishop's cypress 60 years old") (also, Italian cypress)
Datura (also "red datura")
Dianthus
Drought of [illegible]
Elephant ear
Fan palm
Fig, climbing (along sacristy wall)
Fuchia
Genista
Geranium
Grasses (also "var grasses")
Grasses, variegated
Guava
Heliotrope
Hens and chickens
Lantana
Lebanon rose
Libonia
Lily
Linam

Lobelia
Marguerettes
Marygold
Maudeville [?] vine (along church)
Morning glory (in pots along shed)
Moutbretta / moutbrotia
Myrtle
Narcissi
Nebumebrum plant (in central fountain)
Norfolk pine
Nymphea plant (in central fountain)
Oleander, white
Orange tree ("old")
Oxalie border
Pansies
Passion vine (along shed)
Penstomine (along church)
Phoenix Palm
Pointiaxa
Pointsettia
Polangonia
Pomegranate
Ponstem [?]
Poppy
Prickly pear cactus
Primula
Rama plant
Rose
Rosemary
Rudbekia
Salvia
Smilax
Smoke tree
Snowball
Solanum
Spider Lily
St. John's Bread tree
Tree dahlia
Tulips
Umbrella grass
Veronica
Vinca
Violets
Wall flower
Wire vine [?] (along shed)
Yucca

Plant labels at Brand Park, San Fernando, received by Park Department, April 21, 1925

Aloysia citriodora lemon verbena
Genista hispanica Spanish broom
Mimulus glutinosus California monkey flower
Audibertia polystachya California white sage
Encelia californica California bush sunflower
Aquilegia truncata California columbine
Calycanthus occidentalis California spice bush
Pentstemon centranthifolius California scarlet bugler
Pentstemon heterophyllus California violet beard tongue
Berberis nevinii California barberry
Rhamnus crocea California red berry
Pentstemon cordifolius California scarlet honeysuckle
Malvastrum fasciculatum false mallow
Romneya coulteri matilija poppy
Carpenteria californica California tree anemone
Dendromecon rigida California tree poppy
Heteromeles arbutifolia California holly
Cercidium torreyanum palo verde
Citrus aurantium var. Orange
Citrus limonia lemon
Salix pendula weeping willow
Prunus integrifolia catalina cherry
Sambucus glauca elderberry

Casimiroa edulis white sapota
Libocedrus decurrens California incense cedar
Acer macrophyllum California maple
Aesculus californicus California buckeye
Punica granatum pomegranate
Caesalpinia gilliesii bird of paradise tree
Ceanothus arboreus California tree lilac
Nerium oleander oleander
Umbellularia californica California bay tree
Juniperus californica California juniper
Rhamnus californica California coffee berry
Pentstemon antirrhinoides yellow beard-tongue
Cestrum parqui night scented jasmine
Garrya elliptica California silk tassel shrub
Rhus ovata California sumach
Ribes speciosum California fuchsia flowering gooseberry
Ribes malvaceum California pink flowering currant
Astriplex lentiformis California desert salt bush
Lupinus arboreus California tree lupine
Lupinus cytisoides California canyon lupine
Lobelia fulgeus var. Mexican lobelia
Fuchsia gracilis Mexican fuchsia
Trichostema lanatus California woolly blue curls
Zauschneria californica California fuchsia
Ceanothus verucosus fine leaved California lilac
Fremontia californica California slippery elm
Plumbago capensis leadwort
Rosmarinus officinalis rosemary
Lycium richii California box thorn
Pentstemon spectabilis blue beard tongue
Mission grape from San Gabriel
Mission grape from Santa Clara
Rose of Castile from San Jose
Rose of Castile from San Luis Rey
Clematis from San Juan Bautista
Honeysuckle from San Luis Obispo
Rose "Seven Sisters" from Monterey
Jasmine from Santa Barbara
Choisya ternata Mexican mock orange
Ceanothus thyrsiflorius California lilac
Collection of California ferns and fern allies
Collection of California cactus and allied plants

Labels for "representative plants" from selected missions

In addition to the mission name, each label also included the founding date of the mission and the title "Representative Plants"

MISSION SANTA CRUZ: Apple, Clanothus [Ceanothus?], Cestrum, Poppy, Lupine, Geranium

MISSION SAN JOSE DE GUADELUPE: Olive, Grape, Spanish Broom, Rose, Pelargonium, Geranium

MISSION SANTA CLARA DE ASIS: Plum, Rhamnus, Spiraea, Thyme, Pinks, Furarcea [Furfuracea?]

MISSION SAN RAFAEL: Apricot, Rose, Fuchsia, Iris, Geranium, Calla-Lily

MISSION DOLORES, S. F.: Fig, Heliotrope, Pomegranate, Crassula, Candy tuft, Hydrangea

MISSION SAN FRANCISCO DE SOLANO: Cestrum, Hydrangea, Rosemary, Rose, Geranium

MISSION SANTA INES: Apple, Oleander, Pomegranate, Yucca, Cactus, Sage

MISSION LA PURISSIMA CONCEPCION: Quince, Cestrum, Rose, Geranium, Iris, Calla-Lily

MISSION SAN LUIS OBISPO DE TOLOSA: Pear, Salvia, Rose, Thyme, Polly, Geranium

MISSION SAN MIGUEL: Olive, Pomegranate, Rosemary, Tritoma, Santoline [Santolina?], Pinks

MISSION SAN ANTONIO DE PADUA: Fig, Grape, Honeysuckle, Iris, Geranium, Thyme

MISSION LA SOLEDAD: Peach, Jasmine, Rose, Aloe, Poppy, Calla-Lily

MISSION SAN JUAN BAUTISTA: Pomegranate, Oleander, Fuchsia, Rosemary, Geranium, Savory

MISSION SAN CARLOS BORROMEO EL CARMEL: Almond, Rose, Heliotrope, Crassula, Geranium, Savory

Labels for memorial plantings

Planted February 26, 1924, by San Fernando Valley Chapter DAR in memory of Mr. and Mrs. Wm. P. Granger. This tree was raised from an acorn brought from the Charter Oak, Connecticut. By Mr. Wm. P. Granger and presented by Mr. and Mrs. J. C. Maclay.

ROSE OF CASTILE: Planted in memory of Catherine P. Maclay from whose garden these Castilian roses were taken, the original bush was transplanted in early days from Santa Clara.

List of "Native plants," December 30, 1925

Sent for bids to four nurseries: Beverly Hills Nursery, Howard & Smith, Pioneer Nursery Co., and A. E. Simpson

Trichostima lanatum
Pentstemon antirrhinoides
Pentstemon cordifolius
Carpenteria californicus
Rhamnus californica (in tree form)
Umbellularia californica (in tree form)
Fremontia californica
Heteromeles arbutifolia
Ceanothis verucosus
Ceanothus cyaneus
Ceanothus hybridus

Notes

Preface

1. Dienstag, "Alzheimer's and the Spiritual Terrain of Memory."

2. Silliman, "Indigenous Traces in Colonial Spaces."

3. Lonetree, *Decolonizing Museums*; Mihesuah, "American Indian History"; Smith, *Decolonizing Methodologies*; White, *The Content of the Form.*

4. Haas, *Saints and Citizens,* 184.

5. Vizenor, *Manifest Manners.*

6. Weaver, "More Light than Heat," 236.

7. Bruyneel, *The Third Space of Sovereignty.*

8. Delgado and Stefancic, *Critical Race Theory,* 3.

9. Brave Heart-Jordan, "The Return to the Sacred Path."

10. Linklater, *Decolonizing Trauma Work.*

11. Corsane, "Robben Island"; ka Mpumlwana et al., "Inclusion and the Power of Representation."

12. Cook-Lynn, *A Separate Country,* xv.

13. Fixico, *Call for Change*; Hoxie, "Sovereignty's Challenge"; Miller and Riding In, eds., *Native Historians Write Back*; Sleeper-Smith, ed., *Contesting Knowledge.*

14. Herwitz, *Heritage, Culture, and Politics in the Postcolony,* 1.

15. My interest in the missions dates back to 1984, when for my undergraduate thesis at Harvard I analyzed Chumash collections at the Peabody Museum and the Smithsonian Institution National Museum of Natural History. Reid, "Chumash Acculturation." As simplistic and limited as my conclusions were, the far more interesting and important questions have persisted.

Introduction

1. James, *The Old Franciscan Missions of California,* foreword, n.p.

2. The California Missions Foundation was established in 1998; the foundation is "dedicated to preserving the landmark California Missions and associated historical and cultural resources for the benefit of the public." http://californiamissionsfoundation.org/mission-statement. "On January 1, 2016, the California Missions Foundation successfully merged with the California Mission Studies Association, an organization founded in 1984 and dedicated to scholarship, research and membership. Together the combined CMF is the only

statewide organization dedicated to the preservation and studies of the California Missions and their related historical sites." http://californiamissionsfoundation.org/about-us.

3. James, *The Old Franciscan Missions of California,* n.p.

4. These questions of representation and the construction of the past in the microcosm of the California mission landscapes clearly reflect important and powerful processes written at global, national, regional, and local scales. Seminal works such as Benedict Anderson's *Imagined Communities,* Eric Hobsbawm's writings on nationalism, and Michel-Rolph Trouillot's *Silencing the Past* have laid the foundation for a myriad of scholars addressing the complex relationships of state interests, identity, and history.

5. Scholars of colonialism have long recognized that colonizers mobilize the narratives of conquest to privilege and legitimate their own positions while erasing the histories of the colonized: Anderson, *Imagined Communities*; Bernard, *Rhetorics of Belonging*; Bhabha, *The Location of Culture*; Bhabha, ed., *Nation and Narration*; Bodnar, *Remaking America*; Fanon, *Black Skin, White Masks* and *The Wretched of the Earth*; Memmi, *The Colonizer and the Colonized*; Renan, "What Is a Nation?"

6. The terms *Native American, Indigenous,* and *Indian* are all deployed by Native peoples under particular circumstances and with intentional connotations. The terms are used here interchangeably and respectfully. Where relevant, historical terms such as *neophyte* are also referenced with the acknowledgment of the constructions and problematics implied by each term. Similarly, tribal names reflect both historical and contemporary usage as applicable to the time period discussed.

7. This study is part of the transdisciplinary investigation of space and power and, more particularly, the inquiry within landscape history to address issues of power and landscape design around the globe and across human history: Cosgrove and Daniels, eds., *The Iconography of Landscape*; Dinius and Vergara, eds., *Company Towns in the Americas*; Harris, *The Nature of Authority* and "Clean and Bright and Everyone White"; Hayden, *The Power of Place*; Ruggles, *Gardens, Landscape, and Vision*; Siegel, "Contested Places and Places of Contest"; Silverman, "Touring Ancient Times"; Tolia-Kelly, *Landscape, Race and Memory*; Van Slyck, "Mañana, Mañana."

8. For example, Rothberg, *Multidirectional Memory,* 2 (in particular, see his discussion of what happens when these different histories "confront each other in the public sphere"), and Levy and Sznaider, "Memory Unbound." Within the growing literature of critical heritage studies, see De Jong and Rowlands, eds., *Reclaiming Heritage*; Harrison, *Heritage*; Herwitz, *Heritage, Culture, and Politics in the Postcolony*; Logan and Reeves, *Places of Pain and Shame*; Sharp, *Geographies of Postcolonialism*; Silberman, "'Sustainable' Heritage"; Smith, *Uses of Heritage*; Upton, *What Can and Can't Be Said*; Winter, *Post-conflict Heritage, Postcolonial Tourism.*

9. O'Brien, *Firsting and Lasting.*

10. Celebrations of the tercentennial of Father Junípero Serra's birth and his canonization have focused a great deal of attention on both his historical significance and his role as a symbolic figure in the production of California's past. See, for example, Beebe and Senkewicz, *Junípero Serra*; Castillo, "Cultural Chauvinism"; Hackel, *Junípero Serra*; Panich, "After Saint Serra"; and Thomas, "The Life and Times."

11. The literature on Native resistance and agency is vast. Examples of scholarship relevant to the California context include Bouvier, *Women and the Conquest of California*; Castillo, *Native American Perspectives* and "Neophyte Resistance and Accommodation in the Missions of California"; Chávez-García, *Negotiating Conquest*; Haas, *Saints and Citizens*; Hurtado,

Indian Survival on the California Frontier; Lightfoot, *Indians, Missionaries, and Merchants,* 82–113; Monroy, *Thrown among Strangers*; Reyes, "Race, Agency, and Memory in a Baja California Mission" and *Private Women, Public Lives*; Schneider and Panich, "Native Agency at the Margins of Empire."

12. Haas, *Saints and Citizens,* 7.

13. Haas, *Pablo Tac.*

14. Hackel and Wyss, "Print Culture and the Power of Native Literacy in California and New England Missions."

15. Gunther, *Ambiguous Justice*; Hyer, *"We Are Not Savages"*; Rifkin, *Manifesting America,* 149–96.

16. Carrico, *Strangers in a Stolen Land*; Lindsay, *Murder State*; Smith, *Freedom's Frontier*; Trafzer and Hyer, eds., introduction to *Exterminate Them!*

17. Silliman, "Theoretical Perspectives on Labor and Colonialism" and "Indigenous Traces in Colonial Spaces"; Voss, "Colonial Sex." For the colonial history of California, particularly important sources are Anderson, *Tending the Wild*; Chávez-García, *Negotiating Conquest*; Gutiérrez and Orsi, eds., *Contested Eden*; Haas, *Conquests and Historical Identities in California,* "Raise Your Sword," and *Saints and Citizens*; Hackel, *Children of Coyote, Missionaries of Saint Francis*; Hackel, ed., *Alta California*; Jackson and Castillo, *Indians, Franciscans, and Spanish Colonization*; Lightfoot, *Indians, Missionaries, and Merchants*; Monroy, *Thrown among Strangers*; Newell, *Constructing Lives at Mission San Francisco;* Sandos, *Converting California*; and Voss, *The Archaeology of Ethnogenesis.* For historiography of colonial California and the missions see Hilton, "Identities and the Usable Pasts of Colonial Borderlands"; Hurtado, "Fantasy Heritage"; and Weber, "A New Borderlands Historiography." Robinson's "From Ethnohistory to Ethnogenesis" reveals how changing interpretations of the Native deep past reflect changing relationships between archaeologists and Native people.

18. On the more recent history of California and the construction of the "Spanish fantasy past," see DeLyser, *Ramona Memories*; Deverell, *Whitewashed Adobe*; Deverell and Flamming, "Race, Rhetoric, and Regional Identity"; Kropp, *California Vieja*; McClung, *Landscapes of Desire*; McWilliams, *Southern California Country*; Rawls, "The California Mission as Symbol and Myth"; Servin, "California's Hispanic Heritage"; Starr, *Inventing the Dream*; and Thomas, "Harvesting Ramona's Garden." The construction of California history to serve political and social interests in Monterey's landscape is traced by Norkunas, *The Politics of Public Memory,* and by Walton, *Storied Land.*

19. Lightfoot, "A Cubist Perspective," 192.

20. Mission gardens have received little scholarly treatment, and the extensive historical scholarship on the missions has paid little attention to the significance of the colonial landscapes or the role of the later mission gardens in the production and consumption of mission heritage sites. Brown's "California Mission Gardens" is one of the few to argue for the anachronistic nature of the gardens, and Thomas, in "Harvesting Ramona's Garden," pointed out the ideological incongruities of romanticized gardens in the missions. General histories of California gardens have generally overlooked the mission landscapes or misattributed them. For example, Judith Taylor's extensively edited posthumous publication of Harry Morton Butterfield's history of California gardens mistakenly attributes the 1872 Santa Barbara Mission garden to E. Denys Rowe (1881–1954) (Taylor and Butterfield, *Tangible Memories,* 298). The studies that have addressed the mission gardens have been largely descriptive or reproduce a romanticized version of their history; for example, Adams, "Gardens of the Spanish Days of California"; Gebhard, introduction to *An Arcadian Landscape*;

Hendry, "Spanish Mission Gardens of California"; Jacobus, "The Mission Santa Clara Garden"; Padilla, *Southern California Gardens*, 24–25; and Power, *California Gardens*. Garden historian David Streatfield's scholarship is more rigorous in the garden chronology, but does not consider the gardens' broader cultural and ideological significance (Streatfield, *California Gardens*, 25, and "'Californio' Culture and Landscapes, 1894–1942," 104–5). Similarly, Colonial Revival histories such as Hosmer, "The Colonial Revival in the Public Eye," have located the mission gardens within the broader impulses of the Mediterranean Revival and ignored their nineteenth-century origins at Santa Barbara. Patricia Rubertone has argued for the need for archaeologists to pay attention to landscape as well as architecture in "Historical Landscapes." A more detailed discussion of the historiography of the mission landscapes is presented in Kryder-Reid, "'Perennially New.'"

21. For Mission Revival architectural history, see Gebhard, "The Spanish Colonial Revival in Southern California"; Kirker, *California's Architectural Frontier*; Mooney, "Sunny Spain or Our Algeria"; Sagarena, "Building California's Past"; and Weitze, *California's Mission Revival*. On the history of the restorations and reconstruction, see Hackling, "Authenticity in Preservation"; Vaz, "The Northern Missions"; and Weinberg, "Historic Preservation and Tradition in California."

22. Haas, *Saints and Citizens*; Hokowhitu et al., eds., *Indigenous Identity and Resistance*; Mihesuah, "American Indian History as a Field of Study"; Oland, Hart, and Frank, eds., *Decolonizing Indigenous Histories*; Smith, *Decolonizing Methodologies*.

23. Aulich, "Memory, What Is It Good For?"; Bennett, Julius, and Soudien, eds., *City, Site, Museum*; Field, "'No One Has Allowed Me to Cry.'"

24. Colwell-Chanthaphonh and Ferguson, eds., *Collaboration in Archaeological Practice*; Harrison, "'Counter-Mapping' Heritage" and "Heritage as Social Action"; Hodges and Watson, "Community-based Heritage Management"; Hodgkin and Radstone, eds., *Contested Pasts*; Isaac, "Responsibilities toward Knowledge"; Medina, "History, Culture, and Place Making"; Meskell, "Negative Heritage and Past Mastering in Archaeology"; Sather-Wagstaff, *Heritage That Hurts*; Shackel, *Memory in Black and White*; Walkowitz and Knauer, eds., *Contested Histories in Public Space*; Westcoat, "The Indo-Islamic Garden."

25. Blake, "UNESCO's 2003 Convention on Intangible Cultural Heritage"; Martinez, "Wrong Directions and New Maps of Voice"; Read, "'The Truth Will Set Us All Free'"; Laurajane Smith, "Empty Gestures?"; Paul Chaat Smith, *Everything You Know about Indians Is Wrong*; Waterton and Smith, "The Recognition and Misrecognition of Community Heritage"; Zimmerman, "Plains Indians and Resistance to 'Public' Heritage."

26. Braun, ed., *Transforming Ethnohistories*; Hokowhitu et al., eds., *Indigenous Identity and Resistance*; Macdougall and Carlson, "West Side Stories"; Shannon, "The Construction of Native Voice"; Smith and Wobst, eds., *Indigenous Archaeologies*; Smithers and Newman, eds., *Native Diasporas*.

27. Anderson, Barbour, and Whitworth, "A World of Balance and Plenty"; Hull, "A Land of Many People"; Jones and Perry, eds., *Contemporary Issues in California Archaeology*; Simmons, "Indian Peoples of California." For more specific analysis of the lifeways and worldview of the Chumash, Native peoples of the Santa Barbara area, see Flynn, "From Three Worlds to One"; Gamble, *The Chumash World at European Contact*; and Johnson, "Chumash Social Organization."

28. Anderson, "Native Californians as Ancient and Contemporary Cultivators" and *Tending the Wild*; Blackburn and Anderson, eds., *Before the Wilderness*; Cuthrell et al., "A Land of

Fire"; Gamble, *The Chumash World at European Contact*; Lewis, "Patterns of Indian Burning in California"; Lightfoot and Parrish, *California Indians and Their Environment.*

29. Lightfoot and Parrish, *California Indians and Their Environment,* 7. See also Gamble, "A Land of Power," and Hull, "A Land of Many People."

30. Heizer and Elsasser, "World View of California Indians"; Panich, "Spanish Missions in the Indigenous Landscape"; Robinson, "Land Use, Land Ideology"; Rojas, "She Bathes in a Sacred Place."

31. Weber, *Bárbaros,* 124. The term *neophyte,* or moving into the condition of *neófia,* signified not only an individual's new Christian name being recorded in the baptismal registry, but also the person's being classified as a minor under the law and "losing freedom of movement and personal and cultural sovereignty" (Haas, *Saints and Citizens,* 5).

32. While California was officially under Spanish rule until 1822, revolutionary movements in Spain and Mexico in the 1810s meant that Alta California became increasingly isolated and the region's ties to both Spain and central Mexico became tenuous (Hackel, *Children of Coyote,* 370–71).

33. In colonial times 127 Franciscans served in Alta California, nearly all of whom were born and educated in Spain. A relatively small number of missionaries were posted at each mission and, as members of their religious order, served under a president of the California missions. Indian officials, called *alcaldes* and *mayordomos,* helped oversee the social control and labor at the missions (Hackel, "The Staff of Leadership").

34. For a more complete analysis of the missions' agriculture, animal husbandry, and trade, see Archibald, *The Economic Aspects of the California Missions*; Farnsworh and Jackson, "Cultural, Economic, and Demographic Change"; and Jackson and Castillo, *Indians, Franciscans, and Spanish Colonization,* 31–72. Demographic data from the mission registers are publicly available through the online documentary archives of the Huntington Library's Early California Population Project.

35. In addition to site-specific studies and the Historic American Buildings Survey records, key sources for the architecture of the California missions include Baer, *Architecture of the California Missions*; Ettinger, "Hybrid Spaces" and "Spaces of Change"; Hannaford and Edwards, *Spanish Colonial or Adobe Architecture of California*; Judson, "The Architecture of the Mission"; Newcomb, *The Franciscan Mission Architecture of Alta California*; and Smith, *The Architectural History of Mission San Carlos.* For the interior decoration of the missions see Neuerburg, *The Decoration of the California Missions.*

36. The relationship between the mission architecture and the control of vision, including surveillance, is argued more fully in Kryder-Reid, "Sites of Power and the Power of Sight." The function of the architecture as a strategy to influence Native behaviors, including sexual practices, is argued in Voss, "Colonial Sex," and Weber, "Arts and Architecture, Force and Fear."

37. The Franciscans claimed the land as trustees on behalf of the neophytes, to whom title was eventually to be given. The boundaries of the mission lands were, in many cases, never formally established, and with secularization most of the lands were deeded to private citizens (Hackel, *Children of Coyote,* 387). For a more complete history of land tenure in Southern California, see Shipek, *Pushed into the Rocks.*

38. Haas details this process in chap. 5 of *Saints and Citizens,* 140–63.

39. Ibid., 161.

40. Ibid., 163.

41. This simplistic summary necessarily condenses the complex sequence of legal maneuvers and political dynamics of the 1830s through 1850s. For a fuller treatment of the mission land history, see Hackel, *Children of Coyote*, 369–419.

42. Ibid., 369–70. For a fuller discussion of the impact of the dissolution of the missions, changing property ownership and labor relations, and the criminalization of Mexicans, see Monroy, *Thrown among Strangers*. For a cogent exposition of the systematic disenfranchisement of Native peoples following secularization, see Carrico, *Strangers in a Stolen Land*; Haas, *Saints and Citizens* and *Conquest and Historical Identities in California*; Heidenreich, *This Land Was Mexican Once*; Lindsay, *Murder State*; Moore, "We Feel the Want of Protection"; Paddison, "Capturing California"; and Smith, *Freedom's Frontier*.

43. The causes of the demographic collapse are explicated in Hackel, *Children of Coyote*, and Jackson and Castillo, *Indians, Franciscans, and Spanish Colonization*. Kat Anderson details practices such as legalized forced indenture and boarding schools that exacerbated the cultural losses throughout the nineteenth century, particularly for Indian children (Anderson, *Tending the Wild*; see especially chap. 3).

44. Moore, "We Feel the Want of Protection"; Paddison, "Capturing California"; Phillips, *Bringing Them under Subjection, Chiefs and Challengers*, and *Vineyards and Vaqueros*.

45. Heidenreich, *This Land Was Mexican Once*, 144.

46. The missions were featured in Helen Hunt Jackson's hugely popular novel *Ramona* (1884) and were regularly highlighted during the 1880s and 1890s in *Land of Sunshine, Out West*, and other magazines that celebrated California. California's preservation movement paralleled similar efforts in other parts of the country such as the founding of the Society for the Preservation of New England Antiquities (now Historic New England) and the Mount Vernon Ladies' Association.

47. The rise of Anglo-American political and social interests is chronicled in histories such as Almaguer, *Racial Fault Lines*; Camarillo, *Chicanos in a Changing Society*; Monroy, *Thrown among Strangers*; and Pitt, *The Decline of the Californios*. How those shifting power relations were inscribed in architecture, landscape, and other cultural forms in California has been a rich area of inquiry whose seminal works include Deverell, *Whitewashed Adobe*; Kropp, *California Vieja*; and McClung, *Landscapes of Desire*. Wilson has analyzed a similar process in New Mexico in *The Myth of Santa Fe*.

48. In addition to their full, formal names, many of the missions are also known by shortened or alternate names. For example, Mission San Carlos de Borromeo in Monterey is often called the "Carmel Mission" and Mission San Francisco de Asís is called "Mission Dolores," named for the nearby creek.

49. Ramirez, *Native Hubs*, 26. See also Weibel-Orlando, *Indian Country L.A.*

50. Carocci, "Living in an Urban Rez," 263–65.

51. Johnson, "American Indians, Manifest Destiny, and Indian Activism"; Linda Tuhiwai Smith, *Decolonizing Methodologies*; Polly Walker, "Research in Relationship."

52. Bruyneel, *The Third Space of Sovereignty*, 104.

53. Martinez, "Wrong Directions and New Maps of Voice," 559.

54. There are multiple versions of this photograph, attributed variously to George P. Thresher, Charles Betts Waite, and Charles Pierce. Given that the rededication event was well attended, multiple photographers may have been there, but Pierce was also known to purchase other photographers' collections and put his name on them. The Huntington image credits Thresher, and an identical image in the Pierce collection includes a handwritten

description on the back of the photograph: "Mission Indian women at rededication of Mission San Luis Rey—May 12, 1893."

55. Cosgrove, *Social Formation and Symbolic Landscape,* 13.

56. Schein, "Race and Landscape in the United States," 5.

57. Halbwachs, *On Collective Memory,* 200.

58. Mitchell, introduction to *Landscape and Power,* 1.

59. Memmi, *The Colonizer and the Colonized,* 193.

60. Dunbar-Ortiz, *An Indigenous Peoples' History of the United States.*

61. Niezen, *The Origins of Indigenism*; Weaver, "Indigenousness and Indigeneity."

62. This idea of landscape as recognizing the permeability and metaphoric meaning of gardens follows more of a cultural geography than a formalist garden history approach to landscape.

63. The notion of landscape as a social stage builds on the social and architectural history applied to eighteenth-century Virginia by Isaac, *The Transformation of Virginia,* and Upton, *Holy Things and Profane,* as well as more recent scholarship on the performative aspects of heritage spaces, e.g., Gröppel-Wegener, "Creating Heritage Experience through Architecture," and Synnestvedt, "Who Wants to Visit a Cultural Heritage Site?"

64. Margaret Somers's theorizing of identity and narrative is useful for deconstructing the mission landscapes because it "builds from the premise that narrativity and relationality are conditions of *social* being, *social* consciousness, *social* action, institutions, structures, even society itself; the self and the purposes of self are constructed and reconstructed in the context of internal and external relations of *time* and *place* and *power* that are constantly in flux" (Somers, "The Narrative Constitution of Identity," 621; emphasis in the original). Somers identifies particular patterns of relationships that she terms "relational settings," and she argues that "identity-formation takes shape within these relational settings of contested but patterned relations among narratives, people, and institutions . . . [that have] a history . . . over time and space" (626).

65. Scott, *Domination and the Arts of Resistance.* James Sandos also draws on Scott's model to assess Indian resistance to missionization, although he does not explore the significance of landscape in that contest of power. See Sandos, *Converting California,* especially chap. 10, "Indian Resistance to Missionization." On accounting for Indigenous agency, see Gamble, "Subsistence Practices"; Liebman and Murphy, eds., *Enduring Conquests*; Sandos, "Neophyte Resistance in the Alta California Missions"; Sandos and Sandos, "Early California Reconsidered"; and Silliman, "Writing New Archaeological Narratives."

66. Highmore, "Introduction: Questioning Everyday Life," 17.

67. For example, see Bender, "Time and Landscape," and Emerson, *Cahokia and the Archaeology of Power.*

68. Foucault, *Discipline and Punish,* 219.

69. Ibid. See also Foucault, "Space, Knowledge, and Power," for Paul Rabinow's revealing interview. For applications of Foucault's observations on the disciplining power of landscape by other scholars, see Casella, "Landscapes of Punishment and Resistance"; Delle, *An Archaeology of Social Space*; Hauser and Hicks, "Colonialism and Landscape"; Hicks, *"The Garden of the World"*; and Singleton, "Slavery and Spatial Dialectics on Cuban Coffee Plantations."

70. Tuan, *Place and Space,* 5.

71. Upton, "Ethnicity, Authenticity, and Invented Traditions," 4.

72. Certeau, *The Practice of Everyday Life,* xiv.

73. Ibid., xvii. The production of meaning in the landscape in this analysis also draws on the phenomenological perspectives of Martin Heidegger and Maurice Merleau-Ponty as adeptly applied to Mesolithic landscapes by Christopher Tilley. Particularly useful is the awareness in these conceptual models of the dynamic relationship between the physicality of space and body on the one hand and perceptual consciousness—being and dwelling—on the other. The study is also indebted to Henri Lefebvre's understandings of the complex social construction of space; Lefebvre, *The Production of Space.* See also Heidegger, "Building, Dwelling, Thinking"; Merleau-Ponty, *Phenomenology of Perception*; and Tilley, *A Phenomenology of Landscape.*

74. Geertz, "Thick Description"; Turkle, *Evocative Objects.*

75. James Corner, "Introduction: Recovering Landscape"; Hunt, *The Afterlife of Gardens*; Mitchell, *Landscape and Power.*

76. Hunt, *The Afterlife of Gardens.*

77. Lakoff and Johnson, *Metaphors We Live By*, 3.

78. The use of ideology in this study draws on Louis Althusser ("Ideology and Ideological State Apparatuses") and his concept of ideology as the "imaginary relationship of individuals to their real conditions of existence," particularly his premise that ideology has a material existence manifested through practices that constitute individuals as subjects.

79. Certeau, *The Practice of Everyday Life*, 6.

80. This concept of cultural memory (also referred to, with varying emphases, as social memory, public memory, communal memory, collective memory, public history) is laid out in Connerton, *How Societies Remember*; Halbwachs, *On Collective Memory*; Hobsbawm and Ranger, eds., *The Invention of Tradition*; Kansteiner, "Finding Meaning in Memory"; Lipsitz, *Time Passages*; and Olick and Robbins, "Social Memory Studies." For the connections of landscape and memory, see Lowenthal, "Past Time, Present Time"; Schama, *Landscape and Memory*; and Tilley's introduction to the 2006 special issue of the *Journal of Material Culture* on landscape, heritage, and identity. Work beyond California illustrates the potential for more inclusive historical narratives of heritage sites that incorporate Indigenous pasts, such as Colwell-Chanthaphonh and Ferguson, "Memory Pieces and Footprints"; Hirsch, "Landscape, Myth, and Time"; Rappaport, *The Politics of Memory*; and Silverman, "Touring Ancient Times."

81. Olick and Robbins, "Social Memory Studies," 112.

82. Sturken, *Tangled Memories.*

83. Dearborn and Stallmeyer, *Inconvenient Heritage*; Ricoeur, *Memory, History, Forgetting*; Zerubavel, *The Elephant in the Room.*

84. The nostalgia of the sites operates as both restorative and reflective nostalgias, as Svetlan Boym has described them, in the sense that each is seen at various times as both naively essentialist and self-consciously melancholic (Boym, *The Future of Nostalgia*).

85. Turkle, *Evocative Objects*, 311.

86. Ibid.

87. I explore this dating of the beginnings of the reception of the missions as heritage sites further in chap. 2, but I argue an earlier date than others who privilege the organization of formal preservations groups in the 1880s and 1890s. Priests ministering to congregations and residing at the missions even in the 1850s and 1860s wrote of repairs and acknowledged the historic significance of the buildings, and parishioners similarly expressed attachments to the sites perceived as relics of an earlier age.

88. Useful understandings of heritage sites and their landscapes in postcolonial contexts include Appadurai, *The Future as Cultural Fact*; Hall, "Identity, Memory and Countermemory"; and Stoler, *Carnal Knowledge and Imperial Power.*

89. Miller, *Stuff.*

90. Lowenthal, "Fabricating Heritage," 8.

91. Anderson, *Imagined Communities*; Hobsbawm and Ranger, eds., *The Invention of Tradition.*

92. Association for Critical Heritage Studies, Manifesto. See also Harrison, *Heritage*; Laurajane Smith, *Uses of Heritage*; and Smith and Waterton, *Heritage, Communities and Archaeology.*

93. Association for Critical Heritage Studies, Manifesto.

94. Gordon, *Private History in Public,* 8.

95. Schon, *The Reflective Practitioner*; Ševčenko, "Sites of Conscience: Heritage of and for Human Rights" and "Sites of Conscience: New Approaches to Conflicted Memory."

96. Dearborn and Stallmeyer, *Inconvenient Heritage*; Mitthofer, "Competing Narratives on the Future of Contested Heritage"; Silverman and Ruggles, eds., *Cultural Heritage and Human Rights.*

97. Handler and Gable, *The New History in an Old Museum*; Modlin, Alderman, and Gentry, "Tour Guides as Creators of Empathy."

98. Lowenthal, "Fabricating Heritage," 8.

99. Laurajane Smith and Emma Waterton (*Heritage*) have cogently critiqued what they term the "authorized heritage discourse" in perpetuating certain interests. See also Laurajane Smith, *Uses of Heritage.* In the California context, centuries of Catholic sponsorship of publications have produced a vast apologetic or "Christophilic Triumphalism" literature of church history in the state (Sandos, *Converting California,* 154). Other academics, including Native and non-Native scholars, have been advocates for the interests of Native peoples such as gaining tribal recognition. This divisiveness is evident in the scholarship of mission history as well as in approaches to public interpretation at the missions. John Bodnar has written about similar relationships between national agendas and local attitudes surfacing in public ceremonies and commemorations (Bodnar, *Remaking America*).

100. Mitchell, "Imperial Landscape," 17.

101. Brubaker and Cooper, "Beyond 'Identity,'" 4–5.

102. Ibid., 5.

103. Almaguer, *Racial Fault Lines*; Camarillo, *Chicanos in a Changing Society*; Deverell, *Whitewashed Adobe*; Kropp, *California Vieja.*

104. Bender, "Time and Landscape," 103.

105. Bjerregaard, "Dissolving Objects," 74.

106. Soja, *My Los Angeles, Postmodern Geographies,* and *Seeking Spatial Justice*; Bhabha, *The Location of Culture.*

107. Influential in my thinking about memory and the consequences of exclusive and inclusive presentations of the past is Paul Ricoeur's *Memory, History, Forgetting.* For the work of scholars on landscape, heritage, and reconciliation, see Bender and Winer, eds., *Contested Landscapes*; Dwyer and Alderman, *Civil Rights Memorials and the Geography of Memory*; Levin, ed., *Defining Memory*; Mason, "Conflict and Complement"; Olick, *The Politics of Regret*; Simon, *The Touch of the Past*; and Sullivan, "Some Thoughts about Museums, Reconciliation, and Healing." An important context for this larger project of heritage in postcolonial contexts is the role of Indigenous scholars in that work. For example, see Battiste, ed.,

Reclaiming Indigenous Voice and Vision; Bruchac, Hart, and Wobst, eds., *Indigenous Archaeologies*; Hale, ed., *Engaging Contradictions*; and Linklater, *Decolonizing Trauma Work*.

108. Fixico, *Call for Change*, 2.

1. Colonial Mission Landscapes

1. Allen, "Alta California Missions," 77–78.

2. Timbrook, Johnson, and Earle, "Vegetation Burning by the Chumash."

3. Milliken, *A Time of Little Choice*; see also Dartt-Newton and Erlandson, "Little Choice for the Chumash."

4. A number of scholars have concluded that, given the deterioration of traditional resource bases due to drought and sea temperature changes, and given the profound impact of Spanish settlement on indigenous social, economic, and political structures, the decision to join the mission system was one of "risk management." In other words, joining a mission was one of the best options presented to a people in the midst of extreme demographic and environmental stress. Castillo, "Neophyte Resistance and Accommodation in the Missions of California"; Combs and Ploogh, "The Conversion of the Chumash Indians"; Costello and Hornbeck, "Alta California"; Haas, *Saints and Citizens*; Hackel, *Children of the Coyote*; Jackson and Castillo, *Indians, Franciscans, and Spanish Colonization*, 31–72; Larson, Johnson, and Michaelsen, "Missionization among the Coastal Chumash of Central California"; Lightfoot, *Indians, Missionaries, and Merchants*, 82–113; Lightfoot et al., "The Study of Indigenous Political Economies"; Lightfoot, Gonzales, and Schneider, "Refugees and Interethnic Residences."

5. This important research is still in its relatively early phases. See Bernard, Robinson, and Sturt, "Points of Refuge in the South Central California Colonial Hinterlands," and Panich and Schneider "Expanding Mission Archaeology."

6. For example, Archibald, "Indian Labor at the California Missions."

7. Lightfoot, "A Cubist Perspective"; Schneider and Panich, "Native Agency at the Margins of Empire." Archaeologists and anthropologists working on colonial periods and in postcolonial contexts have for more than two decades been embracing Indigenous-centered perspectives and concern with Native agency as part of the broader movement to decolonize the discipline (Smith, *Decolonizing Methodologies*): Ferris, *The Archaeology of Native-Lived Colonialism*; Gallivan, Moretti-Langholtz, and Woodard, "Collaborative Archaeology and Strategic Essentialism"; McGuire, "Why Have Archaeologists Thought the Real Indians Were Dead and What Can We Do About It?"; Preucel, "Becoming Navaho"; Silliman, "Crossing, Bridging, and Transgressing Divides" and "Change and Continuity." Scholars are also publicly debating the political and ethical implications of working on issues related to contemporary sovereignty, advocacy, recognition, and the archaeologies of persistence. See, for example, Bruchac, Hart, and Wobst, eds., *Indigenous Archaeologies*; Field, "Complicities and Collaborations"; Hale, "Activist Research v. Cultural Critique"; Lightfoot et al., "The Study of Indigenous Political Economies"; Watkins, "Beyond the Margin"; and Zimmerman, "Usurping Native American Voice."

8. Haas, *Saints and Citizens*; Newell, *Constructing Lives*; Panich, "Archaeologies of Persistence"; and Schneider et al., "A Land of Cultural Pluralism."

9. Schneider, "Placing Refuge."

10. Lightfoot et al., "Evolutionary Typologies"; Lightfoot et al., "The Study of Indigenous Political Economies."

11. The complexities of Indigenous negotiations of the imposition of colonial power and, particularly, their use of traditional resources and persistence of belief practices and

cosmologies, are emerging in numerous recent studies by Kent Lightfoot, Lee Panich, Lisbeth Haas, and others: Haas, *Saints and Citizens*; Lightfoot, "A Cubist Perspective"; Light foot, Gonzales, and Schneider, "Refugees and Interethnic Residences"; Lightfoot, Luby, and Pesnichak, "Evolutionary Typologies and Hunter-Gatherer Research"; Lightfoot et al., "The Study of Indigenous Political Economies"; Panich, "Missionization and the Persistence of Native Identity."

12. Haas, *Saints and Citizens*.

13. Panich, "Native American Consumption" and "'Sometimes They Bury the Deceased's Clothes and Trinkets.'"

14. In Luiseño, *ayelkwi*.

15. Castañeda, "Engendering the History of Alta California," 235–38; Sandos, *Converting California,* 20–21. Archaeologist David Robinson has proposed that the concept of polyvalence is useful for understanding the cultural metaphors and perceptions through which Native Americans and missionaries interpreted the "media of material culture, animals, embellished architecture, and landscape" and structured colonial interactions (Robinson, "Polyvalent Metaphors," 302).

16. Phoebe A. Hearst Museum of Anthropology, collections catalog, http://hearstmuseum.berkeley.edu/exhibitions/cent/gallery1_3_9.html.

17. The entire text reads: "María Marta, neofita de la mision de el Serafico Doctor San Buenaventura me hizo an . . . (María Marta, neophyte in the mission of the Seraphic doctor [in] San Buenaventura made me in the year . . .) (Mundy and Leibsohn, "History from Things").

18. Sandos, *Converting California,* 28.

19. Schneider and Panich, "Native Agency at the Margins of Empire," 10. For other perspectives on Indigenous knowledge, power, and polity see Gamble, "A Land of Power," and Bettinger, *Sociopolitical Evolution in Aboriginal California*.

20. Anderson, *Tending the Wild,* 1.

21. Fagan, "The House of the Sea."

22. The characterization of the interior courtyards as gardens is an oft-repeated fallacy, generally predicated on the presence of mission gardens in these areas beginning in 1872 at Santa Barbara and replicated at other missions in the twentieth century. For example, Hoover, "The Archaeology of Spanish Colonial Sites," described the "hollow quadrangle of cloisters, corridors, a church, and work or storage spaces. This complex usually surrounded a central garden" (95). For a more complete historiography see Kryder-Reid, "'Perennially New.'"

23. Costello and Hornbeck, "Alta California," 311; Gentilcore, "Missions and Mission Lands of Alta California"; Ressler, "Indian and Spanish Water-Control."

24. Costello, *The Ranches and Ranchos of Mission San Antonio de Padua*; Costello and Hornbeck, "Alta California." For a detailed investigation of Rancho Petaluma, see Silliman, *Lost Laborers in Colonial California*.

25. The ecological impact of colonialism, particularly on Native lifeways, is established globally in Crosby, *Ecological Imperialism,* and for southern New England in Cronon, *Changes in the Land*. In the California context, the significance of introduced plants and animals is explored in depth in Allen, "Alta California Missions"; Anderson, *Tending the Wild*; Blackburn and Anderson, eds., *Before the Wilderness*; Hackel, "Land, Labor, and Production"; and Preston, "Serpent in the Garden." Michael Hardwick has compiled a list of native and introduced plants known to have been cultivated at the missions as well as an overview of the agricultural practices at the missions; Hardwick, *Changes in the Landscape*.

26. Blackburn, ed., *December's Child,* 66.

27. Ibid., 91.

28. See also Heizer and Elsasser, "World View of California Indians"; Panich, "Spanish Missions in the Indigenous Landscape"; Perry, "Chumash Ritual and Sacred Geography"; Robinson, "Land Use, Land Ideology"; Rojas, "She Bathes in a Sacred Place"; and Whitley and Whitley, "A Land of Vision and Dreams." For a broader discussion of applying Indigenous epistemologies to archaeological contexts, see Harris, "Indigenous Worldviews."

29. The task of accounting for Indigenous epistemologies in the diverse landscapes included in the contemporary geopolitical boundaries of California is inherently problematic. Not only does it include a wide range of cultural, linguistic, and environmental contexts, but it is also fraught with the issues of how to understand these views in the terms of hegemonic structures of Western epistemologies. The same challenges of ethnopoetics that Herbert Luthin articulates in his essay "Making Texts" (27) on translating Native California stories and songs apply to understanding their cosmologies. See also on this issue Dell Hymes's seminal *"In Vain I Tried to Tell You."*

30. Father Juan Crespí, translated by Alan Brown and quoted in Timbrook, Johnson, and Earle, "Vegetation Burning by the Chumash," 166.

31. For a more detailed discussion of the personal and institutional influences informing the missionaries' attitudes and beliefs, as well as their relationships with Indigenous people, Spanish colonial settlers, and Spanish civil officials, see Beebe and Senkewicz, *Junípero Serra* and "What They Brought"; Hackel, *Junípero Serra*; and Refugio de la Torre Curiel, "Franciscan Missionaries in Late Colonial Sonora."

32. Sandos, *Converting California.* Haas, in *Saints and Citizens,* details the structure of *castas* and material practices, including clothing, bodily ornament, education, and rituals (chap. 2, "Becoming Indian in Colonial California") and the construction of identities more broadly in *Conquests and Historical Identities.* Gloria Miranda outlines the complexities of the term *gente de razón* in "Racial and Cultural Dimensions of Gente de Razón Status." Barbara Voss's *Archaeology of Ethnogenesis* investigates the San Francisco Presidio and traces the creation of Californio identities and material practices of ethnogenesis. For a hemispheric treatment of this issue see Weber, *Bárbaros.*

33. Marking property lines and establishing dedicated-use areas (pasturage or agricultural) have long been an aspect of colonizing new territory (e.g., Cronon, *Changes in the Land*). For a more in-depth view of the missions' place in the mercantile economy of Alta California, see Hackel, "Land, Labor, and Production," and Jackson, "The Changing Economic Structure."

34. The active management of the environment has been richly documented in numerous recent studies. See Anderson, "Native Californians as Ancient and Contemporary Cultivators" and *Tending the Wild*; Anderson, Barbour, and Whitworth, "A World of Balance and Plenty"; Blackburn and Anderson, eds., *Before the Wilderness*; Farris, "Depriving God and the King of the Means of Charity," 145–46; and Gamble, *The Chumash World at European Contact.*

35. Arnold, ed., *Foundations of Chumash Complexity*; Gamble, "Chumash Architecture" and *The Chumash World at European Contact*; King, *Evolution of Chumash Society.*

36. Baer, *Architecture of the California Missions*; Ettinger, "Spaces of Change"; Hannaford and Edwards, *Spanish Colonial or Adobe Architecture of California*; Johnson, "Chumash Social Organization"; Judson, "The Architecture of the Mission"; Lee, "Spanish Missions"; Newcomb, *The Franciscan Mission Architecture of Alta California.*

37. Costello, *Santa Inés Excavations,* 89.

38. The most comprehensive study of mission water systems is John Ressler's master's thesis, "Spanish Mission Water Systems." Other sources include Browne, *San Buenaventura Mission Water System*; Gentilcore, "Missions and Mission Lands of Alta California"; Hoover, "Excavation at the Santa Inés Mill Complex" and "San Antonio Water-Powered Mill"; and Soto, "Mission San Luis Rey." For a report on one of the most thoroughly excavated water systems, see Cohen-Williams, "Archaeological Excavations of the Sunken Gardens of Mission San Luis Rey, California." The Mission Santa Inés grist and fulling mills have been designated a National Historic Landmark District and the property is being developed as a California State Historic Park. Recent excavations at San Gabriel have recovered remains of the drain system to channel water to the mission; Hoffman and Dietler, "Water at the San Gabriel Mission."

39. Bandini, *A Description of California in 1828,* 5.

40. Farris, "Depriving God and the King of the Means of Charity."

41. Costello, *The Ranches and Ranchos of Mission San Antonio de Padua,* 9. On *diseños* see Lucido, "Plotting Out the Land," and Mendoza "The Diseños Project."

42. Scott, *Domination and the Arts of Resistance,* 120.

43. Sandos, *Converting California,* 57–58. Important archaeological work on Native American dwellings at the missions, particularly recent excavations at San Miguel and Santa Clara, has revealed substantive evidence of the continuities of Indigenous material, social, and political traditional practices and the agency of Native peoples within colonial mission contexts. See Allen, *Native Americans at Mission Santa Cruz*; Arkush, "Native Responses to European Intrusion"; Bennyhoff and Elsasser, *Sonoma Mission*; Deetz, "Archaeological Excavations at La Purísima Mission"; Farnsworth, "Missions, Indians, and Cultural Continuity"; Farris, *Archaeological Testing in the Neophyte Housing*; Foster, "'They're Just Rocks'"; Greenwood, ed., *The Changing Faces of Main Street*; Hoover and Costello, eds., *Excavations at Mission San Antonio*; Howard, "Excavations at Tes-haya"; Panich et al., "Assessing Diversity"; and Peelo, "The Creation of a Carmeleño Identity." See also Kimbro, *Furnishing Plan.*

44. Haas, *Saints and Citizens,* 7. This summary simplifies the complexity among the diverse settings of the twenty-one missions and the variety of Native responses documented by Lightfoot, Panich, Schneider, and others.

45. Indian housing is described by, among others, Bandini, *A Description of California in 1828* (6), and La Pérouse, *Voyage de La Pérouse Autour du Monde.* The account of the visit to Monterey and San Carlos Mission in September 1786, which has been translated and published as *Life in California,* occurs in vol. 2, 247–83 of the original edition.

46. Codero's views are reprinted in the 1989 edition of La Pérouse, *Life in California.* Curators at the Laguna Art Museum, which owns the Deppe painting, note that this first oil on canvas representation of the missions evokes secularization by depicting two dons (former Spanish soldiers and settlers) in the foreground, one at left conversing with a Franciscan and one at right speaking with a Gabrielino/Shoshone. Laguna Art Museum; Ferdinand Deppe, *San Gabriel Mission* (ca. 1832). http://lagunaartmuseum.org/ferdinand-deppe-san-gabriel-mission-1832.

47. Robinson, *Life in California,* 28–29.

48. Although he addresses only "non-Indian homes," Mason's "Adobe Interiors in Spanish California" provides a sense of the period furnishings and spaces.

49. Engelhardt, *Santa Barbara Mission,* 84, 86.

50. There is a similar parallel in the application of technology to control the body in the Franciscans' use of the *corma,* a restrictive device attached to a person's ankles, especially women suspected of adulterous behavior. See Hackel, *Children of Coyote,* 325; and Smith, "Under Lock and Key," 18.

51. Construction of gender in Native communities included a spectrum of sexual orientation and gender assignments and roles; Hollimon, "The Third Gender in Native California" and "Archaeology of the *'Aqi.*" In *Constructing Lives* Newell explicates the complexities of the imposition of Catholic expectations of a nuclear family model for Indigenous familial, social, and political networks in Bay Area societies, as well as the ways in which Indians created new alliances through marriage and godparenting at Mission San Francisco.

52. Voss, "Colonial Sex," 53.

53. Ibid., 46.

54. Baudrillard, "Structures of Interior Design," 309–10.

55. Manriques [L. Frank], oral history.

56. Allen, *Native Americans at Mission Santa Cruz,* 53; see also Allen, "Rethinking Mission Land Use."

57. Mendoza, "Indigenous Landscapes."

58. Numerous scholars have examined the impact of labor practices in the mission contexts, including Archibald, "Indian Labor"; Cook, *The Conflict between the California Indian and White Civilization*; Sandos, *Converting California*; Silliman, *Lost Laborers* and "Theoretical Perspectives on Labor and Colonialism"; Newell, *Constructing Lives,* chap. 2, "Building Faith"; and Voss, "Domesticating Imperialism." Consistent among the arguments has been the recognition of routinized labor practices, with their structured movements in time and space, spatial arrangements, and associated rewards and penalties. Sherburne F. Cook, writing in 1943 about the "mental and moral aspects of labor," argued that "labor . . . has perhaps constituted a more serious obstacle to the racial reorientation of the Indian than the brutal but quite comprehendible physical conflict" (Cook, *The Conflict between the California Indian and White Civilization,* 95).

59. Robinson, *Life in California,* 24.

60. Reply of Tapis and Cortés to Goycoechea's statements, Santa Barbara, October 30, 1800, Santa Barbara Archives, 2:86–143. Quoted in Cook, *The Conflict between the California Indian and White Civilization,* 93.

61. La Pérouse, *Life in a California Mission,* 89. Hackel (*Children of Coyote,* 240–58) and Sandos ("Between Crucifix and Lance," 211) argue that the appointment of alcaldes paralleled and built on the traditional leadership structure of the chiefdom. For a more comprehensive analysis of California Indigenous political organization in environmental contexts, see Bettinger, *Sociopolitical Evolution in Aboriginal California,* and for an accessible overview, see Lightfoot and Parrish, *California Indians and Their Environment.*

62. Peelo, "Baptism among the Salinan Neophytes"; Reddy, "Feeding Family and Ancestors."

63. For example, deer and marine resources (fish and shellfish) have been excavated at most of the coastal missions and as far inland as Santa Inés. See Allen, *Native Americans at Mission Santa Cruz,* and Walker and Davidson, "Analysis of Faunal Remains from Santa Inés Mission."

64. Costello and Hornbeck, "Alta California"; Larson, Johnson, and Michaelsen, "Missionization among the Coastal Chumash of Central California."

65. Robinson, *Life in California,* 50.

66. Historians Robert H. Jackson and Edward Castillo have argued that these changing labor practices also dramatically altered gendered roles and therefore both social relationships and relationships with the natural world; Jackson and Castillo, *Indians, Franciscans, and Spanish Colonization,* 38–39.

67. Lasuén, "From the Refutation of Charges," 273.

68. Voss, *The Archaeology of Ethnogenesis,* 147.

69. The material and spatial practices of colonization at the missions have been explored by a number of scholars: Jackson and Castillo, *Indians, Franciscans, and Spanish Colonization;* Kryder-Reid, "Footprints of Domination and Resistance" and "Sites of Power and the Power of Sight"; Silliman, "Theoretical Perspectives on Labor and Colonialism" and "Indigenous Traces in Colonial Spaces"; and Voss, "Colonial Sex."

70. La Pérouse, *Life in a California Mission,* 85, 87–88.

71. Reply of Tapis and Cortés to Goycoechea's statements, Santa Barbara, October 30, 1800, Santa Barbara Archives, 2:86–143. Quoted in Cook, *The Conflict between the California Indian and White Civilization,* 93. Piecework referred to quotas for tasks such as grinding grain or making adobe bricks.

72. Arkush, "Native Responses to European Intrusion"; Castillo, "Neophyte Resistance and Accommodation in the Missions of California"; Hackel, "Land, Labor, and Production," 124–28; Sandos, "Neophyte Resistance in the Alta California Missions."

73. Newell, *Constructing Lives at Mission San Francisco*; Robinson, *Life in California,* 24; Sandos, *Converting California,* 100; Silliman, "Theoretical Perspectives on Labor and Colonialism"; Voss, "Colonial Sex."

74. Cook, *The Conflict between the California Indian and White Civilization,* 91–96.

75. Stoler, *Carnal Knowledge and Imperial Power.*

76. Castañeda, "Engendering the History of Alta California" and "Sexual Violence in the Politics and Policies of Conquest"; Castillo, "Gender Status Decline"; Haas, *Conquests and Historical Identities in California*; Heidenreich, *This Land Was Mexican Once*; Hollimon, "The Third Gender in Native California"; Newell, *Constructing Lives,* chap. 4, "Love and Marriage"; Voss, "Colonial Sex."

77. Casteñeda, "Engendering the History of Alta California," 232; Chávez-García, *Negotiating Conquest,* 1–24; Peelo, "The Creation of a Carmeleño Identity" and "Pottery Making."

78. Casteñeda, "Engendering the History of Alta California."

79. Voss, "Domesticating Imperialism," 196–98.

80. Voss, *The Archaeology of Ethnogenesis,* 291–92.

81. Robinson, *Life in California,* 48–49.

82. Peyri, "Informe de la Mision San Luis Rey," quoted in Soto, "Mission San Luis Rey," 37.

83. Tac, "Indian Life and Customs at Mission San Luis Rey," 97.

84. Farnham, *Travels in the Californias and Scenes in the Pacific Ocean,* 109.

85. George Simpson described the Santa Barbara fountain and lavandería in 1842: "The covered channel, which rests partly on an artificial aqueduct, terminates in front of the church with a classical urn, throwing out a number of graceful jets into a circular basin that surrounds it; this basin empties itself into a second, through the mouth of a grotesque figure of a man lying on his belly; and the second again, through the jaws of a lion, pours its water into a third, which, overflowing its brim, sends forth in every direction a number of rivulets to irrigate the gardens and fields" (Simpson, *An Overland Journey,* 215).

86. Sandos lays out the distinctions between baptism and conversion in *Converting California.*

87. Heizer and Elsasser, "World View of California Indians."

88. Grant, *The Rock Paintings of the Chumash*; Imwalle, *"Fighting the Elements"*; Lee and Neuerburg, "The Alta California Indians as Artists"; Perry, "Chumash Ritual and Sacred Geography"; Robinson, "Land Use, Land Ideology"; Whitely, *The Art of the Shaman.*

89. Hudson and Underhay, *Crystals in the Sky,* 146–47.

90. Rojas, "She Bathes in a Sacred Place."

91. Gamble, *The World of the Chumash,* 150.

92. Boscana, *Chinigchinich,* 37; reprinted in Castillo, "Mission Studies and the Columbian Quincentennial," 13.

93. Hackel, *Children of the Coyote,* 163–64.

94. Father Lasuén brought in artisans and craftsmen on four- or five-year contracts, including stonecutters, carpenters, weavers, and at least six painters; Sandos, *Converting California,* 95.

95. Stilgoe, *Common Landscape of America,* 12–21.

96. Bremer, *Blessed with Tourists,* 19.

97. Robinson, *Life in California,* 59.

98. Duhaut-Cilly, "Duhaut-Cilly's Account of California," 354.

99. Leone, "Rule by Ostentation."

100. Robinson, *Life in California,* 25.

101. For a review of Franciscan thought informing the California missionaries, see González, "'The Child of the Wilderness Weeps for the Father of Our Country'"; Hackel, *Junípero Serra*; and Sandos, *Converting California,* especially chap. 3, "Junípero Serra and Franciscan Evangelization." For insight into the Spanish colonization in the Americas more broadly, see Weber, *The Spanish Frontier in North America* and *Bárbaros.* On the role of violence and coercion in the missions, see Hackel, *Children of the Coyote*; Heidenreich, chap. 2, "Stories of the Settler-Colonizers and of the Colonized," in *This Land Was Mexican Once*; Lightfoot, *Indians, Missionaries, and Merchants,* 92–93; Saunt, "'My Medicine Is Punishment'"; Silliman, "Theoretical Perspectives on Labor and Colonialism"; and Voss, "Colonial Sex." It is also useful to consider colonial era violence within the context of pre-contact warfare in California; see Allen, "A Land of Violence."

102. Robinson, *Life in California,* 25–26, 31–32.

103. Sandos, *Converting California,* 49.

104. The extensive decorative painting in the San Fernando convento is documented in the Index of American Design Record, National Gallery of Art, Washington, D.C. There is a rich literature on the decorative programs and visual culture of missions in California and Latin America. Haas's "The Politics of the Image" (chap. 3 of *Saints and Citizens*) is an excellent synthesis of the import of images for understanding Indigenous–colonial relationships through this iconography. For the role of visual culture in California missions, see also Kimbro and Costello, *The California Missions,* chap. 6, "Painting and Painters in Early California"; Neuerburg, *The Decoration of the California Missions,* "The Function of Prints in the California Missions," and "Painting in the California Missions"; and Phillips, "The Stations of the Cross Revisited." For the broader context of imagery in colonial settings in the Americas, see Bargellini and Komanecky, eds., *The Art of the Missions of Northern New Spain*; Cummins, "The Indulgent Image" and "Representation in the Sixteenth Century"; Gruzinski, *Painting the Conquest*; and Peterson, *The Paradise Garden Murals of Malinalco.*

105. Haas, *Saints and Citizens,* 85. A line of future inquiry about these decorative paintings is to explore how the WPA Federal Art Project's sponsored "restorations" may have

distorted or influenced our contemporary understandings of the original schemes. Those restorations are documented in the Index of American Design housed at the National Gallery of Art, Washington, D.C. For more on the IAD, see Clayton, "Picturing a 'Usable Past,'" and Doss, "American Folk Art's 'Distinctive Character.'"

106. Haas, *Saints and Citizens,* 83.

107. A productive example for this line of inquiry is Gwyneira Isaac's investigation of colonial and Indigenous knowledge systems in the context of the Zuni Museum, and particularly the process of reproduction through which knowledge is transmitted, practiced and circulated; see "Responsibilities toward Knowledge."

108. Dean, "The Renewal of Old World Images" and *Inka Bodies and the Body of Christ*; Haas, *Saints and Citizens*; Huckins, "Seeing Is Believing"; Lara, *Christian Texts for Aztecs* and *City, Temple, Stage;* Newell, *Constructing Lives.*

109. Kimbro and Costello, *The California Missions,* 129.

110. As Haas notes, others have read Indigenous colonial painting as incorporating elements of both colonial and Indigenous culture, as well as producing a uniquely original art form in the process. For more on colonial Indigenous painting, see Carolyn Dean, *Inka Bodies and the Body of Christ,* and Peterson, *The Paradise Garden Murals of Malinalco.*

111. Haas, *Saints and Citizens,* 88. See also Walker and Hudson, *Chumash Healing.*

112. Kimbro and Costello, *The California Missions,* 137.

113. Haas, *Saints and Citizens,* 87.

114. Freedberg, *The Power of Images.*

115. Synnestvedt, "Who Wants to Visit a Cultural Heritage Site?"; Tuan, *Place and Space.*

116. Kimbro and Costello, *The California Missions,* 131.

117. Monsignor Francis J. Weber, personal communication, May 29, 2008: "While incense was not often mentioned, I am sure that it was used whenever it was available. In fact, its absence was noted several times, for example on July 16, 1769, when the great cross was erected at San Diego. Mass was offered by Fray Junípero Serra in a brushwood shelter, and 'since the incense was lacking, fumes and smoke from the gunpowder served instead.' Then, there were censors at all the missions, and that would presume the use of incense for Benediction and High Mass."

118. Russell, *From Serra to Sancho,* provides a detailed account of the blending of influences, instruments, styles, and cultural practices to produce a new form of sacred music at the missions. See Sandos, *Converting California* (chap. 9, "Music and Conversion") and "Identity through Music" for a discussion of the role of music in converting California Indians to Roman Catholicism.

119. Russell, *From Serra to Sancho.*

120. Robinson, *Life in California,* 114.

121. Duflot de Mofras, *Duflot de Mofras' Travels,* 221.

122. Ibid.

123. Foucault, "Of Other Spaces."

124. This notion of the construction of placemaking draws on Tilley's *A Phenomenology of Landscape* and is reflected in the popularity of sites of public commemoration; Schama, *Landscape and Memory*; Shaffer, *See America First.*

125. Samuels, "Of Other Scapes," 70.

126. While it accounts for subjectivity and agency, this reading of the mission landscapes also parallels similar analyses in other colonial and institutional settings that draw on Foucault's concept in *Discipline and Punish* of disciplining spaces of surveillance and control.

See, for example, Delle, *An Archaeology of Social Space*; Hickman, *Therapeutic Landscapes*; Lenik, "Mission Plantations, Space, and Social Control"; Mrozowski and Beaudry, "Archaeology and the Landscape of Corporate Ideology"; Truett, *Fugitive Landscapes*; and Yanni, *The Architecture of Madness.*

127. Robinson, *Life in California*, 25–26.

128. Sandos, *Converting California*, 45.

129. Mendoza, "Sacrament of the Sun," 87. For the operations of architecture in Spanish missionary settings, see also Lara, *City, Temple, Stage.*

130. Mendoza, "The Liturgy of Light," 16. See also Gentry "Chronicles of Light," and Mendoza and Lucido, "Of Earth, Fire, and Faith."

131. Kimbro and Costello, *The California Missions*, 136, 138. An unsigned, undated drawing in the Santa Barbara archives provides a third example; Neuerburg, *The Decoration of the California Missions*, 43; Kryder-Reid, "Sites of Power."

132. Mendoza, "The Liturgy of Light."

133. Garnett, *San Francisco One Hundred Years Ago*, n.p.

134. Neuerburg, "Indian Pictographs at Mission San Juan Capistrano" and *The Decoration of the California Missions*; Lee and Neuerburg, "The Alta California Indians as Artists before and after Contact."

135. For a review of resistance manifested in the decorative programs of the mission churches, see Sandos, "Between Crucifix and Lance," 207–9.

136. Sandos, *Converting California*, 149. See also Beebe and Senkewicz, "The End of the 1824 Chumash Revolt in Alta California," and Hudson, "Chumash Revolt of 1824."

137. Corbett, "Chumash Bone Whistles"; Gamble, *The Chumash World.*

138. Garnett, *San Francisco One Hundred Years Ago*, n.p.

139. Boscana, *Chinigchinich*; Hudson et al., eds., *The Eye of the Flute*; Sandos, *Converting California*, 168.

140. Panich, "'Sometimes They Bury the Deceased's Clothes and Trinkets.'"

141. Tarlow, "Emotion in Archaeology."

142. Bhabha, *Our Neighbors, Ourselves*, 17; see also Soja, *Thirdspace.* Robert Preucel and Frank Matero have applied this concept to the Coronado State Monument in "Placemaking on the Northern Rio Grande."

143. On paradoxical communities, see Kristeva, *Strangers to Ourselves*, 194.

144. Bhabha, *Our Neighbors, Ourselves*, 18.

2. Inventing Heritage

1. Jackson, *Ancient Missions and Churches*, 1.

2. Ibid.

3. Ibid.

4. Stoddard, *John L. Stoddard's Lectures.*

5. Lummis, "In the Lion's Den," 43.

6. Ibid.

7. Heizer, introduction to *The Destruction of California Indians*; Meighan, "Indians and the California Missions."

8. Heidenreich, *This Land Was Mexican Once*, 144.

9. Schwarzer, *Riches, Rivals & Radicals.*

10. Between 1769 and 1812 the leader or "president-general" of the Catholic missions in California was appointed by his apostolic college in Mexico City and, following Mexican

independence, by the commissary general of the Indies, a Franciscan residing in Spain. After 1812 the leader of the California missions was formally called the commissary prefect, although the title president-general is more commonly used. Following secularization, the leadership of the missions became more complicated as missions fell under various diocesan authorities whose boundaries shifted over time, and as different orders, such as the Cistercians and the Comboni Fathers, along with the Franciscans and diocesan priests, took over the ministries of various mission parishes. Weber, *Encyclopedia of California's Catholic Heritage.*

11. For a survey of the transition to Anglo-American government in the 1850s, see Lyman, "The Beginnings of Anglo-American Local Government in California," 199.

12. Nordstrom, *Danger on the Doorstep*; Roy, *Rhetorical Campaigns of the Nineteenth-Century.*

13. For a discussion of historic materiality and Gilded Age discourses of Americanization deployed to enforce racial values in the East Coast context of two Jamaica, Queens, sites, see Matthews, "Gilded Ages and Gilded Archaeologies."

14. McGroarty, "The Place of the Sacred Garden," 247.

15. The Santa Barbara portion of this chapter builds on a more detailed history of the Santa Barbara Mission garden and its influence on the other missions and on regional landscape design; see Kryder-Reid, "'Perennially New.'" The Chumash are one of the best-known examples of Indigenous peoples who were able to support relatively high population levels without agriculture. They lived off the abundant resources of their coastal and island homes, harvesting fish, shellfish, and marine mammals from the ocean, hunting animals in the upland/mountain ranges, gathering berries, nuts, and wild grasses, and processing acorns as a staple crop. The Chumash lived in large villages, maintained extensive trade networks, and organized themselves in complex chiefdoms with hereditary leaders, religious leaders, and specialized craftspeople (Gamble, *The Chumash World at European Contact*). Eighty-six separate Chumash villages are mentioned in the baptismal registers for the current Santa Barbara County region (Johnson, "Chumash Social Organization," 83).

16. Geiger (*Mission Santa Barbara,* 41) describes the first structures as log cabins; Jackson and Castillo identify them as wattle and daub (*Indians, Franciscans, and Spanish Colonization,* 157). Catherine R. Ettinger has argued that these early wood, reed, and mud mission structures relied on traditional Indigenous construction methods as well as the Native Americans' skilled labor (Ettinger, "Hybrid Spaces," 88–89). The architectural history of Mission Santa Barbara is well documented thanks to the meticulous work of Father Maynard Geiger, who served as the first archivist at the mission from 1937 to 1977.

17. Robinson, *Life in California,* 44–45.

18. At one point only four friars remained at Santa Barbara, and they had to share the residence with families from the town, a fate the priest at the time described as "being martyred with needles" (Father Narcisco Durán to San Fernando College, September 25, 1837; cited in Geiger, *Mission Santa Barbara,* 116).

19. Camarillo, *Chicanos in a Changing Society,* 34.

20. Document 106, Santa Bárbara Mission Archive-Library; cited in Geiger, *Mission Santa Barbara,* 164.

21. Simpson, *Narrative of a Journey round the World,* 396.

22. The Franciscans' title to the mission was sold to Don Richard Den on June 10, 1846, for 7,500 pesos (Geiger, *Mission Santa Barbara,* 139). An apostolic college was originally founded in town, but moved to the mission building itself in 1856 (ibid., 155–56). The title was restored to the Franciscans in 1861.

23. Brewer, *Up and Down California in 1860–1864,* 56. William Henry Brewer (1828–1910) was a professor of chemistry at Washington College in Pennsylvania when in 1860 he joined the staff of California's first state geologist, Josiah Dwight Whitney; in 1864 Brewer accepted a position as professor of agriculture at Yale University.

24. The college was closed with loan debt of more than $16,000 (Geiger, *Mission Santa Barbara,* 187–89).

25. Romo, [Diary]. Entries through November 28, 1871, were translated by Father Geiger, For remaining entries I consulted the original handwritten document in Spanish. Romo departed from Port Said, Egypt, and stopped in Sicily and Naples, where he visited the Cardinal's Palace, the "principal churches," including St. Martin, the Church of St. Lucy al Monte, and the Church of Mt. Calvary, the royal palace, the new Campo Santo, and the Church of San Severino. There is no record of his time in Rome, but when the diary begins again in October 1871, he records stops in France at Marseilles, Avignon, Valenze, and Paris, staying in convents in each city. In one of the few specific mentions of a garden, he notes that the convent on the rue des Fourneaux has "two magnificent gardens." In Paris he visits the Church of Carmen, Church of the Dominicans (currently called the Panthéon), Church of St. Gervaise, the Cathedral, St. Eustachus, the municipal palace, Church of St. Thomas, the Louvre, Versailles, and the Church of Our Lady of Victory.

26. The college, which had been the brainchild of Bishop Amat of Los Angeles, was intended to provide an English-based classical education at a time when California's educational system was still developing. The courses of instruction included mathematics, classical and modern languages, and various courses in history, geography, rhetoric, moral and natural philosophy, and religion (Geiger, *Mission Santa Barbara,* 187).

27. Ibid. The timing of the garden construction might have been influenced by the fact that in 1872 Bishop Amat was negotiating with the town of Santa Barbara regarding the purchase of rights to share the mission's extensive water system; the arrangement was to include the provision of free water for the mission.

28. Bishop Amat to Romo, June 10, 1872, document 324, CLS Santa Bárbara Mission Archive-Library.

29. Romo's diary includes a small sketch of a fountain in the margins, but its tiered basins do not match the basin and jet that were executed on the patio, and he may have been sketching the front 1808 fountain or considering other possibilities for the patio.

30. Ford, *An Artist Records the California Missions,* 31.

31. Although the 1903 plan in the Santa Bárbara Mission Archive-Library was executed thirty years after the garden was planted, its record of species appears fairly consistent with earlier photos, suggesting it is a relatively accurate representation of the plants in the garden from at least 1885 on. The dating of specific garden features in this study is based on the photographic evidence in the Santa Bárbara Mission Archive-Library and published in Geiger, *A Pictorial History of the Physical Development of Mission Santa Barbara.* The photographs' dates are, in turn, based on the documentary record in the mission records of changing rooflines, conversions of doors to windows, and other architectural changes, which were more meticulously recorded than improvements to the landscape.

32. While some of the plant species listed on the 1903 plan were represented in the garden as of 2008, none was in the same location, which suggests major replantings in the mid-twentieth century, likely in the 1930s, when the design was simplified with lawn replacing the central flower beds. The current patio garden is maintained by a contract with the landscaping company that cares for the whole mission grounds.

33. The circular frame around the central basin does not appear to have been planted and was removed between November 1888 and August 1889. The arched wooden arbor along the east side of the garden parallel to the church is visible in photographs until 1890 and was planted with climbing vines, possibly grape, which provided shade in the garden.

34. For more on the local politics of Santa Barbara, see also Camarillo, *Chicanos in a Changing Society.*

35. Ibid., 10.

36. Ibid., 41–51.

37. Ibid., 53.

38. Lummis, "The Patio," 15.

39. Father Romo felt increasingly frustrated at his inability to renegotiate the archdiocese's stranglehold on the mission's efforts to generate income, and he returned to Egypt, where he died in Alexandria in 1890 (Geiger, *Mission Santa Barbara,* 203). In 1915 the mission became a parish serving the people of Santa Barbara.

40. Ibid., 234.

41. Illustrations accompanying an 1891 article include captions with the note "From a photograph taken especially for the 'Examiner'" (Bigelow, "Christmas at the Mission").

42. For a discussion of the significance of the Santa Barbara Mission garden in the historiography of Mission Revival architecture, see Kryder-Reid, "'Perennially New.'"

43. Byne and Byne, *Spanish Gardens and Patios*; Fox, *Patio Gardens*; Latham, *The Gardens of Italy*; Nichols, *Spanish and Portuguese Gardens*; Villiers-Stuart, *Spanish Gardens*; Wharton, *Italian Villas and Their Gardens.*

44. Alfred Korzybski (1879–1950), in *The Manhood of Humanity,* proposed the concept of "time binding" as part of a new discipline called "general semantics."

45. McCan, "Mission Garden Restored," 10.

46. McCan's self-reflective observations presaged later academic studies of the importance of place in the construction of "imagined communities" through public history, memorials, civic rituals, and other memory practices: Anderson, *Imagined Communities*; Connerton, *How Societies Remember*; Hobsbawm, *Nations and Nationalism*; Hobsbawm and Ranger, eds., *The Invention of Tradition*; Holtorf and Williams, "Landscapes and Memories."

47. Barraclough, *Making the San Fernando Valley,* 29. For a more in-depth discussion of the construction of whiteness during this period, see chap. 1.

48. "A Southern California Paradise," 97; quoted in Barraclough, *Making the San Fernando Valley,* 31.

49. Barraclough, *Making the San Fernando Valley,* 33–34.

50. Sandul, *California Dreaming,* 1.

51. In records of the first two years of the park's development, it was usually described as a "Mission Garden" and occasionally a "Spanish garden" or "Historic Garden," and the proposed buffer zone to preserve the area around the mission was coined a "safety park" by Charles Lummis, president of the Landmarks Club of California, writing to the Right Reverend John J. Cantwell, bishop of Los Angeles, September 24, 1921. Beginning in the spring of 1923, when the park was close to completion, it became known as the "Memory Garden," but there is no record of the explicit reasons for the change. The desire to differentiate the city park from the neighboring mission may have been a factor, and there may have been criticism about the extent to which the garden was an authentic re-creation, but at this point the evidence is only circumstantial.

52. Park Commission superintendent to Mr. Sylvester E. Weaver, president, Chamber of Commerce, Los Angeles, September 22, 1921, City of Los Angeles, Records Management Division, Recreation and Parks Board, Facilities Files, Brand Park.

53. Park Commission secretary to the city council, February 21, 1924, City of Los Angeles, Records Management Division, Recreation and Parks Board, Facilities Files, Brand Park.

54. McGroarty, *Los Angeles from the Mountains to the Sea,* 595–96. McGroarty's biographical entry for McCan describes her as "one of the most brilliant and popular women of Southern California."

55. McCan, "Mission Garden Restored," 10.

56. Ibid.

57. Bingham, *Charles F. Lummis*; Fiske and Lummis, *Charles F. Lummis*; Thompson, *American Character.*

58. Making the trip with McCan in April and May 1922 were Mr. Shearer and the commission president, William A. Bowen. Somewhat surprisingly, there are no notes describing the garden at Mission San Juan Capistrano, which would have been the only other mission besides Santa Barbara with an extensive garden at the time, but it may be that the mission to the south of Los Angeles was close enough that it was assumed everyone involved in the project was already familiar with it.

59. On April 29, 1922, they visited San Francisco, where at Mission Dolores they "saw the resident Pastor, Father Sullivan, and obtained cuttings of some old plants in the Mission Garden—Olives, willow, pomegranate and old Spanish rose," and at Mission Santa Clara they "secured some cuttings of old olives and fig trees. We met the celebrated Father Ricardi, the weather prophet, and he told us of having saved cuttings of the Mission grape from the original vines planted by the Padres, and which were dug up many years ago to make room for a new building in connection with the college. These cuttings are now old vines and Father Ricardi agreed to send us cuttings from those vines to plant on our pergolas in the San Fernando Mission Garden" ("A report [to the Board of Park Commissioners] of a trip made to visit the old Missions of California for the purpose of securing plants, etc. to be used in connection with the restoration of an old Mission garden in Brand Park at San Fernando Mission," May 1922, City of Los Angeles, Records Management Division, Recreation and Parks Board, Facilities Files, Brand Park).

60. Typescript of an article by Martha Nelson McCan submitted on March 10, 1924, for publication in the Native Sons magazine, *Grizzly Bear* (City of Los Angeles, Records Management Division, Recreation and Parks Board, Facilities Files, Brand Park). The article does not appear to have been published in *Grizzly Bear* (American Library Internet Archives, digitized by the San Francisco Public Library).

61. Lummis pleaded with the bishop to move the fountain intact rather than following the contractor's recommendation to dismantle and reassemble it, and his advice was heeded (Charles Lummis, president, Landmarks Club of California Inc. to the Right Reverend John J. Cantwell, September 24, 1921, correspondence on file, City of Los Angeles, Records Management Division, Recreation and Parks Board, Facilities Files, Brand Park).

62. According to a plaque on the relocated fountain, it is reportedly dated as 1812–14 and is modeled on a fountain in Cordoba. These origins have not yet been substantiated, but the influence of the fountain, variously described as flower or star shaped, as a model on other gardens is clear, and it was often mentioned as a highlight in descriptions of the Brand Park garden. A replica of it was later built in the central courtyard of the San Fernando Mission.

63. Park Commission superintendent to Miss Eva L. Hettinger, November 21, 1924, City of Los Angeles, Records Management Division, Recreation and Parks Board, Facilities Files, Brand Park.

64. Martha Nelson McCan to Criswell, president, Los Angeles city council, and acting mayor, September 20, 1922, City of Los Angeles, Records Management Division, Recreation and Parks Board, Facilities Files, Brand Park.

65. Anonymous, "Brand Mission Park," n.p.

66. McCan, "A Spanish Landscape Garden," n.p.

67. Anonymous, "Brand Mission Park," n.p.

68. Park Commission superintendent to Mr. Sylvester E. Weaver, president, Chamber of Commerce, September 22, 1921, correspondence on file, City of Los Angeles, Records Management Division, Recreation and Parks Board, Facilities Files, Brand Park.

69. Park Commission president to Mrs. Mary Griswold, chairman, Landmarks Committee, Ebell Club, October 2, 1923, correspondence on file, City of Los Angeles, Records Management Division, Recreation and Parks Board, Facilities Files, Brand Park. Farnham's first name is spelled variously as Sallie and Sally.

70. Ibid.

71. The statue by Douglas Tilden was dedicated by the Native Sons of the Golden West, November 17, 1907 (Anonymous, "Tilden's Latest Statue," 81).

72. Kirk argues that the commemoration of emancipation in public monuments reveals the nationalistic and racial discourses negotiated through statues in which the relationships of white nation and black body were represented in figural form. See Savage, *Standing Soldiers, Kneeling Slaves.*

73. McCan, "Mission Garden Restored," 10.

74. San Fernando women's clubs pledged a total of $1,750 while individual residents of the town pledged $4,500. There is no indication that McCan approached any of the clubs formed by African Americans, Latinas, or Asian Americans in Los Angeles in the wake of the decisions of most women's clubs at the turn of the twentieth century to exclude people of color (Davis, "An Era and Generation of Civic Engagement California," 139).

75. Gullett, "Women Progressives and the Politics of Americanization in California," 72. See also *Becoming Citizens,* Gullett's more developed study of the California women's movement during the period 1880–1911.

76. The *Clubwoman* (1921): 1; quoted in Gullett, "Women Progressives and the Politics of Americanization in California," 76.

77. Los Angeles's Friday Morning Club, one of the largest women's club's in the nation, met from 1900 to 1924 in a Mediterranean-style clubhouse designed by Arthur B. Benton.

78. Anonymous, "Restoration of Mission Park O.K.'d"; unidentified newspaper clipping on file, City of Los Angeles, Records Management Division, Recreation and Parks Board, Facilities Files, Brand Park.

79. McCan, "Mission Garden Restored," 10.

80. Park Commission superintendent to Sylvester E. Weaver, president, Chamber of Commerce, September 22, 1921; secretary of the Board of Park Commissioners to John S. McGroarty, November 22, 1921, City of Los Angeles, Records Management Division, Recreation and Parks Board, Facilities Files, Brand Park.

81. Hageman notes that the basins for the fountains were based on those at San Fernando and San Luis Rey; Hageman, "An Architectural Study of Mission La Purísima Concepción," 125.

82. Park Commission to Rev. Father Mestres, pastor, Monterey Mission, Monterey; Rev. Father Buckler, pastor, Santa Ines Mission, Solvang; and Rev. Rather John Gleibe, pastor, Santa Barbara Mission, Santa Barbara, May 1922, City of Los Angeles, Records Management Division, Recreation and Parks Board, Facilities Files, Brand Park.

83. When the Mission San Fernando grounds were developed, Brand Park became a model for the creation of a garden in the inner courtyard of the mission, complete with a reproduction of the "star" fountain in its center constructed in 1964.

84. Hayes, *Pioneer Notes from the Diaries of Judge Benjamin Hayes,* 207–8.

85. Krekelberg, *Mission San Juan Capistrano,* 9.

86. For an account of Lummis's and the Landmarks Club's efforts to preserve the missions, see chap. 18, "To the Rescue of the Missions," in Fiske and Lummis, *Charles F. Lummis,* 87–92.

87. A local paper noted that Mrs. Ryan was "spending a number of months at the old semi-Mexican town of Capistrano" and also commented that "Mrs. Ryan will make no definite announcements of her plans, but one may look for an interesting description of native California life at no very distant day if the close study of the local conditions by the gifted writer is any indication" (*El Viajante,* Saturday, October 1, 1904, clipping on file, Southwest Museum Archives). Two years after leaving the mission, Mrs. Ryan published a romantic novel, *For the Soul of Rafael,* set in San Juan Capistrano. It not only included photographs staged in the mission ruins but was also based closely enough on some of the characters she had met during her sojourn there that some of the locals were offended (Krekelberg, *Mission San Juan Capistrano,* 61).

88. Marah Ellis Ryan to Charles Lummis, September 5, 1904, correspondence on file, Southwest Museum Archives.

89. Ibid.

90. Egan to Lummis, August 31, 1904; quoted in Krekelberg, *Mission San Juan Capistrano,* 67. O'Reilly led services at the mission as well as served as rector of St. Joseph's Parish in Santa Ana. Krekelberg adds a note that Egan was "at times suspicious and unfriendly toward the clergy," which Krekelberg attributes to the disputes between the Juaneños and the Capistrano settlers in which Father Mut had taken the part of the Indians and Egan had held it against the Church. Krekelberg also points out that Egan was not above removing property from the mission for personal purposes, and that he had sent floor tiles from the mission for Lummis to use in the construction of his home; Krekelberg, *Mission San Juan Capistrano,* 67.

91. For example, a 1912 report on the restoration funds lists donors that include the Landmarks Club ($150), Native Sons of the Golden West ($15), John and Frank Foster ($25 each), "various persons" ($35), and "through Fr. Quentu" (then rector of the parish) ($200); Krekelberg, *Mission San Juan Capistrano,* 77.

92. O'Sullivan to Monsignor Cawley, January 1923; quoted in Krekelberg, *Mission San Juan Capistrano,* 134.

93. O'Sullivan, *Little Chapters about San Juan Capistrano.* Entries regarding the construction sequence and admission fee can be found in the *Mission Ledger* and are quoted in Krekelberg, *Mission San Juan Capistrano,* 95, 105.

94. The statue was sculpted by John Van Rennselaer, and at O'Sullivan's request Father Zephyrin Engelhardt spoke at its first dedication on August 13, 1914. A second more secular dedication took place three months later with Lummis, McGroarty, and other civic leaders in attendance; Krekelberg, *Mission San Juan Capistrano,* 80–81.

95. It is not known if the 1922 fountain restorations in Brand Park were a specific model for O'Sullivan, who had already completed the small fountain in the "sacred garden" in 1920, but he had a car and traveled to Los Angeles for meetings (Lummis journal, November 21, 24, 1916; quoted in Krekelberg, *Mission San Juan Capistrano,* 96).

96. Lummis journal; quoted in Krekelberg, *Mission San Juan Capistrano,* 87.

97. Quoted in Krekelberg, *Mission San Juan Capistrano,* 140–41.

98. Rexford Newcomb to Wallace Penfield, September 17, 1936, La Purísima Mission State Park Archives.

99. Hallan-Gibson, "Mission San Juan Capistrano," 63.

100. Anonymous, "Is She in Your Album?" *Los Angeles Times,* June 13, 1929, 8.

101. Anonymous, "Restorer of Mission Dies," 7.

102. The fountain in the middle of the central courtyard is called the "Fountain of the Four Evangelists" and was constructed in 1930. The development of the garden was likely delayed by the Depression, which sharply reduced tourism at the mission. At the time of O'Sullivan's death in 1933 the fountain had been completed and the walks laid out, but the plantings were not completed until the spring of 1934; Krekelberg, *Mission San Juan Capistrano,* 161–63.

103. Anonymous, "Garden Club Gives Seeds," n.p.

104. Anonymous, "Jubilee Celebration."

105. Through gifts and the joint purchase by the state and Santa Barbara County, 520 acres were assembled and in 1935 the property was vested in the state of California and designated as La Purísima State Historical Monument, to be managed by the California Department of Natural Resources, Division of State Parks (Whitehead, ed., *California's Mission La Purísima Concepción,* xxvi). In one of the few studies of the garden at La Purísima, Charles Hosmer draws interesting parallels between the Colonial Revival designs at La Purísima and Colonial Williamsburg. His research seems to include only the Hageman and Ewing documents reprinted in Whitehead, and he therefore misses some of the subtleties of divergent agendas each of the parties brought to the negotiations regarding the mission garden design; Hosmer, "The Colonial Revival in the Public Eye." Similarly, Christine Savage's account of the garden relies heavily on Hageman and Rowe's publication, which overlooks some of the revealing debates among project principals (Savage, *New Deal Adobe,* 123–30).

106. The restoration project was managed jointly by the State Department of Natural Resources, Division of State Parks, and by the National Park Service with the understanding that the site would be administered by the California State Parks Department once the construction was finished. It was dedicated December 7, 1941, as La Purísima State Historical Monument and became a California State Park in 1963.

107. At La Purísima, Company #1951 served from July 1934 until June 1942, the longest assignment of any company to a camp in the California program (NPS National Register Nomination National-State Park Cooperative Program and the Civilian Conservation Corps in California State Parks, 1933–1942, draft, E8). The dormitory, church, and outbuildings were reconstructed with hundreds of thousands of hand-made adobe bricks but architects adapted the traditional building methods to modern construction standards because of seismic activity in the area. The workers, most of whom were from the Los Angeles area, apparently recognized the significance of their endeavors to rebuild such a historic monument, and many reenrolled for multiple tours at the site (Savage, *New Deal Adobe,* 100). As recently as 2008 the CCC laborers returned to La Purísima for a reunion to celebrate the

seventy-fifth anniversary of the CCC (1933–2008); personal communication, Ann Boggess, State Park interpreter, May 7, 2008.

108. A group of citizens called the Advisory Committee, chaired by Santa Barbara County Engineer Wallace Penfield, was invited by the CCC to offer expertise and to coordinate with local planning efforts. Committee members included Dr. Frederic Clements, director of the Santa Barbara Ecological Station of the Carnegie Institute; Carleton Monroe Wilson, architect and vice-chairman of the Historic Buildings Committee; Kelley Hardenbrook, an attorney based in Lompoc who was familiar with the land acquisitions for the park; Marion Parks, a researcher and historian of the Santa Barbara Parlor of Native Daughters of the Golden West; and Pearl Chase, general chairman of the Plans and Planting Committee of the Community Arts Association of Santa Barbara and chairman of the County Roadside Committee. Ex officio members were Ronald Adam, county supervisor of the Lompoc District; L. Deming Tilton, director of the State Planning Commission and director of the Santa Barbara County Planning Commission; Frank Dunne, Santa Barbara County forester; and Wallace C. Penfield, engineer of the Santa Barbara County Planning Commission (Hageman, "An Architectural Study of the Mission La Purísima Concepción," 199). Senior foreman Fred C. Hageman, a staff architect of the National Park Service, directed the CCC labor force while Russell Ewing, the Park Service's "regional historical inspector," provided research on documentary evidence for the reconstruction.

109. Report of September 24, 1935; quoted in subsequent report by W. C. Penfield, chairman, La Purisima Advisory Committee, "Standards and Policies of the La Purisima Advisory Committee Concerning the Grounds of the La Purisima Mission," June 15, 1936.

110. Wallace Penfield to Mr. Newton B. Drury, February 25, 1936, La Purísima Mission State Park Archives, Advisory Committee file.

111. The challenge of resolving the divergent opinions was magnified by the need for the landscaping to keep pace with the building restoration in time for the public opening, and partly because the County of Santa Barbara had, based on the plan approved in 1935, purchased additional land and paid for reconfiguring a road and other improvements to accommodate a garden in the front of the mission.

112. Ewing, "Mission La Purisima Conception, California," 236.

113. Russell C. Ewing to Lawrence C. Merriam, regional officer, U.S. Department of the Interior, National Park Service, Branch of Planning and State Cooperation, May 22, 1936, La Purísima Mission State Park Archives, Advisory Committee file.

114. The mission is sited at the base of a mesa so that there is limited space behind the mission buildings. Today this area is interpreted as a small walled courtyard in which crafts and daily chores are demonstrated (there is an oven for baking bread). There seems to have been no consideration of this space as a site for the garden during the 1930s restoration.

115. Emerson Knight, regional inspector, "Basic principles which should govern design of La Purisima Mission Garden near Lompoc," enclosure in memo to Mr. Wallace C. Penfield from Lawrence C. Merriam, May 25, 1936, La Purísima Mission State Park Archives, Advisory Committee file.

116. Russell C. Ewing to Lawrence C. Merriam, regional officer, U.S. Department of Interior, National Park Service, Branch of Planning and State Cooperation, May 22, 1936, La Purísima Mission State Park Archives, Advisory Committee file.

117. Emerson Knight, regional inspector, "Basic principles which should govern design of La Purísima Mission Garden near Lompoc," enclosure in memo to Mr. Wallace C.

Penfield from Lawrence C. Merriam, May 25, 1936, La Purísima Mission State Park Archives, Advisory Committee file.

118. Daniel R. Hull to Lawrence C. Merriam, regional officer, National Park Service, June 1, 1936, La Purísima Mission State Park Archives, Advisory Committee file.

119. Minutes of the La Purisima Advisory Committee, April 16, 1936, La Purísima Mission State Park Archives.

120. Wallace C. Penfield, "Standards and Policies of the La Purisima Advisory Committee Concerning the Grounds of the La Purisima Mission," June 15, 1936, 1–2 (emphasis in the original), La Purísima Mission State Park Archives, Advisory Committee file.

121. Ibid., 4. Penfield's reference is to Rexford Newcomb, *The Old Mission Churches and Historic Houses of California.*

122. It can hardly be coincidental that Newcomb's drawing of the restored plan of San Juan Capistrano with its patio garden and central fountain was reprinted in the Hageman report with the caption "Comparative California Mission Plans"; Hageman, "An Architectural Study of the Mission La Purísima Concepción," 31.

123. Shepherd's original proposal, which was subsequently modified by the Park Service, was for a four-acre patio "enclosed by a low wall, enframed along one side by an arbor completely embowered with grapes, wisteria, clematis, jasmine and climbing roses, and along the other side trees for windbreak and shelter. These plants have been with us for centuries throughout Spain, Mexico, and in California. . . . The sketch . . . gives the proper conception of the informal grouping of old favorites as creeping thyme, carnations, stocks, iris, larkspur, lavender, poppy, violets, calendula, hollyhocks, and other ground covers. The planting of woody shrubs as roses, myrtle, crepe myrtle, . . . germander, rosemary, pomegranates and oleander along these walks is very typical of the informal arrangement found in many early Mission gardens. The fact that evidence is not always found of the early presence of some of these plants does not indicate that they did not exist in many of the Mission gardens"; Harry Shepherd, "Report of the Landscape Development of Mission La Purisima, Lompoc Calif." Submitted to the Advisory Committee of La Purisima Mission, April 13, 1936, p. 1, La Purísima Mission State Park Archives, Advisory Committee file.

124. Wallace C. Penfield, "Standards and Policies of the La Purisima Advisory Committee Concerning the Grounds of the La Purisima Mission," June 15, 1936, 5, La Purísima Mission State Park Archives, Advisory Committee file.

125. Ibid., 7–8.

126. The tropes of nostalgia and its underlying ideology are discussed in more detail in chapter 4.

127. Emerson Knight, regional inspector, "Basic principles which should govern design of La Purisima Mission Garden near Lompoc," enclosure in memo to Mr. Wallace C. Penfield from Lawrence C. Merriam, May 25, 1936, La Purísima Mission State Park Archives, Advisory Committee file.

128. Wallace C. Penfield, "Standards and Policies of the La Purisima Advisory Committee Concerning the Grounds of the La Purisima Mission," June 15, 1936, 4, La Purísima Mission State Park Archives, Advisory Committee file.

129. Hageman, "An Architectural Study of the Mission La Purísima Concepción," 124–35, 177; Ewing, "Mission La Purisima," includes photographs of the water features being excavated and restored, raising questions of how much of the architectural detail was based on archaeologically recovered evidence, and what was based on comparative models such as San Fernando's fountain (287–88).

130. Shepherd and Rowe tried to reduce the formality of the geometric beds by planting trailing plants along the edges of the paths.

131. Wallace Penfield to Mr. H. Dana Bowers, July 6, 1937, La Purísima Mission State Park Archives, Advisory Committee file.

132. Rowe, "The Story of a Garden."

133. Hageman, "An Architectural Study of the Mission La Purísima Concepción," 8.

134. A cross had been erected in the garden in 1951, and by 1957, when the Advisory Committee met to address maintenance issues in the then twenty-year-old garden and develop more educational programs, it was treated as just another garden feature whose plantings needed a "sound pruning program" (minutes of the Advisory Committee, September 21, 1957, La Purísima Mission State Park Archives, Advisory Committee file). As of 2008, a cross stands in front of the church.

135. Wallace Penfield to Newton B. Drury, December 5, 1936, La Purísima Mission State Park Archives, Advisory Committee file.

136. Guy L. Fleming, superintendent, Southern District, to J. H. Covington, December 14, 1936, La Purísima Mission State Park Archives, Advisory Committee file.

137. Newton B. Drury to Wallace Penfield, February 27, 1936, La Purísima Mission State Park Archives, Advisory Committee file.

138. Ford, "Some Detached Notes," 240–41.

139. Ibid., 240.

140. Benthold, "Uncovering the Mission's Secrets," 187.

141. Anonymous, "Colegio de San Gabriel," 198.

142. Anonymous, "Old Mission Will Boast New Garden," n.p.

143. This phenomenon of connecting descent groups to the preservation of significant places in the geography of their ancestors was common across the country. For case studies elsewhere in the United States, see Brundage, *The Southern Past,* and Lindgren, *Preserving the Old Dominion.*

144. Hand-lettered posted sign next to the models, April 2008.

145. Hidalgo, "A Meaningful Rededication at San Gabriel Mission."

146. Interview with Manuel Ramirez and Bernardo Casas, Mission San Gabriel, 2008.

147. While I have not done a systematic survey of the maintenance arrangements at all the mission gardens, a number contract with outside landscaping companies. For example, at Mission San Diego a landscaping crew drives up from Tijuana to tend the garden. At Santa Barbara a firm is contracted to tend the central courtyard garden. At San Juan Capistrano the landscape volunteers (the "Gardening Angels") have collaborated with the archaeologists and preservationists to devise landscaping guidelines that preserve the integrity of the buildings, but the exuberant floral displays are the work of the volunteers. At San Antonio de Padua the newly renovated garden is tended by a group of volunteers from a nearby town who have no connection to the parish. At San Antonio de Pala, a part-time staff person tends the garden, and the mission curator is trying to recruit volunteers. This information on the contemporary site management was gathered through personal communication with maintenance staff, docents, and curators at the missions.

148. While technically an "asistencia" of Mission San Luis Rey and not one of the original twenty-one missions, Pala is included in this study. It is generally considered part of the corpus of California missions as it is older and larger than some of the "official" missions, and it is included in the official list of missions eligible for Mission Foundation funds under the California Missions Preservation Act. The parcel that includes the mission (two-thirds

of an acre) was conveyed in 1961 without compensation from the Pala Reservation to the Diocese of San Diego Education and Welfare Corporation to be used for educational purposes; 75 U.S. Statutes at Large 79, May 1961.

149. Hyer, *"We Are Not Savages,"* 32–33. Hyer's book is an excellent source for a more detailed history of the Cupeño, Luiseños, Kumeyaays, and the Pala Reservation, particularly the history of violence and legal dispossession of Native lands and the strategies of resistance throughout.

150. Ibid., 97–101; see also Carillo, *The Story of Mission San Antonio de Pala.* Activist and author Helen Hunt Jackson visited the Pala reservation in 1883 and reported on the poor conditions. Jackson and Kinney, *Report,* 29.

151. Pala Band of Mission Indians, http://www.palatribe.com. The Cupeños joined the Luiseños on the reservation in 1903 following their forced removal from the traditional Cupa lands forty miles away at what is known today as Warner Springs.

152. The Comboni Fathers were called the Sons of the Sacred Heart at the time they came to Pala. Now called the Comboni Missionaries, they are also known as Verona Fathers. In May 1991 the mission was returned to the Diocese of San Diego. The Barnabite Fathers were in charge of the Pala Mission from June 1996 to July 2005, at which point the Diocese of San Diego resumed administration and pastoral care of the mission.

153. 75 U.S. Statutes at Large 79 (1961).

154. Pala Casino Spa Resort, http://www.palacasino.com.

155. Other prominent donors included Dr. Eugene Vinograd, Colonel Irving Salomon, Mr. and Mrs. Thomas Leavey, and the Bureau of Catholic Indian Missions; Carillo, *The Story of Mission San Antonio de Pala,* 32–37.

156. Ibid., 35.

157. Ibid., 37.

158. This "do it yourself" resourcefulness has led to some ongoing problems with drainage and failing masonry in the garden; personal communication, Sister Barbara Jackson, May 2008.

159. Rindge, *Ceramic Arts of the Malibu Potteries,* 111–15. I am grateful to Father Jack Clark Robinson for telling me of the Franciscan connections with Malibu tile and for pointing out its use in the Santa Barbara fountain (note: this fountain is in a different courtyard than the original Romo fountain and garden); Father Jack Clark Robinson, personal communication, April 2008.

160. The Santa Barbara fountain with Malibu tile is in a courtyard of the Retreat Center, to the west of the site of Romo's 1872 garden in the main quadrangle patio.

161. Avente Tile, LLC, an online tile showroom and catalog founded in 2002 by Bill Buyok; http://www.aventetile.com.

162. "History and Culture," Pala Band of Mission Indians, accessed July 11, 2014, http://www.palatribe.com.

163. Father Bonaventure Oblasser, 1954 letter to Bishop Charles Francis Buddy; quoted in Durchholz, *Defining Mission,* 67.

164. Mission San Antonio de Pala, http://www.missionsanantonio.org/Home_Page.php. The site also notes that "the submissions of St. Bartholomew's on the Rincon Indian Reservation, Our Lady of Refuge on the La Jolla Indian Reservation, and St. James on the Pauma Indian Reservation [Pauma Band of Luiseño Indians] continue to work through Mission San Antonio de Pala" ("A Summarized History," http://www.missionsanantonio.org/History.html).

165. See Harrison, *Shared Landscapes,* for an analysis of the physically and mentally constructed landscapes of both Aboriginal and settler pastoralists on the grazing lands of Australia.

166. Byrne, "An Archaeology of Attachment."

167. "Fr. Herman Manuel, SVD," http://www.svdvocations.org.

168. *Fallbrook and Bonsall Village News,* "Corpus Christi Fiesta at Pala June 1."

169. Plans and Planting Committee, La Purisima, memo from Pearl Chase, chairman Sub-Committee, October 1, 1954.

170. *Santa Barbara News Press,* January 24, 1948; quoted in Geiger, *Mission Santa Barbara,* 244.

171. Sherman, "Historic Mission's New Master Plan Has Been Tweaked."

172. Engelhardt, *Mission San Antonio de Padua,* 131–32.

173. Krekelberg, *Mission San Juan Capistrano,* 120.

174. McCan, "Mission Garden Restored," 10.

3. Cultivating Heritage

1. Anonymous, *Santa Barbara News Press,* January 24, 1948.

2. Kropp, *California Vieja,* 13.

3. Dyer, "To Preserve the Early Landmarks."

4. For analysis of the construction of the "Spanish fantasy past" in the cultural landscape, see DeLyser, *Ramona Memories*; Kropp, *California Vieja*; McClung, *Landscapes of Desire*; McWilliams, *Southern California Country*; and Thomas, "Harvesting Ramona's Garden."

5. Kropp, *California Vieja,* 5.

6. Heidenreich, *This Land Was Mexican Once,* chap. 5.

7. Flower, *A Child's History of California,* 55.

8. Halbwachs, *On Collective Memory,* 200; Somers, "The Narrative Constitution of Identity."

9. Sharp, *Geographies of Postcolonialism,* 37.

10. Examples of similarly contested and constructed meanings have been explored at heritage sites around the world. See, for example, Dearborn and Stallmeyer, *Inconvenient Heritage,* and Eggleton, "Re-envisioning the Alhambra."

11. Lummis, McGroarty, and Forbes, "Old Mission One of *Your* Big Assets."

12. Angier, *The Garden Book of California,* 34–35.

13. Ibid., 49–50.

14. Kryder-Reid, "'Perennially New,'" 396–400.

15. French, *The California Garden,* 75.

16. De Forest, "Old Santa Barbara Gardens"; Streatfield, "Where Pine and Palm Meet," 65–66.

17. Byne and Byne, *Spanish Gardens and Patios*; Fox, *Patio Gardens*; Latham, *The Gardens of Italy*; Nichols, *Spanish and Portuguese Gardens*; Wharton, *Italian Villas and Their Gardens.* These lavishly illustrated books tended to present the European gardens as timeless remnants of a classical age when in fact many were influenced by contemporary design trends and international influences in their own right.

18. Warner, *Our Italy,* 9.

19. Aiken, "Upon the King's Highway," 691.

20. Garnett, "Stately Homes of California."

21. Deverell and Flamming investigate a similar construction of Los Angeles's emerging regional and racialized identity through the rhetoric of constructed "other," whether "the East" or a romanticized distant past ("Race, Rhetoric, and Regional Identity"); Abigail Van Slyck has similarly examined the construction of architecture and racial identity in the Southwest ("Mañana, Mañana").

22. Dr. Ezra Carr, "Art and Nature," *Southern California Horticulturalist* 2, no. 1 (1878): 1; quoted in Sackman, "A Garden of Worldly Delights," 251.

23. Dyer, "To Preserve the Early Landmarks."

24. Within the rich literature on this topic, see studies on the intersection of photography, landscape, tourism, and public memory, in particular, Barron, Bernstein, and Fort, eds., *Reading California*; Edwards and Hart, eds., *Photographs Objects Histories*; Kroes, *Photographic Memories*; Redding, ed., *Through the Lens*; Respini, ed., *Into the Sunset*; Sandweiss, *Print the Legend*; Schwartz and Ryan, *Picturing Place*; Strain, *Public Places, Private Journeys*; and Urry, *The Tourist Gaze,* chap. 6. For the Southern California context, see Watts, "Picture Taking in Paradise" and "Photography in the Land of Sunshine."

25. Watts, "Picture Taking in Paradise," 218; see also Crang, "Knowing, Tourism, and Practices of Vision."

26. For a more comprehensive treatment of Watkins, see Nickel, *Carleton Watkins,* and Palmquist, *Carleton E. Watkins.*

27. It should be noted that in some of the better-preserved missions, such as San Luis Rey, Watkins included figures in the foreground, a technique that serves to highlight the scale of the facades. Watkins also documented Native peoples living at the perimeter of the missions, such as his view of "Indian Huts at Mission San Gabriel."

28. Watts and others have noted that certain views become privileged at each mission and are replicated by amateur and professional photographers alike (Watts, "Picture Taking in Paradise," 226). See also Burton-Carvajal, "The Carmel Mission in Art."

29. Taber, *California Scenery.* Until it was destroyed in the 1906 earthquake and fire, Taber's San Francisco studio dealt largely in portraits and views, and he both published scenic views of his own and purchased work of other photographers (often unattributed), including Carleton Watkins's stock, which Taber acquired in 1881 following Watkins's bankruptcy; Getty Museum, "I. W. Taber."

30. Neuerburg, "Biographical Introduction." Ford exhibited his mission engravings in 1893 at the Chicago World's Fair and at the California Midwinter Exposition the following year in San Francisco. The Fine Arts Dealers Association entry for Henry Chapman Ford credits his exhibition of mission etchings at the Chicago World's Fair in 1893 for "sparking real interest in the Spanish heritage of the state of California"; http://www.fada.org/browse_by_essay.html?essay=722&lookfor=Henry+Chapman+Ford.

31. Jorgensen exhibited his mission watercolor series in Washington, D.C., in 1906 as well as in a number of galleries in California, including the Bohemian Club in San Francisco, and they are now on display at Mission Solano in Sonoma. Significantly, Santa Barbara is the only mission in which Jorgensen included human figures.

32. See Burton-Carvajal, "The Carmel Mission in Art"; Neuerburg, "The California Missions in Art"; and Stern, "Art in California."

33. Vaughn, "The Joining of Historical Pageantry and the Spanish Fantasy Past."

34. Guy's painting won the Gold Medal at San Diego's Panama-California Exposition in 1915 and was donated by a private collector to the San Diego History Center in 2011

(San Diego History Center press release, July 3, 2011, http://www.sandiegohistory.org/press/5818).

35. Vaughn, "The Joining of Historical Pageantry and the Spanish Fantasy Past," 218. Monroy makes something of the opposite argument in "Making Mexico in Los Angeles" by tracing how Mexicans in Los Angeles in the 1920s "placed themselves on the landscape" through theater, sports, and religion (161).

36. Jackson, *Ancient Missions and Churches of America,* n.p.

37. The source for Harry Fenn's engravings is an intriguing question that reveals the interplay of media and the role of the Franciscans' own promotional efforts. Fenn (1838–1911), one of the founders of the American Watercolor Society, was a prolific book and magazine illustrator, producing 111 images for *Harper's* alone from 1869 to 1908 (Henry, "History of the Picture Postcard"). When Fenn was touring the United States in 1870 gathering material for Bryant, ed., *Picturesque America,* the Santa Barbara garden had yet not been created. Fenn's view, however, mirrors the perspectives of the 1885 photographs of the garden, suggesting he worked from those early photos for the 1887 *Harper's* story.

38. It is interesting to note that the view looking east with the Santa Barbara towers in the background is only possible from a vantage point in the garden or, for the more elevated perspectives, from the upper story of the south wing of the quadrangle. The entry into the garden was forbidden to women and access to the second floor would have required special permission, making the postcard a portal for views otherwise not available to everyone.

39. Henry, "The History of the Picture Postcard," 3; Willes, foreword to *Picturing Berkeley.* Real-photo postcards (sometimes called RPPCs) involve developing a negative onto photo paper with a preprinted postcard backing.

40. For a more extensive discussion of McCan's development of Brand Park in San Fernando, see chap. 2.

41. McGroarty, "The Place of the Sacred Garden," 239.

42. In this regard they partake in what Denis Cosgrove has described as the "dialectics of modernity" (Cosgrove, "Landscape, Culture, Modernity," 45).

43. Mitchell (*The Lie of the Land*) and Sackman ("A Garden of Worldly Delights") have argued that this sense of spatial segregation has been critical to the marginalization of the labor that actually produced California's agricultural bounty. The walled and bounded gardens of elite residences and suburban tracts were examples of Veblen's "polite environments" that "inscribed social hierarchy into the landscape" (Sackman, "Garden of Worldly Delights," 255).

44. Engle, "'Roughing It' at Ft. Hunter Liggett."

45. Boucher, "Mission Project," L4.

46. Hallan-Gibson, "Mission San Juan Capistrano," 71. Exhibition curator Jean Stern describes Hallan-Gibson as an expert in the acknowledgments to *Romance of the Bells* (13).

47. Anonymous, "Old Spanish Missions Standing."

48. Gunthorp, *With a Sketch Book along the Old Mission Trail,* 146.

49. Downie, *A Visit to San Carlos,* n.p.

50. Amero, "The Making of the Panama-California Exposition," 17. For an analysis of the fair's inculcation of the Spanish heritage narrative, see Bokovoy, *The San Diego World's Fairs and Southwestern Memory,* and Kropp, *California Vieja,* chap. 3. For a history of the exposition's landscape design and its influence on the Mediterranean Revival landscape architectural movement, see Montes, "Balboa Park, 1909–1911." In a similar display, the cast of *The Mission Play* accompanied a float representing Mission San Gabriel in the Rose Bowl Parade

in 1924 (*Los Angeles Times* photo archives), http://framework.latimes.com/2011/12/30/the-rose-parade/#/7.

51. Goodhue, introduction to *The Architecture and the Gardens of the San Diego Exposition,* 6.

52. The pageant was staged by Henry Kabierski and the writer John Steven McGroarty to perform historical dramas about the mission era in California. Bokovoy, "Humanist Sentiment, Modern Spanish Heritage, and California Mission Commemoration."

53. The miniatures are cast from sculptures by Lompoc, California, artist Alvin Cabral. The Cameo Guild manufactures the missions using a cold-cast porcelain method that involves pouring a liquid blend of resin and ground porcelain into a mold that is placed into a vacuum chamber. After cooling, the sculpture is removed from the mold and hand painted. Seiden, "Monuments to the Missions."

54. The standard size measures approximately 3″ H × 7″ W × 5″ D and the smaller cameo version is 2″ H × 3″ W × 3″ D. Because their price exceeds that of the typical souvenir and because they are also sold through high-end boutiques and directly from the Cameo Guild website, it is likely these objects are typically consumed by "collectors" as well as souvenir shoppers, but the Cameo Guild does not share their consumer profile information.

55. Cameo Guild Studios, "Mission de Oro Collection," product brochure.

56. Seiden, "Monuments to the Missions."

57. Cameo Guild Studios, "California Mission Gifts, Souvenirs, and Collectibles," http://www.cameoguildstore.com.

58. Cameo Guild Studios, "Mission de Oro Collection," product brochure.

59. This ideology of the vacant, picturesque landscape is implicated in the nostalgic invention of the English "cottage garden" tradition, which similarly has been reproduced through the visual culture of paintings, cookie tins, and miniatures. Helmreich, "Domesticating the Nation" and "The Marketing of Helen Allingham."

60. Cameo Guild Studios, "Mission de Oro Collection," product brochure.

61. This construction of meaning of the missions parallels other heritage sites. Eggleton's analysis of the Alhambra similarly details how "a series of visualizing tropes and tendencies within both textural and image based media . . . dislocated 'the site' from its Nasrid origins and post-conquest reinvention, while being absorbed into an idea of Spain and its Islamic heritage that has endured to the present day." As at the missions, reenvisioning space at the Alhambra had implications for site design as it was remade "in accordance with the desires, anxieties, apprehensions and expectations of visitors in the late eighteenth and early nineteenth centuries" (Eggleton, "Re-envisioning the Alhambra," 6).

62. Jackson, *Ancient Missions and Churches,* 1.

63. Sandos, *Converting California,* 154.

64. Weber, "San Fernando," 397–98.

65. Downie, *Mission San Carlos Borromeo del Rio Carmelo,* 1; two-page pamphlet (on file, Bancroft Library, Berkeley).

66. Saunders, "Historic Gardens in California," 394.

67. Reynolds, "The Story of Alta California's Bountiful Mission Gardens," 12.

68. This consumption of the landscape as destination and pilgrimage is discussed more fully in chap. 4.

69. *In the Path of the Padres,* n.p.

70. "Path of the Padres" hikes are offered by California State Parks staff at the San Luis Reservoir State Recreation area; see http://www.parks.ca.gov/?page_id=28070.

71. In addition to glowing descriptions of the mission garden itself, the story embeds its mission garden style in the cottage residence the group rents for the season: "the garden surrounding it [the house] contained a profusion of flowers, vines, and trees. To the right stood a gnarled old pine. . . . Just beyond its shadow was the garden, divided into different beds by a series of walks that radiated from a fountain. By the side of the latter, shading and half hiding it grew a banana-tree; and at different corners of the beds were orange and lemon trees" (Roberts, "A Santa Barbara Holiday," 816).

72. Ibid., 822.

73. Ibid., 824.

74. Ibid.

75. Steele, *Old Californian Days.* As noted, Warner's *Our Italy* (1890) included an image of the garden with a friar, as did Stoddard in 1900 in the Southern California volume of his published lecture series (Stoddard, *John L. Stoddard's Lectures*). In *The Missions of California,* Smyth (1899) used an image of the garden as a frontispiece, in this case with a padre standing on the steps of the church looking into the garden.

76. Henry, "Alice Hare," 159–62.

77. Shurtleff, *The Old Missions of California,* n.p.

78. Eggleton, "Re-envisioning the Alhambra," 198, 201. Eggleton also explores the dynamic relationship between viewing and constructed meaning at the Alhambra over time in "'A Living Ruin.'"

79. Watts, "Picture Taking in Paradise," 219.

80. A 1949 *San Francisco Chronicle* article cited in the California Missions Museum text uses the spelling "Leon Bayard de Vale" but records associated with Miniature Fabricators and the mission models created for Knott's Berry Farm use "Leon Bayard de Volo." The models range in size from approximately 59″ × 38″ to 36″ × 28″. Edmondson's career was primarily in Southern California with a particular focus on Spanish Colonial Revival residential architecture. He had worked with George Washington Smith, a leader in the Spanish Colonial Revival style. Stanton's career was based in Carmel, and he worked primarily in Northern California. His architectural legacy includes a number of public buildings such as the city hall and library in King City and the Monterey County Courthouse in Salinas (Pacific Coast Architecture Database).

81. While Native Americans were not included in models or in other Mission Trails Building exhibits, there were extensive exhibits of Native American art, history, and culture at the Exposition, but mainly located in the Federal Building and representing over 100 tribes from around the United States (*San Francisco Chronicle,* February 17, 1939, 37E).

82. For a more detailed history of the mission models, see Kryder-Reid, "Crafting the Past."

83. According to museum curator Nancy Butler (personal communication, October 30, 2008), "The California Model Missions Museum is a supported organization of the National Heritage Foundation. All of the 990 tax information is reported under the umbrella of the National Heritage Foundation. The museum was accepted by their Board of Directors as a nonprofit project on 4/1/1999 and therefore shares the nonprofit 501(c)(3), 509(a)(1) federal tax status. All donations to this foundation are tax deductible." The National Heritage Foundation (http://nhf.org), which administered multiple donor-managed funds, declared bankruptcy in 2009 (Barrett, "Controversial Charity Files for Bankruptcy").

84. Jenkins, "The Catholic Menace," 29. See also Nordstrom, *Danger on the Doorstep.*

85. Roy has argued that the popularity of the anti-Catholic rhetoric of the 1910s was due in part to its mobilization of themes of progressivism, masculinity, and nationalism; Roy, *Rhetorical Campaigns of the Nineteenth-Century.*

86. Saunders and Chase, *The California Padres and Their Missions,* v.

87. Saunders and Chase, "Love in the Padres' Garden," 173.

88. Ibid., 176.

89. Bremer, "Tourists and Religion."

90. Starr, *Inventing the Dream,* 89.

91. "A Task above Church or Creed" is the title of an illustration in which a female figure reminiscent of Lady Liberty with a crown inscribed "California" holds a scroll reading, "The restoration of the most important landmark in California's history." The image, signed by "Gale," is from an unnamed newspaper in the clipping file of the Coy Collection, California State Library, Sacramento.

92. Anonymous, "Will You Help Restore California Landmark?"

93. Americans United for Separation of Church and State ("Americans United") filed a federal lawsuit (Doe v. Norton, No. 04CV02089—D.D.C. filed December 2, 2004) challenging the constitutionality of the Missions Act on October 2, 2004, two days after the passage of the original legislation. Cooperman, "Federal Aid for Churches Is Criticized."

94. Mahaney, "The California Missions Preservation Act."

95. Senator Barbara Boxer, http://www.boxer.senate.gov, accessed March 12, 2008.

96. Samuel Farr, congressional testimony, November 17, 2004. Farr is the U.S. representative for California's Twentieth Congressional District, which includes Carmel.

97. Rev. Barry W. Lynn, letter submitted for inclusion in the *Congressional Record,* November 17, 2004. Lynn is the executive director of Americans United for Separation of Church and State.

98. Cosgrove and Daniels, eds., *The Iconography of Landscape*; Crary, *Techniques of the Observer*; Harley, *Maps, Knowledge, and Power*; Neal, "Practice Makes Perfect"; Urry, *The Tourist Gaze.*

99. Cosgrove, "Landscape, Culture and Modernity," 32.

100. Daniels, *Humphrey Repton.*

101. Edmonds, "Who Said Romance Was Dead?"

102. Sutton and Stroulia, "Archaeological Sites and the Chasm between Past and Present."

103. Anthony Wayne Vodges's album in the Huntington Library collection records his California travels (1888–92) and contains nine photographs of the Santa Barbara Mission, including two views of the garden taken in 1888. Other examples include photo albums in collections of the Bancroft Library, the Huntington Library, and the California Historical Society. These albums attest to the growing importance of photographs as a way for tourists to commemorate their mission visits. For example, the Bancroft collection includes 106 photographic prints, albumen, 11 × 19 cm., mounted and compiled in an album of unknown authorship titled "Scenic Views in California and the Columbia River Gorge" (ca. 1880–ca. 1890?).

104. For the changing meaning and messages of photography over time, see Barthes, *Camera Lucida.* This notion of the enduring emotional geography of personal photos is a rich line of inquiry in its own right. One example of the value of such research is Rose, "'Everyone's Cuddled Up.'"

105. The translation of photographs into placemaking devices is also explored in Chambers, "Family as Place," and Sontag, *On Photography,* 8–9.

106. Stewart, *On Longing,* 137–38.

107. Carroll, "The Influence of the Missions on Present-Day California."

108. For an in-depth history of the development of the El Camino Real and the placement of the bell markers in the early twentieth century, see Kropp, *California Vieja,* chap. 2, and "In Search of History and Romance." For a more detailed history of the bells and their manufacture, see Kurillo and Tuttle, *California's El Camino Real and Its Historic Bells.*

109. For a more complete analysis of mission gift shops, see Pedelty, "The New California Mission System." The role of material culture in religious experience and tourism is explored more fully in Wharton, *Selling Jerusalem.*

110. The story of this family's RV tour of all twenty-one missions is posted at http://varley.net/nonfiction/adventures21-missions-part-1 and http://varley.net/nonfiction/adventures/21-missions-part-2.

111. The pleasure of collecting was explored in 1931 by Benjamin, *Illuminations,* and more fully by Muensterberger, *Collecting.* The links between collecting and identity are extensively mined in the four-volume series *The Collector's Voice,* edited by Susan Pearce and Paul Martin, particularly in vol. 4, *Contemporary Voices.*

112. Daniel Miller argues for the material environment's role in creating us as subjects/selves and speaks to the role of consumption in constituting the contexts of human subjectivity; Miller, *The Comfort of Things* and *Stuff,* and Miller, ed., *Materiality.*

113. Pearce and Martin, introduction to *Contemporary Voices,* vol. 4 of *The Collector's Voice,* xxi.

114. Gordon, *Private History in Public.* For an in-depth study of archaeological approaches to material consumption in American history, see Mullins, *The Archaeology of Consumer Culture.*

115. For a fuller history of the roadside mission bell markers, see Kropp, *California Vieja,* chap. 2. Listings for vintage mission memorabilia in online sellers also include commemorative plates and cups, linen wall hangings, pillows, automobile association maps and brochures, lapel pins, albums, teaspoons, and postcards.

116. Kryder-Reid, "Crafting the Past."

117. As part of an informal heritage practice, there is little record of model making in official archives. Evidence of the practice can be traced, however, to examples such as Harry Downie's boyhood model of the mission he would go on to help restore as an adult; Anonymous, "Mission Models Were Harry Downie's Hobby." Norman Neuerburg, an architectural historian who studied the missions extensively, has written about visiting another mission scholar and enthusiast, Edith Webb, in her backyard in 1941 to view her meticulously researched model of Mission San Diego; Neuerburg, "The Little Mission." The practice is continued by amateurs and professionals who offer their models for sale. For example, a documentary series on the missions hosted by Huell Howser includes coverage of hobbyist Luis Tur, who is described as making "nineteen of the twenty-one mission models using nothing but pieces of junk" (Huell Howser Productions, *California Missions #110*). Professional artist Gene Gill has created miniatures of all twenty-one California mission buildings as part of his miniature series based on historical architecture and landmarks from around the world (http://www.genegillminiatures.com/index.html). The California missions are in the personal collection of Dr. and Mrs. Richard Dyke, Los Angeles.

118. According to Bradley Fogo (personal communication), the 1981 History-Social Science Framework was the first state curriculum framework to suggest the study of California history in fourth grade, but the 1949 textbook's inclusion of mission projects in its

"suggested activities" clearly indicates the time depth of the practices, even if not mandated. The general learning objectives have been revised several times, but the particular curriculum materials and teacher's lesson plans are developed at the local level. Fogo, "What Every Student Should Know and Be Able to Do"; Walker and Gonzalez, "Missions Accomplished for Fourth-Graders"; Quinio blog entry, September 7, 2008, http://quinio.wordpress.com/2008/09/07/scenes-from-oc-lincoln-at-the-mission.

119. Flower, *A Child's History of California,* 198.

120. Myers-Lim, "Educating Elementary School Children about California Missions," 42 (the article's byline gives the name as Meyers-Lim). See also Medina, "The Truth Shall Set Us Free"; O'Brien, "Indians and the California Gold Rush"; Pacini-Ketchabaw and Taylor, eds., *Unsettling the Colonial Places and Spaces*; and Sleeper-Smith et al., eds., *Why You Can't Teach.*

121. Gutfreund, "Standing up to Sugar Cubes," 164. Gutfreund traces the evolution of Native American and Latino activism regarding the California mission curriculum, and his analysis, including the responses of the state's Board of Education, demonstrates the symbolic significance of education debates in state politics. There is a wealth of curriculum resources online that employ critical historical perspectives. For example, in response to the question, "why study the missions?" website author Tricia Anne Weber notes, "the Missions can provide our students with a better understanding of both California's rich Native and Spanish heritages as well as the devastating effects of colonialism" (Weber, California Missions Resource Website, http://www.californias-missions.org).

122. Presidio of San Francisco, "Mission Possible," press release, June 17, 2010, http://www.presidio.gov/trust/press/pressreleases/mission10.htm.

123. Diepenbrock, "Call It California 'Mission: Possible'" (emphasis in the original), http://www.ocregister.com/articles/strong-555288-http-href.html.

124. California Missions Foundation, http://www.californiamissionsfoundation.org/the-foundation.html.

125. Baudrillard, *The System of Objects,* 73.

126. Stewart, *On Longing,* xii–xiii.

127. Dean MacCannell has explored cultural experiences such as visiting tourist attractions and argues that every experience is composed of two parts—the "model" or "embodied ideal" and the "influence" or the "changed, created, intensified belief or feeling based on the model." He writes that the "medium" is the agency that connects the model and its influence. In this paradigm, the mission models are the "medium" that refer to the "model" of mission sites, and the influence is the associated feelings and beliefs about the meaning of California's colonial past (MacCannell, *The Tourist,* 23–25).

128. Bodnar, *Remaking America.*

129. The general theme of the California State Standards for fourth grade, "California: A Changing State," charges that "students learn the story of their home state, unique in American history in terms of its vast and varied geography, its many waves of immigration beginning with pre-Columbian societies, its continuous diversity, economic energy, and rapid growth. In addition to the specific treatment of milestones in California history, students examine the state in the context of the rest of the nation, with an emphasis on the U.S. Constitution and the relationship between state and federal government" (California State Board of Education, History-Social Science Content Standards). For a discussion of how the Spanish fantasy past influenced state history textbooks from 1920 to 1965, see Kropp, "Sugar Cube Missions," and Pohlmann, "California's Mission Myth."

130. Gutfreund, "Standing Up to Sugar Cubes."

131. Commenting in 2008 on the annual crop of mission models being showcased in classrooms across the state, blogger Andrew Quinio mused, "The highlight of every California student's fourth grade experience is the Mission project. . . . If you went to a public school in California, you will remember staying up late gluing miniature plastic trees on a wooden base, delicately placing colored cellophane in the windows to mimic stained glass, forcing your parents to drive you to the arts and crafts store across town because it was the only place that sold tiny bells that you could mount in the belfry of your scale model of Mission Santa whoever, and bringing it in the next morning only to discover that most of your friends bought their projects at Toys R Us (no assembly required) and would still receive the same grade as you. Ahhh, memories" (http://quinio.wordpress.com/2008/09/07/scenes-from-oc-lincoln-at-the-mission).

132. Create-A-Mission, Mission Parts and Accessories page, Donaco Sales Company, Modesto, Calif., http://www.schooltimecreateaproject.com/parts.html#_cam.

133. Magee, "A Model of Tradition"; Templeton, "Model Behavior."

134. Castillo, "Mission Studies and the Columbian Quincentennial," 12.

135. The curriculum is in the Costo papers at the University of California Riverside (Costo Archive, UCR n.d., box 31, folder 11.1). Reprinted in Gutfreund, "Standing Up to Sugar Cubes," 179.

136. Gutfreund, "Standing Up to Sugar Cubes," 179.

137. Ibid.

138. Miranda, "Post-Colonial Thought Experiment."

139. Miscolta, "An Interview with Deborah Miranda."

140. Huell Howser Productions, *California Mission #110*.

141. Newcomb, *The Old Mission Churches and Historic Houses of California*, 5.

142. Almaguer, *Racial Fault Lines*, 33.

4. Consuming Heritage

1. Farr, congressional debate.

2. Pomeroy, *In Search of the Golden West*; Shaffer, *See America First*; Wrobel, *Promised Lands*; Wrobel and Long, eds., *Seeing and Being Seen*.

3. Deverell, *Railroad Crossings*; Ott, "Landscapes of Consumption."

4. Anonymous, "Mission Proves Good That Was Done for the Indians"; Anonymous, "Tells of Trip to Mission." For more on the promotion of auto tourism, see Ott, "Landscapes of Consumption."

5. Field, "A Southwest Sleepy Hollow"; Gates, "Motoring among the Missions."

6. There is a wealth of literature exploring how the California tourism industry and heritage sites have been implicated in the production of a "Spanish fantasy past"; see DeLyser, *Ramona Memories*; Deverell, *Whitewashed Adobe*; Kropp, *California Vieja*; McClung, *Landscapes of Desire*; McWilliams, *Southern California Country*; Rawls, "The California Mission as Symbol and Myth"; Riggin-Walden, "The Spanish Missions," especially chap. 4, "Manufactured Icons of Heritage"; Starr, *Inventing the Dream*; and Thomas, "Harvesting Ramona's Garden."

7. For a detailed study of the community of writers and artists (including Charles Lummis) centered on the Arroyo Seco area of Los Angeles County who were influential in the early construction of southwestern identity and active in collecting, preservation, and interpretation from 1880 to 1920, see Yeoman, "Messages from the Promised Land."

8. Moore, *In the Footsteps of the Padres.* For a more complete analysis of El Camino's place in a constructed past, see Kropp, "The Road: El Camino Real and Mission Nostalgia," chap. 2 in *California Vieja.*

9. This notion of a canonized tradition, laid forth by Edward Said as a central tenet of Orientalism, has been part of the production of travel writing and cultural tourism practices globally; Said, *Orientalism,* 176–77.

10. Bremer, "Sacred Spaces and Tourist Places," 29.

11. Models for these approaches include Baker, *Captured Landscape*; Bruner, "Abraham Lincoln as Authentic Reproduction"; Cohen, "A Phenomenology of Tourist Experiences"; and Gregory, "Colonial Nostalgia and Cultures of Travel." For an example of the dynamic relationship of landscapes and the practices of tourists, see Handler and Gable, *The New History in an Old Museum,* and Minca, "The Tourist Landscape Paradox."

12. Examples of volunteer groups include the "gardening angels" at Mission San Juan Capistrano and the rose garden guild of Mission San Antonio de Padua. At other missions dedicated staff and resident clergy have taken on the landscaping, including John Gebhard and Brother Columcille at Santa Inés (Mission Santa Ines, "Old Mission Santa Ines"), and Manuel Ramirez and Bernardo Casas at Mission San Gabriel. Even missions run by the State Parks rely on volunteers to help interpret and maintain the gardens. La Purísima, for example, is supported by an affiliated nonprofit organization called Prelado de los Tesoros de La Purísima, which helps raise funds, recruit volunteers, train docents, and advocate for the park (www.lapurisimamission.org).

13. In many cases these faith community members can be described as parishioners and the ordained and lay leadership, but in some settings, such as San Luis Rey and Santa Clara, those who attend retreats at the mission and those who are students at the university are important constituencies as well.

14. These two aspects of the experience MacCannell terms the "model" and the "influence," while the agency connecting the two is the "medium"; these elements (model, influence, and medium), along with the people who make it happen, are called "cultural productions" (MacCannell, *The Tourist,* 23–24).

15. Numerous scholars have interrogated tourism and its associated practices as a productive form of cultural analysis; see Coleman and Crang, eds., *Tourism*; Edensor, *Tourists at the Taj*; MacCannell, *The Tourist*; Minca and Oakes, eds., *Travels in Paradox*; and Urry, *The Tourist Gaze.*

16. Within the broader field of the embodied experience of architecture (e.g., Psarra, *Architecture and Narrative*), the literature of the experience of religious architecture, material culture, and visual culture is vast and addressed only tangentially in this study. See, for example, Morgan, "Religion and Embodiment in the Study of Material Culture" and *The Sacred Gaze*; Morgan and Promey, eds., *The Visual Culture of American Religions*; Nelson, ed., *American Sanctuary*; and Wynn, *Faith and Place.* Similarly, the California missions are also part of the global phenomenon of religious tourism (e.g., Bremer, *Blessed with Tourists*; Norman, *Spiritual Tourism*).

17. MacCannell, *The Tourist,* 26. For a more particular examination of archaeological sites as visual and embodied experiences, see Synnestvedt, "Who Wants to Visit a Cultural Heritage Site?"

18. Garden, "The Heritagescape," 408.

19. Farr, congressional debate.

20. Brubaker and Cooper, "Beyond 'Identity,'" 4–5.

21. Kimbro and Costello, *The California Missions,* 4.

22. For example, George Simpson's published account of his travels around the world in the 1840s described anticipating his mission visit during the "tedious voyage" at sea by reading Forbes's history of California "with its many curious details." When he arrived at Mission San Francisco in 1842 he was prepared to see that "the mission, though dead, still spake through its interesting associations. . . . Every object in the present solitude, not even excepting the mouldering adobe, had its own tale to tell of the motley life of bygone days" (Simpson, *Narrative of a Journey,* 332–33).

23. Dean MacCannell, *The Tourist,* 123–24.

24. For example, Huell Howser Productions, *California Missions #109.*

25. Virtual Video Tours, accessed May 2015, http://www.visualtraveltours.com/tours_show.html?id=65. The Purísima tour was the first one developed by travel writer Gordon Burgett for this company (now called Tours4Mobile). The Purísima tour has since been revised; the current URL is http://tours4mobile.com/tours/California-tours/California-mission-la-purisima.

26. Giaccardi and Palen, "The Social Production of Heritage through Cross-Media Interaction."

27. A great quantity of information about the missions is available online, particularly for the fourth-grade target audience. For example, the California Missions Resource Center offers an image gallery and an interactive map with a time line, associated images, maps, and architectural drawings, as well as historical statistics for each mission.

28. There are numerous blogs and online accounts of mission tours. Their descriptions reveal the range of reception from cynicism to nostalgia and enthusiasm and often a combination of conflicting responses. For example, the author of the blog *Tamerlane's Thoughts* described a visit to Mission San Fernando: "I arrive at the San Fernando mission to find a very plasticky, Southern California mission. Manicured lawns, palm trees, and a facade and roof that looked identical to the thousands of tract homes in southern Orange County. There was no character at all. It was a rip-off at four dollars (for the entrance fee)" (http://karakullake.blogspot.com/search/label/California%20Missions). Many express the desire to visit all the sites as if collecting the experiences. For example, a blogger posting pictures of her mission visits commented, "Four down, seventeen to go!!" (Karla Novoa, "The Missions," http://karlanovoa.1000words.kodak.com/default.asp?item=2305699). An online review of Mission Dolores (as Mission San Francisco is popularly known) reported, "I learned about 'mission fever' from them [the gift shop staff]—which is apparently what makes people want to travel to all of the missions in California. Yeah—I bought a map—what of it?" (Valerie D., "Review of Mission Dolores," http://www.yelp.com/biz/mission-dolores-san-francisco?start=80, posted May 2, 2007).

29. For a discussion of approaches to the body in the landscape and for an example of an analysis of walking through a landscape, see Veder, "Walking through Dumbarton Oaks." Other examples of combining phenomenological and post-structural understandings of the embodied experience include Conan, "Fragments of a Poetic of Gardens"; Wood and Latham, "The Thickness of Things"; and Wylie, *Landscape.*

30. The exception to the limited interpretation is that some of the more developed sites offer prerecorded audio tours, such as the handheld devices linked to listening stations at San Juan Capistrano.

31. Gregson and Rose, "Taking Butler Elsewhere." Upton offers a useful historiographical essay on these complex intersections of the sensory and the personal with the social and

the cultural in the formation of selfhood, identity, and agency in the context of the everyday; Upton "Architecture in Everyday Life."

32. Secretary to Mr. C. L. Kalix, Memory Garden, Brand Park, October 29, 1923, City of Los Angeles, Records Management Division, Recreation and Parks Board, Facilities Files, Brand Park.

33. Saunders and Chase, "Love in the Padres' Garden," 175–76.

34. For examples of the importance of a multisensory understanding of history and culture, see Smith, *The Smell of Battle* and *Sensing the Past*; Howes and Classen, *Ways of Sensing*; Classen, *The Deepest Sense*; and Reinarz, *Past Scents*.

35. See, for example, Bachelard, *The Poetics of Space*; Hunt, *Afterlife of Gardens*; Ingold, *The Perception of the Environment*; Lefebvre, *The Production of Space*; and Tuan, *Topophilia*.

36. Cole, "Crematoria, Barracks, Gateway," 105.

37. Rodriguez, *Days of Obligation*, 125.

38. Boucher, "Mission Project."

39. Abbott, *Santa Ines Hermosa*.

40. Parishioners and staff who walk through the landscape on a daily or weekly basis clearly engage in entirely different ways than tourists. While these experiences are also a vital part of many missions, they go beyond the scope of this analysis.

41. Bernard Ventures was hired to design a new group entry, new front gate, museum store, and entry plaza completed in 2013, http://barnardventures.com/project/historic-mission-san-juan-capistrano; Mission San Juan Capistrano, *Annual Report, 2011–2012*.

42. This bell-ringing practice was established in 2015 as part of the celebrations of the three-hundredth anniversary of Serra's birth. http://www.missionsjc.com/activities/bell-ringing.php, accessed July 31, 2015.

43. Mission San Juan Capistrano audio tour, Great Stone Church Walking Tour, stop 16.

44. Sorensen, personal communication, interview at Mission San Juan Capistrano, April 2008.

45. Pedelty, "The New California Mission System." Deana Dartt-Newton's Ph.D. dissertation, "Negotiating the Master Narrative," has contributed a much needed study and Native perspective to the analysis of the public interpretation of California's past.

46. Geoffrey Holt, "Restoration Drawing."

47. As Lynn Meskell has argued, archaeological materials are potent tools in the political discourses of modern life because objects can be "mobilized and deployed in identity struggles . . . and the reproduction of social inequalities" (Meskell, "Archaeologies of Identity,"189).

48. Interpretive sign posted at the Santa Barbara lavandería, recorded April 2013.

49. Mitchell, *The Lie of the Land*, 199.

50. The exception to this main message is the interpretation offered at the two Park Services sites, Purísima and Solano, which privilege more fully the Native American past and, particularly at Purísima, include the twentieth-century restorations as part of the sites' history.

51. Dartt-Newton, "California's Sites of Conscience" and "Negotiating the Master Narrative." Michelle Lorimer's dissertation, "Reconstructing the Past," similarly explores the presentation of the past in mission museums.

52. Vaughn, "Locating Absence."

53. Pedelty, "The New California Mission System," 83.

54. Interpretive sign, Mission San Juan Capistrano, recorded April 2008. Although there have been no interpreters or demonstrations on view when I have been at the mission, the sign notes, "Members of the Acjachemen tribe regularly demonstrate traditional basket weaving in this area."

55. Interpretive sign, Mission San Gabriel, recorded 2013.

56. The reconstructed dwelling was close to the location of the last house of the Chumash village to exist to the late nineteenth century; Tina Foss, personal communication, May 27, 2015.

57. Quoted in Hidalgo, "A Meaningful Rededication."

58. The reference is to *Ramona* (1884), a novel by Helen Hunt Jackson that was hugely influential in raising awareness of the unjust treatment of and policies concerning California Native peoples.

59. An interesting side note to the layering of heritage practices around these historic plant specimens was the recent excavation at the Monterey Presidio of a 1905 marble marker for the "Junípero Oak." The marker commemorated the tree under whose shade Junípero Serra stood during the ceremony "taking possession of California for Spain" (Mendoza, "The Cross and the Spade," 48). For an interpretation of California's citrus heritage and its place in the cultural landscape, visit the California Citrus State Historic Park in Riverside.

60. Other examples of historical and devotional sculptures include Father Palou at Mission San Fernando and the Virgin Mary at numerous missions, including San Antonio de Pala and Mission San Gabriel. At Mission San Diego sculptures representing the saints for whom each of the missions is named are displayed in a reconstructed colonnade facade at the entrance to the mission. I have discussed Serra sculptures in the mission landscapes in the context of interpreting identity in "Greenwashed."

61. Monroy has examined this paternalistic rhetoric in colonial context; *Thrown among Strangers*, 44–50.

62. In 2008–9 the foundation that administers Mission San Juan Capistrano and supports its preservation undertook a restoration of the cast concrete 1913 sculpture by John Van Rennselaer, which had been relocated from the center of the forecourt to the bell wall near the Stone Church ruins in 1928. The restoration included replacing a cross that was part of the original composition. The sculpture is a popular backdrop for group photos.

63. Rawls, *Indians of California*.

64. Flowers, *A Child's History of California*, 46.

65. Mission San Juan Capistrano website, Restoration Projects, http://www.missionsjc.com/history-preservation/preservation-efforts/highlights.

66. This reading of time markers in the Mission San Gabriel was first explored in Kryder-Reid, "Marking Time."

67. The California mission ruins share many of the same formal and associative aspects of ruins in other designed landscapes. See, for example, Hunt, "Picturesque Mirrors," and King on fabricated ruins in the nineteenth-century southern Maryland landscape in *Archaeology, Narrative, and the Politics of the Past*.

68. Robinson, *Life in California*, 57.

69. Farnham, *Travel in the Californias*, 111–12.

70. This description is based on site visits by the author in 1994, 2008, and 2013.

71. The complex practices associated with touristic spaces are implicated in this study, but not fully explored. For examples of other, closer readings of tourism geographies, see Cartier and Lew, eds., *Seductions of Place*.

72. These interpretations of mission history in the San Gabriel mission garden are consistent with the main messages and underlying ideologies in other mission museums as has been demonstrated by Dartt-Newton's analysis in "Negotiating the Master Narrative."

73. The plaque is mounted on the wall of the winery to the right of the McGurrin mural.

74. Interpretive signage, Mission San Gabriel, recorded 2008.

75. Engelhardt, *San Gabriel Mission,* 354. For a more comprehensive study of the missions' system of punishment and justice, including corporal punishment, see also Hackel, *Children of the Coyote,* 321–66, and Lightfoot, *Indians, Missionaries, and Merchants,* 82–113.

76. Hill, "The Museum Indian"; Lonetree, *Decolonizing Museums.*

77. The cross and crucifix were restored and rededicated in 2012 after being damaged in a storm.

78. Benthold, "Uncovering the Mission's Secrets," 187.

79. While the San Gabriel sundial is modern, sundials were used in the colonial era as timekeeping devices; Francis J. Weber, *The California Missions,* 126.

80. The label posted next to the mural credits it to Buckley McGurrin, unveiled in 1939, "practically disappeared by 1950; Reconstructed and elaborated mural by Hendrick Keyzer and Vivian Flores (600 hours)."

81. Claretian Missionaries, USA Province, "100 Years of Service at San Gabriel Mission," http://www.claretian.com/SanGabrielMissionCentennialCelebration.php.

82. Interpretive signage, Mission San Gabriel, recorded 2008.

83. Anonymous, "Belgian Monarchs at Ancient Mission."

84. Sorensen, personal communication, Mission San Juan Capistrano, April 2008.

85. Mission San Antonio de Padua website, http://missionsanantonio.net/cutting-of-the-roses.

86. According to Tina Foss, director of the Santa Barbara Mission Museum, "We have a widely disparate group of volunteers in the Huerta. Hispanic, Chumash and Anglo. Most just love gardens and history"; personal communication, May 27, 2015.

87. Sortomme, "Restoring Heritage Plants from California's Missions." The partnership was started by Sortomme and Santa Barbara Mission curator Tina Foss; in 2003 the project was formally named La Huerta Project.

88. Hayes, "La Heurta Project."

89. Julius Herman Boeke coined the term "dual economy" to describe the coexistence of traditional and developed economies such as those he studied in Dutch Indonesia; Boeke, *Economics and Economic Policy of Dual Societies.*

90. Even limiting the scope to missions that serve as parishes leaves a diverse range of audiences given the missions' varying relationships with their local communities. Mission San Antonia de Pala, for instance, is in the middle of the Pala Indian Reservation, which generally has little to do with the parish. San Antonio de Padua is on an army base, which is a distinctive setting and creates a unique relationship with the local civilian community. San Luis Rey runs an active retreat center as well as a parish, and Mission Santa Clara is part of a Catholic university founded by the Society of Jesus, a Roman Catholic religious order commonly referred to as the Jesuits. The Santa Clara mission garden is absorbed into the campus and the mission building functions as a college chapel as well as parish church.

91. Rodriguez, *Days of Obligation,* 123.

92. This idea of layered landscapes has been usefully applied to plantations in the American South where captive slaves traversed the landscape gardens of Monticello and Gunston Hall differently than the planter gentry and their guests; see Epperson, "Panoptic Plantations," and Upton, "White and Black Landscapes in Eighteenth-Century Virginia."

93. Personal communication, Jerome "Jerry" S. Nieblas, project manager, Mission San Juan Capistrano, April 2008.

94. Personal communication, Sister Barbara Jackson, parish administrator, Antonio de Pala, 2008.

95. Mission San Carlos Borroméo de Carmelo, http://www.carmelmission.org/museum.

96. Mission San Juan Capistrano, http://www.missionsjc.com. Since 2013, the "Catholic Visitor" page has been removed in a subsequent redesign of the website, and a new page for "religion and spirituality" substituted.

97. Franciscan Pilgrimage Program, http://www.franciscanpilgrimages.com.

98. The William H. Hannon Foundation website, Junípero Serra page, http://www.hannonfoundation.org/juniperoserra.html. Hannon died in 1999, but the Hannon Foundation, founded in 1983, continues to sponsor essay contests about Serra and to carry on Hannon's philanthropic support of Catholic schools, hospitals, and other organizations.

99. Rimbert, "Junípero Serra Statue Unveiled and Blessed."

100. Castillo, "Cultural Chauvinism."

101. Author's observation, February 2013.

102. The William H. Hannon Foundation, http://www.hannonfoundation.org.

103. For a discussion of the implications and opportunities for changing interpretation of the missions in the wake of the Serra canonization, see Panich, "After Saint Serra."

104. The history of Serra is intertwined with California history and identity construction in a myriad of ways. For example, a statue of Serra sculpted by Ettore Cadorin is one of two statues representing California in the National Statuary Hall Collection in the U.S. Capitol.

105. Hudson, *The Famous Missions of California,* 69–70.

106. Rodriguez, *Days of Obligation,* 125.

107. Boucher, "Mission Project," L4.

108. Ibid.

Conclusion

1. Castillo, "Cultural Chauvinism"; Dartt-Newton, "California's Sites of Conscience"; Wyand, "Pilgrimage to California."

2. Atalay, *Community-Based Archaeology* and "Indigenous Archaeology as Decolonizing Practice"; Bruchac, "Decolonization in Archaeological Theory"; Bruchac, Hart, and Wobst, eds., *Indigenous Archaeologies*; Habu, Fawcett, and Matsunaga, eds., *Evaluating Multiple Narratives*; Hokowhitu et al., eds., *Indigenous Identity and Resistance*; King, *Unsettling America*; Mertens, Cram, and Chilisa, eds., *Indigenous Pathways into Social Research*; Miller and Riding In, eds., *Native Historians Write Back*; Panich, "Interpretive Issues"; Watkins, *Indigenous Archaeology.*

3. Castillo, "Mission Studies and the Columbian Quincentennial," 12.

4. Martinez, "Wrong Directions and New Maps of Voice," 545–46.

5. For a broader discussion of the interface of art and politics in California, see Selz, *Art of Engagement,* particularly chap. 3, "On Racism, Discrimination, and Identity Politics," and Landauer's introductory essay in the volume, "Countering Cultures."

6. LaPena, "The Arts," 56.

7. *California Mission Daze,* a collaborative, mixed-media installation created by David Avalos, James Luna, Deborah Small, and William Weeks at Installation Gallery, San Diego, in 1988. The project was supported by a project grant from COMBO, the Combined Arts and Education Council of San Diego County, funded by the National Endowment for the Arts and the City of San Diego as part of the NEA's Test Program of Support for Local Arts Agencies (David Avalos, personal communication, August 2015).

8. LaPena, "Exhibitions/Exposure."

9. Ollman, "Exhibit Paints Serra in Un-saintly Glow."

10. Ibid.

11. Ibid.

12. Cultural Conservancy, "Biography of L. Frank Manriquez," http://www.nativeland.org/directors.html.

13. *Acorn Soup* was a regular feature in *News from Native California* between 1992 and 2006; Bernardin, "Acorn Soup Is Good Food," 6. See Barnardin for an assessment of Frank's work within California Indian visual and literary arts.

14. Ibid., 7, 11.

15. Frank, *Acorn Soup,* 26, 32. Other projects such as L. Frank's documentary and YouTube posts for the L. Frank Project are ongoing. See the BACIPIX documentary, http://www.bacipix.com/documentary.php; and the L. Frank Project on YouTube, http://www.youtube.com/watch?v=KA32en5G7lM.

16. California Museum, *California Indians: Making a Difference,* http://www.californiamuseum.org/california-indians-making-difference.

17. Huntington Library, *Junípero Serra and the Legacies of the California Missions,* exhibition, August 17, 2013–January 6, 2014.

18. Steven Hackle, quoted in Huntington Library press release dated August 8, 2013, "Major International Exhibition on Junípero Serra," http://www.huntington.org/WebAssets/Templates/content.aspx?id=14509.

19. Soja, *Seeking Spatial Justice*; Harrison, "'Counter-Mapping' Heritage" and *Shared Landscapes.*

20. Upton, "Authentic Anxieties," 300.

21. Russell, "Towards an Ethics of Oblivion and Forgetting," 249; Borić, "Happy Forgetting?"; Field, "Complicities and Collaborations"; Meskell, "Negative Heritage."

22. Bhabha, *The Location of Culture*; Bruyneel, *The Third Space of Sovereignty*; Martinez, "Wrong Directions and New Maps of Voice."

23. Corrin, ed., *Mining the Museum.*

24. Thelen, introduction to *History as a Catalyst for Civic Dialogue,* ed. Korza and Schaffer Bacon, vii.

25. Baird, "'The Breath of the Mountain Is My Heart'"; Gröppel-Wegener, "Creating Heritage Experience through Architecture"; Ševčenko, "Sites of Conscience."

26. Bennett, Julius, and Soudien, eds., *City, Site, Museum.*

27. Matthews, "Unconventional Archaeologies in Setauket, New York"; McDavid, "Beyond Strategy and Good Intentions"; Mullins, "Politics, Inequality, and Engaged Archaeology." See also Praetzellis, Praetzellis, and Van Buren, "Remaking Connections."

28. International Coalition of Sites of Conscience, http://www.sitesofconscience.org/about-us.

29. Cameron, "World Heritage Sites of Conscience and Memory."

30. International Coalition of Sites of Conscience, http://www.sitesofconscience.org/about-us.

31. The potential for the public sphere, including museums, heritage sites, and cultural landscapes, to be a force for political and societal reconciliation is explored in Olick, *The Politics of Regret,* especially chap. 9, "Collective Memory and Chronic Differentiation."

32. Farr, congressional debate. Samuel Farr is U.S. representative for California's Twentieth Congressional District.

33. For examples of landscapes and museums as forces for reconciliation, see Bender and Winer, eds., *Contested Landscapes;* Mason, "Conflict and Complement"; Simon, *The Touch of the Past*; and Sullivan, "Some Thoughts about Museums, Reconciliation, and Healing."

34. Ashworth and Hartmann, eds., *Horror and Human Tragedy Revisited*; Barnes, ed., *The Materiality of Freedom*; Cohen, "Educational Dark Tourism at an In Populo Site"; Duffy, "Museums of 'Human Suffering' and the Struggle for Human Rights"; Williams, *Memorial Museums.*

35. Dartt-Newton, "California's Sites of Conscience."

36. Myers-Lim, "Educating Elementary School Children about California Missions," 43.

37. Gibbons, congressional debate. James Gibbons is the U.S. representative for Nevada's Second Congressional District.

38. Capps, congressional debate. Lois Capps is the U.S. Representative for California's Twenty-Fourth Congressional District, which includes Mission Santa Barbara, an image of which appears on the congresswoman's website banner.

39. The mural had been modified by February 2013.

40. Savage, *Standing Soldier, Kneeling Slave,* 4.

41. Doss reports the details of the Oñate case in her broader analysis of contested identity and memorials in *Memorial Mania*; see esp. 313–16 on the Oñate protest incident.

42. Elvia Díaz, "Statue of Spaniard Loses Foot," *Albuquerque Journal,* January 8, 1998; quoted in Doss, *Memorial Mania,* 313.

43. Doss, *Memorial Mania,* 316.

44. Bruyneel, *The Third Space of Sovereignty.*

45. Bhabha, "Cultural Diversity and Cultural Differences," 208.

46. Bhabha, *The Location of Culture.*

47. Galvan, the first Native American curator of a California mission, traces his ancestors to Liberato, who was baptized in 1801 at age fourteen at Mission Dolores; on Galvan, see Russell, "Bones of Discontent"; see also Nunez, "Journeys."

48. Nakata and David, "Archaeological Practice at the Cultural Interface."

49. Along with other activist archaeology projects (e.g., Shackel and Gadsby, eds. "Archaeologies of Engagement"; Smith, "Empty Gestures?"), Kent Lightfoot and others have written about the political implications for archaeologists working on California mission–period sites, particularly given the criteria for federal tribal recognition; Lightfoot et al., "The Study of Indigenous Political Economies."

50. Lightfoot et al., "The Study of Indigenous Political Economies"; Panich, "After Saint Serra"; Whitley and Whitley, "A Land of Vision and Dreams."

51. Bhabha, "Cultural Diversity and Cultural Differences," 208.

52. Nunez, "Journeys," 47.

53. Preucel and Matero, "Placemaking on the Northern Rio Grande."

54. *California Mission Daze,* group exhibition by David Avalos, James Luna, and Deborah, Small Installation Gallery, San Diego, 1988. According to the National Museum of the

American Indian's *Emendatio* website, the NMAI team included curators Paul Chaat Smith and Truman T. Lowe, and the exhibition was "created, designed and developed with James Luna for the Venice Biennale in 2005; the artist was consulted to provide direction and advice throughout the exhibition re-design and installation process" for exhibition at the George Gustav Heye Museum in New York in 2008; accessed July 19, 2015, http://www.nmai.si.edu/exhibitions/emendatio/jamesluna.html.

55. National Museum of the American Indian, http://www.nmai.si.edu/exhibitions/emendatio.

56. Luna, "The Performance Art of James Luna," http://www.jamesluna.com/oldsite.

57. For example, a special issue of *News from Native California* titled "Saying Our Share: Surviving the Missions," guest-edited by James Luna, features the work of Gerald Clarke Jr., Ed Drew, Lewis deSoto, James Luna, Steven Hackel, Catherine Nelson-Rodriguez, Annelia Hillman, Judith Lowry with David McKay, Sheila Tishla Skinner, Guillermo Gomez-Peña, and L. Frank.

58. While the term *post-Indian* is not in wide circulation, it speaks to the ongoing debate over constructed identities and their political implications, particularly in Native American contemporary art criticism. See, for example, Lomayesva, "Indian Identity—Post Indian Reflections," and the 1998 exhibition *Remix: New Modernities in a Post-Indian World,* curated by Joe Baker (Delaware) and Gerald McMaster (Plains Cree) for NMAI and the Heard Museum in Phoenix.

59. Watson, "Jimmie Durham's *Building a Nation.*"

60. Association of Critical Heritage Studies, 2012 Manifesto, http://www.criticalheritagestudies.org/history.

61. Lewis, *An Experiment in Criticism,* 140–41.

62. Birnbaum, *Preservation Brief 36*; Coffin, *Guide to Developing a Preservation Maintenance Plan for a Historic Landscape.*

63. Gable and Handler, "Public History, Private Memory," 60.

64. Manriques [L. Frank], oral history video interview, *California Indians: Making a Difference,* http://www.californiamuseum.org/california-indians.

Bibliography

Abbott, Mamie Goulet. *Santa Ines Hermosa: The Journal of the Padre's Niece*. 3rd ed. Los Olivos, Calif.: Olive Press Publications, 2002.

Adair, Bill, Benjamin Filene, and Laura Koloski. *Letting Go? Sharing Historical Authority in a User-Generated World*. Philadelphia: Pew Center for Arts & Heritage; Walnut Creek, Calif.: Left Coast Press, 2011.

Adams, Charles Gibbs. "Gardens of the Spanish Days of California." *Annual Publications of the Historical Society of Southern California* 45 (1932): 347–55.

Aiken, Charles Sedgwick. "Upon the King's Highway: Life To-day along the Royal Road of the California's Motor Cars and Polo Ponies—Golf, Bridge and Country Clubs by the Pathways of the Padres." *Sunset* 21, no. 8 (December 1908): 689–715.

Allen, Mark W. "Land of Violence." In Jones and Perry, *Contemporary Issues in California Archaeology*, 197–215.

Allen, Rebecca. "Alta California Missions and Pre-1849 Transformations of Coastal Lands." *Historical Archaeology* 44, no. 3 (2010): 69–80.

———. *Native Americans at Mission Santa Cruz, 1791–1834*. Vol. 5 of *Perspectives in California Archaeology*. Los Angeles: Institute of Archaeology, University of California, Los Angeles, 1998.

———. "Rethinking Mission Land Use and the Archaeological Record in California: An Example from Santa Clara." *Historical Archaeology* 44, no. 2 (2010): 72–96.

Almaguer, Tomás. *Racial Fault Lines: The Historical Origins of White Supremacy in California*. Berkeley: University of California Press, 1994.

AlSayyad, Nezar, ed. *Consuming Tradition, Manufacturing Heritage: Global Norms and Urban Forms in the Age of Tourism*. London: Routledge, 2001.

Althusser, Louis. "Ideology and Ideological State Apparatuses." In *Lenin and Philosophy and Other Essays*. Translated from the French by Ben Brewster, 121–76. New York: Monthly Review Press, 1971.

Amero, Richard W. "The Making of the Panama-California Exposition, 1909–1915." *Journal of San Diego History* 36, no. 1 (Winter 1990): 1–47.

Anderson, Benedict R. O'G. *Imagined Communities: Reflections on the Origin and Spread of Nationalism*. Rev. and extended ed. London: Verso, 1991

Anderson, M. Kat. "Native Californians as Ancient and Contemporary Cultivators." In Blackburn and Anderson, *Before the Wilderness,* 151–74.

———. *Tending the Wild: Native American Knowledge and the Management of California's Natural Resources.* Berkeley: University of California Press, 2005.

Anderson, M. Kat, Michael G. Barbour, and Valerie Whitworth. "A World of Balance and Plenty: Land, Plants, Animals, and Humans in Pre-European California." In Gutiérrez and Orsi, *Contested Eden,* 12–47.

Angier, Belle Sumner. *The Garden Book of California.* San Francisco: Paul Elder, 1906.

Anonymous. "Belgian Monarchs at Ancient Mission." *New York Times,* October 13, 1919. Retrieved online, New York Times Archive, http://www.NYTimes.com.

———. "Brand Mission Park: An Asset to the Valley." *San Fernando Democrat,* February 3, 1922. Clipping on file, City of Los Angeles, Records Management Division, Recreation and Parks Board, Facilities Files, Brand Park.

———. "Colegio de San Gabriel." *Tidings,* August 25, 1922. Reprinted in Weber, *The Pride of the Missions,* 198–99.

———. "Garden Club Gives Seeds: Presentation to Mission Made by Dr. Smyley at Ceremonies." November 17, 1934. Clipping from an unidentified newspaper, San Juan Capistrano Archives.

———. "Is She in Your Album?" *Los Angeles Times,* June 13, 1929, 8.

———. "Jubilee Celebration." *Pasadena Star-News,* July 22, 1934. Clipping, San Juan Capistrano Archives.

———. "Mission Models Were Harry Downie's Hobby." *Monterey Peninsula Herald,* June 1, 1970, 17A.

———. "Mission Proves Good That Was Done for the Indians: San Juan Relics, Seen During Motor Tour, Attest Works of Faith and Husbandry Directed by the Franciscan Padres." *San Francisco Examiner,* June 27, 1920.

———. "Old Mission Will Boast New Garden: Natives of California Plan Restoration and Will Have Benefit at San Gabriel." *Los Angeles Times,* March 6, 1930. Clipping in the Owen C. Coy Collection, box 1303, folder 5, California State Library, Sacramento.

———. "Old Spanish Missions Standing as Silent Symbols of Peace amid Tumult of World at Arms to Be Preserved as Monument to Christian Brotherhood." *San Francisco Chronicle,* January 16, 1918, 40.

———. "Restoration of Mission Park O.K.'d: San Fernando Chamber of Commerce Pledges Aid to Plan for Improved Garden" [ca. November/December 1921]. Unidentified newspaper clipping on file, City of Los Angeles, Records Management Division, Recreation and Parks Board, Facilities Files, Brand Park.

———. "Restorer of Mission Dies." *Tidings,* July 28, 1933, 7.

———. "Scenic Views in California and the Columbia River Gorge," ca. 1880–ca. 1890. Bancroft Library Collections (BANC PIC 1984.043), University of California, Berkeley.

———. "Tells of Trip to Mission: A Visit to the San Juan Capistrano Mission by a Reo Six from the Reo Motor Car Co. of California, Containing a Party Sent out by Manager Byron C. Foy." *Los Angeles Herald,* June 17, 1922.

———. "Tilden's Latest Statue." *Silent Worker* 20, no. 5 (February 1908): 81.

———. [Untitled article about Mrs. Marah Ellis Ryan.] *El Viajante,* October 1, 1904. Clipping on file, Southwest Museum Archives, Los Angeles.

———. "Will You Help Restore California Landmark?" Clipping from an unnamed newspaper in the Owen C. Coy Collection, California State Library, Sacramento.

Appadurai, Arjun. *The Future as Cultural Fact: Essays on the Global Condition.* London: Verso, 2013.

Archibald, Robert. *The Economic Aspects of the California Missions.* Washington, D.C.: Academy of American Franciscan History, 1978.

———. "Indian Labor at the California Missions: Slavery or Salvation?" *Journal of San Diego History* 24, no. 2 (1978): 172–82.

Architecture, Physical Environment, and Society in Alta California. Proceedings of the Twenty-Second Annual Conference of the California Mission Studies Association. Santa Clara: California Mission Studies Association, 2005.

Arkush, Brooke S. "Native Responses to European Intrusion: Cultural Persistence and Agency among Mission Neophytes in Spanish Colonial California." *Historical Archaeology* 45, no. 4 (2011): 62–90.

Arnold, Jeanne E., ed. *Foundations of Chumash Complexity.* Vol. 7 of *Perspectives in California Archaeology.* Los Angeles: Cotsen Institute of Archaeology, University of California, 2004.

Ashworth, Gregory, and Rudi Hartmann, eds. *Horror and Human Tragedy Revisited: The Management of Sites of Atrocities for Tourism.* New York: Cognizant Communication Corporation, 2005.

Atalay, Sonya. *Community-Based Archaeology: Research with, by, and for Indigenous and Local Communities.* Berkeley: University of California Press, 2012.

———. "Indigenous Archaeology as Decolonizing Practice." *American Indian Quarterly* 30, nos. 3, 4 (2006): 280–310.

Aulich, Jim. "Memory, What Is It Good For? Forced Labour, Blockhouses and Museums in Nord-Pas de Calais, Northern France." In Purbrick, Aulich, and Dawson, *Contested Spaces,* 191–210.

Bachelard, Gaston. *The Poetics of Space.* Boston: Beacon, 1964.

Baer, Kurt. *Architecture of the California Missions.* Berkeley: University of California Press, 1958.

Baird, Melissa F. "'The Breath of the Mountain Is My Heart': Indigenous Cultural Landscapes and the Politics of Heritage." *International Journal of Heritage Studies* 19, no. 4 (2013): 327–40.

Baker, Kate. *Captured Landscape: The Paradox of the Enclosed Garden.* New York: Routledge, 2012.

Bandini, José. *A Description of California in 1828.* Translated by Doris Marion Wright. Bancroft Library Publication, no. 3. Berkeley: Friends of the Bancroft Library, 1951. [Originally *Documentos para la historia de California, 1776–1850.*]

Bargellini, Clara, and Michael Komanecky, eds. *The Art of the Missions of Northern New Spain.* Mexico City: Antiguo Colegio de San Ildefonso, 2009.

Barnes, Jodi A., ed. *The Materiality of Freedom: Archaeologies of Postemancipation Life.* Columbia: University of South Carolina Press, 2011.

Barraclough, Laura R. *Making the San Fernando Valley: Rural Landscapes, Urban Development, and White Privilege.* Athens: University of Georgia Press, 2011.

Barrett, William P. "Controversial Charity Files for Bankruptcy." *Forbes,* January 28, 2009.

Barron, Stephanie, Sheri Bernstein, and Ilene Susan Fort. *Reading California: Art, Image, and Identity, 1900–2000.* Los Angeles: Los Angeles County Museum of Art, with the University of California Press, 2000. Exhibition catalog.

Barthes, Roland. *Camera Lucida: Reflections on Photography.* Translated by Richard Howard. New York: Hill and Wang, 1981.

Battiste, Marie, ed. *Reclaiming Indigenous Voice and Vision.* Vancouver: University of British Columbia Press, 2000.

Baudrillard, Jean. "Structures of Interior Design." In *The Everyday Life Reader*, edited by Ben Highmore, 308–18. London: Routledge, 2002.

———. *The System of Objects*. Translated by James Benedict. London: Verso Books, 1996.

Bauer, William J., Jr. *We Were All like Migrant Workers Here: Work, Community, and Memory on California's Round Valley Reservation, 1850–1941*. Chapel Hill: University of North Carolina Press, 2009.

Beebe, Rose Marie, and Robert M. Senkewicz. "The End of the 1824 Chumash Revolt in Alta California: Father Vincente Serría's Account." *Americas* 53 (1996): 273–83.

———. *Junípero Serra: California, Indians, and the Transformation of a Missionary*. Norman: University of Oklahoma Press, 2015.

———. "What They Brought: The Alta California Franciscans before 1769." In Hackel, *Alta California*, 17–46.

———, eds. *Architecture, Physical Environment, and Society in Alta California*. Proceedings of the Twenty-Second Annual Conferences of the California Mission Studies Association. Bakersfield: California Mission Studies Association, 2005.

Bender, Barbara. "Time and Landscape." *Current Anthropology* 43, no. 4 (2002): 103–12.

Bender, Barbara, and Margot Winer, eds. *Contested Landscapes: Movement Exile and Place*. Oxford: Berg, 2001.

Benjamin, Walter. *Illuminations*. Edited and with an introduction by Hannah Arendt. Translated by Harry Zohn. New York: Harcourt, Brace & World, 1968.

Bennett, Bonnie, Chrischené Julius, and Crain Soudien, eds. *City, Site, Museum: Reviewing Memory Practices at the District Six Museum*. Cape Town: District Six Museum, 2008.

Bennyhoff, James A., and Albert B. Elsasser. *Sonoma Mission: An Historical and Archaeological Study of Primary Constructions, 1823–1913*. University of California Archaeological Survey Report, 25. Berkeley: University of California, 1954.

Benthold, Dwinelle. "Uncovering the Mission's Secrets." *Los Angeles Sunday Times*, February 6, 1921. Reprinted in Weber, *The Pride of the Missions*, 186–90.

Bernard, Anna. *Rhetorics of Belonging: Nation, Narration, and Israel/Palestine*. Liverpool: Liverpool University Press, 2013.

Bernard, Julienne, David Robinson, and Fraser Sturt. "Points of Refuge in the South Central California Colonial Hinterlands." In Panich and Schneider, *Indigenous Landscapes and Spanish Missions*, 154–71.

Bernardin, Susan. "Acorn Soup Is Good Food: L. Frank, News from Native California, and the Intersections of Literary and Visual Arts." *Studies in American Indian Literatures* 27, no. 3 (2015): 1–33.

Bettinger, Robert L. *Sociopolitical Evolution in Aboriginal California: The Rise of Orderly Anarchy*. Berkeley: University of California Press, 2015.

Bhabha, Homi K. "Cultural Diversity and Cultural Differences." In *The Post-Colonial Studies Reader*, edited by Bill Ashcroft, Gareth Griffiths, and Helen Tiffin, 206–9. New York: Routledge, 1994.

———. *The Location of Culture*. New York: Routledge, 1994.

———. *Our Neighbours, Ourselves: Contemporary Reflections on Survival*. Berlin: De Gruyter, 2011.

———, ed. *Nation and Narration*. New York: Routledge, 1990.

Bigelow, Henry. "Christmas at the Mission." *San Francisco Examiner*, December 1891. Clipping on file, Santa Barbara Archives (OLS DOC 747d).

Bingham, Edwin R. *Charles F. Lummis: Editor of the Southwest*. San Marino, Calif.: Huntington Library Press, 2006.

Birnbaum, Charles A. *Preservation Brief 36: Protecting Cultural Landscapes: Planning, Treatment and Management of Historic Landscapes.* Washington, D.C.: U.S. Department of the Interior, National Park Service Cultural Resources, Preservation Assistance Division, 1994.

Bjerregaard, Peter. "Dissolving Objects: Museums, Atmosphere and the Creation of Presence." *Emotion, Space and Society* 15 (May 2015): 74–81.

Blackburn, Thomas C., ed. *December's Child: A Book of Chumash Oral Narratives, Collected by J. P. Harrington.* Berkeley: University of California Press, 1975.

Blackburn, Thomas C., and Kat Anderson, eds. *Before the Wilderness: Environmental Management by Native Californians.* Menlo Park, Calif.: Ballena Press, 1993.

Blake, J., 2009. "UNESCO's 2003 Convention on Intangible Cultural Heritage: The Implications of Community Involvement in 'Safeguarding.'" In *Intangible Heritage,* edited by Laurajane Smith and Natsuko Akagawa, 45–73. London: Routledge, 2009.

Bodnar, John. *Remaking America: Public Memory, Commemoration, and Patriotism in the Twentieth Century.* Princeton, N.J.: Princeton University Press, 1992.

Boeke, Julius Herman. *Economics and Economic Policy of Dual Societies, as Exemplified by Indonesia.* New York: International Secretariat, Institute of Pacific Relations, 1953.

Bokovoy, Matthew F. "Humanist Sentiment, Modern Spanish Heritage, and California Mission Commemoration, 1769–1915." *Journal of San Diego History* 48, no. 3 (Summer 2002): 177–203.

———. *The San Diego World's Fairs and Southwestern Memory, 1880–1940.* Albuquerque: University of New Mexico Press, 2005.

Borić, Dusan. "Happy Forgetting? Remembering and Dismembering Dead Bodies." In *Archaeology and Memory,* edited by Dusan Borić, 48–67. Oxford: Oxbow Books, 2010.

Boscana, Gerónimo. *Chinigchinich: A Revised and Annotated Version of Alfred Robinson's Translation of Father Gerónimo Boscana's Historical Account of the Beliefs, Usages, Customs, and Extravagancies of the Indians of This Mission of San Juan Capistrano Called the Acagchemem Tribe.* Annotations by John P. Harrington; reprint of 1933 ed. with a new preface by William Bright. Banning, Calif.: Malki Museum Press, Morongo Indian Reservation, 1978.

Boucher, Geoff. "Mission Project: Not Bad, Dad." *Los Angeles Times,* March 11, 2008, L4–5.

Bouvier, Virginia Marie. *Women and the Conquest of California, 1542–1840: Codes of Silence.* Tucson: University of Arizona Press, 2004.

Boym, Svetlana. *The Future of Nostalgia.* New York: Basic Books, 2001.

Braun, Sebastian Felix, ed. *Transforming Ethnohistories: Narrative, Meaning, and Community.* Norman: University of Oklahoma Press, 2013.

Brave Heart-Jordan, Maria Yellow Horse. "The Return to the Sacred Path: Healing from Historical Trauma and Historical Unresolved Grief among the Lakota; A Dissertation Based upon an Independent Investigation." Ph.D. diss., Smith College School for Social Work, 1995.

Bremer, Thomas S. *Blessed with Tourists: The Borderlands of Religion and Tourism in San Antonio.* Chapel Hill: University of North Carolina Press, 2004.

———. "Sacred Spaces and Tourist Places." In *Tourism, Religion, and Spiritual Journeys,* edited by Dallen J. Timothy and Daniel H. Olsen, 25–35. New York: Routledge, 2006.

———. "Tourists and Religion at Temple Square and Mission San Juan Capistrano." *Journal of American Folklore* 113, no. 450 (2001): 422–35.

Brewer, William Henry. *Up and Down California in 1860–1864: The Journal of William H. Brewer.* Edited by Francis P. Farquhar. New Haven, Conn.: Yale University Press, 1930. http://www.yosemite.ca.us/library/up_and_down_california.

Brown, Tom. "California Mission Gardens." *Pacific Horticulture* 49, no. 1 (1988): 3–11.

Browne, Robert O. *San Buenaventura Mission Water System.* Ventura County Archaeological Society, Thousand Oaks, Calif. Submitted to the Ventura City Council, Ventura, 1974.

Brubaker, Rogers, and Frederick Cooper. "Beyond 'Identity.'" *Theory and Society* 29, no. 1 (2000): 1–47.

Bruchac, Margaret M. "Decolonization in Archaeological Theory." In *Encyclopedia of Global Archaeology,* edited by Claire Smith, 2069–77. New York: Springer, 2014.

Bruchac, Margaret M., Siobhan M. Hart, and H. Martin Wobst, eds. *Indigenous Archaeologies: A Reader on Decolonization.* Walnut Creek, Calif.: Left Coast Press, 2010.

Brundage, William Fitzhugh. *The Southern Past: A Clash of Race and Memory.* Cambridge, Mass.: Harvard University Press, 2005.

Bruner, Edward M. "Abraham Lincoln as Authentic Reproduction: A Critique of Postmodernism." In *The Political Nature of Cultural Heritage and Tourism: Critical Essays,* vol. 3, edited by Dallen J. Timothy, 19–37. Aldershot, UK: Ashgate, 2007.

Bruyneel, Kevin. *The Third Space of Sovereignty: The Postcolonial Politics of U.S.–Indigenous Relations.* Minneapolis: University of Minnesota Press, 2007.

Bryant, William Cullen, ed. *Picturesque America; or, The Land We Live In.* 2 vols. New York: D. Appleton, 1872, 1874.

Burns, John F., and Richard J. Orsi, eds. *Taming the Elephant: Politics, Government, and Law in Pioneer California.* Berkeley: University of California Press, 2003.

Burton-Carvajal, Julianne. "The Carmel Mission in Art." *American Art Review* 20, no. 1 (2008): 82–89.

Byne, Mildred Stapley, and Arthur Byne. *Spanish Gardens and Patios.* New York: Architectural Record, 1924.

Byrne, Denis. "An Archaeology of Attachment: Cultural Heritage and the Post-contact." In *After Captain Cook: The Archaeology of the Recent Indigenous Past in Australia,* edited by Rodney Harrison and Christine Williamson, 135–46. Walnut Creek, Calif.: Alta Mira Press, 2004.

———. *Counterheritage: Critical Perspectives on Heritage Conservation in Asia.* New York: Routledge, 2014.

California Mission Buildings. Brochure Series of Architectural Illustration 4, no. 7 (1898): 110–20.

California State Board of Education. *History–Social Science Content Standards for California Public Schools: Kindergarten through Grade Twelve.* Adopted October 1998. Sacramento: California Department of Education, 1998. http://www.cde.ca.gov/be/st/ss/documents/histsocscistnd.pdf.

Camarillo, Albert. *Chicanos in a Changing Society: From Mexican Pueblos to American Barrios in Santa Barbara and Southern California, 1848–1930.* Cambridge, Mass.: Harvard University Press, 1979.

Cameron, Christina. "The Spirit of Place: The Physical Memory of Canada." *Journal of Canadian Studies* 35, no. 1 (2000): 77–94.

———. "World Heritage Sites of Conscience and Memory." In *World Heritage and Cultural Diversity,* edited by Dieter Offenhäusser, Walther Ch. Zimmerli, and Marie-Theres Albert, 112–19. Cottbus: German Commission for UNESCO, 2010.

Capps, Lois. [Congressional debate, November 17, 2004.] Congressional Record, 108th Congress, 2nd Session, House of Representatives (2003–4). California Missions Preservation Act. https://www.congress.gov/congressional-record/2004/11/17/house-section/article/H9828-1.

Carillo, J. M. *The Story of Mission San Antonio de Pala.* Oceanside, Calif.: North County Printers, 1959.

Carocci, Max. "Living in an Urban Rez: Constructing San Francisco as Indian Land." In Porter, *Place and Native American Indian History and Culture,* 263–82.

Carrico, Richard L. *Strangers in a Stolen Land: American Indians in San Diego, 1850–1880.* Sacramento: Sierra Oaks Pub., 1987.

Carroll, Mary Pius. "The Influence of the Missions on Present-Day California." Newman Prize essay. Berkeley, Newman Club of the University of California, 1916. Berkeley. MSS on file, Bancroft Library, 1916. Reprinted from the *University of California Chronicle* 18, no. 4 (October 1916).

Cartier, Carolyn, and Alan A. Lew, eds. *Seductions of Place: Geographical Perspectives on Globalization and Touristed Landscapes.* London: Routledge, 2005.

Casella, Eleanor Conlin. "Landscapes of Punishment and Resistance: A Female Convict Settlement in Tasmania, Australia." In Bender and Winer, *Contested Landscapes,* 113–20.

Castañeda, Antonia. "Engendering the History of Alta California, 1769–1848: Gender, Sexuality, and the Family." In Gutiérrez and Orsi, *Contested Eden,* 230–59.

———. "Sexual Violence in the Politics and Policies of Conquest: Amerindian Women in the Spanish Conquest of Alta California." In *Building with Our Hands: New Directions in Chicana Studies,* edited by Adela de la Torre and Beatríz M. Pesquera, 15–33. Berkeley: University of California Press, 1993.

Castillo, Edward D. "Cultural Chauvinism Offered to Justify Serra Canonization." In Costo and Costo, *The Missions of California,* 67–80.

———. "Gender Status Decline, Resistance, and Accommodation among Female Neophytes in the Missions of California: A San Gabriel Case Study." *American Indian Culture and Research Journal* 18, no. 1 (1994): 67–93.

———. "Mission Studies and the Columbian Quincentennial." *News from Native California* 5 (May–July 1991): 12–13.

———, ed. *Native American Perspectives on the Hispanic Colonization of Alta California.* New York: Garland, 1991.

———. "Neophyte Resistance and Accommodation in the Missions of California." In *The Spanish Missionary Heritage of the United States: Selected Papers and Commentaries from the November 1990 Quincentenary Symposium,* edited by Howard Benoist and María Carolina Flores, 60–75. San Antonio: National Park Service, 1993.

Chambers, Deborah. "Family as Place: Family Photograph Albums and the Domestication of Public and Private Space." In Schwartz and Ryan, *Picturing Place,* 96–114.

Chávez-García, Miroslava. *Negotiating Conquest: Gender and Power in California, 1770s to 1880s.* Tucson: University of Arizona Press, 2004.

Chilcote Olivia. "Pow Wows at the Mission: Identity and Federal Recognition for the San Luis Rey Band of Luiseño Mission Indians." *Boletín: Journal of the California Missions Studies Association* 31, no. 1 (2015): 79–87.

Classen, Constance. *The Deepest Sense: A Cultural History of Touch.* Urbana-Champaign: University of Illinois Press, 2012.

Clayton, Virginia Tuttle. "Picturing a 'Usable Past.'" In *Drawing on America's Past: Folk Art, Modernism, and the Index of American Design,* 1–43. Washington, D.C.: National Gallery of Art, 2002.

Coffin, Margaret. *Guide to Developing a Preservation Maintenance Plan for a Historic Landscape.* Olmsted Center for Landscape Preservation, Cultural Landscape Publication no. 7. Washington, D.C.: National Park Service, U.S. Department of the Interior, 1995.

Cohen, Erik. "Educational Dark Tourism at an In Populo Site: The Holocaust Museum in Jerusalem." *Annals of Tourism Research* 38, no. 1 (January 2011): 193–209.

———. "A Phenomenology of Tourist Experiences." *Sociology* 13, no. 2 (May 1979): 179–201.

Cohen-Williams, Anita G. "Archaeological Excavations of the Sunken Gardens of Mission San Luis Rey, California." In Beebe and Senkewicz, *Architecture, Physical Environment, and Society in Alta California*, 13–64.

Cole, Tim. "Crematoria, Barracks, Gateway: Survivors' Return Visits to the Memory Landscapes of Auschwitz." *History and Memory* 25, no. 2 (Fall/Winter 2013): 102–31.

Coleman, Simon, and Mike Crang, eds. *Tourism: Between Place and Performance.* New York: Berghahn Books, 2002.

Colwell-Chanthaphonh, Chip, and T. J. Ferguson. "Memory Pieces and Footprints: Multivocality and the Meanings of Ancient Times and Ancestral Places among the Zuni and Hopi." *American Anthropologist* 108, no. 1 (2006): 148–62.

———, eds. *Collaboration in Archaeological Practice: Engaging Descendant Communities.* Lanham, Md.: Rowman & Littlefield, 2007.

Combs, Gary, and Fred Ploogh. "The Conversion of the Chumash Indians." *Human Ecology* 5 (1977): 309–28.

Conan, Michel. "Fragments of a Poetic of Gardens." *Landscape Journal* 25, no. 1 (2006): 1–21.

Connerton, Paul. *How Societies Remember.* Cambridge: Cambridge University Press, 1989.

Cook, Sherburne F. *The Conflict between the California Indian and White Civilization.* Berkeley: University of California Press, 1976.

Cook-Lynn, Elizabeth. *A Separate Country: Postcoloniality and American Indian Nations.* Lubbock: Texas Tech University Press, 2011.

Cooperman, Alan. "Federal Aid for Churches Is Criticized." *Washington Post,* December 3, 2004, A25.

Corbett, Raymond. "Chumash Bone Whistles: The Development of Ceremonial Integration in Chumash Society." In *Foundations of Chumash Complexity,* edited by Jeanne E. Arnold, 65–73. Perspectives in California Archaeology 7. Los Angeles: Cotsen Institute of Archaeology, University of California, Los Angeles, 2004.

Corner, James. "Introduction: Recovering Landscape as a Critical Cultural Practice." In *Recovering Landscape: Essays in Contemporary Landscape Architecture,* edited by James Corner, 1–26. Princeton, N.J.: Princeton Architectural Press, 1999.

Corrin, Lisa, ed. *Mining the Museum: An Installation by Fred Wilson.* Baltimore: Contemporary; New York: New Press, 1994.

Corsane, Gerard. "Robben Island: Facing the Challenges of Creating a National Museum in a World Heritage Site." In *Re-mapping the Field: New Approaches in Conflict Archaeology,* edited by John Schofield, Axel Klausmeier, and Louise Purbrick, 64–71. Bonn: Westkreuz-Verlag, 2006.

Cosgrove, Denis. "Landscape, Culture and Modernity." In *Geographical Imagination and the Authority of Images: Hettner-Lecture 2005 with Denis Cosgrove,* 29–52. Stuttgart: Franz Steiner Verlag, 2006.

———. *Social Formation and Symbolic Landscape.* Towata, N.J.: Barnes and Noble Books, 1985.

Cosgrove, Denis, and Stephen Daniels, eds. *The Iconography of Landscape: Essays on the Symbolic Representation, Design and Use of Past Environments.* Cambridge: Cambridge University Press, 1988.

Costello, Julia G. *The Ranches and Ranchos of Mission San Antonio de Padua*. Bakersfield: California Mission Studies Association, 1994.

———. *Santa Inés Excavations, 1986–1988*. California Historical Archaeology, no. 1. Salinas, Calif.: Coyote Press, 1989.

Costello, Julia G., and David Hornbeck. "Alta California: An Overview." In *Columbian Consequences*. Vol. 1, *Archaeological and Historical Perspectives on the Spanish Borderlands West*, edited by David Hurst Thomas, 303–31. Washington, D.C.: Smithsonian Institution Press, 1991.

Costo, Rupert, and Jeanette Costo. *The Missions of California: A Legacy of Genocide*. San Francisco: Indian Historian Press, 1987.

Crang, Mike. "Knowing, Tourism and Practices of Vision." In *Leisure/Tourism Geographies: Practices and Geographical Knowledge*, edited by David Crouch, 238–56. London: Routledge, 1999.

Crary, Jonathan. *Techniques of the Observer: On Vision and Modernity in the Nineteenth Century*. Cambridge, Mass.: MIT Press, 1990.

Cronon, William. *Changes in the Land: Indians, Colonists, and the Ecology of New England*. New York: Hill and Wang, 1983.

Crosby, Alfred W. *Ecological Imperialism: The Biological Expansion of Europe, 900–1900*. 2nd ed. Cambridge: Cambridge University Press, 2004.

Cummins, Tom. "The Indulgent Image: Prints in the New World." In *Contested Visions*, edited by Ilona Katzew, 203–25. Los Angeles: Los Angeles Museum of Art, 2011. Exhibition catalog.

———. "Representation in the Sixteenth Century and the Colonial Image of the Inca." In *Writing without Words: Alternative Literacies in Mesoamerica and the Andes*, edited by Elizabeth Boone and Walter Mignolo, 188–219. Durham, N.C.: Duke University Press, 1994.

Cuthrell, Rob Q., Chuck Striplen, Mark Hylkema, and Kent G. Lightfoot. "A Land of Fire: Anthropogenic Burning on the Central Coast of California." In Jones and Perry, *Contemporary Issues in California Archaeology*, 153–72.

Daniels, Stephen. *Humphrey Repton: Landscape Gardening and the Geography of Georgian England*. New Haven, Conn.: Yale University Press, 1999.

Dartt-Newton, Deana. "California's Sites of Conscience: An Analysis of the State's Historic Mission Museums." *Museum Anthropology* 34, no. 2 (2011): 97–108.

———. "Negotiating the Master Narrative: Museums and the Indian/Californio Community of California's Central Coast." Ph.D. diss., University of Oregon, 2009.

Dartt-Newton, Deana, and Jon M. Erlandson. "Little Choice for the Chumash: Colonialism, Cattle, and Coercion in Mission Period California." *American Indian Quarterly* 30, no. 3/4 (2006): 416–30.

Davis, Clark. "An Era and Generation of Civic Engagement: The Friday Morning Club in Los Angeles, 1891–1931." *Southern California Quarterly* 84, no. 2 (Summer 2002): 135–68.

Dean, Carolyn. *Inka Bodies and the Body of Christ: Corpus Christi in Colonial Cuzco, Peru*. Durham, N.C.: Duke University Press, 1999.

———. "The Renewal of Old World Images and the Creation of Colonial Peruvian Visual Culture." In *Converging Culture: Art and Identity in Spanish America*, edited by Diane Fane, 171–82. Brooklyn: Brooklyn Museum Press, 1996.

Dearborn, Lynne M., and John C. Stallmeyer. *Inconvenient Heritage: Erasure and Global Tourism in Luang Prabang*. Walnut Creek, Calif.: Left Coast Press, 2010.

de Certeau, Michel. *The Practice of Everyday Life.* Translated by Steven Rendall. Berkeley: University of California Press, 1984.

Deetz, James. "Archaeological Investigations at La Purisima." *Annual Report of the Archaeological Survey, Department of Anthropology, University of California, Los Angeles, 1962/1963,* 5 (1963): 161–241.

De Forest, Elizabeth. "Old Santa Barbara Gardens and How They Came to Be." *Pacific Horticulture* 38 (1977–78): 31–36.

De Jong, Ferdinand, and Michael Rowlands, eds. *Reclaiming Heritage: Alternative Imaginaries of Memories in West Africa.* Walnut Creek, Calif.: Left Coast Press, 2007.

Delgado, Richard, and Jean Stefancic. *Critical Race Theory: An Introduction.* 2nd ed. New York: NYU Press, 2012.

Delle, James. *An Archaeology of Social Space: Analyzing Coffee Plantations in Jamaica's Blue Mountains.* New York: Plenum Press, 1998.

DeLyser, Dydia. *Ramona Memories: Tourism and the Shaping of Southern California.* Minneapolis: University of Minnesota Press, 2005.

Deverell, William. *Railroad Crossings: Californians and the Railroad, 1850–1910.* Berkeley: University of California Press, 1994.

———. *Whitewashed Adobe: The Rise of Los Angeles and the Remaking of Its Mexican Past.* Berkeley: University of California Press, 2004.

Deverell, William, and Douglas Flamming. "Race, Rhetoric, and Regional Identity: Boosting Los Angeles, 1880–1930." In *Power and Place in the North American West,* edited by Richard White and John Findlay, 117–43. Seattle: University of Washington Press, 1999.

Dienstag, Alan. "Alzheimer's and the Spiritual Terrain of Memory." *On Being with Krista Tippett,* March 19, 2015, http://www.onbeing.org/program/alan-dienstag-alzheimers-and-the-spiritual-terrain-of-memory/64.

Diepenbrock, William. "Call It California 'Mission: Possible.'" *Orange County Register,* February 20, 2009. http://www.ocregister.com/articles/strong-555288-http-href.html.

Dinius, Oliver J., and Angela Vergara, eds. *Company Towns in the Americas: Landscape, Power, and Working-Class Communities.* Athens: University of Georgia Press, 2011.

Doss, Erika. "American Folk Art's 'Distinctive Character': The Index of American Design and New Deal Notions of Cultural Nationalism." In *Drawing on America's Past: Folk Art, Modernism and the Index of American Design,* 61–73. Washington, D.C.: National Gallery of Art, 2002. Exhibition catalog.

———. *Memorial Mania: Public Feeling in America.* Chicago: University of Chicago Press, 2010.

Downie, Harry. *Mission San Carlos Borromeo del Rio Carmelo.* Carmel, Calif.: Carmel Press, n.d. [ca. 1940]. Visitor brochure, Bancroft Library Collection, University of California, Berkeley.

———. *A Visit to San Carlos: The Father of the Missions.* San Francisco: Alex. Dulfer Printing, 1938.

Duffy, Terence M. "Museums of 'Human Suffering' and the Struggle for Human Rights." *Museum International* 53 (2001): 10–16.

Duflot de Mofras, Eugène. *Duflot de Mofras' Travels on the Pacific Coast.* 2 vols. Translated and edited by Marguerite Eyer Wilbur. Santa Ana, Calif.: Fine Arts Press, 1937. Translation of 1844 ed.

Duhaut-Cilly, Auguste Bernard. "Duhaut-Cilly's Account of California in the Years 1827–1828." Translated by Charles Franklin Carter. *California Historical Society Quarterly* 8, no. 2–4 (June–December 1929): 131–66, 214–50, 306–36.

Dunbar-Ortiz, Roxanne. *An Indigenous Peoples' History of the United States.* Boston: Beacon Press, 2014.

Durchholz, Patricia. *Defining Mission: Camboni Missionaries in North America.* Lanham, Md.: University Press of America, 1999.

Dwyer, Owen J., and Derek H. Alderman. *Civil Rights Memorials and the Geography of Memory.* Chicago: Center for American Places at Columbia College Chicago, 2008.

Dyer, Frank J. "To Preserve the Early Landmarks." *San Francisco Chronicle,* March 1, 1896. Archived in Richard N. Schellens Papers, 155, California Historical Society, San Francisco.

Edensor, Tim. *Tourists at the Taj: Performance and Meaning at a Symbolic Site.* London: Routledge, 1998.

Edmonds, Mark. "Who Said Romance Was Dead?" *Journal of Material Culture* 11, no. 1–2 (2006): 167–88.

Edwards, Elizabeth, and Janice Hart, eds. *Photographs Objects Histories: On the Materiality of Images.* London: Routledge, 2004.

Eggleton, Lara. "'A Living Ruin': Palace, City, and Landscape in Nineteenth-Century Travel Descriptions of Granada." *Architectural Theory Review* 18, no. 3 (2013): 372–87.

———. "Re-envisioning the Alhambra: Readings of Architecture and Ornament from Medieval to Modern." Ph.D. diss., University of Leeds, May 2011.

Emerson, Thomas E. *Cahokia and the Archaeology of Power.* Tuscaloosa: University of Alabama Press, 1997.

Engelhardt, Zephyrin. *Mission San Antonio de Padua.* Santa Barbara: Mission Santa Barbara, 1929.

———. *San Gabriel Mission and the Beginnings of Los Angeles.* San Gabriel: Mission San Gabriel, 1927.

———. *Santa Barbara Mission.* San Francisco: James H. Barry, 1923.

Engle, Jan. "'Roughing It' at Ft. Hunter Liggett." *Los Angeles Times,* August 17, 2008.

Engstrand, Iris H. W. "Perception and Perfection: Picturing the Spanish and Mexican Colonial West." *Western Historical Quarterly* 36, no. 1 (2005): 4–21.

Epperson, Terrence W. "Panoptic Plantations: The Garden Sights of Thomas Jefferson and George Mason." In *Lines That Divide: Historical Archaeologies of Race, Class, and Gender,* edited by James. A. Delle, Stephen A. Mrozowski, and Robert Paynter, 58–77. Knoxville: University of Tennessee Press, 2000.

Ettinger, Catherine R. "Hybrid Spaces, Indigenous Contributions to Mission Architecture." In Beebe and Senkewicz, *Architecture, Physical Environment, and Society in Alta California,* 77–89.

———. "Spaces of Change: Architecture and the Creation of a New Society in the California Missions." *Boletín: Journal of the California Mission Studies Association* 21, no. 1 (2004): 23–44.

Ewing, Russell C. [Memo to L. C. Merriam, regional officer, U.S. Department of Interior, National Park Service, Branch of Planning and State Cooperation.] May 22, 1936. La Purísima Mission State Park Archives, Advisory Committee file.

———. "Mission La Purisima Conception, California." In Whitehead, *California's Mission La Purísima Concepción,* 235–98.

Fagan, Brian. "The House of the Sea: An Essay on the Antiquity of Planked Canoes in Southern California." *American Antiquity* 69, no. 1 (2004): 7–16.

Fallbrook and Bonsall Village News. "Corpus Christi Fiesta at Pala June 1," 18, no. 19 (May 8, 2014). Accessed June 1, 2014, http://www.thevillagenews.com/story/78015.

Fanon, Frantz. *Black Skin, White Masks.* Translated by Charles Lam Marmann. New York: Grove Press, 1967.

———. *The Wretched of the Earth.* Translated by Constance Farrington. New York: Grove Press, 1963.

Farnham, Thomas Jefferson. *Travels in the Californias and Scenes in the Pacific Ocean.* New York: Saxton & Miles, 1844.

Farnsworth, Paul. "Missions, Indians, and Cultural Continuity." *Historical Archaeology* 26, no. 1 (1992): 22–36.

Farnsworth, Paul, and Robert H. Jackson. "Cultural, Economic, and Demographic Change in the Missions of Alta California: The Case of Nuestra Señora de las Soledad." In *The New Latin American Mission History,* edited by E. Langer and Robert H. Jackson, 109–29. Lincoln: University of Nebraska Press, 1995.

Farr, Samuel. [Congressional Debate, November 17, 2004.] Congressional Record, 108th Congress, 2nd Session, House of Representatives (2003–4). California Missions Preservation Act. https://www.congress.gov/congressional-record/2004/11/17/house-section/article/H9828-1.

Farris, Glenn J. *Archaeological Testing in the Neophyte Housing Area at Mission San Juan Bautista California.* Resource Protection Division, California Department of Parks and Recreation, Sacramento, 1991.

———. "Depriving God and the King of the Means of Charity: Early Nineteenth-Century Missionaries' Views of Cattle Ranchers near Mission La Purísima, California." In Panich and Schneider, *Indigenous Landscapes and Spanish Missions,* 135–53.

Ferris, Neal. *The Archaeology of Native-Lived Colonialism: Challenging History in the Great Lakes.* Tucson: University of Arizona Press, 2009.

Field, Anna Caroline. "A Southwest Sleepy Hollow." *Land of Sunshine* 15 (1901): 126–38.

Field, Les W. "Complicities and Collaborations: Anthropologists and the 'Unacknowledged Tribes' of California." *Current Anthropology* 40 (1999): 193–209.

Field, Sean. "'No One Has Allowed Me to Cry': Trauma, Memorialization and Children in Post-Conflict Rwanda." In Purbrick, Aulich, and Dawson, *Contested Spaces,* 211–32.

Fiske, Turbesé Lummis, and Keith Lummis. *Charles F. Lummis: The Man and His West.* Norman: University of Oklahoma Press, 1975.

Fixico, Donald L. *Call for Change: The Medicine Way of American Indian History, Ethos, and Reality.* Lincoln: University of Nebraska Press, 2013.

Fleming, Guy. L. [Letter to J. H. Covington from superintendent, Southern District.] December 14, 1936. La Purísima Mission State Park Archives, Advisory Committee file.

Flower, Enola. *A Child's History of California.* California State Series. Sacramento: California State Department of Education, 1949.

Flynn, Johny Preston. "From Three Worlds to One: An Analysis of Chumash Religious History." Ph.D. diss., University of California, Santa Barbara, 1991.

Fogo, Bradley. "What Every Student Should Know and Be Able to Do: The Making of California's Framework, Standards, and Tests for History-Social Science." Ph.D. diss., Stanford University, 2010.

Ford, Henry Chapman. *An Artist Records the California Missions.* Edited with an Introduction by Norman Neuerburg. San Francisco: Book Club of California, 1989.

———. "Some Detached Notes by Henry Chapman Ford on the Missions of California." *California Historical Society Quarterly* 3, no. 3 (1924): 238–44.

Foster, John M. "'They're Just Rocks': San Miguel Mission Native Quarters, Making Sense of Tragedy." *Boletín: Journal of the California Mission Studies Association* 31, no. 1 (2015): 169–84.

Foucault, Michel. *Discipline and Punish.* Translated by Alan Sheridan. New York: Vintage Books, 1979.

———. "Of Other Spaces." *Diacritics* 16, no. 1 (1986.): 22–27.

———. "Space, Knowledge, and Power." In *Foucault Reader,* edited by Paul Rabinow, 239–56. New York: Pantheon Books, 1984.

Fox, Helen Morgenthau. *Patio Gardens.* New York: Macmillan, 1929.

Frank, L. *Acorn Soup.* Berkeley: Heyday Books, 1999.

Freedberg, David. *The Power of Images: Studies in the History and Theory of Response.* Chicago: University of Chicago Press, 1989.

French, Jere Stuart. *The California Garden: And the Landscape Architects Who Shaped It.* Washington, D.C.: Landscape Architecture Foundation, 1993.

Gable, Eric, and Richard Handler. "Public History, Private Memory: Notes from the Ethnography of Colonial Williamsburg, Virginia, USA." In Levin, *Defining Memory,* 47–62.

Gallivan, Martin, Danielle Moretti-Langholtz, and Buck Woodard. "Collaborative Archaeology and Strategic Essentialism: Native Empowerment in Tidewater Virginia." *Historical Archaeology* 45, no. 1 (2011): 10–23.

Gamble, Lynn H. "Chumash Architecture: Sweatlodges and Houses." *Journal of California and Great Basin Anthropology* 17 (1995): 54–92.

———. *The Chumash World at European Contact: Power, Trade, and Feasting among Complex Hunter-Gatherers.* Berkeley: University of California Press, 2008.

———. "A Land of Power: The Materiality of Wealth, Knowledge, Authority, and the Supernatural." In Jones and Perry, *Contemporary Issues in California Archaeology,* 175–96.

———. "Subsistence Practices and Feasting Rites: Chumash Identity after European Colonization." *Historical Archaeology* 49, no. 2 (2015): 115–35.

Garden, Mary-Catherine E. "The Heritagescape: Looking at Landscapes of the Past." *International Journal of Heritage Studies* 12, no. 5 (September 2006): 394–411.

Garnett, Porter. *San Francisco One Hundred Years Ago. Translated from the French of Louis Choris with Illustrations from Drawings Made by Choris in the Year 1816, to Which Are Added Certain Views of San Francisco at the Present Day.* San Francisco: Taylor, Nash & Taylor; A. M. Robertson, 1913. http://www.books-about-california.com/Pages/SF_100_Years_Ago/SF_100_Years_ago_text.html.

———. "Stately Homes of California: El Fureidis." *Sunset* 32 (1914): 1060.

Gates, Eleanor. "Motoring among the Missions: A Real Joy Ride through the Cathedral Towns of California." *Sunset* 28 (1912): 305–14.

Gebhard, David. Introduction to *An Arcadian Landscape: The California Gardens of A. E. Hansen, 1920–1932,* edited by David Gebhard and Sheila Lynds, vi–xiv. Los Angeles: Hennessey and Ingalls, 1985.

———. "The Spanish Colonial Revival in Southern California (1895–1930)." *Journal of the Society of Architectural Historians* 26 (May 1967): 131–47.

Geertz, Clifford. "Thick Description: Toward an Interpretive Theory of Culture." In *The Interpretation of Cultures: Selected Essays,* 3–30. New York: Basic Books, 1973.

Geiger, Maynard. *Mission Santa Barbara, 1782–1965.* Santa Barbara: Franciscan Fathers of California, 1965.

———. *A Pictorial History of the Physical Development of Mission Santa Barbara from Brush Hut to Institutional Greatness, 1786–1963*. San Francisco: Franciscan Fathers of California, 1963.

Gentilcore, R. Louis. "Missions and Mission Lands of Alta California." *Annals of the Association of American Geographers* 51, no. 1 (March 1961): 53–55.

Gentry, Jewel, "'Chronicles of Light': San Carlos Borromeo, Solar Geometry, and the Architecture of the California Missions." *Boletín: Journal of the California Missions Studies Association* 28, no. 1–2 (2011–12): 85–94.

Giaccardi, Elisa, and Leysia Palen. "The Social Production of Heritage through Cross-Media Interaction: Making Place for Place-Making." *International Journal of Heritage Studies* 14, no. 3 (2008): 281–97.

Gibbons, James. [Congressional debate, November 17, 2004.] Congressional Record, 108th Congress, 2nd Session, House of Representatives (2003–4). California Missions Preservation Act. https://www.congress.gov/congressional-record/2004/11/17/house-section/article/H9828-1.

González, Michael J. "'The Child of the Wilderness Weeps for the Father of Our Country': The Indian and the Politics of Church and State in Provincial California." In Gutiérrez and Orsi, *Contested Eden*, 147–72.

Goodhue, Bertram Grosvenor. Introduction to *The Architecture and the Gardens of the San Diego Exposition*, 3–9. Described by Carleton Monroe Winslow together with an essay by Clarence S. Stein. Illustrated from photographs by Harold A. Taylor. San Francisco: Paul Elder, 1916.

Gordon, Tammy S. *Private History in Public: Exhibition and the Settings of Everyday Life*. Lanham, Md.: Alta Mira Press, 2010.

Grant, Campbell. *The Rock Paintings of the Chumash: A Study of a California Indian Culture*. Berkeley: University of California Press, 1965.

Greenwood, Roberta S., ed. *The Changing Faces of Main Street*. Ventura, Calif.: Ventura Redevelopment Agency, 1976.

Gregory, Derek. "Colonial Nostalgia and Cultures of Travel: Spaces of Constructed Visibility in Egypt." In AlSayyad, *Consuming Tradition, Manufacturing Heritage*, 111–51.

Gregson, Nicky, and Gillian Rose. "Taking Butler Elsewhere: Performativities, Spatialities, and Subjectivities." *Environment and Planning D: Society and Space* 18 (2000): 433–52.

Gröppel-Wegener, Alke. "Creating Heritage Experience through Architecture." In *Performing Heritage: Research, Practice and Innovation in Museum Theatre and Live Interpretation*, edited by Anthony Jackson and Jenny Kidd, 39–52. Manchester: Manchester University Press, 2011.

Gruzinski, Serge. *Painting the Conquest: The Mexican Indians and the European Renaissance*. Paris: Flammarion, 1992.

Gullett, Gayle. *Becoming Citizens: The Emergence and Development of the California Women's Movement, 1880–1911*. Champaign: University of Illinois Press, 2000.

———. "Women Progressives and the Politics of Americanization in California, 1915–1920." *Pacific Historical Review* 64, no. 1 (1995): 71–94.

Gunther, Vanessa Ann. *Ambiguous Justice: Native Americans and the Law in Southern California. 1848–1890*. East Lansing: Michigan State University Press, 2007.

Gunthorp, Maude Robson. *With a Sketch Book along the Old Mission Trail*. Caldwell, Idaho: Caxton Printers, 1940.

Gutfreund, Zevi. "Standing Up to Sugar Cubes: The Contest over Ethnic Identity in California's Fourth-Grade Mission Curriculum." *Southern California Quarterly* 92, no. 2 (Summer 2010): 161–97.

Gutiérrez, Ramón A., and Richard J. Orsi, eds. *Contested Eden: California before the Gold Rush.* Berkeley: University of California Press, 1998.

Haas, Lisbeth. *Conquests and Historical Identities in California, 1769–1936.* Berkeley: University of California Press, 1997.

———. *Pablo Tac, Indigenous Scholar: Writings on Luiseño Language and Colonial History, c. 1840.* Berkeley: University of California Press, 2011.

———. "'Raise Your Sword and I Will Eat You': Luiseño Scholar Pablo Tac, ca. 1841." In Hackel, *Alta California,* 79–110.

———. *Saints and Citizens: Indigenous Histories of Colonial Missions and Mexican California.* Berkeley: University of California Press, 2014.

Habu, Junko, Clare Fawcett, and John M. Matsunaga, eds. *Evaluating Multiple Narratives: Beyond Nationalist, Colonialist, Imperialist Archaeologies.* New York: Springer, 2008.

Hackel, Steven W. *Children of the Coyote, Missionaries of Saint Francis: Indian–Spanish Relations in Colonial California, 1769–1850.* Chapel Hill: University of North Carolina Press, 2005.

———. *Junípero Serra: California's Founding Father.* New York: Hill and Wang, 2013.

———. "Land, Labor, and Production: The Colonial Economy of Spanish and Mexican California." In Gutiérrez and Orsi, *Contested Eden,* 111–46.

———. "The Staff of Leadership: Indian Authority in the Missions of Alta California." *William and Mary Quarterly,* 3rd ser., 54, no. 2 (1997): 347–76.

———, ed. *Alta California: Peoples in Motion, Identities in Formation, 1769–1850.* Berkeley: Published for Huntington-USC Institute on California and the West by University of California Press, Berkeley, and Huntington Library, San Marino, Calif., 2010.

———. and Hilary E. Wyss. "Print Culture and the Power of Native Literacy in California and New England Missions." In *Native Americans, Christianity, and the Reshaping of the American Religious Landscape,* edited by Joel W. Martin and Mark A. Nicholas, 201–22. Chapel Hill: University of North Carolina Press, 2010.

Hackling, Joan Helen. "Authenticity in Preservation Thought: The Reconstruction of Mission La Purísima Concepción." Master's thesis, University of California, Los Angeles, 1989.

Hageman, Frederick C. "An Architectural Study of the Mission La Purísima Concepción." In *California's Mission La Purísima Concepción: The Hageman and Ewing Reports,* prepared and edited for publication by Richard S. Whitehead, 1–234. Santa Barbara: Santa Barbara Trust for Historic Preservation, 1991.

Halbwachs, Maurice. *On Collective Memory.* Chicago: University of Chicago Press, 1992.

Hale, Charles R. "Activist Research v. Cultural Critique: Indigenous Land Rights and the Contradictions of Politically Engaged Anthropology." *Cultural Anthropology* 21 (2006): 96–120.

———, ed. *Engaging Contradictions: Theory, Politics, and Methods of Activist Scholarship.* Berkeley: University of California Press, 2008.

Hall, Martin. "Identity, Memory and Countermemory: The Archaeology of an Urban Landscape." *Journal of Material Culture* 11, no. 1–2 (2006): 189–209.

Hallan-Gibson, Pamela. "Mission San Juan Capistrano." In Stern and Miller, *Romance of the Bells,* 45–71.

Handler, Richard, and Eric Gable. *The New History in an Old Museum: Creating the Past at Colonial Williamsburg.* Durham, N.C.: Duke University Press, 1997.

Hannaford, Donald R., and Revel Edwards. *Spanish Colonial or Adobe Architecture of California, 1800–1850*. Stamford, Conn.: Architectural Book Publishing, 1931 [reprinted 1990].

Hardwick, Michael R. *Changes in the Landscape: The Beginnings of Horticulture in the California Missions*. 2nd ed. Orange, Calif.: Paragon Agency, 2005.

Harley, John Brian. *Maps, Knowledge, and Power*. Cambridge: Cambridge University Press, 1988.

Harris, Dianne. "Clean and Bright and Everyone White: Seeing the Postwar Domestic Landscape in the United States." In Harris and Ruggles, eds., *Sites Unseen*, 241–62.

———. *The Nature of Authority: Villa Culture, Landscape, and Representation in Eighteenth-Century Lombardy*. University Park: Pennsylvania State University Press, 2003.

Harris, Dianne, and D. Fairchild Ruggles, eds. *Sites Unseen: Landscape and Vision*. Pittsburgh: University of Pittsburgh Press, 2007.

Harris, Heather. "Indigenous Worldviews and Ways of Knowing as Theoretical and Methodological Foundations behind Archaeological Theory and Method." In Smith and Wobst, *Indigenous Archaeologies*, 33–41.

Harrison, Rodney. "'Counter-Mapping' Heritage, Communities, and Places in Australia and the UK." In *Local Heritage, Global Context: Cultural Perspectives on Sense of Place*, edited by John Schofield and Rosy Szymanski, 79–98. Farnham, UK: Ashgate, 2011.

———. *Heritage: Critical Approaches*. New York: Routledge, 2012.

———. "Heritage as Social Action." In *Understanding Heritage in Practice*, edited by Susie West, 240–76. Manchester: Manchester University Press and Open University, 2010.

———. *Shared Landscapes: Archaeologies of Attachment and the Pastoral Industry in New South Wales*. Sydney: University of New South Wales Press, 2004.

Hauser, Mark W., and Dan Hicks. "Colonialism and Landscape: Power, Materiality and Scales of Analysis in Caribbean Historical Archaeology." In *Envisioning Landscape*, edited by Dan Hicks, Laura McAtackney, and Graham J. Fairclough, 251–74. Walnut Creek, Calif.: Left Coast Press, 2007.

Hayden, Dolores. *The Power of Place: Urban Landscapes as Public History*. Cambridge, Mass.: MIT Press, 1997.

Hayes, Benjamin Ignatius. *Pioneer Notes from the Diaries of Judge Benjamin Hayes, 1849–1875*. Edited by Marjorie Tisdale Wolcott. Los Angeles: Printed privately, 1929.

Hayes, Virginia. "La Huerta Project: Restoring S.B. Mission's Crop Garden." *Santa Barbara Independent*, January 23, 2007.

Heidegger, Martin. "Building, Dwelling, Thinking." In *Basic Writings: Martin Heidegger*, edited by David Ferrell Krell, 319–40. London: Routledge, 1977.

Heidenreich, Linda. *This Land Was Mexican Once: Histories of Resistance from Northern California*. Austin: University of Texas Press, 2007.

Heizer, Robert F. Introduction to *The Destruction of California Indians*, xiii–xvii. 1974. Reprint, Lincoln: Bison Books, 1993.

Heizer, Robert F., and Albert B. Elsasser. "World View of California Indians." In *The Natural World of the California Indians*, 202–20. Berkeley: University of California Press, 1980.

Helmreich, Anne. "Domesticating the Nation: The Cottage Garden." In *The English Garden and National Identity*, 66–90. Cambridge: Cambridge University Press, 2002.

———. "The Marketing of Helen Allingham." In *Gendering the Landscape*, edited by Anna Roberts and Steven Adams, 45–60. Manchester: Manchester University Press, 2000.

Hendry, G. H. "Spanish Mission Gardens of California." *California Arts and Architecture* 46 (1934): 3.

Henry, Ed. "The History of the Picture Postcard . . . and the Postcard as History." In *Picturing Berkeley: A Postcard History,* edited by Burlington Willes, 3–13. Salt Lake City: Gibbs Smith, 2005.

Henry, Michael. "Alice Hare: Views of California Beauty." In *Shadowcatchers: A Directory of Women in California Photography 1900–1920.* Vol. 2. Edited by Peter Palmquist, 159–62. Arcata, Calif.: P. E. Palmquist, 1991.

Herwitz, Daniel Alan. *Heritage, Culture, and Politics in the Postcolony.* New York: Columbia University Press, 2012.

Hickman, Clare. *Therapeutic Landscapes: A History of English Hospital Gardens since 1800.* Manchester: Manchester University Press, 2013.

Hicks, Dan. *"The Garden of the World": An Historical Archaeology of Sugar Landscapes in the Eastern Caribbean.* Oxford: Archaeopress, 2007.

Hidalgo, Ellie. "A Meaningful Rededication at San Gabriel Mission." *Tidings,* July 4, 2008.

Highmore, Ben. Introduction to *The Everyday Life Reader,* edited by Ben Highmore, 1–34. London: Routledge, 2002.

Hill, Richard. "The Museum Indian: Still Frozen in Time and Mind." *Museum News* 79, no. 3 (2000): 40–44, 58–61, 63, 66–67, 74.

Hilton, Sylvia L. "Identities and the Usable Pasts of Colonial Borderlands: Spanish Historians and the North Pacific Frontiers of the Spanish Empire." In Hackel, *Alta California,* 235–323.

Hirsch, Eric. "Landscape, Myth, and Time." *Journal of Material Culture* 11, no. 1–2 (2006): 151–65.

Hobsbawm, Eric J. *Nations and Nationalism since 1780: Programme, Myth, Reality.* Cambridge: Cambridge University Press, 1990.

Hobsbawm, Eric J., and Terrence Ranger, eds. *The Invention of Tradition.* Cambridge: Cambridge University Press, 1983.

Hodges, Andrew, and Steve Watson. "Community-Based Heritage Management: A Case Study and Agenda for Research." *International Journal of Heritage Studies* 6, no. 3 (2000): 231–43.

Hodgkin, Katharine, and Susannah Radstone, eds. *Contested Pasts: The Politics of Memory.* London: Routledge, 2003.

Hoffman, Laura, and John Dietler. "Water at the San Gabriel Mission and the Intensification of Production: The Industrial Revolution Comes to California." Paper presented at the Annual Meeting of the Society of American Archaeology Annual Meetings, Honolulu, April 2013.

Hokowhitu, Brendan, Nathalie Kermoal, Chris Andersen, Anna Petersen, Michael Reilly, Isabel Altamirano-Jiménez, and Poia Rewi, eds. *Indigenous Identity and Resistance: Researching the Diversity of Knowledge.* Dunedin, NZ: Otago University Press, 2010.

Hollimon, Sandra E. "Archaeology of the *'Aqi*: Gender and Sexuality in Prehistoric Chumash Society." In Schmidt and Voss, *Archaeologies of Sexuality,* 179–96.

———. "The Third Gender in Native California: Two-Spirit Undertakers among the Chumash and Their Neighbors." In *Women in Prehistory: North America and Mesoamerica,* edited by Cheryl Claassen and Rosemary A. Joyce, 173–88. Philadelphia: University of Pennsylvania Press, 1997.

Holt, Geoffrey. "Restoration Drawing: Wall Decoration over Doorway, Façade of Mission House." Index of American Design. Washington, D.C.: National Gallery of Art, 1937.

Holtorf, Cornelius J., and Howard M. R. Williams. "Landscapes and Memories." In *The Cambridge Companion to Historical Archaeology,* edited by Dan Hicks and Mary C. Beaudry, 235–54. Cambridge: Cambridge University Press, 2006.

Hoover, Robert L. "The Archaeology of Spanish Colonial Sites in California." In *Comparative Studies in the Archaeology of Colonialism,* edited by Stephen L. Dyson, 93–114. Oxford: British Archaeological Record, 1985.

———. "Excavation at the Santa Inés Mill Complex." *Pacific Coast Archaeological Society Quarterly* 28, no. 2 (Spring 1992): 48–65.

———. "San Antonio Water-Powered Mill." *California Mission Studies Association Newsletter* 8, no. 1 (1991): 7.

Hoover, Robert L., and Julia Costello, eds. *Excavations at Mission San Antonio, 1976–1978.* Monograph 26. Los Angeles: Cotsen Institute of Archaeology, University of California, 1985.

Hosmer, Charles B., Jr., "The Colonial Revival in the Public Eye: Williamsburg and Early Garden Restoration." In *The Colonial Revival in America,* edited by Alan Axelrod, 52–70. New York: W.W. Norton for the Henry Francis du Pont Winterthur Museum, 1985.

Howard, Donald M. "Excavations at Tes-haya: The Indian Rancheria at Mission San Antonio de Padua (Mnt-100)." *Monterey County Archaeological Society Quarterly* 2, no. 1 (1972): 1–11.

Howes, David, and Constance Classen. *Ways of Sensing: Understanding the Senses in Society.* New York: Routledge, 2014.

Hoxie, Frederick E. "Sovereignty's Challenge to Native American (and United States) History." *Journal of Nineteenth-Century Americanists* 2, no. 1 (2014): 137–42.

Huckins, Pamela. "Seeing Is Believing: Images of Heaven and Hell in Alta California Missions." *Boletín: Journal of the California Missions Studies Association* 27, no. 1–2 (2010): 73–80.

Hudson, Travis. "The Chumash Revolt of 1824: Another Native Account from the Notes of John P. Harrington." *Journal of California and Great Basin Anthropology* 2 (1980): 123–36.

Hudson, Travis, Thomas Blackburn, Rosario Curletti, and Janice Timbrook, eds. *The Eye of the Flute: Chumash Traditional History and Ritual as Told by Fernando Librado Kitsepawit to John P. Harrington.* Santa Barbara, Calif.: Santa Barbara Museum of Natural History, 1977.

Hudson, Travis, and Ernest Underhay. *Crystals in the Sky: An Intellectual Odyssey Involving Chumash Astronomy, Cosmology, and Rock Art.* Socorro, N.Mex.: Ballena Press, 1978.

Hudson, William Henry. *The Famous Missions of California with Sketches in Color.* New York: Dodge Publishing, 1901.

Huell Howser Productions. *California Missions #109: Mission Gardens.* Video. Los Angeles: Huell Howser Productions, 1998.

———. *California Missions #110: Art of the Missions.* Video. Los Angeles: Huell Howser Productions, 2000.

Hull, Kathleen L. "A Land of Many People: Population Dynamics as Context and Catalyst." In Jones and Perry, *Contemporary Issues in California Archaeology,* 73–92.

Hunt, John Dixon. *The Afterlife of Gardens.* Philadelphia: University of Pennsylvania Press, 2004.

———. "Picturesque Mirrors and the Ruins of the Distant Past." In *Gardens and the Picturesque: Studies in the History of Landscape Architecture,* 171–91. Cambridge, Mass.: MIT Press, 1994.

Huntington Library. "Early California Population Project." Steven W. Hackel, general editor. http://www.huntington.org/Information/ECPPmain.htm.

———. "Major International Exhibition on Junípero Serra and the California Missions Opens Aug. 17." Huntington Library press release, August 8, 2013.

Hurtado, Albert L. "Fantasy Heritage: California's Historical Identities and the Professional Empire of Herbert E. Bolton." In Hackel, *Alta California,* 197–214.

———. *Indian Survival on the California Frontier.* New Haven, Conn.: Yale University Press, 1990.

Hyer, Joel R. *"We Are Not Savages": Native Americans in Southern California and the Pala Reservation, 1840–1930.* East Lansing: Michigan State University Press, 2001.

Hymes, Dell. *"In Vain I Tried to Tell You": Essays in Native American Ethnopoetics.* Lincoln: University of Nebraska Press, 1981.

Imwalle, Michael H. "Fighting the Elements: Conservation of Chumash Painted Cave State Historic Park (CA-SBA-506)." *Boletín: Journal of the California Missions Studies Association* 28, no. 1–2 (2011-2012): 76–83.

In the Path of the Padres: Twentieth Century Presentation in Rotogravure of California's Richest Heritage, Her Franciscan Missions of the Spanish Era. With a foreword by Fra. Zephyrin Engelhardt and editorial text by Stuart N. Lake. Los Angeles: C. Leslie Richards, 1934.

Ingold, Tim. *The Perception of the Environment: Essays on Livelihood, Dwelling and Skill.* London: Routledge, 2000.

Isaac, Gwyneira. "Responsibilities toward Knowledge: The Zuni Museum and the Reconciling of Different Knowledge Systems." In Sleeper-Smith, *Contesting Knowledge,* 303–21.

Isaac, Rhys. *The Transformation of Virginia, 1740–1790.* Chapel Hill: University of North Carolina Press, 1982.

Jackson, Helen Hunt. *Ramona.* Boston: Roberts Brothers, 1884.

Jackson, Helen Hunt, and Abbott Kinney. *Report of Mrs. Helen Hunt Jackson and Abbot Kinney on the Mission Indians in 1883.* Boston: Press of Stanley and Usher, 1887.

Jackson, Robert H. "The Changing Economic Structure of the Alta California Missions: A Reinterpretation." *Pacific Historical Review* 61 (1992): 387–415.

Jackson, Robert H., and Edward Castillo. *Indians, Franciscans, and Spanish Colonization: The Impact of the Mission System on California Indians.* Albuquerque: University of New Mexico Press, 1996.

Jackson, William Henry. *Ancient Missions and Churches of America.* Chicago: White City Art Company, 1894.

Jacobus, Pauline. "The Mission Santa Clara Garden." *Pacific Horticulture* 37, no. 3 (1976): 3.

James, George Wharton. *The Old Franciscan Missions of California.* Boston: Little, Brown, 1913. http://www.gutenberg.org/files/13854/13854-h/13854-h.htm.

Jenkins, Philip. "The Catholic Menace." In *The New Anti-Catholicism: The Last Acceptable Prejudice,* 23–45. Oxford: Oxford University Press, 2003.

Johnson, John Richard. "Chumash Social Organization: An Ethnohistorical Perspective." Ph.D. diss., University of California, Santa Barbara, 1988.

Johnson, Troy. "American Indians, Manifest Destiny, and Indian Activism: A Cosmology of Sense of Place." In Porter, *Place and Native American Indian History and Culture,* 71–92.

Jones, Terry L., and Jennifer E. Perry, eds. *Contemporary Issues in California Archaeology.* Walnut Creek, Calif.: Left Coast Press, 2012.

Judson, William L. "The Architecture of the Mission." *Historical Society of Southern California Publications* 7, no. 2–3 (1909): 114–18.

Jurmain, Claudia K., and William McCawley. *O, My Ancestor: Recognition and Renewal for the Gabrielino-Tongva People of the Los Angeles Area.* Berkeley: Heyday Books; Long Beach, Calif.: Rancho Los Alamitos Foundation, 2009.

ka Mpumlwana, Khwezi, Gerard Corsane, Juanita Pastor-Makhurane, and Ciraj Rassool. "Inclusion and the Power of Representation: South African Museums and the Cultural Politics of Social Transformation." In *Museums, Society, Inequality,* edited by Richard Sandell, 244–61. London: Routledge, 2002.

Kansteiner, Wolf. "Finding Meaning in Memory: A Methodological Critique of Collective Memory Studies." *History and Theory* 41 (May 2002): 179–97.

Kimbro, Edna E. *Furnishing Plan for the Santa Cruz Mission Adobe, Santa Cruz Mission State Historic Park, Santa Cruz, California.* Sacramento: California Department of Parks and Recreation, 1988.

Kimbro, Edna E., and Julia G. Costello, with Tevvy Ball. *The California Missions: History, Art, and Preservation.* Los Angeles: Getty Conservation Institute, 2009.

King, C. Richard. *Unsettling America: The Uses of Indianness in the 21st Century.* London: Rowman and Littlefield, 2013.

King, Chester D. *Evolution of Chumash Society: A Comparative Study of Artifacts Used for Social System Maintenance in the Santa Barbara Channel Region before A.D. 1804.* New York: Garland Press, 1991.

King, Julia A. *Archaeology, Narrative, and the Politics of the Past: The View from Southern Maryland.* Knoxville: University of Tennessee Press, 2012.

Kirker, Harold Clark. *California's Architectural Frontier: Style and Tradition in the Nineteenth Century.* San Marino, Calif.: Huntington Library, 1960.

Korzybski, Alfred. *The Manhood of Humanity: The Science and Art of Human Engineering.* New York: E. P. Dutton, 1921.

Krekelberg, William. *Mission San Juan Capistrano: The Fall and Rise of a California Mission.* Orange, Calif.: Paragon Agency for the Diocese of Orange, 2004.

Kristeva, Julia. *Strangers to Ourselves.* Translated by Leon Roudiez. New York: Columbia University Press, 1991.

Kroes, Rob. *Photographic Memories: Private Pictures, Public Images, and American History.* Hanover, N.H.: Dartmouth College Press, 2007.

Kropp, Phoebe S. *California Vieja: Culture and Memory in a Modern American Place.* Berkeley: University of California Press, 2006.

———. "In Search of History and Romance on El Camino Real." In *The Culture of Tourism, the Tourism of Culture: Selling the Past to the Present in the American Southwest,* edited by Hal K. Rothman, 38–65. Albuquerque: University of New Mexico Press, 2003.

———. "Sugar Cube Missions: Bringing the Spanish Past into the California Classroom." Paper presented at the Ninety-Fourth Annual Meeting of the Organization of American Historians, Los Angeles, April 2001.

Kryder-Reid, Elizabeth. "Crafting the Past: Mission Models and the Curation of California Heritage." *Heritage & Society* 8, no. 1 (2015): 60–83.

———. "Footprints of Domination and Resistance: California's Spanish Mission Landscapes." Paper presented in the session "Post-Structuralism and Architectural History," Annual Meeting of the Society of Architectural Historians, Seattle, 1995.

———. "Greenwashed: Identity and Landscape at the California Missions." In *British Archaeological Reports.* International Series 2709, Landscape and Identity: Archaeology and Human Geography, edited by Kurt D. Springs, 83–102. Oxford: Archaeopress, 2015.

———. "Marking Time in San Gabriel Mission Garden." *Studies in the History of Gardens & Designed Landscapes: An International Quarterly* 34, no. 1 (2014): 15–27.

———. "'Perennially New': Santa Barbara and the Origins of the California Mission Garden." *Journal of the Society of Architectural Historians* 69, no. 3 (2010): 378–405.

———. "Sites of Power and the Power of Sight: Vision in the California Mission Landscapes." In Harris and Ruggles, *Sites Unseen*, 181–212.

Kurillo, Max, and Erline Tuttle. *California's El Camino Real and Its Historic Bells.* San Diego: Sunbelt Books, 2000.

Laguna Art Museum. "Ferdinand Deppe, San Gabriel Mission, 1932." Accessed August 7, 2015, http://lagunaartmuseum.org/ferdinand-deppe-san-gabriel-mission-1832.

Lakoff, George, and Mark Johnson. *Metaphors We Live By.* Chicago: University of Chicago Press, 1980.

Landauer, Susan. "Countering Cultures: The California Context." In Selz, *Art of Engagement*, 1–24.

LaPena, Frank. "The Arts: A Time of Emptiness." *News from Native California* 13, no. 1 (Fall 1999): 56.

———. "Exhibitions/Exposure." *News from Native California* 2, no. 6 (January–February 1989): 19.

La Pérouse, Jean François de Galaup. *Life in a California Mission: The Journals of Jean François de La Pérouse.* Introduction and commentary by Malcolm Margolin. Berkeley, Calif.: Heyday Books, 1989.

———. *Voyage de La Pérouse Autour du Monde.* 4 vols and atlas. Paris: De L'Imprimerie de la République, 1797.

Lara, Jaime. *Christian Texts for Aztecs: Art and Liturgy in Colonial Mexico.* Notre Dame, Ind.: University of Notre Dame Press, 2008.

———. *City, Temple, Stage: Eschatological Architecture and Liturgical Theatrics in New Spain.* Notre Dame, Ind.: University of Notre Dame Press, 2004.

Larson, Daniel O., John R. Johnson, and Joel C. Michaelsen. "Missionization among the Coastal Chumash of Central California: A Study in Risk Minimization Strategies." *American Anthropologist* 96, no. 2 (1994): 263–99.

Lasuén, Fermín Francisco de. "From the Refutation of Charges." In *Lands of Promise and Despair: Chronicles of Early California, 1535–1846*, edited by Rose Marie Beebe and Robert M. Senkewicz, 273–76. Berkeley, Calif.: Heyday Books, 2001.

Latham, Charles, with contributions by E. March Phillips. *The Gardens of Italy.* 2 vols. London: Offices of Country Life, Ltd., and George Newnes, 1905, 1909.

Lee, A. J. "Spanish Missions." *APT Bulletin* 22, no. 3 (1990): 42–54.

Lee, Georgia, and Norman Neuerburg. "The Alta California Indians as Artists before and after Contact." In Thomas, *Columbian Consequences*, vol. 1, 467–80.

Lefebvre, Henri. *The Production of Space.* Translated by Donald Nicholson-Smith. Oxford: Blackwell, 1991.

Lenik, Stephan. "Mission Plantations, Space, and Social Control: Jesuits as Planters in French Caribbean Colonies and Frontiers." *Journal of Social Archaeology* 12, no. 1 (2012): 51–71.

Leone, Mark P. "Rule by Ostentation: The Relationship between Space and Sight in Eighteenth-Century Landscape Architecture in the Chesapeake Region of Maryland." In *Method and Theory for Activity Area Research: An Ethnoarchaeological Approach*, edited by Susan Kent, 604–33. New York: Columbia University Press, 1987.

Lepowsky, Maria. "Indian Revolts and Cargo Cults: Ritual Violence and Revitalization in California and New Guinea." In *Reassessing Revitalization Movements: Perspectives from*

North America and the Pacific Islands, edited by Michael E. Harkin, 1–60. Lincoln: University of Nebraska Press, 2004.

Levin, Amy K., ed. *Defining Memory: Local Museums and the Construction of History in America's Changing Communities.* Lanham, Md.: Alta Mira Press, 2007.

Levy, Daniel, and Natan Sznaider. "Memory Unbound: The Holocaust and the Formation of Cosmopolitan Memory." *European Journal of Social Theory* 5 (2002): 87–106.

Lewis, C. S. *An Experiment in Criticism.* Cambridge: Cambridge University Press, 1961.

Lewis, Henry T. "Patterns of Indian Burning in California: Ecology and Ethnohistory." In Blackburn and Anderson, *Before the Wilderness,* 55–116.

Liebman, Matthew, and Melissa S. Murphy, eds. *Enduring Conquests: Rethinking the Archaeology of Resistance to Spanish Colonialism in the Americas.* Santa Fe, N.Mex.: School for Advanced Research Press, 2010.

Lightfoot, Kent G. "A Cubist Perspective of Indigenous Landscapes and Spanish Missions." In Panich and Schneider, *Indigenous Landscapes and Spanish Missions,* 191–208.

———. *Indians, Missionaries, and Merchants: The Legacy of Colonial Encounters on the California Frontiers.* Berkeley: University of California Press, 2000.

Lightfoot, Kent G., Sara L. Gonzales, and Tsim D. Schneider. "Refugees and Interethnic Residences: Examples of Colonial Entanglements in the North San Francisco Bay Area." *Pacific Coast Archaeological Society Quarterly* 42, no. 1 (2009): 1–21.

Lightfoot, Kent G., Edward M. Luby, and Lisa Pesnichak. "Evolutionary Typologies and Hunter-Gatherer Research: Rethinking the Mounded Landscapes of Central California." In *Hunter-Gatherer Archaeology as Historical Process,* edited by K. E. Sasserman and D. H. Holly, 55–78. Tucson: University of Arizona Press, 2011.

Lightfoot, Kent G., Lee M. Panich, Tsim D. Schneider, Sara L. Gonzales, Matthew A. Russell, Theresa Molino, and Elliott H. Blair. "The Study of Indigenous Political Economies and Colonialism in Native California: Implications for Contemporary Tribal Groups and Federal Recognition." *American Antiquity* 78, no. 1 (2013): 89–104.

Lightfoot, Kent G., and Otis Parrish. *California Indians and Their Environment: An Introduction.* Berkeley: University of California Press, 2009.

Lindgren, James Michael. *Preserving the Old Dominion: Historic Preservation and Virginia Traditionalism.* Charlottesville: University of Virginia Press, 1993.

Lindsay, Brendan C. *Murder State: California's Native American Genocide, 1846–1873.* Lincoln: University of Nebraska Press, 2012.

Linklater, Renee. *Decolonizing Trauma Work: Indigenous Stories and Strategies.* Halifax: Fernwood Publishing, 2014.

Lipsitz, George. *Time Passages: Collective Memory and American Popular Culture.* Minneapolis: University of Minnesota Press, 1990.

Little, Barbara J., and Paul A. Shackel, eds. *Archaeology as a Tool of Civic Engagement.* Lanham, Md.: Alta Mira, 2007.

Logan, William, and Keir Reeves. *Places of Pain and Shame: Dealing with "Difficult Heritage."* New York: Routledge, 2009.

Lomayesva, Fred. "Indian Identity—Post Indian Reflections." *Tulsa Law Review* 35, no. 1 (1999): 63–72.

Lonetree, Amy. *Decolonizing Museums: Representing Native America in National and Tribal Museums.* Chapel Hill: University of North Carolina Press, 2012.

Lorimer, Michelle Marie. "Reconstructing the Past: Historical Interpretations and Native Experiences at Contemporary California Missions." Ph.D. thesis, University of California, Riverside, 2013.

Lowenthal, David. "Fabricating Heritage." *History and Memory* 10, no. 1 (1998): 5–24.

———. *The Past Is a Foreign Country.* Cambridge: Cambridge University Press, 1985.

———. "Past Time, Present Time: Landscape and Memory." *Geographical Review* 65, no. 1 (January 1975): 1–35.

Lucida, Jennifer A. "Plotting out the Land: Diseños and Land Grants in Alta California (1821–1848)." *Boletín: Journal of the California Mission Studies Association* 30, no. 1 (2014): 142–43.

Lummis, Charles F. "In the Lion's Den." *Land of Sunshine* 4, no. 1 (Dec. 1895): 43.

———. Letter to Rt. Rev. John J. Cantwell, Bishop of Los Angeles, September 24, 1921. City of Los Angeles, Records Management Division, Recreation and Parks Board, Facilities Files, Brand Park.

———. "The Patio." *Land of Sunshine* 3, no. 1 (June 1895): 12–16.

Lummis, Charles, John B. McGroarty, and Mrs. A. S. C. Forbes. "Old Mission One of *Your* Big Assets." *Los Angeles Examiner,* July 10, 1925. Clipping, Owen C. Coy Collection, California State Library, Sacramento.

Luna, James, ed. "Saying Our Share: Surviving the Missions." *News from Native California* 28, no. 2 (Winter 2014–15): 4–16.

Luthin, Herbert. "Making Texts, Reading Translations." In *Surviving through the Days: Translations of Native California Stories and Songs,* 21–54. Berkeley: University of California Press, 2001.

Lydon, Jane, and Uzma Z. Rizvi, eds. *Handbook of Postcolonial Archaeology.* Walnut Creek, Calif.: Left Coast Press, 2010.

Lyman, Edward Leo. "The Beginnings of Anglo-American Local Government in California." *California History* 81, no. 3–4 (2003): 199–223.

Lynn, Barry W. [Congressional debate, November 17, 2004.] Congressional Record, 108th Congress, 2nd Session, House of Representatives (2003–4). California Missions Preservation Act. https://www.congress.gov/congressional-record/2004/11/17/house-section/article/H9828-1.

MacCannell, Dean. *The Tourist: A New Theory of the Leisure Class.* New York: Schocken Books, 1976.

Macdougall, Brenda, and M. Teresa Carlson. "West Side Stories: The Blending of Voice and Representation Through a Shared Curatorial Practice." In Sleeper-Smith, *Contesting Knowledge,* 156–91.

Madley, Benjamin. "'Unholy Traffic in Human Blood and Souls': Systems of California Indian Servitude under U.S. Rule." *Pacific Historical Review* 83, no. 4 (2014): 626–67.

Magee, Maureen. "A Model of Tradition." Posted on Kumeyaay.com, April 22, 2008. http://www.kumeyaay.com/2008/04/a-model-of-tradition.

Mahaney, Stacey L. "The California Missions Preservation Act: Safeguarding Our History or Subsidizing Religion?" *American University Law Review* 55 (2006): 1523–55.

Mann, Kristin Dutcher. *The Power of Song: Music and Dance in the Mission Communities of Northern New Spain, 1590–1810.* Palo Alto: Stanford University Press, 2010.

Martinez, Doreen E. "Wrong Directions and New Maps of Voice, Representation, and Engagement: Theorizing Cultural Tourism, Indigenous Commodities, and the Intelligence of Participation." *American Indian Quarterly* 36, no. 4 (2012): 545–73.

Mason, Rhiannon. "Conflict and Complement: An Exploration of the Discourses Informing the Concept of the Socially Inclusive Museum in Contemporary Britain." *International Journal of Heritage Studies* 10, no. 1 (March 2004): 49–73.

Mason, William M. "Adobe Interiors in Spanish California." *Southern California Quarterly* 70, no. 3 (Fall 1988): 235–63.

Matthews, Christopher N. "Gilded Ages and Gilded Archaeologies of American Exceptionalism." *International Journal of Historical Archaeology* 16, no. 4 (2012): 717–44.

———. "Unconventional Archaeologies in Setauket, New York." *Anthropology Now* 5, no. 2 (September 2013): 26–34.

McCan, Martha Nelson. "Mission Garden Restored." *Clubwoman* 16, no. 4 (January 1924): 10.

———. "A Spanish Landscape Garden." *Friday Morning Club Bulletin,* January 1922. Clipping on file, City of Los Angeles, Records Management Division, Recreation and Parks Board, Facilities Files, Brand Park.

———. [Untitled typescript of article submitted on March 10, 1924, for publication in the Native Sons of California magazine, *Grizzly Bear.*] City of Los Angeles, Records Management Division, Recreation and Parks Board, Facilities Files, Brand Park.

McCawley, William. *The First Angelinos: The Gabrielino Indians of Los Angeles.* Banning, Calif.: Malki Museum Press; Ballena Press, 1996.

McClung, William Alexander. *Landscapes of Desire: Anglo Mythologies of Los Angeles.* Berkeley: University of California Press, 2000.

McDavid, Carol. "Beyond Strategy and Good Intentions: Archaeology, Race, and White Privilege." In Little and Shackel, *Archaeology as a Tool of Civic Engagement,* 67–88.

McGroarty, John S. *Los Angeles from the Mountains to the Sea: With Selected Biography of Actors and Witnesses of the Period of Growth and Achievement,* vol. 3, 595–96. Chicago: American Historical Society, 1921.

———. *The Mission Play: A Pageant Play in Three Acts.* Los Angeles: Mission Curio and Art Shop, 1911.

———. "The Place of the Sacred Garden." *West Coast Magazine* 6 (1909): 237–48.

McGuire, Randall. "Why Have Archaeologists Thought the Real Indians Were Dead and What Can We Do About It?" In *Indians and Anthropologists: Vine Deloria, Jr., and the Critique of Anthropology,* edited by Thomas Biolsi and Larry J. Zimmerman, 63–91. Tucson: University of Arizona Press, 1997.

McWilliams, Carey. *Southern California Country: An Island on the Land.* New York: Duell, Sloan and Pearce, 1946.

Medina, Laurie Kroshus. "History, Culture, and Place Making: 'Native' Status and Maya Identity in Belize." *Journal of Latin American Anthropology* 4, no. 1 (1998): 134–65.

Medina, Vincent. "The Truth Shall Set Us Free: Tips for Teaching California History to Kids." *News from Native California* 28, no. 2 (Winter 2014–15): 48–58.

Meighan, Clement W. "Indians and the California Missions." *Southern California Quarterly* 69, no. 3 (Fall, 1987): 183–201.

Memmi, Albert. *The Colonizer and the Colonized.* Translated by Howard Greenfield. Boston: Beacon Press, 1967.

Mendoza, Rubén G. "The Cross and the Spade: Archaeology and the Discovery of the Earliest Serra Chapels at the Royal Presidio of Monterey, 1770–1772." *Boletín: California Mission Studies Association* 29, no. 1 (2013): 30–58.

———. "The Diseños Project: A Geospatial Visualization of the Environmental History of California, 1769–1892." *Boletín: Journal of the California Mission Studies Association* 30, no. 1 (2014): 152–53.

———. "Indigenous Landscapes: Mexicanized Indians and the Archaeology of Social Networks in Alta California." In Panich and Schneider, *Indigenous Landscapes and Spanish Missions,* 114–31.

———. "The Liturgy of Light: Solar Geometry and Kinematic Liturgical Iconography in an Early 19th Century California Mission." *Boletín: The Journal of the California Mission Studies Association* 28, no. 1–2 (2011/2012): 6–20.

———. "Mission Possible: Safeguarding the Heritage of the California Missions." *Boletín: The Journal of the California Mission Studies Association* 24, no. 2 (2007): 56–69.

———. "Sacrament of the Sun: Eschatological Architecture and Solar Geometry in a California Mission." *Boletín: The Journal of the California Mission Studies Association* 22, no. 1 (Spring 2005): 87–110.

Mendoza, Rubén G., and Jennifer A. Lucido. "Of Earth, Fire, and Faith: Architectural Practice in the Fernando Missions of Alta California, 1769–1821." *Colonial Latin American Historical Review,* 2nd series 2, no. 2 (Spring 2014): 191–237.

Merleau-Ponty, Maurice. *Phenomenology of Perception.* Translated by Colin Smith. London: Routledge, 1962.

Merrill, William L. "Indigenous Societies, Missions, and the Colonial System in Northern New Spain." In Bargellini and Komanecky, *The Art of the Missions of Northern New Spain,* 122–53.

Mertens, Nonna M., Fiona Cram, and Bagele Chilisa, eds. *Indigenous Pathways into Social Research: Voices of a New Generation.* Walnut Creek, Calif.: Left Coast Press, 2013.

Meskell, Lynn. "Archaeologies of Identity." In *Archaeological Theory Today,* edited by Ian Hodder, 187–213. Cambridge: Polity, 2001.

———. "Negative Heritage and Past Mastering in Archaeology." *Anthropological Quarterly* 75, no. 3 (2002): 557–74.

Meyers-Lim, Nicole. See Myers-Lim, Nicole.

Mihesuah, Devon Abbott. "American Indian History as a Field of Study." In *Indigenizing the Academy: Transforming Scholarship and Empowering Community,* edited by Devon Abbott Mihesuah and Angela Cavender Wilson, 143–60. Lincoln: University of Nebraska Press, 2004.

Miller, Daniel. *The Comfort of Things.* Cambridge: Polity, 2008.

———. *Stuff.* Cambridge: Polity, 2009.

———, ed. *Materiality.* Durham, N.C.: Duke University Press, 2005.

Miller, Susan A., and James Riding In, eds. *Native Historians Write Back: Decolonizing American Indian History.* Lubbock: Texas Tech University Press, 2011.

Milliken, Randall. *A Time of Little Choice: The Disintegration of Tribal Culture in the San Francisco Bay Area, 1769–1820.* Menlo Park, Calif.: Ballena Press, 1995.

Minca, Claudio. "The Tourist Landscape Paradox." *Social and Cultural Geography* 8, no. 3 (June 2007): 433–53.

Minca, Claudio, and Tim Oakes, eds. *Travels in Paradox: Remapping Tourism.* London: Rowman & Littlefield, 2006.

Miranda, Deborah A. "The Blessings and the Genocide; Or, Ten Reasons Why This Issue of News Is Necessary." *News from Native California* 28, no. 2 (Winter 2014–15): 34–36.

———. "Post-Colonial Thought Experiment." In *Bad Indians: A Tribal Memoir,* 186–91. Berkeley: Heyday, 2013. [Originally posted as a blog, "4th Grade California Mission Projects: A Thought Experiment for Parents, Educators, and Students." *When Turtles Fly,* December 30, 2009.]

Miranda, Gloria E. "Racial and Cultural Dimensions of Gente de Razón Status in Spanish and Mexican California." *Southern California Quarterly* 70, no. 3 (1988): 265–78.

Mission Santa Inés. "Old Mission Santa Ines: A Walk with Warwick." Taped oral history with William Warwick. Two-disk DVD set, Mission Santa Ines Archives.

Mitchell, Don. *The Lie of the Land: Migrant Workers and the California Landscape*. Minneapolis: University of Minnesota Press, 1996.

Mitchell, W. J. T. "Imperial Landscape." In *Landscape and Power*. 2nd ed. Edited by W. J. T. Mitchell, 5–34. Chicago: University of Chicago Press, 1994.

———. Introduction to Mitchell, *Landscape and Power*, 1–4.

———, ed. *Landscape and Power*. 2nd ed. Chicago: University of Chicago Press, 1994.

Mitterhofer, Johanna. "Competing Narratives on the Future of Contested Heritage: A Case Study of Fascist Monuments in Contemporary South Tyrol, Italy." *Heritage & Society* 6, no. 1 (2013): 46–61.

Modlin, E. Arnold, Derek H. Alderman, and Glenn W. Gentry. "Tour Guides as Creators of Empathy: The Role of Affective Inequality in Marginalizing the Enslaved at Plantation House Museums." *Tourist Studies* 11, no. 1 (April 2011): 3–19.

Monroy, Douglas. "Making Mexico in Los Angeles." In *Metropolis in the Making: Los Angeles in the 1920s*, edited by Tom Sitton and William Deverell, 161–78. Berkeley: University of California Press, 2001.

———. *Thrown among Strangers: The Making of Mexican Culture in Frontier California*. Berkeley: University of California Press, 1990.

Montes, Gregory. "Balboa Park, 1909–1911: The Rise and Fall of the Olmsted Plan." *Journal of San Diego History* 28, no. 1 (Winter 1982): 46–67.

Mooney, Barbara Burlison. "Sunny Spain or Our Algeria: The Other Colonial Revival." In *Re-creating the American Past: Essays on the Colonial Revival*, edited by Richard Guy Wilson, Shaun Eyring, and Kenny Marotta, 367–89. Charlottesville: University of Virginia Press, 2006.

Moore, Charles Irwin Douglas. *In the Footsteps of the Padres*. Los Angeles: Pacific Mutual Life Insurance Company of California, 1930.

Moore, Shirley Ann Wilson. "'We Feel the Want of Protection': The Politics of Law and Race in California, 1848–1878." In *Taming the Elephant: Politics, Government, and Law in Pioneer California*. Edited by John F. Burns and Richard J. Orsi, 96–125. Berkeley: University of California Press, 2003.

Morgan, David. "Religion and Embodiment in the Study of Material Culture." In *Religion: Oxford Research Encyclopedias*. March 2015. http://religion.oxfordre.com/view/10.1093/acrefore/9780199340378.001.0001/acrefore-9780199340378-e-32.

———. *The Sacred Gaze: Religious Visual Culture in Theory and Practice*. Berkeley: University of California Press, 2005.

Morgan, David, and Sally M. Promey, eds. *The Visual Culture of American Religions*. Berkeley: University of California Press, 2001.

Mrozowski, Stephen A., and Mary C. Beaudry. "Archaeology and the Landscape of Corporate Ideology." In *Earth Patterns: Essays in Landscape Archaeology*, edited by William M. Kelso and Rachel Most, 189–208. Charlottesville: University Press of Virginia, 1990.

Muensterberger, Werner. *Collecting: An Unruly Passion; Psychological Perspectives*. Princeton, N.J.: Princeton University Press, 1994.

Mullins, Paul R. *The Archaeology of Consumer Culture*. Gainesville: University of Florida Press, 2011.

———. "Politics, Inequality, and Engaged Archaeology: Community Archaeology along the Color Line." In Little and Shackel, *Archaeology as a Tool of Civic Engagement,* 89–108.

Mundy, Barbara E., and Dana Leibsohn. "History from Things: Indigenous Objects and Colonial Latin America." *World History Connected* 9, no. 2 (2012). Accessed July 19, 2015, http://worldhistoryconnected.press.illinois.edu/index.html.

Myers-Lim, Nicole. "Educating Elementary School Children about California Missions and the Perpetuation of Genocide." *News from Native California* 28, no. 2 (Winter 2014/15): 42–54. [The article's byline gives the last name as Meyers-Lim.]

Nakata, Martin, and Bruno David. "Archaeological Practice at the Cultural Interface." In Lydon and Rizvi, *Handbook of Postcolonial Archaeology,* 429–43.

Neal, Tim. "Practice Makes Perfect: A Discussion of the Place of the Brochure Image in Landscape Tourism." In Russell, *Images, Representations, and Heritage,* 297–314.

Nelson, Louis P., ed. *American Sanctuary: Understanding Sacred Spaces.* Bloomington: Indiana University Press, 2006.

Neuerburg, Norman. Biographical introduction to *An Artist Records the California Missions: Henry Chapman Ford,* edited by Norman Neuerburg, xiv–xl. San Francisco: Book Club of California, 1989.

———. "The California Missions in Art, 1786 to 1890." In Stern and Miller, *Romance of the Bells,* 85–95.

———. *The Decoration of the California Missions.* 2nd ed. Santa Barbara: Bellerophon Books, 1991.

———. "The Function of Prints in the California Missions." *Southern California Quarterly* 63, no. 3 (1985): 263–80.

———. "Indian Pictographs at Mission San Juan Capistrano." *Masterkey* 56, no. 2 (1982): 55–58.

———. "The Little Mission: History at an Inch to the Foot." *Journal of San Diego History* 33, no. 4 (Fall 1987): 179–96.

———. "Painting in the California Missions." *American Art Review* 4, no. 1 (1977): 72–88.

Newcomb, Rexford. *The Franciscan Mission Architecture of Alta California.* 1916. Reprint, New York: Dover, 1988.

———. *The Old Mission Churches and Historic Houses of California: Their Story, Architecture, and Lore.* Philadelphia: J.B. Lippincott, 1925.

Newell, Quincy D. *Constructing Lives at Mission San Francisco: Native Californians and Hispanic Colonists, 1776–1821.* Albuquerque: University of New Mexico Press, 2009.

Nichols, Rose Standish. *Spanish and Portuguese Gardens.* Boston: Houghton Mifflin, 1924.

Nickel, Douglas R. *Carleton Watkins: The Art of Perception.* San Francisco: San Francisco Museum of Modern Art, with Harry N. Abrams, 1999. Exhibition catalog.

Niezen, Ronald. *The Origins of Indigenism: Human Rights and the Politics of Identity.* Berkeley: University of California Press, 2003.

Nordstrom, Justin. *Danger on the Doorstep: Anti-Catholicism and American Print Culture in the Progressive Era.* Notre Dame, Ind.: University of Notre Dame Press, 2006.

Norkunas, Martha. *The Politics of Public Memory: Tourism, History and Ethnicity in Monterey, California.* Albany: SUNY Press, 1993.

Norman, Alex. *Spiritual Tourism: Travel and Religious Practice in Western Society.* London: Continuum, 2011.

Nunez, Jacque Tahuka. "Journeys." *News from Native California* 28, no. 2 (Winter 2014–15): 46–47.

O'Brien, Jean. *Firsting and Lasting: Writing Indians Out of Existence in New England.* Minneapolis: University of Minnesota Press, 2010.

———. "Indians and the California Gold Rush." In Sleeper-Smith et al., *Why You Can't Teach United States History without American Indians,* 101–17.

Oland, Maxine, Siobahn M. Hart, and Liam Frank, eds. *Decolonizing Indigenous Histories: Exploring Prehistoric/Colonial Transitions in Archaeology.* Tucson: University of Arizona Press, 2012.

Olick, Jeffrey K. *The Politics of Regret: On Collective Memory and Historical Responsibility.* New York: Routledge, 2007.

Olick, Jeffrey K., and Joyce Robbins. "Social Memory Studies: From 'Collective Memory' to the Historical Sociology of Mnemonic Practices." *Annual Review of Sociology* 24 (1998): 105–40.

Ollman, Leah. "Exhibit Paints Serra in Un-Saintly Glow: *California Mission Daze* Joins Fray over Treatment of Indians." *Los Angeles Times,* October 12, 1988.

O'Sullivan, John. *Little Chapters about San Juan Capistrano.* 1912. Reprint, Orange, Calif.: Paragon Agency, 1998.

Ott, John. "Landscapes of Consumption: Auto Tourism and Visual Culture in California, 1920–1940. In Barroñ, Bernstein, and Fort, *Reading California,* 50–67.

Pacini-Ketchabaw, Veronica, and Affrica Taylor, eds. *Unsettling the Colonial Places and Spaces of Early Childhood Education.* New York: Routledge, 2015.

Paddison, Joshua. "Capturing California." In Burns and Orsi, *Taming the Elephant,* 126–36.

Padilla, Victoria. *Southern California Gardens.* Berkeley: University of California Press, 1961.

Palmquist, Peter E. *Carleton E. Watkins: Photographer of the American West.* Fort Worth, Tex.: Amon Carter Museum of American Art, with the University of New Mexico Press, 1983. Exhibition catalog.

Panich, Lee M. "After Saint Serra: Unearthing Indigenous Histories at the California Missions." *Journal of Social Archaeology* 16, no. 2 (2016): 238–58.

———. "Archaeologies of Persistence: Reconsidering the Legacies of Colonialism in Native North America." *American Antiquity* 78 (2013): 105–22.

———. "Interpretive Issues and the California Missions." *Proceedings of the Society for California Archaeology* 18 (2005): 189–92.

———. "Missionization and the Persistence of Native Identity on the Colonial Frontier of Baja California." *Ethnohistory* 57 (2010): 225–62.

———. "Native American Consumption of Shell and Glass Beads at Mission Santa Clara De Asís." *American Antiquity* 79, no. 4 (October 2014): 730–48.

———. "'Sometimes They Bury the Deceased's Clothes and Trinkets': Indigenous Mortuary Practices at Mission Santa Clara de Asís." *Historical Archaeology* 49, no. 4 (2015): 110–29.

———. "Spanish Missions in the Indigenous Landscape: A View from Mission Santa Catalina, Baja California." *Journal of California and Great Basin Archaeology* 30, no. 1 (2010): 69–86.

Panich, Lee M., Helga Afaghani, and Nicole Mathwich. "Assessing the Diversity of Mission Populations through the Comparison of Native American Residences at Mission Santa Clara de Asís." *International Journal of Historical Archaeology* 18, no. 3 (2014): 467–88.

Panich, Lee M., and Tsim D. Schneider. "Expanding Mission Archaeology: A Landscape Approach to Indigenous Autonomy in Colonial California." *Journal of Anthropological Archaeology* 40 (2015): 48–58.

———, eds. *Indigenous Landscapes and Spanish Missions: New Perspectives from Archaeology and Ethnohistory*. Tucson: University of Arizona Press, 2014.

Pearce, Susan, and Paul Martin. Introduction to *The Collector's Voice: Critical Readings in the Practice of Collecting*. Vol. 4, *Contemporary Voices*, xii–xxii. Edited by Susan Pearce and Paul Martin. Aldershot, UK: Ashgate, 2002.

Pedelty, Mark. "The New California Mission System: Museums, Gift Shops, and Historical Archaeologists." *Kroeber Anthropological Society Papers* 73–74 (1992): 80–91.

Peelo, Sarah. "Baptism among the Salinan Neophytes of Mission San Antonio de Padua: Investigating the Ecological Hypothesis." *Ethnohistory* 56 (2009): 589–624.

———. "The Creation of a Carmeleño Identity: Marriage Practices in the Indian Village at Mission San Carlos Borromeo del Rio Carmel." *Journal of California and Great Basin Anthropology* 30 (2010): 117–39.

———. "Pottery Making in Spanish California: Creating Multi-Scalar Social Identity through Daily Practice." *American Antiquity* 76 (2011): 642–66.

Perry, Jennifer E. "Chumash Ritual and Sacred Geography on Santa Cruz Island, California." *Journal of California and Great Basin Anthropology* 27, no. 2 (2007): 103–24.

Peter, Carolyn. "California Welcomes the World: International Expositions, 1894–1940, and the Selling of a State." In Barron, Bernstein, and Fort, *Reading California*, 68–83.

Peterson, Jeanette Favrot. *The Paradise Garden Murals of Malinalco: Utopia and Empire in Sixteenth-Century Mexico*. Austin: University of Texas Press, 1993.

Phillips George H. *Bringing Them under Subjection: California's Tejón Indian Reservation and Beyond, 1852–1864*. Lincoln: University of Nebraska Press, 2004.

———. *Chiefs and Challengers: Indian Resistance and Cooperation in Southern California*. Berkeley: University of California Press, 1975.

———. "The Stations of the Cross Revisited, Reconsidered, and Revised (Sort Of)." *Boletín: The Journal of the California Mission Studies Association* 24, no. 2 (2007): 76–87.

———. *Vineyards and Vaqueros: Indian Labor and the Economic Expansion of Southern California, 1771–1877*. Norman: University of Oklahoma Press, 2010.

Phoebe A. Hearst Museum of Anthropology, Online Collections Catalog. http://hearstmuseum.berkeley.edu/exhibitions/cent/gallery1_3_9.html.

Pitt, Leonard. *The Decline of the Californios: A Social History of the Spanish-Speaking Californians, 1846–1890*. Berkeley: University of California Press, 1966.

Pohlman, John Ogden. "California's Mission Myth." Ph.D. diss., University of California, Los Angeles, 1974.

Pomeroy, Earl. *In Search of the Golden West: The Tourist in Western America*. New York: Alfred A. Knopf, 1957.

Porter, Joy, ed. *Place and Native American Indian History and Culture*. Oxford: Peter Lang, 2007.

Power, Nancy Goslee. *California Gardens: Four Centuries of Design from Mission to Modern*. New York: Clarkson Potter, 1995.

Praetzellis, Mary, Adrian Praetzellis, and Thad Van Buren. "Remaking Connections: Archaeology and Community after the Loma Prieta Earthquake." In Little and Shackel, *Archaeology as a Tool of Civic Engagement*, 109–30.

Preston, William. "Serpent in the Garden: Environmental Change in Colonial California." In Gutiérrez and Orsi, *Contested Eden*, 260–98.

Preucel, Robert W. "Becoming Navajo: Refugees, Pueblitos, and Identity in the Dinétah." In *Enduring Conquests: Rethinking the Archaeology of Resistance to Spanish Colonialism in the*

Americas, edited by Matthew Liebmann and Melissa S. Murphy, 223–42. Santa Fe, N.Mex.: School for Advanced Research Press, 2010.

Preucel, Robert W., and Frank G. Matero. "Placemaking on the Northern Rio Grande: A View from Kuaua Pueblo." In *Archaeologies of Placemaking: Monuments, Memories, and Engagement in Native North America,* edited by Patricia E. Rubertone, 81–93. Walnut Creek, Calif.: Left Coast Press, 2008.

Psarra, Sophia. *Architecture and Narrative: The Formation of Space and Cultural Meaning.* London: Routledge, 2009.

Purbrick, Louise, Jim Aulich, and Graham Dawson, eds. *Contested Spaces: Sites, Representations and Histories of Conflict.* New York: Palgrave Macmillan, 2007.

Rappaport, Joanne. *The Politics of Memory: Native Historical Interpretation in the Columbian Andes.* Cambridge: Cambridge University Press, 1990.

Rawls, James J. "The California Mission as Symbol and Myth." *California History* 71, no. 3 (1992): 342–61.

———. *Indians of California: The Changing Image.* Norman: University of Oklahoma Press, 1984.

Read, Peter. "'The Truth Will Set Us All Free': An Uncertain History of Memorials to Indigenous Australians." In Purbrick, Aulich, and Dawson, *Contested Spaces,* 146–87.

Redding, Mary Anne, ed. *Through the Lens: Creating Santa Fe.* Santa Fe: Museum of New Mexico Press, 2008. Exhibition catalog.

Reddy, Seetha N. "Feeding Family and Ancestors: Persistence of Traditional Native American Lifeways during the Mission Period in Coastal Southern California." *Journal of Anthropological Archaeology* 37 (2015): 48–66.

Refugio de la Torre Curiel, José. "Franciscan Missionaries in Late Colonial Sonora: Five Decades of Change and Conflict." In Hackel, *Alta California,* 47–75.

Reid, Elizabeth B. "Chumash Acculturation: Spanish Historic Contact in the Santa Barbara Area." B.A. thesis, Harvard University, 1984.

Reinarz, Jonathan. *Past Scents: Historical Perspectives on Smell.* Urbana-Champaign: University of Illinois Press, 2014.

Renan, Ernest. "What Is a Nation?" In Bhabha, *Nation and Narration,* 8–22.

Respini, Eva. *Into the Sunset: Photography's Images of the American West.* New York: Museum of Modern Art, 2009. Exhibition catalog.

Ressler, John Q. "Indian and Spanish Water-Control on New Spain's Northwest Frontier." *Journal of the West* 7, no. 1 (January 1968): 10–17.

———. "Spanish Mission Water Systems, Northwest Frontier of New Spain." M.A. thesis, University of Arizona, 1966.

Reyes, Bárbara O. *Private Women, Public Lives: Gender and the Missions of the Californias.* Austin: University of Texas Press, 2009.

———. "Race, Agency, and Memory in a Baja California Mission." In *Continental Crossroads: Remapping U.S.–Mexico Borderlands History.* Edited by Samuel Truett and Elliott Young, 97–120. Durham, N.C.: Duke University Press, 2004.

Reynolds, Dorothy. "The Story of Alta California's Bountiful Mission Gardens." *Pacific Discovery* 9, no. 4 (July–August 1956): 12–19.

Ricoeur, Paul. *Memory, History, Forgetting.* Translated by Kathleen Blamey and David Pellauer. Chicago: University of Chicago Press, 2004.

Rifkin, Mark. *Manifesting America: The Imperial Construction of U.S. National Space.* Oxford: Oxford University Press, 2009.

Riggin-Walden, Lisa. "The Spanish Missions: The Death and Resurrection of a California Institution." Ph.D. diss., University of California, Riverside, June 2006.

Rimbert, Eric. "Junípero Serra Statue Unveiled and Blessed." *Los Angeles Times,* May 30, 1998. http://articles.latimes.com/1998/may/30/local/me-54783.

Rindge, Ronald L. *Ceramic Arts of the Malibu Potteries, 1926–1932.* Seattle: University of Washington Press, published for Malibu Lagoon Museum, 1988.

Roberts, Edwards. "A Santa Barbara Holiday." *Harper's New Monthly Magazine* 74, no. 450 (November 1887): 813–35.

Robinson, Alfred. *Life in California: During a Residence of Several Years in That Territory, Comprising a Description of the Country and the Missionary Establishments.* New York: Wiley and Putnam, 1846.

Robinson, David W. "From Ethnohistory to Ethnogenesis: A Historiography of Hunter-Gatherer Cultural Anthropology in California and the Great Basin." In *The Oxford Handbook of the Archaeology and Anthropology of Hunter-Gatherers,* edited by Vicki Cummings, Peter Jordan, and Marek Zvelebil, 973–90. Oxford: Oxford University Press, 2014.

———. "Land Use, Land Ideology: An Integrated Geographic Information Systems Analysis of Rock Art within South Central California." *American Antiquity* 75 (2010): 792–818.

———. "Polyvalent Metaphors in South-Central California Missionary Processes." *American Antiquity* 78, no. 2 (April 2013): 302–21.

Rodriguez, Richard. *Days of Obligation: An Argument with My Mexican Father.* New York: Penguin, 1992.

Rojas, Mary Virginia. "She Bathes in a Sacred Place: Rites of Reciprocity, Power, and Prestige in Alta California." *Wicazo Sa Review* 18, no. 1 (Spring 2003): 129–56.

Romo, José María. [Diary.] Santa Bárbara Mission Archive-Library.

Rose, Gillian. "'Everyone's Cuddled Up and It Just Looks Really Nice': An Emotional Geography of Some Mums and Their Family Photos." *Social and Cultural Geography* 5, no. 4 (December 2004): 549–64.

Rothberg, Michael. *Multidirectional Memory: Remembering the Holocaust in the Age of Decolonization.* Stanford, Calif.: Stanford University Press, 2009.

Rowe, E. D. "The Story of a Garden." Clipping from unidentified newspaper, La Purisima Mission State Park Archives.

Roy, Jody M. *Rhetorical Campaigns of the Nineteenth-Century[:] Anti-Catholics and Catholics in America.* Lewiston, N.Y.: Edwin Mellen Press, 2000.

Rubertone, Patricia. "Historical Landscapes: The Archaeology of Place and Space." *Man in the Northeast* 31 (1986): 123–38.

Ruggles, D. Fairchild. *Gardens, Landscape, and Vision in the Palaces of Islamic Spain.* University Park: Pennsylvania State University Press, 2000.

———. *Islamic Gardens and Landscapes.* Philadelphia: University of Pennsylvania Press, 2008.

Russell, Craig H. *From Serra to Sancho: Music and Pageantry in the California Missions.* Oxford: Oxford University Press, 2012.

Russell, Ian, ed. *Images, Representations, and Heritage: Moving beyond Modern Approaches to Archaeology.* New York: Springer, 2006.

Russell, Ian Alden. "Towards an Ethics of Oblivion and Forgetting: The Parallax View." *Heritage & Society* 5, no. 2 (2012): 249–72.

Russell, Ron. "Bones of Discontent—Andrew Galvan Carves a Unique, Controversial Role in Relocating Native American Skeletons." *San Francisco Weekly,* November 21, 2007. Accessed August 4, 2015, http://www.sfweekly.com/sanfrancisco/bones-of-discontent

-andrew-galvan-carves-a-unique-controversial-role-in-relocating-native-american-skeletons/Content?oid=2165208.

Ryan, Marah Ellis. *For the Soul of Rafael.* Chicago: A.C. McClurg, 1906.

Sackman, Douglas C. "A Garden of Worldly Delights." In *Land of Sunshine: An Environmental History of Metropolitan Los Angeles,* edited by William Deverell and Greg Hise, 245–66. Pittsburgh: University of Pittsburgh Press, 2005.

Sagarena, Roberto Lint. "Building California's Past: Mission Revival Architecture and Regional Identity." *Journal of Urban History* 28, no. 4 (2002): 429–44.

Said, Edward. *Orientalism.* New York: Vintage Books, 1979.

Sampson, Michael P. "Continuity in Stone Tool Use during the Historic Period in San Diego County, California." *Pacific Coast Archaeological Society Quarterly* 45, no. 1–2 (2011): 49–77.

Samuels, Joshua. "Of Other Scapes: Archaeology, Landscape, and Heterotopia in Fascist Sicily." *Archaeologies* 6, no. 1 (April 2010): 62–81.

Sandos, James A. "Between Crucifix and Lance: Indian-White Relations in California, 1769–1848." In Gutiérrez and Orsi, *Contested Eden,* 196–229.

———. *Converting California: Indians and Franciscans in the Missions.* New Haven, Conn.: Yale University Press, 2004.

———. "Identity through Music: Choristers at Missions San Jose and San Juan Bautista." In Hackel, *Alta California,* 111–28.

———. "Neophyte Resistance in the Alta California Missions." In *Columbus, Confrontation, Christianity: The European-American Encounter Revisited,* edited by Timothy J. O'Keefe, 170–78. Palo Alto, Calif.: Forbes Mill Press, 1994.

Sandos, James A., and Patricia B. Sandos. "Early California Reconsidered: Mexicans, Anglos, and Indians at Mission San José." *Pacific Historical Review* 83, no. 4 (November 2014): 592–625.

Sandul, Paul. *California Dreaming: Boosterism, Memory, and Rural Suburbs in the Golden State.* Morgantown: West Virginia University Press, 2014.

Sandweiss, Martha A. *Print the Legend: Photography and the American West.* New Haven, Conn.: Yale University Press, 2002.

Sather-Wagstaff, Joy. *Heritage That Hurts: Tourists in the Memoryscapes of September 11.* Walnut Creek, Calif.: Left Coast Press, 2011.

Saunders, Charles Francis. "Historic Gardens in California." In *Gardens of Colony and State,* edited by Alice B. Lockwood, 391–402. New York: Garden Club of America, 1934.

Saunders, Charles Francis, and J. Smeaton Chase. *The California Padres and Their Missions.* Boston: Houghton Mifflin, 1915.

———. "Love in the Padres' Garden." In Saunders and Chase, *The California Padres and Their Missions,* 166–76.

Saunt, Claudio. "'My Medicine Is Punishment': A Case of Torture in Early California, 1775–1776." *Ethnohistory* 57, no. 4 (2010): 679–708.

Savage, Christine E. *New Deal Adobe: The Civilian Conservation Corps and the Reconstruction of Mission La Purísima, 1934–1942.* Santa Barbara, Calif.: Fithinan Press, 1991.

Savage, Kirk. *Standing Soldiers, Kneeling Slaves: Race, War, and Monument in Nineteenth-Century America.* Princeton, N.J.: Princeton University Press, 1997.

Schama, Simon. *Landscape and Memory.* New York: Vintage Books, 1996.

Schein, Richard H. "Race and Landscape in the United States." In *Landscape and Race in the United States,* edited by Richard H. Schein, 1–22. New York: Routledge, 2006.

Schmidt, Robert A., and Barbara L. Voss, eds. *Archaeologies of Sexuality.* London: Routledge, 2000.

Schneider, Tsim D. "Placing Refuge: Shell Mounds and the Archaeology of Colonial Encounters in the San Francisco Bay Area, California." Ph.D. diss., University of California, Berkeley, 2010.

Schneider, Tsim D., Sara L. Gonzalez, Kent G. Lightfoot, Lee M. Panich, and Matthew A. Russell. "A Land of Cultural Pluralism: Case Studies from California's Colonial Frontier." In Jones and Perry, *Contemporary Issues in California Archaeology,* 319–37.

Schneider, Tsim D., and Lee M. Panich. "Native Agency at the Margins of Empire: Indigenous Landscapes, Spanish Missions, and Contested History." In Panich and Schneider, *Indigenous Landscapes and Spanish Missions,* 5–22.

Schon, Donald A. *The Reflective Practitioner: How Professionals Think in Action.* New York: Basic Books, 1983.

Schwartz, Joan M., and James R. Ryan, eds. *Picturing Place: Photography and the Geographical Imagination.* London: I. B. Tauris, 2006.

Schwarzer, Marjorie. *Riches, Rivals & Radicals: 100 Years of Museums in America.* Washington, D.C.: American Association of Museums, 2006.

Scott, James C. *Domination and the Arts of Resistance: Hidden Transcripts.* New Haven, Conn.: Yale University Press, 1990.

Seiden, Ellen. "Monuments to Missions." *Figurines & Collectibles* 4, no. 1 (March/April 1998): 68–71.

Selz, Peter. *Art of Engagement: Visual Politics in California and Beyond.* Berkeley: University of California Press; San Jose: San Jose Museum of Art, 2006.

Servín, Manuel Patricio. "California's Hispanic Heritage: A View into the Spanish Myth." In *New Spain's Far Northern Frontier: Essays on Spain in the American West, 1540–1821,* edited by David J. Weber, 204–16. Albuquerque: University of New Mexico Press, 1979.

Ševčenko, Liz. "Sites of Conscience: Heritage of and for Human Rights." In *Heritage, Memory & Identity.* Cultures and Globalization Series 4, edited by Helmut Anheier and Yudhishthir Raj Isar, 114–24. London: SAGE Publications, 2011.

———. "Sites of Conscience: New Approaches to Conflicted Memory." *Museum International* 62, no. 1–2 (2010): 20–25.

Shackel, Paul A. *Memory in Black and White: Race, Commemoration, and the Post-Bellum Landscape.* Walnut Creek, Calif.: Left Coast Press, 2003.

———. "Public Memory and the Search for Power in American Historical Archaeology." *American Anthropologist* 103, no. 3 (2001): 655–70.

Shackel, Paul A., and Erve J. Chambers, eds. *Places in Mind: Public Archaeology as Applied Anthropology.* New York: Routledge, 2004.

Shackel, Paul A., and David Gadsby, eds. "Archaeologies of Engagement, Representation, and Identity." *Historical Archaeology* 45, no. 1 (2011): 1–166.

Shaffer, Marquerite S. *See America First: Tourism and National Identity.* Washington, D.C.: Smithsonian Institution Press, 2001.

Shannon, Jennifer. "The Construction of Native Voice at the National Museum of the American Indian." In Sleeper-Smith, *Contesting Knowledge,* 218–47.

Sharp, Joanne P. *Geographies of Postcolonialism: Spaces of Power and Representation.* Los Angeles: SAGE, 2009.

Sherman, Lola. "Historic Mission's New Master Plan Has Been Tweaked." *San Diego Union-Tribune,* September 6, 2008. http://www.sandiegouniontribune.com/uniontrib/20080906/news_1mc6mission.html.

Shipek, Florence C. *Pushed into the Rocks: Southern California Land Tenure, 1769–1986*. Lincoln: University of Nebraska Press, 1987.

Shurtleff, Ernest Warburton. *The Old Missions of California*. Illustrations by Louis K. Harlow. Boston: L. Prang, 1897.

Siegel, P. E. "Contested Places and Places of Contest: The Evolution of Social Power and Ceremonial Space in Prehistoric Puerto Rico." *Latin American Antiquity* 10, no. 3 (1999): 209–38.

Silberman, Neil Asher, "'Sustainable' Heritage? Public Archaeological Interpretation and the Marketed Past." In *Archaeology and Capitalism: From Ethics to Politics*, edited by Yannis Hamilakis and Philip Duke, 179–94. Walnut Creek, Calif.: Left Coast Press, 2007.

Silliman, Stephen W. "Change and Continuity, Practice and Memory: Native American Persistence in Colonial New England." *American Antiquity* 74 (2009): 211–30.

———. "Crossing, Bridging, and Transgressing Divides in the Study of Native North America." In *Across a Great Divide: Continuity and Change in Native North American Societies, 1400–1900*, edited by Laura L. Scheiber and Mark D. Mitchell, 258–76. Tucson: University of Arizona Press, 2010.

———. "Indigenous Traces in Colonial Spaces: Archaeologies of Ambiguity, Origin, and Practice." *Journal of Social Archaeology* 10, no. 1 (2010): 28–58.

———. *Lost Laborers in Colonial California: Native Americans and the Archaeology of Rancho Petaluma*. Tucson: University of Arizona Press, 2004.

———. "Theoretical Perspectives on Labor and Colonialism: Reconsidering the California Missions." *Journal of Anthropological Archaeology* 20, no. 4 (2001): 379–407.

———. "Writing New Archaeological Narratives: Indigenous North America." In Lydon and Rizvi, *Handbook of Postcolonial Archaeology*, 145–63.

Silverman, Helaine. "Touring Ancient Times: The Present and Presented Past in Contemporary Peru." *American Anthropologist* 104, no. 3 (2002): 881–902.

Silverman, Helaine, and D. Fairchild Ruggles, eds. *Cultural Heritage and Human Rights*. New York: Springer, 2007.

Simmons, William S. "Indian Peoples of California." In Gutiérrez and Orsi, *Contested Eden*, 48–77.

Simon, Roger I. *The Touch of the Past: Remembrance, Learning, and Ethics*. New York: Palgrave MacMillan, 2005.

Simpson, George. *Narrative of a Journey round the World: During the Years 1841 and 1842*. London: H. Colburn, 1847.

———. *An Overland Journey round the World: During the Years 1841 and 1842*. Philadelphia: Lea and Blanchard, 1847.

Singleton, Theresa A. "Slavery and Spatial Dialectics on Cuban Coffee Plantations." *World Archaeology* 33, no. 1 (2001): 98–114.

Skowronek, Russell K. "Sifting the Evidence: Perceptions of Life at the Ohlone (Costanoan) Missions of Alta California." *Ethnohistory* 45 (1998): 675–708.

Sleeper-Smith, Susan, ed. *Contesting Knowledge: Museums and Indigenous Perspectives*. Lincoln: University of Nebraska Press, 2009.

Sleeper-Smith, Susan, Juliana Barr, Jean M. O'Brien, Nancy Shoemaker, and Scott Manning Stevens, eds. *Why You Can't Teach United States History without American Indians*. Chapel Hill: University of North Carolina Press, 2015.

Smith, Claire, and H. M. Wobst, eds. *Indigenous Archaeologies: Decolonizing Theory and Practice*. Routledge: London, 2005.

Smith, Frances Rand. *The Architectural History of Mission San Carlos Borromeo, California.* Berkeley: California Historical Survey Commission, 1921.

Smith, Laurajane. "Empty Gestures? Heritage and the Politics of Recognition." In Silverman and Ruggles, *Cultural Heritage and Human Rights,* 159–71.

———. *Uses of Heritage.* London: Routledge, 2006.

Smith, Laurajane, and Emma Waterton. *Heritage, Communities and Archaeology.* London: Duckworth, 2009.

Smith, Linda Tuhiwai. *Decolonizing Methodologies: Research and Indigenous Peoples.* London: Zed Books, 1999.

Smith, Mark M. *Sensing the Past: Seeing, Hearing, Smelling, Tasting, and Touching in History.* Berkeley: University of California Press, 2007.

———. *The Smell of Battle, the Taste of Siege: A Sensory History of the Civil War.* Oxford: Oxford University Press, 2014.

Smith, Paul Chaat. *Everything You Know about Indians Is Wrong.* Minneapolis: University of Minnesota Press, 2009.

Smith, Stacey L. *Freedom's Frontier: California and the Struggle over Unfree Labor, Emancipation, and Reconstruction.* Chapel Hill: University of North Carolina Press, 2013.

Smith, Terria. "Under Lock and Key." *News from Native California* 28, no. 2 (Winter 2014–15): 17–20.

Smithers, Gregory D., and Brooke N. Newman, eds. *Native Diasporas: Indigenous Identities and Settler Colonialism in the Americas.* Lincoln: University of Nebraska Press, 2014.

Smyth, Eugene Leslie. *The Missions of California.* Chicago: A. Belford, 1899.

Soja, Edward. *My Los Angeles: From Urban Restructuring to Regional Urbanization.* Berkeley: University of California Press, 2014.

———. *Postmodern Geographies: The Reassertion of Space in Critical Social Theory.* New York: Verso, 1989.

———. *Seeking Spatial Justice.* Minneapolis: University of Minnesota Press, 2010.

———. *Thirdspace: Journeys to Los Angeles and Other Real-and-Imagined Places.* Oxford: Blackwell, 1996.

Somers, Margaret. "The Narrative Constitution of Identity: A Relational and Network Approach." *Theory and Society* 23 (1994): 605–49.

Sontag, Susan. *On Photography.* New York: Dell, 1977.

Sortomme, Jerry. "Restoring Heritage Plants from California's Missions." California Museum Studies Association website, n.d. http://californiamissionsfoundation.org/articles/restoringheritageplantsfromcaliforniasmissions.

Soto, Anthony. "Mission San Luis Rey, California: Excavations in the Sunken Garden." *Kiva* 26, no. 4 (1961): 34–43.

Starr, Kevin. *Inventing the Dream; California through the Progressive Era.* New York: Oxford University Press, 1985.

Steele, James. *Old Californian Days.* Chicago: Belford-Clarke, 1889.

Stern, Jean. "Art in California: 1880–1930." In Stern and Miller, *Romance of the Bells,* 73–83.

Stern, Jean, and Gerald J. Miller, eds. *Romance of the Bells: The California Missions in Art.* Irvine, Calif.: Irvine Museum, 1995. Exhibition catalog.

Stewart, Susan. *On Longing: Narratives of the Miniature, the Gigantic, the Souvenir, the Collection.* Durham, N.C.: Duke University Press, 1993.

Stilgoe, John R. *Common Landscape of America, 1580 to 1845.* New Haven, Conn.: Yale University Press, 1982.

Stoddard, John L. *John L. Stoddard's Lectures.* Vol. 10, *Southern California, Grand Cañon of the Colorado River, Yellowstone National Park.* Boston: Balch Bros., 1900. Accessed online, http://www.gutenberg.org/etext/15526.

Stoler, Ann Laura. *Carnal Knowledge and Imperial Power: Race and the Intimate in Colonial Rule.* Berkeley: University of California Press, 2002.

Strain, Ellen. *Public Places, Private Journeys: Ethnography, Entertainment, and the Tourist Gaze.* New Brunswick, N.J.: Rutgers University Press, 2003.

Streatfield, David C. *California Gardens: Creating a New Eden.* New York: Abbeville Press, 1994.

———. "'Californio' Culture and Landscapes, 1894–1942." In *Design with Culture: Claiming America's Landscape History,* edited by Charles A. Birnbaum and Mary V. Hughes, 103–35. Charlottesville: University of Virginia Press, 2005.

———. "Where Pine and Palm Meet: The California Garden as Regional Expression." *Landscape Journal* 4, no. 2 (Fall. 1985): 61–74.

Sturken, Marita. *Tangled Memories: The Vietnam War, the AIDS Epidemic, and the Politics of Remembering.* Berkeley: University of California Press, 1997.

Sullivan, Martin E. "Some Thoughts about Museums, Reconciliation, and Healing." In *Stewards of the Sacred,* edited by Lawrence E. Sullivan and Alison Edwards, 19–25. Washington, D.C.: American Association of Museums, 2004.

Sutton, Susan Buck, and Anna Stroulia. "Archaeological Sites and the Chasm between Past and Present." In *Archaeology in Situ: Sites, Archaeology, and Communities in Greece,* edited by Anna Stroulia and Susan Buck Sutton, 3–50. Lanham, Md.: Lexington Books, 2010.

Synnestvedt, Anita. "Who Wants to Visit a Cultural Heritage Site? A Walk through an Archaeological Site with a Visual and Bodily Experience." In Russell, *Images, Representations, and Heritage,* 333–51.

Taber, Isaiah West. *California Scenery.* Photograph album, Bancroft Library collection, University of California, Berkeley, c. 1885.

Tac, Pablo. "Indian Life and Customs at Mission San Luis Rey: A Record of California Mission Life Written by Pablo Tac, and Indian Neophyte (Rome, ca. 1835)." Edited by Minna Hewes and Gordon Hewes. *The Americas* 9, no. 1 (1952): 87–106.

Tarlow, Sarah. "Emotion in Archaeology." *Current Anthropology* 41, no. 5 (2000): 713–46.

Taylor, Bayard, ed. *Picturesque Europe.* 3 vols. New York: Appleton, 1875–79.

Taylor, Judith M., and Harry Morton Butterfield. *Tangible Memories: Californians and Their Gardens, 1800–1950.* Philadelphia: Xlibris Press, 2003.

Teej T. "Review of Mission Dolores." Posted June 4, 2008, on Yelp San Francisco, http://www.yelp.com/biz/mission-dolores-san-francisco.

Templeton, David. "Model Behavior: Is It Time to Burn Down the Mission?" *Northern California Bohemian,* August 16, 2001. http:www.metroactive.com/papers/sonoma/08.16.01/mission-0133.html.

Thelen, David. "Introduction." In *History as a Catalyst for Civic Dialogue: Case Studies from Animating Democracy,* edited by Pam Korza and Barbara Schaffer Bacon, v–vii. Washington, D.C.: Americans for the Arts, 2005.

Thomas, David Hurst, ed. *Columbian Consequences, Volume 3, The Spanish Borderlands in Pan-American Perspective.* Washington, D.C.: Smithsonian Institution Press, 1991.

Thomas, David Hurst. "Harvesting Ramona's Garden: Life in California's Mythical Mission Past." In *Columbian Consequences,* vol. 3, 119–57.

———. "The Life and Times of Fr. Junípero Serra: A Pan-Borderlands Perspective." *Americas* 71, no. 2 (October 2014): 185–225.

Thompson, Mark. *American Character: The Curious Life of Charles Fletcher Lummis and the Rediscovery of the Southwest.* New York: Arcade Publishing, 2001.
Tilley, Christopher. "Introduction: Identity, Place, Landscape and Heritage." *Journal of Material Culture* 11, no. 1–2 (2006): 7–32.
———. *A Phenomenology of Landscape: Places, Paths, and Monuments.* Oxford: Berg, 1994.
Timbrook, Jan, John R. Johnson, and David D. Earle. "Vegetation Burning by the Chumash." *Journal of California and Great Basin Anthropology* 4, no. 2 (1982): 163–86.
Tolia-Kelly, Divya P. *Landscape, Race and Memory: Material Ecologies of Citizenship.* Farnham: Ashgate, 2010.
Trafzer, Clifford E., and Joel R. Hyer. Introduction to *Exterminate Them! Written Accounts of the Murder, Rape, and Enslavement of Native Americans during the California Gold Rush,* edited by Clifford E. Trafzer and Joel R. Hyer, 1–34. East Lansing: Michigan State University Press, 1999.
Trafzer, Clifford E., and Michelle Lorimer. "Silencing California Indian Genocide in Social Studies Texts." *American Behavioral Scientist* 58, no. 1 (2014): 64–82.
Trouillot, Michel-Rolph. *Silencing the Past: Power and the Production of History.* Boston: Beacon Press, 1996.
Truett, Samuel. *Fugitive Landscapes: The Forgotten History of the U.S.–Mexico Borderlands.* New Haven, Conn.: Yale University Press, 2006.
Tuan, Yi-Fu. *Place and Space: The Perspective of Experience.* Minneapolis: University of Minnesota Press, 1977.
———. *Topophilia: A Study of Environmental Perception, Attitudes, and Values.* New York: Columbia University Press, 1974.
Turkle, Sherry, ed. *Evocative Objects: Things We Think With.* Cambridge, Mass.: MIT Press, 2007.
Upton, Dell. "Architecture in Everyday Life." *New Literary History* 33, no. 4 (2002): 707–23.
———. "Authentic Anxieties." In AlSayyad, *Consuming Tradition, Manufacturing Heritage,* 298–306.
———. "Ethnicity, Authenticity, and Invented Traditions." *Historical Archaeology* 30, no. 2 (1996): 1–7.
———. *Holy Things and Profane: Anglican Parish Churches in Colonial Virginia.* New York: Architectural History Foundation, 1996.
———. *What Can and Can't Be Said: Race, Uplift, and Monument Building in the Contemporary South.* New Haven, Conn.: Yale University Press, 2015.
———. "White and Black Landscapes in Eighteenth-Century Virginia." In *Material Culture in America, 1600–1860,* edited by Robert Blair St. George, 357–69. Boston: Northeastern University Press, 1988.
Urry, John. *The Tourist Gaze: Leisure and Travel in Contemporary Societies.* London: Sage Publications, 1990.
Van Slyck, Abigail A. "Mañana, Mañana: Racial Stereotypes and the Anglo Rediscovery of the Southwest's Vernacular Architecture, 1890–1920." In *Gender, Class, and Shelter.* Vol. 5 of *Perspectives in Vernacular Architecture,* edited by Elizabeth Collins Cromley and Carter L. Hudgins, 95–108. Knoxville: University of Tennessee Press, 1995.
Vaughn, Chelsea K. "The Joining of Historical Pageantry and the Spanish Fantasy Past: The Meeting of Señora Josefa Yorba and Lucretia del Valle." *Journal of San Diego History* 52, no. 4 (Fall, 2011): 213–35.
———. "Locating Absence: The Forgotten Presence of *Monjeríos* in Alta California Missions." *Southern California Quarterly* 93, no. 2 (Summer 2011): 141–74.

Vaz, August Mark. "The Northern Missions: A History of Their Preservation and Reconstruction." Master's thesis, University of California, Los Angeles, 1949.

Veder, Robin. "Walking through Dumbarton Oaks: Early Twentieth-Century Bourgeois Bodily Techniques and Kinesthetic Experience of Landscape." *Journal of the Society of Architectural Historians* 72, no. 1 (March 2013): 5–27.

Villiers-Stuart, Constance M. *Spanish Gardens: Their History Types and Features.* London: B. T. Batsford, 1929.

Vizenor, Gerald Robert. *Manifest Manners: Postindian Warriors of Survivance.* Hanover, N.H.: Wesleyan University Press, 1999.

Vodges, Anthony Wayne. [Photograph album containing views of the Presidio in San Francisco, Angel Island, Santa Barbara, etc.] 1888–92. Huntington Library Collections (Hunt. HM 29204).

Voss, Barbara L. *The Archaeology of Ethnogenesis: Race and Sexuality in Colonial San Francisco.* Berkeley: University of California Press, 2008.

———. "Colonial Sex: Archaeology, Structured Space, and Sexuality in Alta California's Spanish-Colonial Missions." In Schmidt and Voss, *Archaeologies of Sexuality,* 35–61.

———. "Domesticating Imperialism: Sexual Politics and the Archaeology of Empire." *American Anthropologist* 110, no. 2 (2008): 191–203.

Walker, Phillip L., and Katherine D. Davidson. "Analysis of Faunal Remains from Santa Inés Mission." In Julia Costello, *Santa Inés Excavations: 1986–1988,* 162–76. Salinas, Calif.: Coyote Press, 1989.

Walker, Phillip L., and Travis Hudson. *Chumash Healing: Changing Health and Medical Practices in an American Indian Society.* Banning, Calif.: Malki Museum Press, 1993.

Walker, Polly. "Research in Relationship with Humans, the Spirit World, and the Natural World." In Mertens, Cram, and Chilisa, *Indigenous Pathways into Social Research,* 299–315.

Walker, Theresa, and Ron Gonzalez. "Missions Accomplished for Fourth-Graders." *Orange County Register,* June 17, 2010.

Walkowitz, Daniel J., and Lisa Maya Knauer. *Contested Histories in Public Space: Memory, Race, and Nation.* Durham, N.C.: Duke University Press, 2009.

Walton, John. *Storied Land: Community and Memory in Monterey.* Berkeley: University of California Press, 2001.

Warner, Charles Dudley. *Our Italy.* New York: Harper and Brothers, 1891.

Waterton, Emma, and Laurajane Smith. "The Recognition and Misrecognition of Community Heritage." *International Journal of Heritage Studies* 16, no. 1–2 (2010): 4–15.

Watkins, Joe E. "Beyond the Margin: American Indians, First Nations, and Archaeology in North America." *American Antiquity* 68 (2003): 273–85.

———. *Indigenous Archaeology: American Indian Values and Scientific Practice.* Walnut Creek, Calif.: Left Coast Press, 2000.

Watson, Mark. "Jimmie Durham's *Building a Nation* across Post-Indian, Post-American Modernities." *American Art* 28, no. 1 (Spring 2014): 16–24.

Watts, Jennifer A. "Photography in the Land of Sunshine: Charles Fletcher Lummis and the Regional Ideal." *Southern California Quarterly* 87, no. 4 (Winter 2005): 339–76.

———. "Picture Taking in Paradise: Los Angeles and the Creation of Regional Identity, 1880–1920." In *The Nineteenth-Century Visual Culture Reader,* edited by Vanessa R. Schwartz and Jeannene M. Przyblyski, 218–32. New York: Routledge, 2004.

Weaver, Jace. "Indigenousness and Indigeneity." In *A Companion to Postcolonial Studies,* edited by Henry Schwarz and Sangeeta Ray, 221–35. London: Blackwell, 2000.

———. "More Light than Heat: The Current State of Native American Studies." *American Indian Quarterly* 31, no. 2 (2007): 233–55.

Weber, David J. "Arts and Architecture, Force and Fear: The Spanish-Indian Struggle for Sacred Space." In Bargellini and Komanecky, *The Art of the Missions of Northern New Spain*, 9–23.

———. *Bárbaros: Spaniards and Their Savages in the Age of Enlightenment*. New Haven, Conn.: Yale University Press, 2005.

———. "A New Borderlands Historiography: Constructing and Negotiating the Boundaries of Identity." In Hackel, *Alta California*, 215–34.

———. *The Spanish Frontier in North America*. New Haven, Conn.: Yale University Press, 1992.

Weber, Francis J. *The California Missions*. Strasbourg: Éditions du Signe, Archdiocese of Los Angeles, 2005.

———. *Encyclopedia of California's Catholic Heritage*. Mission Hills, Calif.: St. Francis Historical Society and the Arthur H. Clark Company, 2000.

———, ed. *The Pride of the Missions: A Documentary History of San Gabriel Mission*. Los Angeles: F. J. Weber, 1978.

———. "San Fernando, Rey de España: Its Role in the New Millennium." *Southern California Quarterly* 79, no. 3 (Fall 1997): 383–404.

Weibel-Orlando, Joan. *Indian Country L.A.: Maintaining Ethnic Community in Complex Society*. Rev. ed. Urbana: University of Illinois Press, 1999.

Weinberg, Nathan. "Historic Preservation and Tradition in California: The Restoration of the Missions and the Spanish-Colonial Revival." Ph.D. diss., University of California, Davis, 1974.

Weitze, Karen J. *California's Mission Revival*. Los Angeles: Hennessey and Ingalls, 1984.

Westcoat, James L., Jr. "The Indo-Islamic Garden: Conflict, Conservation, and Conciliation in Gujarat, India." In Silverman and Ruggles, *Cultural Heritage and Human Rights*, 53–77.

Wharton, Annabel Jane. *Selling Jerusalem: Relics, Replicas, Theme Parks*. Chicago: University of Chicago Press, 2006.

Wharton, Edith. *Italian Villas and Their Gardens*. New York: Century Company, 1903.

White, Hayden. *The Content of Form: Narrative Discourse and Historical Representation*. Baltimore: Johns Hopkins University Press, 1987.

Whitehead, Richard S., ed. *California's Mission La Purísima Concepción: The Hageman and Ewing Reports*. Santa Barbara: Santa Barbara Trust for Historic Preservation, 1991.

Whitley, David S. *The Art of the Shaman: Rock Art of California*. Salt Lake City: University of Utah Press, 2000.

Whitley, David S., and Tamara K. Whitley. "A Land of Vision and Dreams." In Jones and Perry, *Contemporary Issues in California Archaeology*, 255–71.

Willes, Burlington. Foreword to *Picturing Berkeley: A Postcard History*, edited by Burlington Willes, 1. Salt Lake City: Gibbs Smith, 2005.

Williams, Paul. *Memorial Museums: The Global Rush to Commemorate Atrocities*. Oxford: Berg, 2007.

Wilson, Charles William, ed. *Picturesque Palestine, Sinai and Egypt*. 4 vols. New York: D. Appleton, 1881–84.

Wilson, Chris. *The Myth of Santa Fe: Creating a Modern Tradition*. Albuquerque: University of New Mexico Press, 1997.

Winter, Tim. *Post-Conflict Heritage, Postcolonial Tourism: Culture, Politics, and Development at Angkor*. London: Routledge, 2007.

Wood, Elizabeth, and Kiersten F. Latham. "The Thickness of Things: Exploring the Museum

Curriculum through Phenomenological Touch." *Journal of Curriculum Theorizing* 27, no. 2 (2011): 51–65.

Wrobel, David M. *Promised Lands: Promotion, Memory, and the Creation of the American West.* Lawrence: University Press of Kansas, 2002.

Wrobel, David, and Patrick T. Long, eds. *Seeing and Being Seen: Tourism in the American West.* Lawrence: University Press of Kansas, 2001.

Wyand, Mary Ann. "Pilgrimage to California Includes Missions and Historic Sites. *Criterion Online Edition,* June 10, 2011, accessed July 15, 2014, https://www.archindy.org/criterion/local/2011/06-10/pilgrimage.html.

Wylie, John. *Landscape.* London: Routledge, 2007.

Wynn, Mark R. *Faith and Place: An Essay in Embodied Religious Epistemology.* Oxford: Oxford University Press, 2009.

Yanni, Carla. *The Architecture of Madness: Insane Asylums in the United States.* Minneapolis: University of Minnesota Press, 2007.

Yeoman, Sharyn Wiley. "Messages from the Promised Land: Bohemian Los Angeles, 1880–1920." Ph.D. diss., University of Colorado, Boulder, 2003.

Zerubavel, Eviatar. *The Elephant in the Room: Silence and Denial in Everyday Life.* Oxford: Oxford University Press, 2006.

Zimmerman, Larry J. "Plains Indians and Resistance to 'Public' Heritage Commemoration of Their Pasts." In Silverman and Ruggles, *Cultural Heritage and Human Rights,* 144–58.

———. "Usurping Native American Voice." In *The Future of the Past: Archaeologists, Native Americans and Repatriation,* edited by Tamara L. Bray, 169–84. New York: Garland, 2001.

Internet Resources

California Missions Foundation, http://www.californiamissionsfoundation.org

California Missions Resource Center, http://www.missionscalifornia.com

Claretian Missionaries, USA Province, http://www.claretian.com/SanGabrielMissionCentennialCelebration.php

Franciscan Pilgrimage Programs, http://www.franciscanpilgrimages.com

Hornbeck Collection. Historical Land Use in California. California State University, Monterey Bay, Digital Commons @ CSUMB, http://digitalcommons.csumb.edu/hornbeck

Huntington Library, Early California Population Project, http://www.huntington.org/information/ecppmain.htm

International Coalition of Sites of Conscience, http://www.sitesofconscience.org

Mission San Antonio de Padua, Cutting of the Roses, http://missionsanantonio.net/cutting-of-the-roses

Mission San Antonio de Pala website, http://www.missionsanantonio.org

Mission San Carlos Borroméo website, http://www.carmelmission.org/museum

Mission San Juan Capistrano, audio tour, http://www.missionsjc.com/fun-learning/audiotour.php

———. Catholic Visitor page, http://www.missionsjc.com/visit/catholicvisitors.php

———. Mission San Juan Capistrano Annual Report, 2011–2012, http://www.missionsjc.com/about/MSJC_AnnualReport2012.pdf

Tours4Mobile, http://tours4mobile.com/tours/California-tours

Weber, Tricia Anne. California Missions Resource, http://www.californias-missions.org/teachers.htm

William H. Hannon Foundation website, Junípero Serra page, http://www.hannonfoundation.org/juniperoserra.html

Index

Page numbers in italics refer to figures.

ELIZABETH KRYDER-REID is professor of anthropology and museum studies, director of the Cultural Heritage Research Center in the Indiana University School of Liberal Arts (IUPUI), and former director of the IUPUI museum studies program.